ANNUAL EDITIONS

Urban Society
Sixteenth Edition

EDITOR

Myron A. Levine
Wright State University

Myron Levine is a Professor of Urban Affairs and Geography at Wright State University in Dayton, Ohio. He is the author of *Urban Politics: Power in Metropolitan America.* His writings on urban policy in the United States and Europe have appeared in the *Journal of Urban Affairs,* the *Journal of the American Planning Association,* and the *Urban Affairs Review.* He has been a Fulbright Professor in Germany, Latvia, the Netherlands, and the Slovak Republic, as well as a NEH Fellow in France.

Connect
Learn
Succeed™

ANNUAL EDITIONS: URBAN SOCIETY, SIXTEENTH EDITION

Published by McGraw-Hill, a business unit of The McGraw-Hill Companies, Inc., 1221 Avenue of the Americas, New York, NY 10020. Copyright © 2014 by The McGraw-Hill Companies, Inc. All rights reserved. Previous editions 2012, 2010, and 2008. No part of this publication may be reproduced or distributed in any form or by any means, or stored in a database or retrieval system, without the prior written consent of The McGraw-Hill Companies, Inc., including, but not limited to, in any network or other electronic storage or transmission, or broadcast for distance learning.

Some ancillaries, including electronic and print components, may not be available to customers outside the United States.

Annual Editions® is a registered trademark of The McGraw-Hill Companies, Inc.

Annual Editions is published by the **Contemporary Learning Series** group within the McGraw-Hill Higher Education division.

3 4 5 6 7 8 QVS/QVS 21 20 19 18 17

ISBN 978-0-07-813612-2
MHID 0-07-813612-1
ISSN 0735-2425 (print)
ISSN 2158-4087 (online)

Acquisitions Editor: *Joan L. McNamara*
Marketing Director: *Adam Kloza*
Marketing Manager: *Nathan Edwards*
Senior Developmental Editor: *Jade Benedict*
Senior Project Manager: *Joyce Watters*
Buyer: *Nichole Birkenholz*
Cover Designer: *Studio Montage, St. Louis, MO*
Content Licensing Specialist: *DeAnna Dausener*
Media Project Manager: *Sridevi Palani*

Compositor: Laserwords Private Limited
Cover Images: © Purestock/SuperStock (inset); Richard Nowitx/Digital Vision/Getty Images (background)

Editors/Academic Advisory Board

Members of the Academic Advisory Board are instrumental in the final selection of articles for each edition of ANNUAL EDITIONS. Their review of articles for content, level, and appropriateness provides critical direction to the editors and staff. We think that you will find their careful consideration well reflected in this volume.

ANNUAL EDITIONS: Urban Society
16th Edition

EDITOR

Myron A. Levine
Wright State University

ACADEMIC ADVISORY BOARD MEMBERS

Preface

We live in an urban society. The world has reached the "Metropolitan Moment" where more than half its population resides in cities and suburbs.

Throughout history, cities have been important centers of commerce, administration, and industrial production. Cities are also the places where science and the arts flourish. Today, cities continue to serve as hubs of innovation where the face-to-face exchange of ideas helps to produce technological advances and other innovations vital to a nation's economic growth.

But, despite their strengths, not all is well with cities. In lesser developed countries (LDCs) urban centers are overwhelmed by the continuing arrival of migrants from the countryside who seek a better life in the city. In too many cities, the poor often wind up living in slums and shanty towns, places that lack clean drinking water, trash pickup, the provision of public schools, and even basic toilet facilities and sewage disposal.

Cities in more developed countries (MDCs) are facing the loss of population and economic activity to the suburbs. The national economic stagnation of the early twenty-first century further hurt cities, increasing the stock of vacant properties while diminishing a city's local tax base. Faced with their own budgetary problems, the federal and state governments reduced urban aid. By 2012, Stockton, San Bernardino, and Compton (all in California) declared bankruptcy. Scranton (Pennsylvania) and other cities across the nation dealt with similar fiscal emergencies.

The suburbs, too, have exhibited new weaknesses. "Suburbia" is *not* a uniform ring of affluent residential communities. Declining "first suburbs" and other working-class and inner-ring communities confront the loss of commercial activity and costs of dealing with an increased number of vacant properties and boarded-up homes.

This book observes how cities and suburbs compete for new economic development and jobs. But, in pursuing growth, will localities be able to give sufficient attention to policies that protect the natural environment? Will cities be able to adopt programs that provide for the needs of more vulnerable residents?

This volume probes globalization, how the disappearance of meaningful national borders has undermined the stability of cities. The outsourcing of jobs to "call centers" in India, the competition offered by factory cities in China, and the connections that immigrant entrepreneurs maintain to their homelands all point to the global nature of the contemporary setting in which cities in the United States must govern.

Annual Edition: Urban Society, Sixteenth Edition continues to pay special attention to questions of race and ethnicity. Gunnar Myrdal once called the problem of race the "American dilemma." The book points to the troubling resegregation of public school classrooms. It also reviews the story of a group of poor African-Americans that attempted to flee on foot from flood-ridden and devastated New Orleans after Hurricane Katrina, only to be turned back on the bridge by armed police in suburban Gretna. Such incidents serve as reminders that cities and suburbs have not yet fully resolved the American dilemma.

This edition describes patterns of urban development not just in the United States but also in Mexico, Brazil, China, Japan, India, Nigeria, Egypt, and countries in Europe. The volume's material on cities around the globe is so extensive that the book can be used as a text in courses on world cities and globalization.

This book advocates no single ideological point of view. It reviews both government-based and market-oriented approaches to solving urban ills. It recognizes the critical importance of establishing public–private partnerships in such policy areas as local economic development, education, law enforcement, and the production of affordable housing. But it also recognizes the limitations of market-based and partnership approaches. The book provides much material for debate. It is up to the reader to decide which policies and courses of action should be chosen.

At the back of the book, you will find a card to mail to the publisher. Your insights will help determine which articles are kept, and which are swept aside, when the time comes to publish the seventeenth edition of *Urban*

Society. You can also help identify new magazine, journal, and "web-zine" articles for inclusion in future volumes. Your participation will continue to make *Annual Editions: Urban Society* a lively and informative classroom resource.

The author owes a great debt to Leonard Loeppke at MHHE for his continuing faith in this volume and to Jade Benedict for her fine editing and helpful suggestions. There is also one special acknowledgment: To Nancy, for her love and endless support over the years.

Myron A. Levine
Wright State University
Editor

The Annual Editions Series

VOLUMES AVAILABLE

Adolescent Psychology

Aging

American Foreign Policy

American Government

Anthropology

Archaeology

Assessment and Evaluation

Business Ethics

Child Growth and Development

Comparative Politics

Criminal Justice

Developing World

Drugs, Society, and Behavior

Dying, Death, and Bereavement

Early Childhood Education

Economics

Educating Children with Exceptionalities

Education

Educational Psychology

Entrepreneurship

Environment

The Family

Gender

Geography

Global Issues

Health

Homeland Security

Human Development

Human Resources

Human Sexualities

International Business

Management

Marketing

Mass Media

Microbiology

Multicultural Education

Nursing

Nutrition

Physical Anthropology

Psychology

Race and Ethnic Relations

Social Problems

Sociology

State and Local Government

Sustainability

Technologies, Social Media, and Society

United States History, Volume 1

United States History, Volume 2

Urban Society

Violence and Terrorism

Western Civilization, Volume 1

World History, Volume 1

World History, Volume 2

World Politics

Contents

UNIT 1
Why Cities? The Importance of Cities

UNIT 2
The Contemporary Urban Situation: The Growth, Decline, and Renaissance of Cities

The concepts in bold italics are developed in the article. For further expansion, please refer to the Topic Guide.

UNIT 3
Gentrification, Globalization, and the City

The concepts in bold italics are developed in the article. For further expansion, please refer to the Topic Guide.

UNIT 4
Competitive Pressures and Economic Development

The concepts in bold italics are developed in the article. For further expansion, please refer to the Topic Guide.

UNIT 5
Citizen Participation

Unit Overview 88

The concepts in bold italics are developed in the article. For further expansion, please refer to the Topic Guide.

UNIT 6
School Choice and School Reform

The concepts in bold italics are developed in the article. For further expansion, please refer to the Topic Guide.

UNIT 7
Policing and Crime

The concepts in bold italics are developed in the article. For further expansion, please refer to the Topic Guide.

UNIT 8
A Suburban Nation: Suburban Growth, Diversity, and the Possibilities of "New Urbanism" and "New Regionalism"

The concepts in bold italics are developed in the article. For further expansion, please refer to the Topic Guide.

UNIT 9
Toward Sustainable Cities and Suburbs?

UNIT 10
Cities and Urban Problems Around the Globe

The concepts in bold italics are developed in the article. For further expansion, please refer to the Topic Guide.

corporations and their high-end workforces. In historic Kyoto, new growth projects threaten the traditional character of a city that is the center of Japanese heritage and culture.   **205**

The concepts in bold italics are developed in the article. For further expansion, please refer to the Topic Guide.

for the lethal battles between government forces and heavily armed drug cartels. But violence in Ciudad Juárez actually precedes the more recent surge in bloody gang wars. Hundreds of **femicides** (by current estimates, over 700), or murders of women, have occurred in Juárez. Women are the backbone of the low-wage workforces of the **maquiladoras,** the border factories that have grown as a result of **globalization** and international **free-trade agreements.** In their daily travel to and from jobs, often at night and at odd hours along dark streets, women and young girls are especially vulnerable. Both the government and private employers have failed to provide for the physical safety of women.   **227**

UNIT 11
The Future of Cities and Suburbs: The United States and the World

The concepts in bold italics are developed in the article. For further expansion, please refer to the Topic Guide.

Topic Guide

This topic guide suggests how the selections in this book relate to the subjects covered in your course. You may want to use the topics listed on these pages to search the Web more easily.

On the following pages a number of websites have been gathered specifically for this book. They are arranged to reflect the units of this Annual Editions reader. You can link to these sites by going to www.mhhe.com/cls.

All the articles that relate to each topic are listed below the bold-faced term.

Internet References

The following Internet sites have been selected to support the articles found in this reader. These sites were available at the time of publication. However, because websites often change their structure and content, the information listed may no longer be available. We invite you to visit www.mhhe.com/cls for easy access to these sites.

Annual Editions: Urban Society 16/e

General Sources

Yahoo Social Science/Urban Studies
http://dir.yahoo.com/social_science/urban_studies

Yahoo provides links to sources on urban growth, urban ecology, sprawl, and urban theory and theorists.

Unit 1

"City Centered, Investing in Metropolitan Areas to Build the Next Economy," The Brookings Institution
www.brookings.edu/research/articles/2010/10/21-metro-economy-katz

Bruce Katz, vice-president of The Brookings Institution, calls on governments to undertake "smart" investments that will enhance the productive capacity of metropolitan areas. The site also contains links to videos in which Katz explains the importance of urban regions to national economic prosperity.

Edward Glaeser, Papers on the Web
www.economics.harvard.edu/faculty/glaeser/papers_glaeser

Harvard University economist Edward Glaeser has written on a vast array of urban topics, including entrepreneurship and the city, the importance of social capital (investment in people and skill development), the "clustering" industries, and how cities offer the advantages of "agglomeration" to businesses.

New York: A Documentary Film, Online
www.pbs.org/wnet/newyork

The Web companion to Ric Burns's excellent documentary series contains numerous supporting documents and video clips that reveal how the functions served by New York City have evolved over the years.

Planetizen: The Urban Planning, Design, and Development Network
www.planetizen.com

This site contains a wide range of commentary by urban observers, including articles on the functions of cities, how cities foster creativity, post-industrial transformation, and alternative strategies for local economic development.

Unit 2

Coney Island History Site
www.westland.net/coneyisland

A fun site with wonderful photos that reveal how New York City has changed over the years, as seen in the evolution of the city's fabled beachfront boardwalk and entertainment center.

First Suburbs, The Brookings Institution
www.brookings.edu

Documents the state of the nation's older, more mature suburbs. To find the most relevant reports and articles, be sure to paste the phrase "first suburbs" into the site's search engine.

Katrina Reading Room, The Brookings Institution
www.brookings.edu/metro/katrina-reading-room.aspx

Examines the rebuilding of New Orleans (and the larger Gulf Coast region) after Hurricane Katrina and the subsequent flooding that destroyed much of the city.

Kirwan Institute, The Ohio State University
http://kirwaninstitute.org

The interconnections between race and patterns of urban development.

National Fair Housing Alliance
www.nationalfairhousing.org

An alliance of nonprofit housing organizations and civil rights groups that seeks to fight discrimination in the nation's housing markets.

Public Policy Institute of California
www.ppic.org/main/policyareas.asp

The development choices faced by cities in California.

Resource Centres on Urban Agriculture and Food Security
www.ruaf.org

Web links to reports, videos, and newspaper articles on how cities can promote community gardens and urban farming and thereby bring fresh produce to the "food deserts" of impoverished inner-city neighborhoods.

Urban Agriculture News
http://urbanagriculture-news.blogspot.com

How cities can repurpose vacant land for community gardens and urban farming.

Unit 3

The Brookings Institution, Immigration
www.brookings.edu/topics/immigration.aspx

Studies of the impact of immigration on U.S. communities.

The Brookings Institution, "Dealing with Neighborhood Change: A Primer on Gentrification and Policy Choices"
www.brookings.edu/es/urban/gentrification/gentrification.pdf

Alternative approaches to gentrification, as seen in Atlanta, Cleveland, Washington, D.C., and the San Francisco Bay Area.

Center for an Urban Future
www.nycfuture.org/content/search/topicsearch.cfm?topicarea=39

A New York think tank looks at immigration, technological change, and the future of cities.

Center for Immigration Studies
www.cis.org

The consequences of uncontrolled immigration.

Creative Class
http://creativeclass.com

This website reflects the writings and ideas of economist Richard Florida, who seeks to identify the various means by which cities can attract and support the "creative class." The site maintains

Internet References

a Media Showcase that includes various television and radio interviews with Dr. Florida.

Gentrification Web
http://members.lycos.co.uk/gentrification

This website, designed by Tom Slater, provides a bibliography and various articles on the impacts of gentrification. Highly critical of market-led gentrification, the site provides links to works that rebut the claim that gentrification brings substantial benefits to the residents of poorer communities.

Gotham Gazette
www.gothamgazette.com/city

A review of politics and economic and community development in New York City.

Great Cities Institute, University of Illinois–Chicago
http://uic.edu/cuppa/gci/index.shtml

The GCI explores the changes that post-industrialism and globalization have brought to Chicago and other major cities in the national and world economy. Be sure to look at the series of GCI Working Papers that GCI sometimes makes available online.

National Immigration Forum
www.immigrationforum.org

This advocacy group welcomes continued immigration as congruent with the best of America's traditions and values. The Forum argues that immigrants contribute to the national and local economies as well as to the vibrant life of local communities. The Forum seeks to rebut many of what it sees as the specious arguments that exaggerate the negative impacts of immigration.

Partnership for a New American Economy
www.renewoureconomy.org

A bipartisan group of mayors and business leaders underscore the contributions that immigrants make to the U.S. economy.

Right to the City
www.righttothecity.org

Fights gentrification, land speculation, and displacement.

Urban Institute
www.urban.org

Reports on a vast range of urban housing and development issues, including gentrification and policies that can mitigate displacement.

Urban Land Institute
www.uli.org

The ULI seeks policies that balance economic growth with competing environmental and community priorities. See, in particular, *Managing Gentrification: A ULI Community Catalyst Report* (2006).

Unit 4

American Public Transportation Association, Center for High-Speed Rail
www.highspeedrailonline.com

APTA supports high-speed rail.

Californians for High-Speed Rail
www.ca4hsr.org

A grassroots organization that seeks the construction of complete HSR systems, including HSR stations located in the centers of major cities that are fed by local mass transit.

Field of Schemes
www.fieldofschemes.com

A large collection of newspaper articles and research reports on cost overruns, extravagance, and the one-sided nature of numerous sports stadium projects.

Legislative Analyst's Office (LAO), State of California: 2011 report *High-Speed Rail Is at a Critical Juncture*
www.lao.ca.gov/reports/2011/trns/high_speed_rail/high_speed_rail_051011.pdf

The LAO recommended major modification in a California HSR system, given the fiscal difficulties suffered by the state.

Midwest High-Speed Rail Association
www.midwesthsr.org

Argues that investment in high-speed rail will help transform the ailing economy of the American Midwest.

The Railist: High-Speed Rail News, a Project of Planetizen
www.therailist.com

Tons of discussion of various urban planning issues, including transportation.

Reason Foundation
www.reason.org

Insights that are highly critical of the government's use of eminent domain powers and of the provision of taxpayer subsidies for new sports stadiums and high-speed rail.

U.S. Conference of Mayors. 2010 Report *The Economic Impacts of High-Speed Rail on Cities and Their Metropolitan Areas*
www.usmayors.org/highspeedrail

Argues that HSR stations can serve as the hubs of both local and national economic growth.

U.S. High-Speed Rail Association
www.ushsra.com

The rail industry envisions a 17,000-mile dedicated-track system with trains running at speeds of up to 220 mph.

Unit 5

CommunityWealth.Org, the Democracy Collaborative of the University of Maryland
http://community-wealth.org/strategies/panel/cdcs/articles.html

Contains links to a variety of articles and reports on community development corporations (CDCs).

E-Governance Institute: Citizen Participation
http://andromeda.rutgers.edu/~egovinst/Website/citizenspg.htm

National Civic Review
www.ncl.org/publications/ncr

Reports on the large variety of participatory mechanisms available to local governments.

Internet References

Shelterforce
www.shelterforce.org

Focuses on housing and community development matters, including the contributions of CDCs and other community-based organizations.

Unit 6

Brookings Institution: School Choice; School Vouchers; Charter Schools; Urban and Inner-City Schools
www.brookings.edu/topics/school-choice.aspx

www.brookings.edu/topics/school-vouchers.aspx

www.brookings.edu/topics/charter-schools.aspx

www.brookings.edu/topics/urban-and-inner-city-schools.aspx

This Washington "think tank" presents research reports and the transcripts of scholarly forums that review the evidence regarding choice programs and other reform measures undertaken and an effort to improve inner-city education.

Carnegie Foundation for the Advancement of Teaching
www.carnegiefoundation.org

This is an independent educational policy and research center.

Center for Education Reform
www.edreform.com

This advocacy group urges that governments expand school choice.

Center for Research on Educational Outcomes (CREDO), Stanford University
www.credo.stanford.edu/research-reports.html

Through its affiliation with Stanford University, this organization works to improve the empirical evidence about education reform and student performance.

Center for School Reform at the Heartland Institute
www.heartland.org/schoolreform-news.org/index.html

An organization committed to school choice.

Civil Rights Project, UCLA
www.civilrightsproject.ucla.edu

This group looks to create a new generation of research in social science and law, on the critical issues of civil rights and equal opportunity.

Friedman Foundation for Educational Choice
www.edchoice.org

An organization committed to school choice.

National Alliance for Public Charter Schools
www.publiccharters.org

The nation's leading nonprofit organization committed to advancing the charter school movement.

National Center on School Choice, Vanderbilt University
www.vanderbilt.edu/schoolchoice/research-home.html

The aim of this organization is to provide national intellectual leadership on the study of school choice in all its forms.

National Education Association (NEA)
www.nea.org

The nation's largest organization of teachers has been quite skeptical of plans for school choice.

School Choice, Wisconsin
www.schoolchoiceinfo.org

A collection of news articles and more scholarly studies that analyze the impact of school choice programs, with a special focus on the Milwaukee school voucher program and Milwaukee's use of charter schools.

Thomas B. Fordham Institute
www.fordhaminstitute.org/template/index.cfm

An organization committed to school choice.

Unit 7

California Cities Gang Prevention Network
www.ccgpn.org

The National Council on Crime and Delinquency (NCCD) is a California-based, nonprofit research and consulting firm specializing in child welfare, juvenile justice, and adult criminal justice issues.

Gang Reduction, City of Los Angeles
http://mayor.lacity.org/issues/gangreduction/index.htm

The mayor of Los Angeles has consolidated the delivery of gang prevention and intervention services in the Office of Gang Reduction and Youth Development.

National Forum on Youth Violence Prevention
www.findyouthinfo.gov

The forum aims to build a national conversation about youth and gang violence to increase awareness, drive action, and build local capacity to more effectively address youth violence.

Prof. Wesley G. Skogan Home Page: Community Policing; Crime and Disorder
www.skogan.org

Professor Skogan has studied community policing strategies in Chicago and in cities around the world.

The Urban Institute, Policing and Crime Prevention
www.urban.org/center/jpc/projects/Policing-and-Crime-Prevention.cfm

A Washington-based "think tank" that explores a variety of urban policy initiatives including the effectiveness of various approaches to reducing crime in the city and in public housing.

Unit 8

The Brookings Institution: First Suburbs
www.brookings.edu/topics/first-suburbs.aspx

This Washington-based "think tank" presents numerous research reports and newspaper articles as it examines the current state of America's older suburbs and the policies that can prevent their decline.

Congress for a New Urbanism
www.cnu.org

CNU is one of the strongest voices for New Urbanism. Its numerous publications and reports, including the *Charter for a New Urbanism,* detail the principles of the New Urbanism movement and various efforts to create more livable and sustainable inner-city communities and suburbs.

First Suburbs Coalition
www.marc.org/firstsuburbs

How should the nation deal with the jobs, housing, and infrastructure problems of America's aging suburbs—communities that enjoyed rapid growth following World War II, but many of which are suffering decline today? The focus of this site is on efforts in Missouri and Kansas. Be sure to look at the links to similar efforts undertaken in other Midwest states, including Michigan and Ohio.

Internet References

National Geographic Magazine, Urban Sprawl
http://ngm.nationalgeographic.com/ngm/data/2001/07/01/html/ft_20010701.3.html

Useful and quite readable material on sprawled development and its impacts.

Newurbanism.org
www.newurbanism.org

This is another excellent site that presents more reports, ideas, and illustrative examples from the New Urbanism movement as it seeks to build livable and sustainable communities by reducing sprawl and promoting both walkable communities and the use of mass transit.

Sierra Club, Stopping Sprawl
www.sierraclub.org/sprawl

The Sierra Club is the long-serving advocate for preserving the natural environment of the United States.

Smart Communities Network: Urban Growth Boundaries
www.smartcommunities.ncat.org/landuse/urban.shtml

This site provides links to various resources on urban growth boundaries in metropolitan (Portland) Oregon, and in other U.S. and foreign cities.

Sprawl Watch Clearinghouse
www.sprawlwatch.org

A wealth of articles on sprawl, its impact, and on various policies for containing future sprawled development.

Unit 9

The Brookings Institution: Transportation
www.brookings.edu/topics/transportation.aspx

The Brookings Institution presents a discussion of numerous alternative transportation policies for urban America.

Business First, London
www.p-londonfirst.co.uk

A business group that supports congestion pricing as a key to improving the business climate of central London.

Green Cities
http://greencities.com

Explores green construction practices and various measures that can be taken to make urban development more compatible with environmental values.

International Transport Forum
www.internationaltransportforum.org

A forum with 52 member countries that describes a variety of approaches to reduce traffic congestion.

The Keep NYC Congestion Tax Free Coalition
www.keepnycfree.com

Arguments critical of Mayor Michael Bloomberg's attempt to introduce a system of congestion charges in lower Manhattan.

London (England) Chamber of Commerce
www.londonchamber.co.uk/lcc_public/home.asp

A business association that argues that London's congestion zone is "bad for business."

Our Green Cities, Dr. Kent Portney, Tufts University
http://ourgreencities.com

Dr. Portney is one of the leading experts on sustainable cities, attempting to discover policies that advance all three legs of the sustainable development triangle.

Planner's Web: Sprawl and Growth
www.plannersweb.com/articles/sprawl-articles.html

Various articles from *Planning Commissioners Journal* present competing views on urban sprawl and the desirability of smart-growth policies.

Reason Foundation
http://reason.org

A conservative "think tank" that is skeptical of many of the policies that promise "smart growth" and urban sustainability

Resources for the Future (RFF): Transportation and Urban Land
www.rff.org/Focus_Areas/Pages/Transportation_and_Urban_Land.aspx

Sierra Club: Stopping Sprawl
www.sierraclub.org/sprawl

Founded in 1892, the Sierra Club is America's oldest environmental organization. As part of its agenda of environmental protection, the Sierra Club seeks alternatives to continued sprawled development. Particularly noteworthy are the organization's reports on *Building Better*.

Smart Growth America
http://smartgrowthamerica.org

This advocacy group seeks to curb sprawled development in order to promote historic preservation, the protection of farmland and green spaces, and the development of "healthy" cities and suburbs.

Sustainable Cities
http://sustainablecities.net

The name of this organization says it all. Can policies be adopted to make urban growth and development more compatible with environmental values?

Unit 10

Planetizen
www.planetizen.com

Tons of discussion of various urban planning issues, including transportation, and the environment.

Planum
www.planum.net

The e-zine of the *European Journal of Planning,* this online forum presents a large number of articles on various aspects of European urban planning, including the impact of immigration and the European city of the future.

Rio On Watch
http://rioonwatch.org

Highlights the evictions and other threats to Rio de Janeiro's *favelas* as Brazil prepares to host the 2014 soccer World Cup and the 2016 Summer Olympics.

Squatter City, the blog of Robert Neuwirth, author of
Shadow Cities: A Billion Squatters, A New Urban World
http://squattercity.blogspot.com

Internet References

United Nations Human Settlements Programme
www.unhabitat.org

UN-Habitat seeks to promote shelter for all, with a particular focus on providing alternatives to the slum/squatter communities in lesser developed countries. Particularly noteworthy are the UN-Habitat reports on such topics as *Cities in a Globalizing World* and *The Challenge of Slums*.

Unit 11

The Atlantic: Cities
www.theatlanticcities.com

The Atlantic magazine features articles and discussion on evolving patterns of urban development and the future of cities.

Livable Cities
www.livablecities.org

Website of the International Livable Cities Council.

Urban Visions: The Future of Cities
www.scientificamerican.com/report.cfm?id=future-cities

In-depth reports by *Scientific American*.

UNIT 1

Why Cities? The Importance of Cities

Unit Selections

1. **Why Cities Matter,** Edward Glaeser
2. **The Metropolitan Moment,** Bruce Katz

Learning Outcomes

After reading this unit, you should be able to:

- Describe the functions of cities, that is, why cities exist and the purposes that cities serve.

- Explain why cities and metropolitan areas remain important even in an age where transportation and telecommunications allow the shift of population and economic activity to nonurban areas.

- Explain how cities and metropolitan areas contribute to national economic growth.

- Identify how cities like Chicago have drawn strength as immigration ports of entry.

Student Website

www.mhhe.com/cls

Internet References

"City Centered, Investing in Metropolitan Areas to Build the Next Economy," The Brookings Institution
www.brookings.edu/research/articles/2010/10/21-metro-economy-katz

Edward Glaeser, Papers on the Web
www.economics.harvard.edu/faculty/glaeser/publications

New York: A Documentary Film, Online
www.pbs.org/wnet/newyork

Planetizen: The Urban Planning, Design, and Development Network
www.planetizen.com

Why do cities exist? Simply put, cities perform necessary functions. Cities are hubs of commerce and industry. They are also centers where the exchange of ideas helps to advance a society's economic, intellectual, and cultural growth.

Early cities also served a protective function: A city's walls and fortifications kept out bandits and invading armies. Preindustrial cities were also important administrative centers, the places from which kings and churches extended their command over surrounding areas. In Medieval and Renaissance Europe, cities were also places of learning, the sites of great universities that assembled educators and students from around the country.

Throughout history, cities developed as places of trade; the city was a marketplace where goods could be secured from rural areas and far-off lands. The oldest portions of cities are commonly found along waterways, as harbors, rivers, and canals played a dominant role in early transportation and trade.

During the Industrial Revolution, cities were centers of agglomeration that "brought together" investment capital and the large numbers of workers necessary for factory production. A great migration from the countryside swelled the population of industrial cities, as laborers who were no longer needed for agriculture sought the opportunity presented by factory jobs.

Economist Ed Glaeser recognizes the key roles that cities have played in commerce and manufacturing. Yet, for Glaeser, the importance of cities transcends their traditional economic functions (Article 1, "Why Cities Matter"). Glaeser argues that Chicago's "meteoric growth" was not simply the result of such natural advantages as the city's access to river and lake transportation and its key location as a center for the trade of lumber, grain, and livestock as the United States expanded west.

Cities like Chicago facilitate entrepreneurship, where business owners, scientists, and free thinkers share ideas regarding emerging technologies and possible new ways of organizing production. Glaeser argues that Chicago, for instance, connected entrepreneurs with people of genius and talent, connections that gave birth to such inventions as the elevator and the Pullman sleeping car. Cities like Chicago were also ports of immigration that enabled the cross-fertilization of ideas from people of different cultures. As Ric Burns emphasizes in his documentary history of New York City, only in a city as diverse and cosmopolitan as New York could George Gershwin, the son of a Jewish immigrant, draw on his familiarity with Italian opera, the spirituals and blues of Harlem, and the Yiddish theater to write the all-American musical *Porgy and Bess,* that gives voice to the lives and aspirations of impoverished African-Americans living in post-slavery "Catfish Row," South Carolina.

Bruce Katz observes that the world has reached "The Metropolitan Moment" (Article 2), with over half its population residing in cities and their surrounding suburban areas. The United

© TongRo Image Stock/Alamy

States is even more urban, with 84 percent of the nation's population and 90 percent of the nation's GDP (gross domestic product) coming from metropolitan areas.

For Katz, metropolitan regions are the engines of national economic growth that "agglomerate the world's talented workers, innovative firms and risk-taking entrepreneurs, and concentrate unique assets and industry clusters that define regional competitiveness and drive national economies." As the United States enters the "next economy," Katz calls for federal and state investment in metropolitan economies so that "metros" will continue to "grow" the nation's jobs.

Why Cities Matter

EDWARD GLAESER

Cities often form for obvious and ordinary reasons. An island in the Seine was a good place for Romans and Franks to defend themselves against Huns and Vikings. The tip of Manhattan is a splendid natural port, with access to a deep river that cuts more than three-hundred miles into the American hinterland. But the magic of urban density means that agglomerations of people come together for simple reasons and often achieve amazing things. Most of mankind's cultural, economic, political, and social accomplishments have occurred in cities.

Dominic Pacyga's *Chicago* is a biography of a great and comparatively young city. It provides a comprehensive overview of Chicago's meteoric growth in the nineteenth century and its survival in the leaner years of the late twentieth century. Along the way, Pacyga reminds us of the remarkable things that can result when human beings interact with each other in dense, urban areas.

William Cronon's *Nature's Metropolis,* which appeared in 1991, is the reigning interpretation of Chicago's early growth. The city's natural advantages—its waterways and its proximity to lumber and wheat and livestock—turned a dusty outpost on the American frontier into a metropolis of millions in a few short decades. Pacyga notes that "[t]he city developed into a vast marketplace for lumber, grain, livestock, and produce even as it became a distribution point for eastern goods such as stoves, clothing, and hardware."

In the twentieth century, we became used to accidental urban giants, such as Las Vegas and Los Angeles. Such places are self-reinforcing groups of people who value being near each other (and sunshine), but they could have been located anywhere nearby. No geographical feature determined the placement of Los Angeles. In the nineteenth century, by contrast, when transportation costs were high and natural resources were critical, urban locations in America were practically fixed by geography.

Every one of the twenty largest cities in the United States in 1900 was on a waterway—from the oldest places that perched on the eastern seaboard's natural harbors to the youngest city, Minneapolis, located on the northernmost navigable point of the Mississippi. Pacyga remarks that Chicago's "canal proved to be crucial for the future of the city": it made Chicago the linchpin of a vast watery arc that stretched from New York to New Orleans. As much as cavalrymen and cowboys, city slickers tamed the west by creating the transport network that brought the products of the prairie to the customers of the east.

But Chicago did not grow from a city of 4,500 people in 1840 to a city of 3.4 million ninety years later merely as a center of water-borne, or rail-borne, commerce. The city's vast size reflects its abundance of industrial entrepreneurs. Some, such as Cyrus McCormick and his mechanical reapers, made their inventions in the east and moved to Chicago to be close to agricultural customers. As Pacyga writes, "McCormick moved west because he felt that the natural market for the new machines would be on the prairie." Others, such as George Pullman, produced their ideas in Chicago: "In the winter of 1857–58, he entered into a partnership with two brothers, Benjamin and Norman Field, to construct and operate sleeping cars on two Illinois railroad lines." By connecting people, cities help the spread of ideas, which in turn lead to new inventions, like Pullman's "Palace" cars, thus making inter-continental transportation far more pleasant.

Perhaps the most remarkable of Chicago's collaborative inventions was the skyscraper itself, which did so much to change the shape of cities throughout the world. There is a lively discussion among architectural historians about who deserves the credit for inventing the skyscraper, roughly defined as a building that stands tall thanks to a load-bearing steel skeleton. The Chicago engineer and architect William Le Baron Jenney is often described as the "Father of the Skyscraper," but there is plenty of room to debate that title. Jenney's claim is based on Chicago's Home Insurance Building, which does have metal-framing, but only on two sides. Burnham and Root's earlier Montauk building also had some iron-reinforced walls; such iron-frames were hardly unknown in industrial structures. The case gets even murkier because Burnham had once worked for Jenney, and for his fire-proofing contractor, the remarkable Peter B. Wight, a former disciple of John Ruskin who "proposed a fireproof iron-frame-supported column as early as 1874."

The quest for the skyscraper's paternity often misses the far more important truth: the real father of the skyscraper was Chicago itself. In the wake of the Great Fire of 1871, the city attracted a remarkable collection of architectural and engineering talent that was needed to rebuild a city. After all, even with the buildings gone, Chicago's future remained assured thanks to its enormous geographical advantages. Those minds then learned from each other and borrowed each others' ideas and collectively remade architecture. Ayn Rand's Frank Lloyd Wright, fictionalized as Howard Roark in *The Fountainhead,* is a particularly misleading portrait of an architect. Wright was no Gary Cooper-esque loner who sprang alone into the world as if from the head of Zeus. Wright was part of a chain of Chicago architects, and his ideas built on those of his mentor, Louis Sullivan, who had worked with Jenney himself. They were all part of the great web of creative interchange created by the city that emerged from Chicago's canal and stockyards.

Pacyga is interested in ordinary people, too. In 1900, Chicago attracted a gigantic inflow of immigrants, particularly Germans and Scandinavians. The city offered, after all, some of the highest wages on the planet. In later decades, Chicago provided a way out for many African-Americans, including the writer Richard Wright, fleeing the Jim Crow south. Cities such as this one have always had a comparative advantage in assimilating migrants, who have usually done well in Chicago and helped to give the city its character. When I was a graduate student in Chicago in the late 1980s, the blackboards still had bilingual signs in English and Polish.

Through the 1920s, Chicago was run by native born Americans, such as Big Bill Thompson. A colorful character who once staged a debate with live rats, he was one of the city's many powerful Republicans who "relied on their white American-born base and on African-American votes." After all, Lincoln himself had first been nominated by the Republican Party in the Chicago Wigwam. The Republican Party's commitment to prohibition gave it a natural appeal to Chicago's bootlegging entrepreneurs, notably Al Capone, who had much to lose from the legalization of liquor.

But Anton Cermak, a Czech immigrant and a determined "wet," bested Thompson and turned Chicago into a permanently Democratic city. As Pacyga tells it, "On April 7, 1931, Cermak beat Thompson by 191,916 votes, and the West Side Czech who Thompson had referred to as a 'Bozo' and a 'Bohunk' won all but five wards as Chicago placed the Democrats in power and set the stage for the 1932 presidential election." Cermak and his successors forged a durable Democratic machine that maintained its power through patronage and neighborhood outreach. (Cermak himself died in 1933 taking a bullet that was meant for F.D.R. Pacyga repeats the much-disputed tale that Cermak told the President, "I'm glad it was me instead of you." Others think that Cermak just uttered an expletive.)

In the 1950s, Cermak's machine was inherited by Chicago's first Mayor Daley. Father and son, the two Daleys have led Chicago for forty-two of the last fifty-five years. The durability

of their dominance is a puzzle that Pacyga could have done more to explain. In many large cities, such as New York, the New Deal and the expansion of relatively uncorrupt Federal patronage broke the back of older machines. In Chicago, the Daleys proved remarkably adept at surviving through changing times, much like the city itself. Indeed, one not insignificant reason for their success is that Chicago has managed to thrive despite the declining importance of the natural advantages that once determined the city's growth.

Post-war urban America was hit by changing transportation technologies that enabled families to move to the suburbs and the Sun Belt. All but two of America's ten largest cities in 1950 are less populated now than they were at the time. (The exceptions are New York and Los Angeles.) Chicago is about 23 percent smaller today than it was in that year, but this decline is quite modest compared to the more than 50 percent population drops seen in erstwhile urban giants like Cleveland, Detroit, and St. Louis.

Chicago's continued survival is a reflection of sensible leadership and—even more importantly—smart people who learn from one another in skyscrapers and scattered neighborhoods. The death of distance may have made Chicago's factories far less important, but globalization and new technologies have also increased the returns on being smart. Cities enable people to become smart by learning from other smart people. Like millions of others, I myself have done plenty of learning in the Windy City.

Pacyga's book is a fine introduction to Chicago's history, though it tries to do so much that it lacks the unified narrative and overarching theme that made *Nature's Metropolis* truly great. Pacyga's *Chicago* is closer in spirit to *Gotham,* Edwin Burrows and Mike Wallace's wonderful history of New York up to 1898. If Pacyga does not quite reach their lofty heights, he has still produced a very fine volume that should grace the bookshelves of every Chicago buff and every urbanist.

Critical Thinking

1. Why do cities exist? What are the important functions that cities serve?
2. What factors made Chicago so important; explaining its growth from a prairie town into a major city?

EDWARD GLAESER is the *Glimp Professor of Economics* at Harvard. He directs the Taubman Center for State and Local Government and the Rappaport Institute for Greater Boston.

The Metropolitan Moment

BRUCE KATZ

The early decades of this century are shaping up to be historically disruptive and defining. The global economic order is in a state of radical transition. New environmental imperatives and safety concerns are driving the extreme makeover of national energy systems. Rapid technological innovation is both expanding individual choice and enabling collective action. Social inequities and political volatility are at a fever pitch.

One unifying, simplifying thread emerges in this tumultuous period: the power of cities and metropolitan areas.

The world has arrived at a Metropolitan Moment. For the first time in history, cities and their metropolitan environs house more than half of the world's population. In the United States, metropolitan areas contain 84 percent of the population and generate 91 percent of GDP.

Metropolitan communities, here and abroad, represent the true economic geography. They agglomerate the world's talented workers, innovative firms and risk-taking entrepreneurs, and concentrate unique assets and industry clusters that define regional competitiveness and drive national economies. They are also the undisputed vehicles for environmental sustainability and social inclusion.

Such concentrated power demands new levels of responsibility. With many national and supranational levels of government dangerously adrift, the onus is on cities and metros to act like the engines of national prosperity they are and lead the economy-shaping, talent-preparing, place-making, and environmental-stewarding that this disruptive period demands.

Metros are stepping up to the challenge. In Europe, Munich has become an innovation and production powerhouse by strengthening the relationships between government, research institutions, global companies, and labor skilling institutions. In Asia, Seoul is pursuing a bottom-up effort to grow knowledge-based industrial clusters tied to major development projects in the city.

In the United States, a growing number of metro areas, challenged by an economy stuck in place and a federal government paralyzed by excessive partisanship, are likewise inventing a new playbook for prosperity and a new style of governance.

First, they are innovating locally to engineer the shift from an economy characterized by debt, consumption and income inequities to one driven by exports, powered by low carbon, fueled by innovation and rich with opportunity.

A geographically diverse set of places—Cleveland/Akron, Los Angeles, Louisville/Lexington, Memphis, Minneapolis/St. Paul, Phoenix/Mesa, Portland, Seattle, and Syracuse—are designing and implementing metropolitan business plans to grow jobs for the near term and reshape their economies for the long haul.

These metros are adapting the discipline of private sector business planning—evidence-based, solution-oriented, performance-measured—to the task of revitalizing and restructuring metropolitan economies. The result is the flourishing of deliberate and purposeful strategies that build on the distinctive assets, attributes, and advantages of these very different economies.

Take Greater Seattle, which intent on becoming the global hub of clean IT, is establishing a new facility to test, verify, and rapidly take to market new energy-saving technologies that can be deployed in residential, commercial, industrial, and retail buildings. Or Los Angeles, which is inventing a bottom-up export strategy to build on the distinctive goods and services produced in a diverse metropolis that is expanding trade with Asia, Mexico, and Latin America.

Second, U.S. metros are advocating nationally to enlist the help and support of their states and the federal government.

Greater Seattle, for example, has obtained a commitment from Washington State to match any resources secured to deploy their clean IT strategy. California leaders recently announced a new economic development framework heavily oriented to expanding international trade to scale up the export innovations of Los Angeles and other metros.

More broadly, Colorado, New York, and Tennessee have all initiated state economic development strategies that intentionally build upon and align with the distinctive action plans of cities, counties, and metropolitan areas.

Working together, metros are campaigning for federal support of metropolitan innovations that grow jobs. The U.S. Conference of Mayors jobs agenda, released earlier this month, calls for the federal government to use its substantial export infrastructure (e.g., the Ex Im Bank, the International Trade Administration, the Small Business Administration) to help 25 metros devise their own, home-grown metropolitan export plans over the next two years.

Finally, U.S. metros are networking globally to broaden the possibilities of trade and exchange, particularly with mega-metros in rising nations like China, India, and Brazil. U.S. metros must increasingly look abroad not only for markets for their goods and services but for sources of investment and talent. And that's what many are doing.

In Northern California, for example, the Bay Area Council has become a foundation of respected, actionable, up-to-date information about what the metropolis trades with whom. This platform is supplemented by the activities of private/public organizations like China SF, which acts as a matchmaker between firms wanting to sell goods and provide services to China and Chinese investors looking for investment opportunities in the Bay Area.

The new metropolitan playbook is altering thinking and action across a broad cross section of metropolitan leadership. Transformative initiatives are being delivered and co-produced by networks of corporate, political, civic, and community leaders. Governance is replacing government as the vehicle for change and, in the words of Colorado Governor and former Denver Mayor John Hickenlooper, "collaboration has become the new competition."

America's Metropolitan Moment has arrived and it is making innovative communities sharper in focus, more collaborative and cohesive in action, and more globally fluent and connected. The tantalizing promise is that this Moment will also rebuild the nation—economically, socially, and politically—in the process.

Critical Thinking

1. According to Katz, what contributions do metropolitan areas make to a nation's economic growth?

2. Advances in telecommunications technology have enabled the decentralization of business firms to suburban and to more distant exurban areas. Do these changes diminish the importance of cities?

3. What policies can government enact to help metropolitan areas serve as the engines of national economic growth?

4. What criticisms can be made of Katz's perspective? What arguments can be made against enacting new programs that seek to strengthen the economic capacity of cities?

UNIT 2

The Contemporary Urban Situation: The Growth, Decline, and Renaissance of Cities

Unit Selections

Learning Outcomes

After reading this unit, you should be able to:

- Identify the major population shifts that have reshaped U.S. cities since the 1940s.

- Point to the rise of new economic sectors that have displaced manufacturing in the post-industrial age.

- Explain why a number of older industrial centers have turned to attracting jobs in the medical and educational sectors rather than pursue new "smokestack" industries.

- Explain why numerous former industrial cities have begun to turn to "shrinking" and "greening" strategies.

- Detail the goals and major provisions of the Community Reinvestment Act (CRA).

- Explain how the Reagan–Bush policy of "deregulation" changed home loan practices in cities across the United States.

- Illustrate "balloon payments" and other "predatory" lending practices.

- Compare and evaluate the competing viewpoints of (a) conservatives who blame the CRA for the rash of home foreclosures and boarded-up properties in inner-city neighborhoods, and (b) liberals who absolve the CRA of blame.

- Assess the extent to which "race" continues to be a factor that shapes urban and suburban development in the contemporary United States.

- Come to your own conclusion regarding the causes of urban problems. Are urban problems the result of (a) free-market choice and natural demographic trends, (b) ill-conceived government policies, (c) the manipulations of private-sector institutions, or (d) racial bias?

Student Website
www.mhhe.com/cls

Internet References

Coney Island History Site
www.westland.net/coneyisland

First Suburbs, The Brookings Institution
www.brookings.edu/about/programs/metro/first-suburbs

Katrina Reading Room, The Brookings Institution
www.brookings.edu/metro/katrina-reading-room.aspx

Kirwan Institute, The Ohio State University
http://kirwaninstitute.org

National Fair Housing Alliance
www.nationalfairhousing.org

Public Policy Institute of California
www.ppic.org/main/policyareas.asp

Resource Centres on Urban Agriculture and Food Security
www.ruaf.org

Urban Agriculture News
http://urbanagriculture-news.blogspot.com

Deindustrialization and suburbanization have led to the decline of many former industrial centers. In the United States, cities, especially in the Northeast and the Midwest, have been weakened by a loss of population and manufacturing jobs (Article 3, "Then & Now: 1940–2010: How Has America Changed?"). In the present-day post-industrial economy, service sector and professional jobs have displaced the primacy once enjoyed by manufacturing in big-city economies. Frostbelt cities (in the Northeast and the Midwest United States) have also lost ground as a result of the regional shift of population and economic activity to the Sunbelt, the cities and suburbs of the Southwest and the West.

Advances in transportation and technology undergirded these shifts. The automobile enabled middle-class families to leave central cities for the "good life" of the suburbs. Businesses would soon follow, with trucking enabling the suburbanization of warehousing and manufacturing activities that were once located in central cities. New telecommunications technology helped facilitate the dispersal of office activities both to the suburbs and to the Sunbelt. Region after region has witnessed the rise of edge cities, the dense concentrations of office parks, shopping galleries, and cinema multiplexes that can be viewed as new suburban downtowns.

Throughout their history, U.S. cities have been centers of immigration. In the 1800s and early 1900s, immigrants from Europe poured into U.S. cities. In more recent decades, a new immigration from Mexico, other countries in Latin America, and South and East Asia has continued to fill urban neighborhoods, helping to mask the continued exodus of city residents to the suburbs. Were it not for the new immigration, the long-term decline of central cities would be even more apparent.

Demographic and economic pressures have led city after city to search for its new niche in a post-industrial economy. Many cities have sought to offset their loss of manufacturing jobs by becoming a regional center of universities and medical complexes (Article 4, "Eds, Meds and the Urban Revival"). Cities have also turned to tourism, convention centers, and sports-related development as providing paths to their economic rebirth. New York City reemerged from its flirtation with municipal bankruptcy in the 1970s to become a global center of banks, financial firms, and the headquarters of multinational corporations.

But not all cities have enjoyed a similarly impressive renaissance. Many cities have tried strategy after strategy to not great success. Detroit, St. Louis, Pittsburgh, Buffalo, Cleveland, Dayton, and Youngstown are among the former industrial centers

Digital Vision/PunchStock

that have come to realize that their loss of population is permanent, that they will never return to their peak size. These cities have adopted programs of planned shrinkage, including greening strategies to improve the amenities of urban life while the city tears down the worst of its excessive housing stock and antiquated industrial plants (Article 5, "Can They Save Youngstown?").

As previously described, middle-class families have chosen to leave the central city for the more pleasant environs of suburbia. But it is too simplistic to portray contemporary urban settlement patterns as purely the product of free choice operating in a free market. Discriminatory practices have also helped to determine the shape of the metropolis and the location of urban problems.

The basic patterns of cities and suburbs were established during an age when banks and insurance companies engaged in a practice known as redlining, refusing to finance home mortgages and business start-ups in large portions of inner-city communities that these financial agents dismissed as "non-bankable." At its crudest, banks and other credit institutions drew a red line on a map indicating the portions of the city in which they would make no loans, even to home seekers and business owners who had sound histories of earning and credit repayment. The result was disinvestment, where the unavailability of money for home mortgages and business modernization guaranteed the speedy decline of inner-city neighborhoods. The government itself practiced redlining. In the 1930s and 1940s, the Federal Housing Administration redlined large portions of the central cities, accelerating their decline by refusing to approve loans to applicants who wished to buy properties in these portions of the metropolis.

The Community Reinvestment Act (CRA) of 1975 (strengthened in 1997) finally put an end to redlining and, instead, sought to cure its effects by promoting greenlining, with requirements that banks make loans throughout their service area, including to home seekers and business owners in poorer sections of the city. The CRA has been responsible for the infusion of billions of dollars of investment capital into long-ignored central cities. But, since its enactment, political conservatives have sought to repeal the CRA or diminish its coverage, decrying that the Act's lending requirements constitute an unwise government intrusion into sound business practices. In the early 2000s, conservatives sought to blame the CRA and similar federal programs for helping to produce the crisis in the sub-prime housing market, the rash of home loan foreclosures that jeopardized the United States' economy.

But the defenders of the CRA attribute greater responsibility for foreclosures to Republican-era deregulation policies that enabled smaller and more unscrupulous institutions to enter the home lending field. As a result of deregulation, an increased number of home loans were made that were exempted from CRA regulation and review. As Gregory D. Squires (Article 6, "Predatory Lending: Redlining in Reverse") describes, unregulated entities took quick profits by resorting to creative lending instruments and deceptive practices, convincing borrowers to take out loans that they would be in no position to repay. Squires details the predatory lending practices that quick-profit lenders used to saddle home buyers with unnecessary costs.

The need to maintain a flood of abandoned properties added to cities' burdens at a time of diminished revenues. Declining property values meant shrunken local tax bases. Cutbacks in state and federal assistance further squeezed local governments. The State of California, facing its own fiscal problems and constrained by voter-imposed tax limitation measures, implemented major reductions in social service and urban aid programs, including the elimination of a program that had aided redevelopment agencies in some 400 communities across the state (Article 7, "Out of Cash: The End of the Nation's Largest Redevelopment Program").

Fortunately, many of the most blatant practices of racial discrimination have diminished over the years. Fair housing laws make many discriminatory practices. However, Unit 2 concludes with an important article that points to the continuing influence of race on the shape of the metropolis. Poor African-American residents of New Orleans, attempting to escape the death and devastation of Hurricane Katrina, were met by armed officers from suburban Gretna who blocked the bridge and turned the crowd back to the flood-stricken city (Article 8, "Bridge Blockade after Katrina Remains Divisive Issue"). Racial perceptions and fears still influence patterns of urban development.

Then & Now: 1940–2010: How Has America Changed?

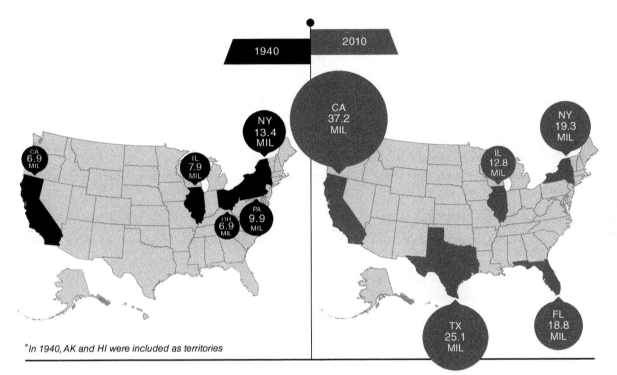

1940   2010

CA
6.9
MIL

NY
13.4
MIL

IL
7.9
MIL

OH
6.9
MIL

PA
9.9
MIL

CA
37.2
MIL

NY
19.3
MIL

IL
12.8
MIL

TX
25.1
MIL

FL
18.8
MIL

*In 1940, AK and HI were included as territories

5 Most Populated States   The overall U.S. population growth has shifted south and west, with Texas and Florida now among the most populous states.

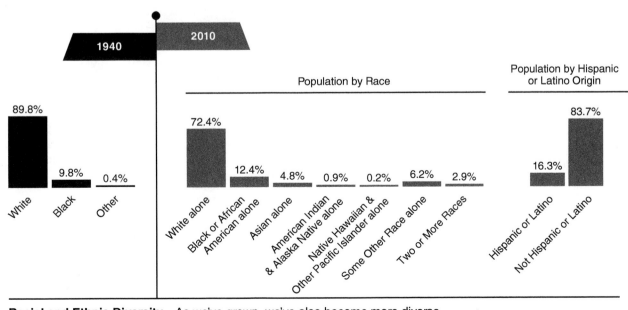

1940   2010

Population by Race

Population by Hispanic or Latino Origin

89.8%

9.8%

0.4%

White   Black   Other

72.4%

12.4%

4.8%

0.9%

0.2%

6.2%

2.9%

White alone

Black or African American alone

Asian alone

American Indian & Alaska Native alone

Native Hawaiian & Other Pacific Islander alone

Some Other Race alone

Two or More Races

16.3%

83.7%

Hispanic or Latino

Not Hispanic or Latino

Racial and Ethnic Diversity   As we've grown, we've also become more diverse.

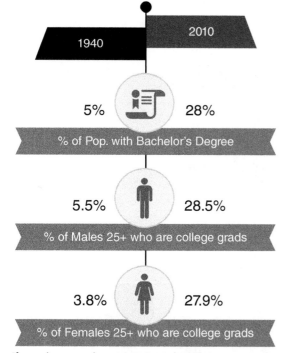

Education   Improved access to education means far more people today are college graduates.

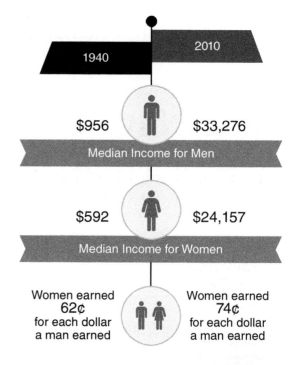

Earnings   Women still make less money in the workplace than men . . . but the wage gap is shrinking.

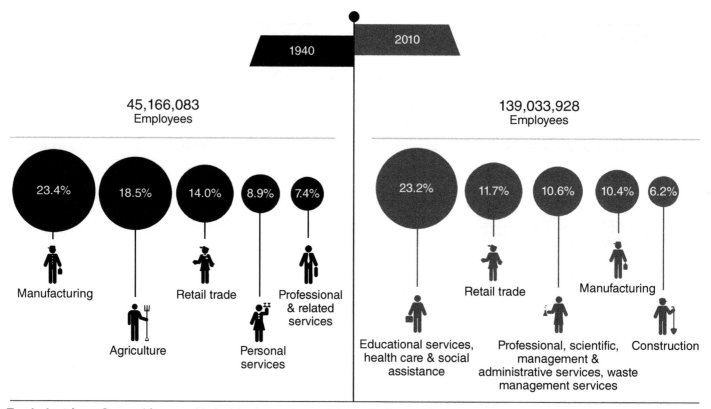

Top Industries   Our workforce and industries have changed dramatically over time.

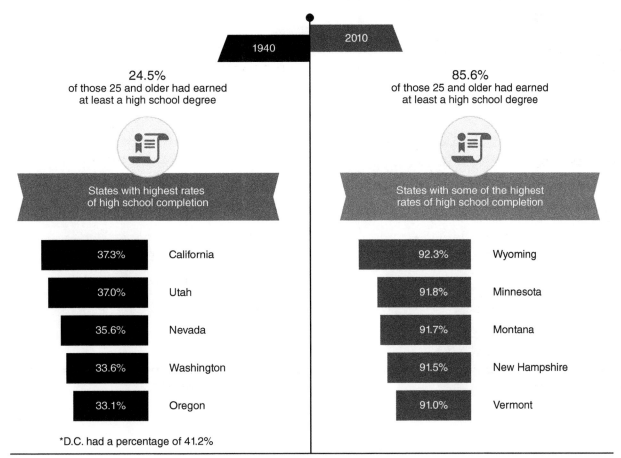

1940

2010

24.5%
of those 25 and older had earned
at least a high school degree

85.6%
of those 25 and older had earned
at least a high school degree

States with highest rates
of high school completion

States with some of the highest
rates of high school completion

37.3%	California
37.0%	Utah
35.6%	Nevada
33.6%	Washington
33.1%	Oregon

*D.C. had a percentage of 41.2%

92.3%	Wyoming
91.8%	Minnesota
91.7%	Montana
91.5%	New Hampshire
91.0%	Vermont

High School Education A far higher percentage of people had high school educations in 2010 than in 1940.

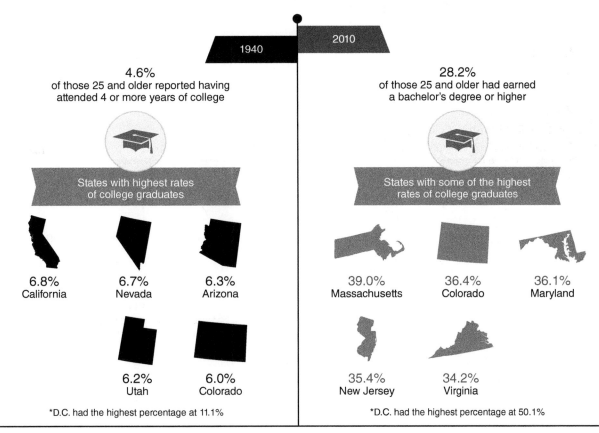

1940

2010

4.6%
of those 25 and older reported having
attended 4 or more years of college

28.2%
of those 25 and older had earned
a bachelor's degree or higher

States with highest rates
of college graduates

States with some of the highest
rates of college graduates

| 6.8% California | 6.7% Nevada | 6.3% Arizona |

| 6.2% Utah | 6.0% Colorado |

*D.C. had the highest percentage at 11.1%

| 39.0% Massachusetts | 36.4% Colorado | 36.1% Maryland |

| 35.4% New Jersey | 34.2% Virginia |

*D.C. had the highest percentage at 50.1%

College Education A bachelor's degree was much more common in 2010 than in 1940.

1940   2010

NEW YORK
7.5
MIL

LOS
ANGELES
1.5
MIL

LOS
ANGELES
3.8
MIL

NEW YORK
8.2
MIL

CHICAGO
3.4
MIL

PHILADELPHIA
1.9
MIL

CHICAGO
2.7
MIL

PHILADELPHIA
1.5
MIL

DETROIT
1.6
MIL

HOUSTON
2.1
MIL

*In 1940, AK and HI were included as territories

Top 5 Cities by Population   The change in America's most-populous cities shows how we've spread across the country.

Critical Thinking

1. What evidence points to the long-term decline of Frostbelt cities and the growth of Sunbelt communities?
2. What evidence points to the transformation of the United States from an industrial to a post-industrial society?

From U.S. Census Bureau, March 2012.

Eds, Meds and Urban Revival

In many cities, a big university is becoming the economic engine that a big corporation used to be.

Rob Gurwitt

L ook out from an upper-floor window of the old Sears building on the edge of downtown Birmingham, Alabama, and you can begin to appreciate the sweep of the city's history.

Close by, just beyond the vacant lot across the street, run the train lines whose arrival in the 1870s gave birth and shape to the city. Away to the south on Red Mountain, his upraised arm like an admonition on the horizon, stands a giant statue of Vulcan, the Roman god of the forge—a bittersweet reminder of the iron and steel works that fed Birmingham's industrial might for close to a century, until U.S. Steel left town in the early 1980s. But it's what lies in the middle that really matters now. Sprawling across 82 city blocks between the tracks and the mountain is the University of Alabama at Birmingham, known to all hereabouts as UAB. It is the largest employer in the city—indeed, in the entire state of Alabama. It has grown at such a prodigious clip in recent decades that locals joke that its initials stand for "the University that Ate Birmingham."

Most of them say this fondly, for the plain truth is that without UAB, Birmingham would have collapsed when U.S. Steel walked away. The university's steady growth, its reach and national prominence as a medical school, hospital system and health sciences complex, its researchers' ability to bring in hundreds of millions of dollars every year in grants and contracts, its 17,000 students and 19,000 employees, its impact on the city's restaurants, arts and entertainment—all of this makes it, in the words of former Mayor Richard Arrington, "our economic life's blood."

It's not that the university is the only economic game in the Birmingham area. Honda and Mercedes now have automotive plants nearby, the insurance and financial sectors remain strong, and one of the country's top 10 banks—Regions—has its headquarters here. Yet for all this, there is a growing conviction in Birmingham that if the city's future dynamism lies anywhere, it is with the researchers, doctors, engineers, faculty members and sheer intellectual heft of UAB. Accustomed to thinking of Birmingham as the undisputed kingpin of Alabama's economy, the city's corporate leaders have watched with dismay in recent years as development momentum has shifted to Mobile, where

the port is bustling, the German steel giant ThyssenKrupp is building a $3.7 billion plant, and the U.S. Air Force's new aerial refueling tanker will be manufactured; and to Huntsville, where a new genetics research institute and companies drawn by NASA's presence have created an air of high-tech vitality. Birmingham used to have four major bank headquarters; Regions' is the only one left. BellSouth, one of the city's most prominent corporate players, has been taken over by AT&T. Other companies have left for New York, Tennessee and Texas.

"With the consolidation of the banking industry, the consolidation of the utility industry, how long will we be like we are?" asks Charles McCrary, the president and CEO of Alabama Power and a boardroom pacesetter both locally and statewide. "UAB is the only sustainable economic development engine we have in Birmingham." The pressing question for both Birmingham and UAB, he has come to believe, is whether they can sort out what to do with it.

Bell Towers for Smokestacks

Plenty of states, cities, academic institutions and medical centers are grappling with a similar challenge. In an era when technological know-how and innovation have become prime economic drivers, "eds and meds" have become indispensable anchors of urban growth. "In many respects," a report by CEOs for Cities and the Initiative for a Competitive Inner City commented a few years ago, "the bell towers of academic institutions have replaced smokestacks as the drivers of the American urban economy."

Yet until relatively recently, most universities and the cities surrounding them went about their business without taking full stock of what each meant to the other. Many local and state government leaders, notes Temple University political scientist Carolyn Adams, "don't see these institutions as having an economic development function much beyond employment and land development." For their part, hospitals and academic institutions aren't accustomed to thinking of themselves as de facto economic bigwigs or pondering the responsibilities that go along with that status; for many, the prevailing attitude toward the communities that host them has essentially been, "You should just thank your lucky stars we're here."

And to a degree, of course, they're right. A 1999 Brookings Institution report by University of Pennsylvania historian Ira Harkavy and Harmon Zuckerman—now the chief planner for Douglas County, Nevada—found that in the 20 largest U.S. cities, "eds and meds" accounted for 35 percent of the workforce employed by the top 10 private employers; in many cities, a university or medical system was the largest private employer, and in four of them—Washington D.C., Philadelphia, San Diego and Baltimore—medical systems and universities generated more than half the jobs among the 10 largest private employers. While no similar study has been done since then, Harkavy, now director of Penn's Netter Center for Community Partnerships, believes all this has only been magnified over the past decade. "There's been a general increase in the size of these institutions," he notes, "especially on the medical side."

Moreover, "eds and meds" have two attributes much appreciated by local political leaders: They have money to spend, and they stay put. As New Haven, Rochester, Philadelphia, Baltimore and other struggling cities all found to their good fortune during the depths of the urban crisis, universities and large medical centers don't get bought out or relocated by their owners. And as their resources have swelled—last year, 76 universities around the country had endowments exceeding $1 billion—institutions such as Harvard, Columbia, Penn, Johns Hopkins and Case Western Reserve have become ambitious and powerful land developers. Sometimes they feel an expand-or-die imperative; sometimes they simply want to improve life in nearby neighborhoods and have grown tired of waiting for financially pressed local governments to jump-start the process.

Yet as Birmingham's example suggests, universities and medical centers are more than just steadfast employers and major land developers. They are "the generators of development across the city," says Harkavy, coming to shape local economies through the research and activities they sponsor. Universities and research institutions undergird what Carolyn Adams calls "networks of knowledge and entrepreneurship that create new products and processes." In other words, they convene faculty, students, researchers, investors, entrepreneurs and others who can share ideas and dream up new ventures—the old Sears building in Birmingham, for instance, is now the Innovation Depot, an incubator designed in part to take the fruits of UAB's research and spin them into businesses. Coupled with the stable incomes they provide, the cosmopolitan tastes they house and the cultural vibrancy they stimulate, it's no surprise that universities have come to anchor many cities' prospects for growth.

What is just beginning to happen is a mutual coming to terms. Local political and civic leaders are starting to think strategically about how to use academic institutions to spur further economic and community development, while university administrators are getting accustomed to the higher expectations thrust on them by their size, resources and place in the changing economic firmament. Some places are further along on this path than others: Pittsburgh, for instance, where the Allegheny Conference on Community Development and the state's Ben Franklin Partnership began in the 1980s to harness innovative thinking at local universities to the cause of economic development; or Philadelphia, where the University of Pennsylvania has a staggering array of initiatives aimed at improving the city's general well-being; or Atlanta, where the Georgia Research Alliance brings government officials, business leaders and university administrators together to attract world-class researchers and labs to the state and then to help them spin ventures off into the marketplace.

Most communities, however, are more like Birmingham: aware of the possibilities and the need to take advantage of them, but not yet organized to get there. "Our growth and development have been so extraordinarily fast," says Dr. Max Michael, dean of UAB's School of Public Health, "that only within the last few years have folks within the community and at UAB lifted up their heads and said, 'Oh my God, here's this big thing in the city,' and begun figuring out a role and responsibilities for the university. A lot of urban universities are in this position: Now we're here, what do we do?"

Unlikely Colossus

That UAB should be in such a position at all would seem remarkable to those who saw it in its early days. It began in the 1930s as a small extension school of the University of Alabama's main Tuscaloosa campus, then in the mid-1940s added a hospital, dental school and medical college on three blocks of Birmingham's south side, surrounded by a neighborhood of small houses, a few stores and restaurants, a quickie car wash and a miniature golf course.

University administrators now work where Birmingham's kids played putt-putt, and the rest of the neighborhood—along with several others in every direction—is long gone as well. UAB has mushroomed from a medical school and hospital offering extension programs for commuting students to a major university with schools of business, education, engineering, arts and humanities, sciences and mathematics—but most important, a gigantic health complex with a $400 million-a-year research enterprise known internationally for its work on cancer, bioengineering, diabetes, heart disease and social and behavioral medicine. And it continues to grow. The university as a whole adds about 225,000 square feet of space each year, says Sheila Chaffin, its planning director. "That's about as much as we did in the entire City University of New York system when I was there," she adds. "It's very aggressive."

UAB helped Birmingham meet the two biggest challenges of its modern life: overcoming the legacy of the fire hoses, police dogs and church bombing with which the more extreme members of white Birmingham responded to the civil rights movement in the 1960s; and reshaping its economy after the departure of U.S. Steel. The first came in mostly quiet ways, through civic leaders who'd grown up elsewhere and come to Birmingham because of the university, and more parochially through the recruiting of black physicians and faculty members, a university-approved move to desegregate the county medical society, the admission of black students and later, when Arrington was mayor, a push to use minority-owned firms to work on campus expansion. When U.S. Steel left, UAB's expansion and the sheer number of white-collar jobs it generated were crucial to keeping the city afloat.

These days, more people work at UAB than in downtown Birmingham. The hospital system alone is a $1.5 billion-a-year enterprise. "Our research expenditures by themselves probably contribute a couple of hundred million dollars to Birmingham in terms of payroll," says Richard Marchase, the university's vice president for research and economic development. "We expect a [researcher] we bring in will hire eight to 10 people and have half a million dollars in payroll, and we see that avenue as among the most important ways we contribute to the city." The university has started to work with the city's economic development team to lure a major pharmaceutical manufacturer to Birmingham. "They wouldn't even look at us were it not for UAB," says Griffin Lassiter, who does business recruitment for the city.

And the new Innovation Depot, located midway between downtown and UAB, pairs the university with a former county- and city-supported incubator; spinoffs from UAB research—on everything from cancer-preventive drugs to toxin detection to cell modeling and molecular screening—form a significant part of its clientele. The university, says Innovation Depot's CEO, Susan Matlock, "is the way to our future as a city."

Yet for all this, it doesn't take many conversations with leaders from both UAB and the city to get the sense that the two still have a ways to go if they're to become true collaborators. "There's no way Birmingham would be the relatively thriving city it is today without the presence of UAB," says Mark Kelly, a local writer who specializes in the city's business and political history. "The flip side is, the UAB attitude has often been, 'You wouldn't be here without us, so we do our civic part by being the largest employer in the state,' and there really has not been a strong connection in terms of planning or strategic thinking between the city and UAB. UAB is almost a city unto itself."

Saving the Neighborhood

This is hardly a complaint unique to Birmingham; there probably isn't a university community in the country where you can't hear some version of it. Still, Harkavy believes, the picture has begun to change in recent years. "Higher education and medical institutions have begun to understand their role better," he says. "There's much more pressure on higher-ed institutions to illustrate their role in the local environment."

One of the most compelling illustrations is taking place in Baltimore, where Johns Hopkins is far and away the largest private employer. In an effort that joins the university, the city and the mega-developer Forest City Enterprises, the John Hopkins medical system is building an immense new life sciences park aimed at spinning off business opportunities from its research, and is placing the park in the deeply struggling East Baltimore neighborhood the school inhabits. In conjunction with the Annie E. Casey Foundation and the city, it has created a public-private enterprise, East Baltimore Development Inc., whose job is to oversee an ambitious effort to rehabilitate the neighborhood by building new housing for its residents, helping them

with family and health counseling, creating a new elementary and middle school, and perhaps most important, crafting workforce development programs to place East Baltimore residents in the construction, health care and bioscience jobs generated by the project. "The plan acknowledges that Hopkins is a great strength in that community," says Deputy Mayor Andrew Frank, "and Hopkins, in its own enlightened self-interest, felt it was important to work with the community and the city to revitalize the neighborhoods around the huge investment in their campus. So we're looking for a transformation of the community that still connects it to its roots."

UAB's president, Carol Garrison, insists that her university, too, has "a plan and partnership with the larger community in terms of how we all move forward together. I'm fond of saying that as goes the city, so goes UAB, and as goes UAB, so goes the city." She points to the close ties between the university's school of education and teachers in area public schools, research on such issues as homelessness and drug addiction being carried on by the UAB faculty, summer programs for high school students, the school of public health's collaboration with storefront churches on health education, and the huge amounts of outside funding UAB brings into Birmingham through its research. "I would say we're doing considerable things in the community," she says.

But there is a perception both within and outside the university that it could be doing more—not so much in terms of discrete efforts, but as the most powerful institution in Birmingham. "From a public health point of view, it's one thing for the medical center to say we provide a kajillion dollars in uncompensated care," says School of Public Health Dean Max Michael. "It's another to say we have rampant poverty, high homicide rates, breathtaking levels of illiteracy and other problems of urban blight that we ought to have a role in addressing. We have any number of faculty who interact with community groups and have developed great trust; the challenge now is how do you coalesce that and make it a longitudinal culture of partnership?"

What makes this a particular challenge is that the priorities of the university, the city and the state all move in different directions, making intensive collaboration difficult to build. "In terms of how do we need to keep this institution alive and growing," says Bob Corley, who chairs UAB's Global and Community Leadership Program, "we're not looking to the city in particular to help that occur. We're looking to the federal government. We're looking to the state government. We're looking to the families and our students who support us through their tuition. Nearly all of them are somewhere outside the city of Birmingham. So the ways in which we can assist the future development and economic development of Birmingham—it's a consideration, but not at the center of what makes us exist. We're not Alabama Power. We don't rely on or require that continuing kind of growth in the economy to make us go."

Similarly, there's a growing chorus within Birmingham arguing that the city—both its public and private leaders—and the state have failed to recognize just how crucial an economic engine UAB has become. "UAB speaks a different language than the state speaks, it speaks a different language than the city speaks, and in all candor, there's not the strongest relationship between the city's business community and UAB," says Jim Hayes, who directs the corporate-financed Economic Development Partnership of Alabama. "I don't know that there's fault at that—I think it's a matter of putting your head down and doing your business every day and not spending your time with the other. But if we ever let UAB lose its momentum, there's not enough money in the state of Alabama to get it back."

Which is why Hayes, Alabama Power's Charles McCrary and others have begun to argue that the way the Alabama legislature funds UAB—which now gets less than a quarter of its money from the state budget—needs to change. In essence, the university draws its state money from the same pool of funds as elementary and secondary schools, which means that every year it is competing with the powerful Alabama Education Association for legislators' attention, even as neighboring Georgia, with its well-funded research alliance, tries to poach UAB's leading researchers. "Right now, UAB lives from budget cycle to budget cycle," says Hayes. "But that's not a strategy. A dollar here and a dollar there equals two dollars. But if you build a system like Georgia's, a dollar here and a dollar there equals five dollars. That's where we've got to go, but it's a leadership issue. State leaders have to recognize that we have to build a system that fosters this kind of growth. And we as a

community—and this is part UAB's fault and part the private community's fault—could be much better advocates for UAB to help facilitate a change."

McCrary insists that's starting to happen, although slowly. There's more informal communication between the business community and UAB's leadership—President Garrison, for instance, just spent a year as head of the regional chamber of commerce—and collaboration on Innovation Depot and several pharmaceutical ventures also has strengthened ties. "For so long, it was just, 'They're over there, we're over here,'" says McCrary. "But now we're saying, 'We need you,' and whenever you tell someone you need them, they say, 'Gee, yeah, you do need me, and I need you.'"

Critical Thinking

1. How is the economy of big cities like Birmingham and Philadelphia quite different today than a half century ago?

2. Why have cities turned their attention to "Eds and Meds"? How does the growth of Eds and Meds represent a shift in city economic development strategies, from the "smokestack" chasing of old to more contemporary "smart cities" policies?

3. Are all cities capable of attracting Eds and Meds?

Can They Save Youngstown?

Brentin Mock

One frequently asked question in Youngstown is: Who's responsible for cutting my neighbor's grass?

It's hard to imagine hearing this often in any city, but there it is on the "Frequently Asked Questions" page of Youngstown's official website, *cityofyoungstownoh.org*. The page provides the obvious answer: the owner. Concerning what to do if the owner refuses to landscape, Youngstown bluntly instructs: "Call the Police!"

The city council recently raised this "infraction" to a misdemeanor 3—a classification shared by prostitution in Ohio. Youngstown absolutely won't tolerate grass growth. Actually, the city hasn't welcomed growth in general since the '50s, when it began hemorrhaging residents at an average population decline of 16 percent annually, from over 170,000 to 73,817 today. Youngstown is a shrinking city, a municipality of arrested or regressive development, both in financial and demographic terms. Most cities in this predicament hunker down, then spend big on casinos, sports stadiums, convention centers, hotels and nightclubs to attract new residents. The success rate for this model is unpromising, however, especially for smaller cities that will never compete with large metropolises.

Youngstown's plan is to embrace stunted growth. The "shrinking city model," as it's called, reasons that a city suffering post-industrial blues and losing residents by the thousands won't suddenly charm people back by way of huge commercial bells and blockbuster whistles. Instead, the shrunk city demolishes blocks, converting its abandoned buildings and houses into open space for neighborhood enterprises and to nurture greenery. The method is fashionably known in Europe as "unbuilding the city," finding purposes for the "terrain vague"—unused land and property—other than habitation, profit or attraction.

So far, only Eastern Europe has successfully enacted these "smart decline" plans, reducing dozens of cities where deindustrialization had taken hold in the aftermath of World War II. In Germany, cities such as Halle and Leipzig have effectively worked their shrinkage into sustainability in the years following the dismantling of the Berlin Wall. Old mills, factories and abandoned homes were put to creative use by the few residents left behind.

It's a bit like telling a bald guy to shelve the Rogaine and the fancy toupees, and work instead with the little bit of hair he has. Youngstown is by no means the only U.S. city that's balding. Virtually any city in Ohio, Pennsylvania and West Virginia that relied on steel production in the 20th century now struggles with the loss of its assets and former status. Unlike many of these cities, Youngstown is owning its population deficit. Through its "Youngstown 2010" plan, led by Mayor Jay Williams, the city plans to remain competitive by investing in 127 small neighborhoods throughout the region.

> **Virtually any city in Ohio, Pennsylvania and West Virginia that relied on steel production in the 20th century now struggles with the loss of its assets and former status.**

But how exactly does a city sustain itself while shrinking? By 2030, a population of 73,000 will become 54,000, which will eventually become 20,000—and then what? Size may not matter, but density does, especially to solidify a tax base that can support schools and media. Is Youngstown sealing its fate by shrinking out of existence?

A Plan Hatched by Town and Gown

The name, "Youngstown 2010," shouldn't be confused with projected development goals, since none exist (at least none to be met by 2010). The year refers instead to census markers. "We don't know how long this process will take," says Phil Kidd, the city's downtown events director and founder of Defend Youngstown, a self-described "movement dedicated to the advancement of the city of Youngstown" with a popular local Web site. "The implementation stage does not have a timeline. In 2010, we'll stop and ask what's working and what's not working."

William D'Avignon, the city's deputy director of planning, adds, "We're not saying everything we want to carry out will be completed by 2010, but we're going to plan for anything that's achievable by 2010."

The idea of shrinking first occurred to Youngstown after closing out the 20th century with three consecutive decades of decline. On Sept. 19, 1977, "Black Monday," the Sheet and Tube steel company closed doors on its mills, triggering the eventual closure of the rest of Youngstown's steel industry. As population withered so did the housing stock, from over 50,000 units built before 1950 to just over 37,000 today. White flight reduced that demographic from two-thirds of the city in 1980 to less than half today; the black population rose from one-third in 1980 to 45 percent today. And if the 4,213 Hispanic and Latino-American population seems minute, bear in mind that that number is 200 percent higher than in 1990.

In the infant years of the new millennium, the city realized it urgently needed a new vision. Jay Williams was working as the city's director of community development in 2001 when the planning department sought out the expertise of Youngstown State University (YSU), the leading employer for the city and Williams's alma mater. YSU had plans in mind for its own growth, but ended up nurturing a rehabilitative partnership with the city. Williams, along with D'Avignon and Anthony Kobak, the current chief city planner, teamed with YSU academics piqued by the research of new urbanists such as Stephen Graham and Ann Markusen. Youngstown came to recognize itself, in the words of Markusen's theoretical work, not as a "sticky" place—an urban center that continuously draws people (Los Angeles, Atlanta, New York City)—but as "slippery"—one where it's easy for, say, a YSU student to slip into the city, and then slip out due to lack of jobs or housing.

"Our right-sizing plan came out of talks we were having internally acknowledging that although our population wouldn't be going back to the hundreds of thousands, but that smaller didn't mean inferior," says Mayor Williams. "The question we asked was, because we were once so much larger how can we take the remnants of what made us large and build upon that?"

The planning team began to consider a counterintuitive approach to development: rather than grow the city, it should clean and "green" up the unoccupied real estate. They conceived and presented a basic "right-sizing" formula to the Youngstown public, who fleshed out the plan with their ideas and expectations. Or, depending on whom you ask, the planners consulted the public first and then drew up a blueprint for Youngstown 2010.

No matter its genesis, the eventual plan reflected three years of public surveys and town hall meetings aimed at understanding the city's needs. "Overwhelmingly, people said they wanted the city shrunken, and they were for cleaning up the blighted situations that were causing different variations of decay, crime and abandonment," Kidd says. Thousands of citizens were consulted, and hundreds of students and professionals logged the process. The plan went into high gear after Williams was elected mayor in 2005. At 34, he was the youngest mayor Youngstown ever elected, and also the first African American—two identity aspects that resonated with college students and the emerging black majority.

The Antidote to Racism

"He's kind of like the Barack Obama of Youngstown," says Rev. Michael Harrison, pastor of Union Baptist Church in the Northside. "I was pretty skeptical of the 2010 plan in the beginning, only because I did not fully understand it. Once the mayor explained it to a group of us pastors, whom he brought together, and showed us exactly how we all could benefit, I bought it hook, line and sinker."

Like Obama, Williams comes across as a figure whose blackness alone is the presumed antidote to racism. As Kobak says, "A lot of people use Jay Williams's getting elected as mayor as a symbolic gesture of moving on, given our history of racial tension."

African-American steelworkers in Youngstown and Western Pennsylvania have historically struggled with discrimination at least as far back as the late 1910s, when white labor unions went on strike against the steel companies. African Americans who were bussed in at that time were seen as scabs, although from their perspective, they were just taking advantage of previously unavailable opportunities.

Hostility toward African-American steelworkers has remained entrenched ever since. They have worked the least desirable and most dangerous jobs for the least amount of pay and lowest chance for promotion. Not until 1974, when the U.S. Department of Labor enforced a federal consent decree on companies practicing racial discrimination, did working conditions for African Americans begin to improve. But Black Monday arrived three years later, rendering the law moot by leaving scores of black men unemployed. Notoriously racist banks refused African Americans home loans, which left neighborhoods segregated all the way through the 20th century.

Ironically, Williams came from the banking industry before he began working for the city. "I started off as a young loan officer and making sure people weren't signing up with fly-by-night loan predators," says Mayor Williams. "I also spent time going out to neighborhood churches and community organizations to do outreach emphasizing the importance of working with local financial institutions and preparing themselves from a credit standpoint. I told the banks they have an obligation to lend on fair terms. But ultimately we were out there in the community educating the people as well. To this day, I still have people who will walk up to me with tears in their eyes talking about when they got their first home loan."

The Youngstown 2010 plan lists improving residents' quality of life as one of its "major vision principles" (its goals), a component aim of which is to "begin dealing with difficult issues such as public safety and racism." The two often go discomfortingly hand-in-hand. To tackle crime, as one of his first acts, Mayor Williams increased the budget for demolitions of abandoned buildings, understood to be havens for criminals. Race is trickier, however, especially when it's inextricably linked to labor and class. Kobak says the city has produced three television shows based on town hall meetings that address issues of race. But eliminating racism won't be as easy as identifying buildings to tear down—longstanding ideas about race and class can't simply be demolished and erased.

It's acknowledged across the board that when cities shrink, the neighborhoods that end up most expendable are typically low-income and often predominantly African- or Latino-American communities. Kobak says these issues need not be seen as black-and-white—"People make them such."

"What we're trying to do is bring people from all walks of life toward a common cause," says Kobak. "We want to remove all the racial issues and bring the city to the forefront by suggesting that these are neighborhood issues, not black-and-white issues." So far, the consensus approach seems to have worked. Rev. Harrison, who's black, says African Americans have been granted "equal opportunity and access" in the new plan, while Kidd says race hasn't been a "major issue."

Cities Shrink, but Problems Grow

Inevitably, unforeseen problems will impinge on Youngstown's plan. For example, another labor conflict—this one not racially loaded—played out as recently as 2004, when the staff of the daily newspaper *Vindicator* went on strike for improved wages. One thing Youngstown possibly overlooked is that as the city shrinks, so does the circulation, subscription, advertising and revenue base for local media. City hall may not have been concerned with drawing people from other cities for growth, but the *Vindicator* was. With a depleted staff, but a mandate to continue publishing, the independent, family-owned *Vindicator* began recruiting journalists from as far away as New Orleans—while the strike was still in effect.

Another problem with shrinking is that fewer competing investors increases the chance for one or a small few to buy up more than a fair share of property—as is the case with downtown Youngstown, where Louis A. Frangos, the single largest property owner, occasionally poses a problem for those trying to preserve the city.

Among the many bank and realty office buildings he owns is the Stambaugh building, a 13-story structure of 531 windows, some of which had been crashing to the sidewalk. Frangos initially proposed getting rid of the building, calling it a "lost cause." The building, however, has historic preservation status. When Frangos suggested replacing the broken windows with unsightly plywood, the city's elite balked: a letter signed by 17 "prominent players" asked the mayor to have Frangos take better care of his buildings. The letter referred to his properties as "a real-life Monopoly game that is occurring in our downtown."

"By no means do we think we have it all figured out," says Kidd. "We all want to clean and green our city so that at some point we can be positioned for growth again, but right now we just have to clean up the house."

Small Town Business

At the same time that the city prepares to shrink, the mayor and his planners are eyeballing potential growth through regional partnerships, including the neighboring municipalities of Austintown, Boardman, Camfield, Campbell and Struthers. Youngstown wants to establish a joint economic development district (JEDD) plan encompassing the Mahoning River Corridor. In the proposed arrangement, the suburban townships will depend on Youngstown's water supply, and residents who work in the city will pay an income tax directed to business expansion efforts.

Youngstown expects the JEDD to produce some 3,750 jobs and $439 million in revenue over the next 20 years. The only problem is that suburbanites aren't interested in financing Youngstown's growth with their own income and water taxes. Some municipalities have retained lawyers specifically trained in JEDD policies to protect themselves from the plan.

For now, though, the principal growth efforts are community empowerment groups. Six neighborhoods, including Wick Park, which Kidd calls home, have been targeted for investment. In concert with the city and YSU, community organizations from each will establish their own development goals, to be executed by volunteer residents and reinforced by the city. Successfully implemented plans will serve as templates for other neighborhoods, as well as for future city-community governance. "A lot of people in this city are used to taking orders through a chain of command," says Kidd. "In this instance, it's a 50-50 partnership between the communities and the city."

The downtown central business district is also being revived. Under the Youngstown Business Incubator program, start-up knowledge- and technology-based companies are nestled under one roof and assisted by federal grants. The one major requirement for inclusion is that the start-ups exchange notes so that they can build as a cluster. One company from this program, Turning Technologies, has already taken off, voted the top software company in the country last year by *Inc. Magazine.*

After two failed attempts, Youngstown also finally won the National Planning Excellence Award for Public Outreach last year, awarded by the American Planning Association. The lesson, apparently, is that sometimes you have to shrink.

Critical Thinking

1. What factors led to the long-term decline of cities like Youngstown?

2. How does Youngstown's "shrinking cities" model represent a bold attempt to re-imagine the city and to reposition itself for a better future?

3. What, if anything, can be done to reverse the decline of former industrial cities? What specific policies or actions do you suggest?

Predatory Lending: Redlining in Reverse

GREGORY D. SQUIRES

The proverbial American dream of owning a home has become an all-too-real nightmare for a growing number of families. Take the case of Florence McKnight, an 84-year-old Rochester widow who, while heavily sedated in a hospital bed, signed a $50,000 loan secured by her home for only $10,000 in new windows and other home repairs. The terms of the loan called for $72,000 in payments over 15 years, after which she would still owe a $40,000 one-time payment. Her home is now in foreclosure.

Unfortunately, this is not an isolated incident. Predatory lending has emerged as the most salient public policy issue in financial services today. If progress has been made to increase access to capital for racial minorities, low-income families and economically distressed communities, that progress has always come with great struggle. And it appears there are few, if any, permanent victories. The emergence of predatory lending practices demonstrates that the struggle against redlining has not been won, but has simply taken some new turns.

After decades of redlining practices that starved many urban communities for credit and denied loans to racial minorities, today a growing number of financial institutions are flooding these same markets with exploitative loan products that drain residents of their wealth. Such "reverse redlining" may be as problematic for minority families and older urban neighborhoods as has been the withdrawal of conventional financial services. Instead of contributing to homeownership and community development, predatory lending practices strip the equity homeowners have struggled to build and deplete the wealth of those communities for the enrichment of distant financial services firms.

There are no precise quantitative estimates of the extent of predatory lending. But the growth of subprime lending (higher cost loans to borrowers with blemishes on their credit records) in recent years, coupled with growing law enforcement activity in this area, clearly indicates a surge in a range of exploitative practices. Not all subprime loans are predatory, but virtually all predatory loans are subprime. Some subprime loans certainly benefit high-risk borrowers who would not qualify for conventional, prime loans. Predatory loans, however, charge higher rates and fees than warranted by the risk, trapping homeowners

in unaffordable debt and often costing them their homes and life savings. Examples of predatory practices include:

- Balloon payments that require borrowers to pay off the entire balance of a loan by making a substantial payment after a period of time during which they have been making regular monthly payments;
- Required single premium credit life insurance, where the borrower must pay the entire annual premium at the beginning of the policy period rather than in monthly or quarterly payments. (With this cost folded into the loan, the total costs, including interest payments, are higher throughout the life of the loan);
- Homeowners insurance where the lender requires the borrower to pay for a policy selected by the lender;
- High pre-payment penalties that trap borrowers in the loans;
- Fees for services that may or may not actually be provided;
- Loans based on the value of the property with no regard for the borrower's ability to make payments;
- Loan flipping, whereby lenders use deceptive and high-pressure tactics resulting in the frequent refinancing of loans with additional fees added each time;
- Negatively amortized loans and loans for more than the value of the home, which result in the borrower owing more money at the end of the loan period than when they started making payments.

Here are some numbers to illustrate the extent of the problem: The Joint Center for Housing Studies at Harvard University reported that mortgage companies specializing in subprime loans increased their share of home purchase mortgage loans from 1 to 13 percent between 1993 and 2000. Economists at the Office of Federal Housing Enterprise Oversight found that subprime loans are concentrated in neighborhoods with high unemployment rates and declining housing values. Almost 20 percent of refinance loans to borrowers earning less than 60 percent of area median income in 2002 were made by subprime lenders, compared to just over 7 percent for borrowers earning 120 percent of median income or higher, according to research by the Association of Community Organizations for Reform Now (ACORN). The Center for Community Change reported that African Americans are three times as likely as whites to finance their homes with subprime loans; this is true even between upper-income blacks and whites. The Joint Center for Housing Studies has also revealed that race continues to be a factor in the distribution of subprime loans after other individual and neighborhood factors are taken into consideration.

One cost of the sudden increase in subprime lending has been an increase in foreclosure rates. According to the Joint Center for Housing Studies, borrowers with subprime loans are eight times more likely to default than those with prime conventional loans. Yet, it has been estimated that between 30 and 50 percent of those receiving subprime loans would, in fact, qualify for prime loans.

Ironically, some of the steps taken to increase access to credit for traditionally underserved communities have inadvertently created incentives for predatory lending. The Community Reinvestment Act of 1977, which banned redlining by federally chartered banks and savings institutions, provided incentives for lenders to serve minority and low-income areas. So did the Fair Housing Act of 1968, which prohibited racial discrimination in home financing. FHA insurance and securitization of loans (lenders sell loans to the secondary mortgage market, which packages them into securities to sell to investors) reduce the risk to lenders and increase the capital available for mortgage lending. In addition, the federal government established affordable housing goals for the two major secondary mortgage market actors, Fannie Mae and Freddie Mac. Fifty percent of the mortgages they buy must be for low- and moderate-income households.

All these actions have increased access to capital, but sometimes by predatory lenders. Wall Street has become a major player by securitizing subprime loans. The involvement of investment banks in subprime lending grew from $18.5 billion in 1997 to $56 billion in 2000.

With passage of the Financial Services Modernization Act of 1999, the consolidation of financial services providers received the blessing of the federal government. Between 1970 and 1997 the number of banks in the U.S. dropped from just under 20,000 to 9,100, primarily as a result of mergers among healthy institutions. The 1999 Act removed many post–Depression-era laws that had provided for greater separation of the worlds of banking, insurance and securities. Subsequent to this "reform," it became far easier for financial service providers to enter each of these lines of business. One result is that commercial banks and savings institutions, which used to make the vast majority of mortgage loans, now make about a third of them. Mortgage banking affiliates of depository institutions, independent mortgage banks, insurance companies and other institutions that are not regulated by the federal government, including predatory lenders, have become a far bigger part of this market.

A critical implication of deregulation is the declining influence of the Community Reinvestment Act. In conjunction with the Fair Housing Act and other fair lending initiatives, the CRA is credited with generating more than $1 trillion in new investment for low- and moderate-income neighborhoods and for increasing the share of loans going to economically distressed and minority markets. Concentration and consolidation among financial institutions that had taken place for years—trends that were exacerbated by the 1999 Act—reduced the impact of CRA by making it easier for many financial institutions that are not covered by the 1977 law to enter the mortgage market. The share of mortgage loans subject to intensive review under the CRA dropped from 36.1 percent to 29.5 percent between 1993 and 2000. And the share of loans going to low-income and minority markets declined in 2001 after steadily increasing throughout the 1990s.

But these are not the last words in this debate. In many ways, community-based organizations, fair housing groups and elected officials are responding to these developments and the predatory practices that have proliferated.

Reactions to Predatory Lending

Public officials, prodded by aggressive community organizing, have proposed many regulatory and legislative changes. As of the beginning of 2004, at least 25 states and 11 localities, along with the District of Columbia, had passed laws addressing predatory lending. These proposals call for limits on fees, prepayment penalties and balloon payments; restrictions on practices that lead to loan flipping; and prohibitions against loans that do not take into consideration borrowers' ability to repay. They provide for additional disclosures to consumers of the risks of high cost loans and of their right to credit counseling and other consumer protections.

In 2000, the Office of the Comptroller of the Currency reached a $300 million settlement with Providian National Bank in California to compensate consumers hurt by its unfair and deceptive lending practices. Later that year, Household International reached a $484 million agreement with a group of state attorneys general in which it agreed to many changes in its consumer loan practices. Household agreed to cap its fees and points, to provide more disclosure of loan terms and to provide for an independent monitor to assure compliance with the agreement. Household also negotiated a $72 million agreement with ACORN for interest rate reductions, waivers of unpaid late charges, loan principal reductions and other initiatives to help families avoid foreclosure.

In response to information provided and pressure exerted by consumer groups, the Federal Trade Commission (FTC) took enforcement action against 19 lenders and brokers for predatory practices in 2002 and negotiated the largest consumer protection settlement in FTC history with Citigroup. The company agreed to pay $215 million to resolve charges against its subsidiary, The Associates, for various deceptive and abusive practices. The suit was aimed primarily at unnecessary credit insurance products The Associates packed into many of its subprime loans.

A number of nonprofits have developed programs to help victims of predatory lending to refinance loans on more equitable terms that serve the financial interests of the borrowers. Many lenders, often in partnership with community-based groups, have launched educational and counseling programs to steer consumers away from predatory loans.

But progress cannot be assumed. Three federal financial regulatory agencies (Comptroller of the Currency, National Credit

Union Administration, and Office of Thrift Supervision) have issued opinions that federal laws preempt some state predatory lending laws for lenders they regulate. In communities where anti-predatory lending laws have been proposed, lobbyists for financial institutions have introduced state level bills to preempt or nullify local ordinances or to weaken consumer protections. Legislation has also been introduced in Congress to preempt state efforts to combat predatory lending. Preliminary research on the North Carolina anti-predatory lending law—the first statewide ban—suggested that such restrictions reduced the supply and increased the cost of credit to low-income borrowers. Subsequent research, however, found that the law had the intended impact; there was a reduction in predatory loans but no change in access to or cost of credit for high-risk borrowers. Debate continues over the impact of such legislative initiatives. And the fight against redlining, in its traditional or "reverse" forms, remains an ongoing struggle.

The Road Ahead

The tools that have been used to combat redlining emerged in conflict. The Fair Housing Act was the product of a long civil rights movement and probably would not have been passed until several years later if not for the assassination of Martin Luther King Jr. that year. Passage of the CRA followed years of demonstrations at bank offices, the homes of bank presidents and elsewhere. And recent fights against predatory lending reflect the maturation of several national coalitions of community advocacy and fair housing groups that include ACORN, the National Community Reinvestment Coalition, the National Training and Information Center, the National Fair Housing Alliance and others. As Frederick Douglass famously stated in 1857:

"If there is no struggle, there is no progress . . . Power concedes nothing without a demand. It never did, and it never will."

Homeownership remains the American dream, though for all too many it is a dream deferred. As Florence McKnight and many others have learned, it can truly become a family's worst nightmare. The unanswered question remains: for how long will the dream be denied?

Critical Thinking

1. What exactly is predatory lending? Give three or four clear examples of predatory lending practices.

2. Why was the Community Investment Act (CRA) passed in 1978? What are its major provisions?

3. What is deregulation? Who pushed for deregulation? How did deregulation reshape the banking and home mortgage industry?

4. Was it the regulations of the CRA or the policies of deregulation that led to the wave of bad loans and the flood of housing foreclosures that plagued communities in the United States during the early 2000s?

GREGORY D. SQUIRES chairs the Sociology Department at George Washington University and is editor of the book, *Why the Poor Pay More: How to Stop Predatory Lending.*

Out of Cash

The End of the Nation's Largest Redevelopment Program

Josh Stephens

Jerry in Oakland

When former California Governor Jerry Brown became mayor of Oakland some 16 years after leaving statewide office, he pledged to add 10,000 residents to the city's downtown. Had Brown been the mayor of, say, booming Plano or Aurora, he could have spent his first term back at the Buddhist monastery where he once lived and the city would have reached that goal of its own accord.

This was, of course, the mid-2000s. Across the bay, San Francisco probably could have doubled in size were it not for the city's restrictions on growth. Today it can hardly house all the Google employees who take the nerd bus from the city to Mountain View every day, much less the 800,000 others who cram into its 47 square miles.

Thirteen years after Brown's first mayoral inauguration—and 36 after his original gubernatorial stint—Oakland has welcomed nearly all of those 10,000 hoped-for downtown residents. New high rises ring Lake Merritt, a tidal basin near downtown, and the Uptown district has replaced drug-infested empty lots with handsome mixed-use apartments, including affordable and market-rate housing. Meanwhile a new California industry, legalized (medical) marijuana, had sprouted its first trade school in downtown Oakland: Oaksterdam University.

Uptown's Fox Theater, a 1920s movie palace, had by the mid-1970s become known as "the largest outdoor urinal in the world." In March of this year, Bob Weir, the Magnetic Fields and Willie Nelson all played on its restored stage. A charter high school dedicated to performing arts is attached to the theater.

"The Uptown neighborhood of Oakland has to be listed as one of the great redevelopment success stories in California," said Gabriel Metcalf, executive director of San Francisco Planning and Urban Research, a land use think tank. "It has brought life back to that part of downtown Oakland and it is now one of the great urban neighborhoods in California."

Even the Golden State Warriors have escaped the NBA's cellar, and native son MC Hammer is out of bankruptcy. Life in the Bay Area's stepsister city—an industrial port town with historically high rates of poverty, drugs and gang activity—has been looking up, and many credit Mayor Brown.

"Jerry had a very clear idea of what he thought the city needed and he needed and he went about pursuing that," said Oakland-based land use consultant David Rosen.

Oakland being Oakland, none of these changes took place on their own. When Brown breezed in with grand proclamations, he knew full well that he would seek help from a source familiar to roughly 400 of California's 600-plus cities: The state's redevelopment agencies.

In the arcane world of public finance, the power wielded by the Oakland Redevelopment Agencies, and its peers across the state, ranks nearly in a class by itself. In California, as in the 48 other states that use versions of it, local entities harvest the so-called "tax increment" that arises in areas designated for redevelopment. As property values rise, a certain portion of the property tax increases get reinvested into further redevelopment in the designated area, rather than going to the general use fund that typically captures property tax dollars. The whole arrangement is known as tax increment financing, or TIF. Redevelopment agencies do not directly develop property, but they do nearly everything else: They create redevelopment plans, fund local infrastructure improvements, assemble parcels, assist developers, broker deals and sell bonds to pay for all of the above.

In other words, redevelopment agencies mint money for cities.

The idea is to create a virtuous cycle that means Napa Valley Chablis is now for sale in places that were, relatively recently, crack dens. This system worked so well that, by 2011, redevelopment project areas—some covering tens of thousands of acres—accounted for 12 percent of the state's total property tax rolls netting over $5.6 billion in tax money annually, with most of it going right back to cities, to the delight of mayors such as Brown.

Claudia Cappio, director of Planning, Building and Major Projects under Brown in Oakland, gives a great deal of credit to the city's redevelopment agency and the funds that it put into projects like Uptown and the Fox Theater.

"They played an important part in the city's ability to match public improvements that would be commensurate with the investment from developers in the 10K housing effort," said Cappio.

But when Brown became governor for the second time in January 2011—28 years after completing his first two terms, and three years after leaving Oakland City Hall—one of the first actions that Brown took was to declare the end of the very program that had helped the city, long the object of unabashed derision (such as Gertrude Stein's inescapable "there is no there there"), get its game back.

Feb. 1, 2012: RDA, RIP

In a 1978 article for *Rolling Stone* magazine, journalist Mike Royko inadvertently bestowed upon Brown the name "Governor Moonbeam," in reference to his prowess at attracting the New Age vote. At the time, it was a major consistency in California. Royko, since deceased, has said that he regrets the name's indignity and has in fact apologized publicly to Brown.

But even if Royko's recantation has failed in the public mind, Brown's new attitude might do the trick: Gov. Moonbeam has become Gov. Pragmatism.

The $26 billion budget deficit that Brown inherited from former Gov. Arnold Schwarzenegger left precious little room for flights of fancy. It arose in part from the state's disastrous housing crash, which has left some communities riddled with foreclosures and in part from a notoriously ineffective budget-setting process in Sacramento.

Viewing redevelopment from the Capitol rather than from City Hall, Brown did the math.

Using his executive powers, he would simply do away with all of the state's redevelopment agencies, which are the local bodies—sponsored by their respective cities and, in some cases, counties—that create the plans for redevelopment project areas and administer the TIF funds that come in. No agencies, no TIF, no $5.6 billion disappearing into 400 black holes.

Needless to say, those black holes were not happy.

From cities' perspective, there's no other way to describe redevelopment than as a cash cow. Though TIF monies were earmarked only for redevelopment-related activities—and were officially governed by redevelopment agencies and not by city governments—they were still a major infusion of cash. They were the only consistent source of funding for local economic and real estate development.

And, best of all, they came with limited state oversight. Agencies were required to spend 20 percent of their increment on affordable housing. But even that rule got bent all the time, with affordable housing funds often socked away for years. Otherwise, cities could use tax increment funds on everything from building bridges and sports stadiums through direct expenditures to assembling properties and brokering deals on behalf of private developers. Some cities, especially small cities, even used redevelopment funds to partially pay the salaries of employees who worked for both city and redevelopment agency. Few people in Sacramento knew what

they were doing, or cared. And all Brown cared about was the $5.6 billion.

"In a lot of ways, he's being realistic," said Los Angeles-based land use consultant Larry Kosmont, whose firm has consulted with several cities on the shutdown of their RDA's. "If I was sitting in the governor's office and saw a $5.6 billion pile of money, the fact that I used it when I was as a mayor has very little to do with the fact that I need it when I'm a governor."

Brown has been anything but remorseful, saying at times that redevelopment was of dubious value and saying on Jan. 18, "I don't think we can delay this funeral."

In fact, not only did the funeral go ahead as planned, but the grave was dug far deeper than anyone expected.

A Quiet Engine

In many ways, the death of redevelopment was inevitable. Brown's decision, backed up by the Supreme Court, was the atomic bomb detonated at the end of a six-decade war of attrition that had been waged on the balance sheets, in the statutes and, several times, in the voting booths of California.

State sponsored, TIF-aided redevelopment started out modestly enough in the urban renewal era and operated below Sacramento's radar for decades. It's hard to overstate how arcane California's system of redevelopment became. It could appeal only to people like Peter Detwiler, the recently retired chief consultant to the Senate Governance and Finance Committee, whose bemusement over California's system of government is matched only by his encyclopedic understanding of it. To hear him tell it, redevelopment law wasn't mere sausage making. It was, to abuse the metaphor, what happens when sausages collide.

Redevelopment in California first arose in 1945 and was codified more formally in 1954. In those early decades, aligned with federal "slum clearance" and "urban revitalization" policies, redevelopment often consisted of the obliteration of blight, such as that which supposedly plagued Bunker Hill, a little piece of San Francisco in L.A., with Victorian apartment houses lining narrow streets above the city's civic center. Today, thanks to bulldozers wielded by the city's redevelopment agency, all that remains of the old Bunker Hill is the Angels Flight funicular, rebuilt in the shadow of Class-A high rises.

Over time, redevelopment became a gentler tool, but one used with increasing frequency. By the mid-1970s, redevelopment agencies abounded.

The best—or worst, depending on who you ask—thing ever to happen to redevelopment was the 1978 passage of Proposition 13, California's infamous "tax revolt." Prop. 13 froze annual residential and commercial property taxes at 1 percent of their most recent sale price. In a state where assessed property values have generally risen ever since the first Rose Parade enticed eastern transplants to the continent's edge, Prop. 13 gave homeowners a windfall while devastating cities.

Unable to count on perpetually rising property tax revenues, cities cut where their expenses were greatest: schools. In essence, the state government apologized to cities for what it considered the recklessness of the state's voters by pledging to "back-fill" local coffers with money for schools.

Left with precious few ways to raise funds, cities created new redevelopment agencies and project areas at a torrid pace. Well more than half of the agencies in the state were founded after 1978. The total, statewide tax increment grew nearly exponentially, from $1.02 billion in 1989 (the first year with reliable records) to $5.6 billion in 2008. It topped $2 billion in 2001 and increased by roughly $1 billion every two years until 2008.

By 2011, an astounding 12 percent of total property tax receipts statewide were captured by cities through TIF arrangements. With little regulation of what could qualify as blight and thus be eligible for a TIF, some counties took redevelopment to extremes. In Southern California, the booming inland county of San Bernardino had, by 2004, classified 22 percent of the land within its borders as blight. By that same year, Riverside had declared blighted a full quarter of its land. Even rural counties like Yolo and San Benito—with hardly any urban areas, much less urban blight—got in the game, both going from zero percent blight in 1982 to 14 percent in 2004.

Along the way, golf courses, farm land, empty strips of urban fringe, city blocks sullied by a few wisps of graffiti, and parcels with just the slightest risk of flooding ended up being designated as candidates for redevelopment project areas. Eventually Sacramento noticed.

"The city of Diamond Bar declared the whole city blighted," said Detwiler. "When the court stopped giggling, it said no."

Over the years, Sacramento has tightened the definition of blight, and lawmakers imposed the 20 percent affordable housing set-aside. But ultimately, the numbers never worked out for Sacramento, because the greater the statewide TIF diversion grew, the more it had to back-fill from the general fund.

The formula worked roughly like this: When TIF gets diverted, roughly half of it comes from would-be school funds. Because statute binds the state to fully fund schools, Sacramento must fill in the shortfall created by the revenue rerouting. By 2011, this meant that the state was kicking in around $1.3 billion to make up for the diverted school revenue.

"There is no line item in the state general fund that asks, 'do we want to spend $1.3 billion a year on the 400-some redevelopment authorities?'" Detwiler said. "By operation of law it's hidden. It's not deviously hidden, but it's simply built into our obligation to fully fund schools."

The state first seriously took notice of this inequity in the mid-1990s under Gov. Pete Wilson. Wilson enacted the Educational Revenue Augmentation Fund (ERAF) by which redevelopment agencies were forced to contribute a share of their TIF monies to schools in their respective areas. And that's where the escalation began. The more the state tried to increase ERAF payments, the more redevelopment agencies resisted, on the grounds that they had earned their TIF funds fair and square.

"Local officials felt double-crossed, and now we get into a story that begins to look like the Hatfields and the McCoys or the Montagues and Capulets," said Detwiler. "In some ways the origins of the dispute are lost. It just becomes retaliation."

In 2010, the redevelopment community thought it had fashioned a suitable shiv. California's electoral system famously allows initiatives on virtually any issue to go on the state ballot and, if adopted, to become part of the state constitution. The CRA and League of Cities sponsored Proposition 22, which provided that the state could not appropriate funds from local entities in order to balance the state budget.

Prop. 22 passed, with 60 percent of the vote. The TIF was safe, at least until California slid into the ocean, or voters changed their minds. Or at least the redevelopment agencies thought so.

Two months later, Brown realized that if the voters had said he couldn't appropriate funds from redevelopment agencies, he had one strategy left.

Unlikely Foes

It's hard to say how many projects have literally stopped in their tracks due to the governor's decision. One of the incredible things about the multibillion-dollar industry that was redevelopment is that no one knows exactly what it entailed. The most recent study of agencies' efficacy and business practices was a report that State Controller John Chiang published hastily in March 2011. It suggests that agencies do not always spend their monies wisely, and found that agencies often do not properly report their activities. Damning though the report may have been, its sample set was 18.

Whatever their books may look like, nearly every one of the state's 400 redevelopment agencies can tell a story about crucial, transformative projects that are now threatened: Rehabilitated buildings, remediated brownfields, affordable housing developments, gleaming new parks, fire stations and even stadiums. To choose even a poignant random sample would not express the extent of the impact, or its variable effects on communities. One city's mixed-use affordable housing development is as important as another city's light rail maintenance yard.

After the governor dropped his bombshell, the redevelopment community wanted to protect its projects, staff members and funds. Several groups, including the California Redevelopment Association and League of California Cities, as well as a separate consortium of the mayors of the state's 10 biggest cities, tried to broker deals. One compromise would have allowed agencies to make "voluntary" ERAF-style payments.

The CRA took a hard line, though, and rejected several proposed compromises the legislature had been more than happy to offer. Almost no one besides Brown ever wanted redevelopment agencies to go away. Even if Republicans in the state legislature were wary of government-sponsored development, they couldn't support a Democratic governor. And Democrats had historically been champions of redevelopment precisely because of its benefits to poor communities. Therefore, the legislature took pains to defy the governor without actually defying the governor. None of it worked.

It was during these mid-summer discussions that CRA executive director John Shirey stepped down to become city manager of Sacramento.

The legislature's ultimate solution was a pair of assembly bills, passed in August: AB X1 26 and AB X1 27. The former called for the dissolution of redevelopment agencies and outlined the procedure by which they would go out of business. The latter nullified AB X1 26 for those sponsoring jurisdictions—city and county governments—that agreed to return some of their TIF to the state. If all the state's agencies agreed to the provisions of AB X1 27, the total repatriated TIF would be, not coincidentally, around $1.3 billion—exactly the amount that Brown expected to net from wholesale elimination, once outstanding bonds and other obligations were met.

The two-bill solution was meant to get around Prop. 22 by making the payments "voluntary." Some choice, said the redevelopment community. In fact, even though the bills were intended to help redevelopment agencies, they were not written with their cooperation. That's because the redevelopment community all along rejected the notion of any kind of hindrance or transfer payments. They stayed out of the discussion in order to maintain the moral high ground for the fight that was to follow.

"Redevelopment agencies didn't want to help write it because their ideology wouldn't let them, so some of the deadlines and some of the procedures are real clunky," said Detwiler. "They chose not to, so that's what you get. You don't play the game, you don't make up the rule."

A lawsuit that the CRA and League of California cities jointly filed in September 2011 contented that the two bills violated Prop. 22 and therefore should both be overturned, thus restoring the status quo.

"We were basically being asked to undermine Prop. 22," said Julio Fuentes, city manager for the Southern California city of Alhambra and president of the CRA board. "I think in the end we didn't have a choice."

The Supreme Court had a choice, of course. In fact, it had four: It could nullify both, either or none of the bills. The plaintiffs were gunning for both. They would have settled for neither.

"What we pointed out to the court was that this two-bill strategy was a strategy to get around Proposition 22," said Shirey. "It still stuns me that the court did not look at intent and did not recognize what the state was doing with AB 26 and 27 was to craft a scheme to get around the will of the voters in Proposition 22."

One fact is indisputable: If the CRA and League had not filed their lawsuit, redevelopment would still exist. It would be hobbled, but deals would remain and projects would continue. Thousands of staff members would still have jobs. Shirey, who left the CRA in August 2011 to be city manager of Sacramento, might even still have his old job.

And yet, almost no one contends outright that the League and CRA made colossal blunders or points out the obvious: That in filing the suit and losing, they dug their own graves. That hesitancy may owe itself to political sensibilities. But

observers may have expected that, one day, the redevelopment agencies would either stick it to the state or die trying.

As it turned out, the court handed down the redevelopment community's worst-case scenario. A unanimous panel of justices held that 27 did indeed violate Prop. 22's prohibition against transfers to certain local funds to the state general fund. But as the state's lawyers argued, if Prop. 22 had been intended to prevent the state from disbanding redevelopment agencies entirely, its drafters could have included explicit language to that effect.

"I guess if we all had the hindsight that we had today maybe things would have been done differently," said Fuentes. "But given the facts and circumstances that we had at that point I think we made the right call. Unfortunately, the Supreme Court didn't feel that way."

A Hard Sell

Throughout 2011, redevelopment agencies did something that they had never had to do in the previous 57 years since the formal establishment of redevelopment: They tried to explain to the public what they did and why they deserved to exist. It didn't work.

Numerous surveys taken during this time indicate that redevelopment agencies' lack of transparency, reported cozy relationships with developers and occasional but highly controversial use of eminent domain struck skepticism in the hearts of voters. And for every triumphant project that agencies trumpeted, residents suspected that there were untold thousands that conferred little, or no, benefit on their cities—or even worse, had an adverse effect.

But while public perceptions tended towards the cynical, some cities did manage to leverage TIF money in ways that helped their residents.

Before it became the home of the Internet and social networking billionaires, the Bay Area had been the industrial heart of the West Coast, with shipyards and steel mills ringing the bay. When those industries faded, they left places like Emeryville: Flat, toxic landfills with million-dollar views. Redevelopment money paid for environmental remediation, and from the 1980s onward the city implemented an aggressive plan to build apartment towers, retail, hotels and office towers, which have all sprouted proudly. It seems like half the Bay Area's bachelor pads are furnished by its Ikea store.

"Emeryville was a post-industrial wasteland and we put in major infrastructure," said Cappio, redevelopment director for the city from 1995 to 2000. She credits the city's redevelopment agency, with its power of TIF, for making the transformation happen.

But successes like Cappio's in Emeryville are, unfortunately, the exception. And the majority of project areas remain in various states of disrepair—as if after decades, the work of transforming communities may never be finished.

Not surprisingly, such state-sponsored redevelopment has long attracted ardent critics, especially among advocates of small government.

"The whole idea of government redevelopment is that the government can plan the type of development that should occur in a neighborhood," said Timothy Sandefur, principal attorney with the Pacific Legal Foundation, which advocates for private property rights. "It's politicians deciding when it ought to be producers and consumers . . . it ought to be builders and taxpayers who get to decide, not the government."

The demise of California $5.6 billion annual experiment, however, sparked a more widespread—if belated—discussion about the efficacy of using TIFs and other methods of public financing.

Though redevelopment professionals readily point to cause and effect between redevelopment funds and new projects, critics question whether projects would've moved forward, even without the government assistance. They further question whether projects built in redevelopment project areas would not have simply been built nearby: Are states spending billions to subsidize business relocations?

"I think there is quite a bit of evidence that these local economic development programs are just moving things around," said Helsley.

Indeed, while cities contend that the battle has always been between them and the state, it may be equally possible that the battle has been among cities themselves, with developers playing a monumental game of musical chairs.

"Developers can bargain one agency against another," said Painter. "The net benefit for society for those arrangements is likely zero or negative."

Painter says "likely" because redevelopment is notoriously difficult to study. Because every locality and every development is unique, researchers cannot run control experiments. For that reason, redevelopment—despite its multibillion-dollar consequences—is notoriously under-studied.

With "any intervention wherein project selection is not based on some kind of explicit criteria, it's really difficult to determine what's successful or what's not," said Painter. "And anything that has to do with regional activity is going to be challenging."

The most widely cited study of California redevelopment is 14 years old. In 1998, Michael Dardia, then of the Public Policy Institute of California, now a deputy director at New York City's Office of Management and Budget, concluded that California's redevelopment agencies and their TIF arrangements created little value for all the money that they were spending. He found that in only four of 38 agencies studied did tax receipts grow fast enough to justify agencies' commonly held claim that they are solely responsible for the incremental development that takes place in project areas.

Dardia further concluded that more than 50 percent of the land in most project areas was vacant, meaning that agencies were not so much wiping out blight as they were promoting new development.

For something with such dubious value, tax increment financing has a large, loyal following. Forty-eight other states have followed California's lead in establishing their own TIF-powered redevelopment programs. California's experience, does not, however, necessarily provide a cautionary tale

for them. Other states have already, it seems, chosen different paths.

Marianne O'Malley, managing and principal analyst with California's nonpartisan Legislative Analyst's Office, conducted a study comparing California's redevelopment system to those in other states. She found that California cities relied far more heavily on it than cities elsewhere.

"In other states, it was a much smaller feature," said O'Malley. "Typically the maximum length of a district timeline was a lot shorter" than in other states.

Additionally, other states do not set up the inherent rivalry between education and local economic development.

"We also found that oftentimes the affected local agencies would have to approve the creation of a TIF, and/or in some cases they were statutorily not permitted to use the schools' share of the property tax," said O'Malley.

Indeed, it appears that California's was, shall we say, a unique system.

"Take any state—have Illinois or Ohio or Michigan or even Massachusetts put up $1 billion for local economic development—and you would have chambers of commerce dancing in the street," said Detwiler. "No other state . . . spent $1.25 billion per year on local economic development with almost no state strings attached."

New Status Quo

Very few civic leaders in California are happy about its uniqueness now, however.

All lamentation aside, the actual dissolution of agencies is proving to be a monumental headache. Many city officials contend that the legislation ending redevelopment was poorly written, with clunky, unclear provisions for liquidating agencies' assets and determining which projects in progress constitute obligations that the state must honor, even in the wake of the agencies' demise.

The legislation includes what some consider vague language, and it does not offer much direction on matters such as the definition of "enforceable obligations." Each former redevelopment agency will have an oversight board that will approve those obligations, but even then the state Department of Finance must approve of the boards' lists.

Most expect that the result will be endless politicking over partially developed projects. For instance, the legislation does not necessarily pay for projects that have been designed but not yet built, meaning that potentially hundreds of millions of dollars in design work could be tossed out. Moreover, the auditor-controller offices in every county has to audit the books of each defunct redevelopment agency, and the Department of Finance must scrutinize all 400 agencies all at once, delving into an area of law that is arcane even by real estate standards.

"There's a whole series of very unusual, unique and almost unanswerable questions," said Kosmont, the LA real estate consultant.

The obvious reason for AB X1 26's shortcomings, such as they are, is that it was written without any expectation that it was going to be implemented. AB X1 26 was intended only to govern the wind-down of those agencies that opted out of the voluntary payments under the two-bill solution. That number had been expected to be minimal. But the court's decision instantly made it the law of the land, warts and all.

"Now we're dealing with the dissolution, uncertainty and confusion when you do something quickly and rashly," said Kosmont.

The second issue facing California cities is that of long-term economic development. Not long ago, the idea that California would have to so much as bat an eyelash to compete against, and beat out, other states for business and migration would have been a punch line on the Tonight Show. But in the past decade, California's luster has faded, according to some measures—not least of which is the $26 billion deficit that kicked off the redevelopment chaos in the first place.

Supporters of redevelopment contend that, far from a zero-sum game, tax increment financing is crucial for them to create an appealing, functional urban landscape. Otherwise, businesses will have little trouble resisting California's charms. Moreover, TIF is simply part of urban economics in the United States.

"The only other one that doesn't (have TIF) is Arizona," said Kosmont. "And, last time I looked, Arizona was mostly desert without high land prices."

Opponents of redevelopment contend, however, that whatever its economic ramifications, the demise of redevelopment marks a significant moral victory for the state and its taxpayers. No longer will it be so politically easy, or convenient, for governments to use eminent domain. Historically, redevelopment agencies have used the state's authority to seize property using the power of eminent domain far more liberally than other public bodies. Critics blame this on relative anonymity of these agencies—they are often unelected bodies that have little interaction with the public, and thus have little incentive to be accountable to the public.

These agencies are "unnecessary, wasteful, dubious, sometimes corrupt entities that exploit the power of eminent dominant in order to give it to politically well connected developers," said Sandefur. Their end, he says, is a fantastic development for owners of property throughout the state, and to taxpayers."

That view is rare among civic leaders, however. By and large, the consensus in California's beleaguered cities is that the redevelopment process needed to be fixed, not thrown away.

"We need a break of about 3–5 years where we don't have the winking and nudging and lying about blight, and state and local officials can get clean and sober on TIF spending," said Detwiler.

Lawmakers in Sacramento are already discussing the prospects for a brand-new, reformed redevelopment program. Many proposals would do away with the troublesome notion of "blight" and replace it with redevelopment criteria geared towards more specific goals. One suggestion is for tax increment financing to align with Senate Bill 375, California's 2008 law that promotes compact and transit-oriented development for the purposes of reducing greenhouse gas emissions.

If nothing happens, cities will of course be free to pursue their own economic development strategies and to encourage whatever development they see fit. The trouble, however, is that they will not have $5.6 billion with which to do so.

Uncertain in Sacramento

From his vantage point in the statehouse, Jerry Brown has said little about the chaos that has engulfed his former counterparts and colleagues across the state. He has tepidly referred to the merits of redevelopment "such as they are" and said nothing substantive since his "funeral" comment two weeks before the dissolution deadline.

Observers in Sacramento say that the governor shows little appetite for reviving redevelopment. In a recent speech to an anxious audience of developers in Los Angeles, State Sen. Alex Padilla called Brown the number-one obstacle to a new redevelopment scheme. If Brown sticks to his position, the effects could be devastating for cities—especially Oakland and its peers.

"In some number of years . . . areas of cities, probably larger cities, will be deteriorating and that they have no financial wherewithal to address those problems," said Shirey.

But, as almost everyone in the state agrees, Brown has bigger problems. Gone are the days when a mayor in California could focus on building shining new apartments for 10,000 people or when a governor could contemplate sending up his own satellite, as Brown famously did back in those moonbeam days. Even things in Sacramento—the city, not the political maelstrom—have changed.

The first time he was governor, Brown, who at various times had both dated Linda Ronstadt and toyed with the idea of becoming a priest, famously slept on a mattress in a shoebox of an apartment near the State Capitol. He knew what he was missing out on, since his father, the legendary Pat Brown, resided in the governor's mansion from 1959 to 1967. Jerry Brown is now married and older than his father was when he left office. Though not quite so spiritual or ascetic as he once was, Brown still lives in an apartment rather than the governor's mansion. These days, however, the digs are far more upscale.

They're in a converted loft apartment, in a building developed with—you guessed it—redevelopment funds.

Critical Thinking

1. What is the purpose of redevelopment assistance? Can you cite examples of successful redevelopment efforts in California cities?

2. What factors led the State of California to slash state aid for local redevelopment programs? In what ways was the elimination of redevelopment funds inevitable?

3. How can the cutbacks be defended? What charges have critics leveled against the local use of state redevelopment

assistance? Give an example or two of what critics saw as the abuses of local redevelopment programs.

4. Cities across the country have turned to TIF (Tax Increment Financing) arrangements in their efforts to support local economic development projects. Can you explain how a TIF district works?

Josh Stephens has covered planning, land use, and architecture as an editor and freelance journalist for the better part of a decade. He is currently editor of the *California Planning & Development Report*. Josh previously edited *The Planning Report* and *Metro Investment Report*, monthly newsletters covering, respectively, land use and infrastructure in the Los Angeles region.

As a freelance writer Stephens has been a regular contributor to, among others, *Planetizen.com, Next American City, Sierra Magazine, InTransition,* and *Planning Magazine.* He also writes for Planetizen's Interchange blog and serves on the editorial board of *The Planning Report*. Stephens holds a bachelor's degree in English from Princeton University and is a candidate for a master's in public policy at the Harvard University Kennedy School of Government.

Josh's interest in urbanism is the result of an abiding, lifelong love-hate relationship with his native Los Angeles.

From *Next American City Magazine*, vol. 1, no. 1, 2012. Copyright © 2012 by Next American City, Inc. Reprinted by permission. www.americancity.org.

Bridge Blockade after Katrina Remains Divisive Issue

CHRIS KIRKHAM AND PAUL PURPURA

Two years later, anger creeps up in Kim Cantwell Sr. when he thinks about the Jefferson Parish deputy who aimed an assault rifle at his 22-year-old son's face, barring the family with five children in tow, some as young as 8 months old, from walking across the Crescent City Connection to their Algiers Point home in the days after Hurricane Katrina.

"I wonder to this day what was he thinking about?" Cantwell asked recently. "Did he even care? You bet I'm pissed. I bury it every day, but you bet I'm still pissed."

Three miles away in Gretna, Police Chief Arthur Lawson, one of three law enforcement leaders who sanctioned the blockade, makes no excuses for his actions.

"I don't second-guess this decision. I know I made it for the right reasons," said Lawson, referring to law enforcement's desire to prevent the looting and crime in New Orleans from spreading across the river. "I go to sleep every night with a clear conscience."

The two men have never met, but they represent opposite ends of one of the most controversial chapters of Katrina's aftermath: the decision to close the bridge to people, mostly African-Americans, trying to flee the chaos and flooding that engulfed New Orleans.

Not only did the blockade spawn state and federal investigations and five lawsuits targeting Gretna, its police force, Lawson, Jefferson Parish Sheriff Harry Lee and other law enforcement agencies, the episode vaulted the New Orleans area's historical struggle with race and class onto an international stage.

It seared images and stirred racial tensions as tales of white shotgun-toting cops and attack dogs keeping desperate African-Americans from entering the suburban West Bank community began circulating in the hectic days after the storm. But interviews with dozens of those involved, including Gretna officials speaking for the first time, paint a more nuanced picture of the blockade.

On one side are those who say Lawson, who is white, and other suburban police authorities placed more value on property than human life.

On the other are many Gretna residents, black and white, who firmly support law enforcement's decisions.

While they stand by their actions, leaders of the enclave of 17,000 residents—12 percent of whom are African-American, according to the 2000 census—say they welcomed many families flooded out of New Orleans since the storm. They are confident the court of law will correct judgments made about their city in the court of public opinion.

"Am I going to be stuck with the 'racist' legacy of what happened on the bridge?" asked Gretna Mayor Ronnie Harris, who is white. "Maybe so. Do I think it's fair? It's not. There's another chapter to be told, hopefully."

Evacuees Stream In

Versions of the story differ widely. Evacuees say they were turned back at gunpoint by unreasonable officers. West Bank officials talk about monumental miscommunication and strained resources.

In the eyes of Gretna police officials, the Jefferson Parish Sheriff's Office and other West Bank leaders, Gretna went into lockdown immediately after the storm. Armed officers and junk vehicles blocked major entrances into the city.

No one was allowed in without proof of residence, and those who remained in the city were urged to leave if they could.

But beginning Aug. 31, two days after the storm, a stream of evacuees started appearing at Gretna's city limits. Some had walked across the bridge to the Terry Parkway exit; some were brought in by Regional Transit Authority bus drivers desperately trying to ferry people out of the floodwaters.

Gretna officials said storm victims came to Terry Parkway because New Orleans police officers were blocking the exit ramps to General de Gaulle Drive, the first exit on the West Bank end of the bridge which is within the city limits of New Orleans. NOPD spokesman Sgt. Joe Narcisse said officers never blocked the ramps.

As hundreds and eventually thousands of evacuees collected beneath the West Bank Expressway across from Oakwood Center that day, Gretna officials said they had little food or water to offer.

So police and city workers broke into a Jefferson Parish bus barn and hotwired two buses later that afternoon. Another police officer owned a school bus. For more than 12 hours they brought the evacuees across the Huey P. Long Bridge to dry land on the east bank at Causeway Boulevard and Interstate 10 in Metairie, where a makeshift evacuation hub had been established.

Lawson and Harris estimate they evacuated close to 6,000 people, with the help of some Jefferson Parish sheriff's deputies. But the crowds continued to grow under the elevated expressway at Whitney Avenue on the West Bank, they said.

"It was getting to the point where we just couldn't physically continue to run the buses 24 hours a day evacuating people," Lawson said. "The more people we would move, the more were coming."

Waiting for Buses

On Aug. 31, Harris said he reached the governor's office and arranged a hasty, 2 A.M. meeting with the governor's husband, Raymond "Coach" Blanco, and Sam Jones, an aide to the governor. Lawson, Harris, Jefferson Parish Councilman Chris Roberts and other Gretna police officials were present.

At that time, West Bank officials said they were promised that hundreds of buses were coming to evacuate the Superdome and the Ernest N. Morial Convention Center.

In a recent interview, Jones said his recollection of the meeting was vague, but he believed buses naturally would have come up at some point.

"There were buses going in from the beginning, but it was a trickle," said Jones, now special assistant to the governor. "We were operating in the environment of a Mad Max movie. You were scrapping for every drop of gasoline, every set of wheels you could get. You sent them where you heard the screaming."

With the knowledge that buses were arriving, Lawson said he met soon after with the sheriff, who gave the thumbs up to the decision. On the morning of Sept. 1, Lawson and Sheriff's Office Deputy Chief Craig Taffaro met with the Crescent City Connection police and decided to block the bridge to pedestrians. Vehicles were allowed to cross.

Gretna police took the West Bank-bound lanes, the Sheriff's Office the east bank-bound lanes and the bridge police took the commuter lanes.

Around the same time, looters set fire to Oakwood mall.

"Whatever spin anyone puts on it, we do know in our hearts that it was the right thing to do," Taffaro said. "It made no sense to leave one deplorable area to come to another."

Meanwhile, close to 8,000 mostly white evacuees from St. Bernard Parish were being brought to Algiers from the Chalmette ferry landing via boats and barges. Buses were sent to Algiers to evacuate those storm victims, Jones said.

Gretna officials said they knew of that operation but discouraged state officials from directing the evacuees into their city for the same reasons they closed the bridge: They didn't have the resources to provide for them.

Eventually the buses came. But they went to New Orleans, not Gretna, West Bank law enforcement officials said.

Blocked from Their Home

The Cantwells, who are white, rode out the storm at a Canal Street hotel, and their car was trapped in a nearby parking garage. The hotel met their needs, but food and fuel for the generator ran low. They had to make a move, and after hearing a radio report of people walking across the bridge, they decided to go to their Delaronde Street home in Algiers Point, where they could get a car to leave the area.

They set out Sept. 1, 2005, about noon with their children among them. The youngest was 8 months old.

Carrying gear and pushing two baby strollers as they walked up the Camp Street off-ramp from the Pontchartrain Expressway, they encountered some New Orleans police officers and National Guardsmen, who offered them food and water. None told them they could not cross the bridge, Cantwell said.

Others were walking across the bridge to the West Bank too, he said. They snapped pictures of themselves, relieved and smiling because they were going to their home, Cantwell said.

They got no farther than the toll plaza, where the bridge meets the ground in Algiers. There, the Jefferson Parish deputy immediately called out through his car's loudspeaker, "You're not walking into this parish," Cantwell said, puzzled because they never planned to walk into Jefferson.

His son, Kim Cantwell Jr., then 22, tried to show the deputy his driver's license, with their Delaronde Street address. They pointed toward Algiers. It was for naught.

"Instead of talking to us, he pulled an M-16 and pointed it at my son's face," Cantwell said.

Turned back and escorted to the east bank by the deputy and a Crescent City Connection police officer, the Cantwells later trudged through waist-high water, holding the younger children and their gear above the waterline, as they walked to the Superdome, where they spent a harrowing night.

After standing in line for more than 13 hours, they boarded a bus the next evening that took them to Fort Worth, Texas.

Mixed Signals

When the blockade was brought to the public's attention, accusations began to fly about shotguns being fired over evacuees' heads and callous police officers turning away families and people in wheelchairs.

Lawson admits that one of his officers, who is black, fired a warning shot over his shoulder when a crowd started to threaten to throw him off the bridge.

Larry Bradshaw and Lorrie Beth Slonsky, two San Francisco paramedics in the city for a convention, said they were told to cross the bridge by New Orleans police stationed near Harrah's New Orleans Casino. They are white.

"I always think unless there's a compelling reason not to help somebody, that you help somebody in need," Bradshaw said recently. "It's part of the whole American frontier character, and it seemed like Gretna violated that."

The New Orleans Police Department has denied it ever officially directed evacuees over the bridge. However, Mayor Ray Nagin, in an "SOS" statement that was quoted by CNN, said to the thousands of people gathered at the Convention Center that "we are now allowing people to march. They will be marching up to the Crescent City Connection to the (West Bank-bound) expressway to find relief."

In a recent interview, Nagin said the statement was meant to heighten awareness of the problems at the Convention Center, not to encourage people to cross the bridge into Gretna. Even two years later, he referred to police on the bridge using "attack dogs and machine guns," rumors at the time that law enforcement officials vehemently deny.

"All the neighboring parishes—Plaquemines, St. Bernard—were bringing their people here. We were kind of the dropping-off point for all these places," Nagin said. "So for another neighboring parish to say 'no' was pretty unnerving."

Lawson said he has had no communication with New Orleans officials or the mayor's office since the storm. Harris, the Gretna mayor, had a brief conversation with Nagin about the bridge incident in January 2006 at a Louisiana Conference of Mayors meeting, after several unsuccessful attempts. He explained his reasoning to Nagin, who didn't accuse him or Lawson of racism. They haven't spoken since, Harris said.

Support and Scorn

In the weeks after Hurricane Katrina tore through stained-glass windows and flooded parts of his Gretna church, the Rev. Orin Grant's cell phone was abuzz with questions from congregants and longtime friends.

There were the usual concerns: How was his family? When would worship services begin? Then there were the news updates: "The power is back on in Gretna" . . . "Oh, and did you hear about the people on the bridge?"

Though he was in a Houston hotel, details of the bridge blockade flowed in. From the outset, Grant, who is black, quickly threw his support behind law enforcement.

"If I thought this was a negative racial incident, I would have spoken up," said Grant, pastor of St. Paul's Baptist Church in the city's largely African-American McDonoghville neighborhood. "I don't take sides; I take a stand."

Grant's opinion is not unusual among residents.

In the weeks and months after the storm, hundreds of yard signs supporting Lawson and city workers sprang up across town. The Gretna and Jefferson Parish councils passed resolutions supporting the decision, and Lawson was presented with an award for his services by the Jefferson Parish Martin Luther King Jr. Task Force this year.

"Arthur Lawson is our employee, we are his boss," said Joe Roppolo, a white businessman whose Gretna Sign Works printed up about 600 of the support signs. "No matter what the rest of the world thinks, he did what his constituents wanted him to do. So we should take the heat if anyone does."

Some resentment still lingers.

Percy Jupiter Jr., who is black, watched the evacuees stream over the bridge from the Fischer public housing development in Algiers.

"It looked like the New York marathon, except these people were running for their lives," said Jupiter, who now lives in Gretna. "The bottom line is that Gretna and Jefferson Parish thinks everyone across the river is a hoodlum. Gretna did not want them over here."

Others say the issue has largely faded as more pressing issues have come to the forefront. Rhonda Royal and her family saw the blockade, heard the warning shots and decided to turn

around rather than approach the police on the bridge. Her home in eastern New Orleans was flooded, but she's since moved to Gretna.

"Some people might bring it up, but most are just trying to get on and rebuild what they've got," said Royal, who is black.

The Rev. Jesse Pate, pastor of Harvest Ripe Church in Gretna, still comes down on both sides of the debate two years later, but he understands the outrage that persists.

"You can look at it and say, 'It would have been chaotic, people would have looted houses.' It was just one of those crazy moments in time, that anything would have been acceptable," said Pate, who is black. "But during that time, (law enforcement) valued property over the lives of those people. And that's where the tragedy is."

Public Report Elusive

With five lawsuits and a criminal investigation in Orleans Parish looming, Gretna has largely borne the brunt of the fallout from the bridge incident.

"Our community has taken it on the chin at a national level," Harris said. "When civil order was breaking down, we did something about it. Yet when we take a common sense approach when buses are coming, we get our heads knocked in a PR battle."

State Attorney General Charles Foti completed an investigation and turned over his findings to both the Orleans Parish district attorney's office and the U.S. attorney's office in New Orleans a year ago.

Foti's office will not release the findings to the public. New Orleans District Attorney Eddie Jordan also declined to make the report public. In August 2006, Jordan's then-spokeswoman told The Times-Picayune that prosecutors were preparing to present the matter to a grand jury. The district attorney's current spokesman said last week nothing has been presented.

The American Civil Liberties Union and The Times-Picayune also have been spurned in their attempts to get the report released to the public.

"Because the investigation is still pending, my office is unable to provide you with information at this time," Jordan wrote Aug. 15 in rejecting the newspaper's request under the state's public records law.

The U.S. Justice Department, the FBI and the U.S. attorney's office in New Orleans also received Foti's report and monitored the case. The agencies have not found evidence sufficient to move forward with any criminal charges, U.S. Attorney Jim Letten said.

"It's not an active investigation at this time," Letten said.

But attorneys in five civil lawsuits are pressing ahead their query.

Of the lawsuits, filed on behalf of both black and white plaintiffs, one is pending in Orleans Parish Civil District Court. The other four are in U.S. District Court in New Orleans, all allotted to Judge Mary Ann Vial Lemmon, an appointee of President Clinton.

As chairman of the Local and Municipal Affairs Committee, state Sen. Cleo Fields, D-Baton Rouge, monitored the progress Foti's office made in its investigation of the blockade, presiding over a November 2005 hearing at which the attorney general testified on his query.

A month later, Fields' Baton Rouge law firm filed a lawsuit in federal court on behalf of a couple, followed by a second one filed on Aug. 29, 2006, which seeks class-action status.

The federal court cases allege that police violated an array of constitutional rights, including freedom to assemble, freedom from excessive search and seizure and the right to travel.

Most of the cases are still in early stages, although one is scheduled for trial in January.

But one substantive ruling could have reverberations in the other three federal cases.

On March 30, in a victory for Gretna and the Jefferson Parish Sheriff's Office, Lemmon dismissed in one case the claim that the police violated the right to travel—a claim made in other lawsuits.

She ruled that while people have "a fundamental right" to cross state lines, the U.S. Supreme Court has not ruled on the question of intrastate travel, or that within a state.

Gretna's attorney, Franz Zibilich, said at the time the ruling "gutted" the lawsuit. Fields, representing the plaintiffs in that case, said the intrastate travel argument was "a very small portion of the lawsuits."

The ruling also is expected to affect other cases, said attorney Dane Ciolino, a Loyola University law professor who is not involved in the litigation.

"The basis for the dismissal of the intrastate travel argument should also apply to all cases, given that in all cases the plaintiffs were traveling from one point in Louisiana to another," Ciolino said in an e-mail.

Despite Lemmon's ruling, attorney Julian Baudier of New Orleans has kept the right-to-travel argument alive in representing an Algiers family that was turned back by Gretna police and now is suing them.

"My argument was, how do you know where my people were going?" Baudier said, adding that his clients' interstate travel right could have been violated because they considered fleeing to Texas. They ended up in Baton Rouge, he said.

Of the four cases in federal court, two were brought by Algiers families trying to return to their homes from downtown New Orleans.

"If it brings a little more humanity to a future catastrophe, that wouldn't hurt my feelings," Cantwell said of his lawsuit. "If I don't get a nickel out of this, maybe that cop, he'll think a little better."

Other than a general description—"a middle-aged guy with salt and pepper hair and a mustache"—they still do not know the deputy's name.

Despite his anger, Cantwell said he has tried to move on with his life.

"What happened happened," he said. "You can't relive bad parts of your life every day. That's like quicksand. It's going to suck you down."

Critical Thinking

1. What exactly happened at the bridge connecting New Orleans to Gretna?

2. Is urban growth and decline purely the result of a free market and free choice? Are all people in the metropolis free to move to wherever they want, depending on their income and buying power? What do you think the incident at Gretna bridge reveals?

UNIT 3

Gentrification, Globalization, and the City

Unit Selections

Learning Outcomes

After reading this unit, you should be able to:

- Explain how immigration has helped contribute to neighborhood stability and the economic health of many cities.
- Formulate your own opinion as to what would constitute a "wise" immigration policy for the United States, a policy that would recognize the needs of big cities.
- Define "globalization" and identify the various aspects or dimensions of globalization.
- Illustrate how certain cities have been able to find their niche in the global economy while others have not.
- Define "outsourcing" and explain why U.S. firms have begun outsourcing manufacturing, back-office support tasks, and information technology (IT) jobs to firms overseas.
- Explain how China's cities have become the "world's factory." Describe the various actions that China has taken in its efforts to increase the attractiveness of cities like Shenzhen to foreign firms.
- Evaluate Richard Florida's "creative class" theory: Has Dr. Florida accurately identified the critical factors that make an economically healthy city?
- Evaluate how gentrification is transforming numerous inner-city neighborhoods, pointing to both the benefits and to the costs of gentrification.
- Formulate possible policies by which a city can reduce some of the more harmful impacts of gentrification.

Student Website

www.mhhe.com/cls

Internet References

The Brookings Institution, Immigration
www.brookings.edu/topics/immigration.aspx

The Brookings Institution, Gentrification
www.brookings.edu/es/urban/gentrification/gentrification.pdf

Center for an Urban Future
www.nycfuture.org/content/search/topicsearch.cfm?topicarea=39

Center for Immigration Studies
www.cis.org

Creative Class Group
http://creativeclass.com

Gentrification Web
http://members.lycos.co.uk/gentrification

Gotham Gazette
www.gothamgazette.com/city

Great Cities Institute, University of Illinois–Chicago
http://uic.edu/cuppa/gci/index.shtml

National Immigration Forum
www.immigrationforum.org

Partnership for a New American Economy
www.renewoureconomy.org

Right to the City
www.righttothecity.org

Urban Institute
www.urban.org

Urban Land Institute
www.uli.org

Globalization denotes the penetrability of borders. Advances in transportation, computerization, and telecommunications define the contemporary urban environment where cities are influenced by events, decisions, and forces that have their roots in other countries.

Extensive immigration is one such global force that is exerting a strong influence on U.S. cities. The new immigration comes to American cities from Latin America (especially Mexico), East Asia, South Asia, and Africa, a marked contrast to the "old immigration" of the 1800s and early 1900s that came primarily from Europe. Critics point to the added costs of schooling, policing, and public welfare services that result from the new immigration.

Yet, the defenders of immigration point to the important contributions that new arrivals make to both the local and national economies. In New York, Los Angeles, Chicago, Dallas, Miami, San Francisco, and other gateway cities, investment by immigrant entrepreneurs helps to create jobs and bring new life to communities that were once considered beyond hope (Article 9, "Movers & Shakers: How Immigrants Are Reviving Neighborhoods Given up for Dead"). Immigrants help to fill and stabilize inner-city neighborhoods that would otherwise suffer the ills that accompany extensive housing vacancies.

The most dynamic global cities are sites of international corporate headquarters and major international banks and financial firms. These cities are the command and control centers of the global economy. New York, London, and Tokyo each have such a dense concentration of corporate headquarters and financial firms that the three cities are generally recognized to occupy the top tier of the global cities hierarchy. But even cities that are not at the top of the hierarchy can be affected by global influences. In Miami, kinship ties and a new diversity of people, ideas, and cultures have added to the city's vibrancy (Article 10, "Swoons Over Miami").

Globalization also exacerbates the pressures of economic competition that a city confronts. Local leaders must compete for major businesses that oftentimes can choose to locate facilities in any one of the number of cities not just across the country but around the globe. Advances in telecommunications and transportation means that U.S. cities even face competition from such far-off places like Bangalore, Hyderabad, and Mumbai, centers of information technology (IT) and the operation of call centers in India. In a digital age, even firms that have had a long-term loyalty to the United States may find it financially advantageous to outsource data-processing and other back-office and support tasks to low-wage sites located overseas. The competitive pressures of globalization are unrelenting, so much so that Bangalore, Hyderabad, and Mumbai now face the prospect of losing jobs to even lower-wage sites in Russia, Eastern Europe, and China (Article 11, "Outsourcing: Beyond Bangalore").

James Fallows describes the severity of the competitive pressures that often leads firms to outsource production to plants located in factory cities in China (Article 12, "China Makes, the World Takes"). China, once cut off from the world by its inward-looking brand of Maoist communism, now seeks to find strength

© Hisham F. Ibrahim/Getty Images

by building its cities as pivotal production centers in the global economy. Fallows describes the various steps that China has taken to lure firms from the West, making it easy for executives to shift production to factories in China.

How do cities respond to such unrelenting competitive interlocal and global pressures? One commonplace strategy is for a city to reduce local taxes imposed on a firm and to offer the infrastructure improvements and various other incentives that a prospective firm may desire. Such a strategy, however, can be very costly. Such concessions also reduce the revenues a city has available to support schools and other essential municipal services.

But the offer of tax reductions and other subsidies is not the only path that a city can take in its efforts to gain new businesses. Economist Richard Florida argues that technology-oriented firms and other cutting-edge corporations will be especially attracted to cities that are able to provide the talented, educated, and innovative workers that such businesses seek. Tax breaks alone will not suffice to win the competition; as such concessions are easily matched by competitor cities. As Professor Florida has argued in such books as *The Rise of the Creative Class* and *Who's Your City?*, cities attract top-end businesses by nurturing an environment that attracts the creative class—the young, talented, and entrepreneurial professionals that world-class firms desire (Article 13, "The Rise of the Creative Class"). But not all urbanists agree with Dr. Florida's viewpoint that municipal spending on hiking paths, bicycle trails, and the amenities desired by the creative class will have such a great long-term economic payoff.

Other critics worry about displacement, that in the inner-city neighborhoods "rediscovered" by the creative class, rising land values and rents will push out the urban poor. Gentrification refers to the resettlement and upgrading of once-declining inner-city neighborhoods that occurs when young professionals find value in living close to a city's jobs and night life.

Defenders of gentrification argue that such positive developments are good for the city. They also point to the benefits that neighborhood upgrading brings to the poor in terms of higher levels of public safety and municipal service, the ability to select more healthy foods at local supermarkets, and the opportunity to patronize a greater variety of local restaurants and stores (Article 14, "Studies: Gentrification a Boost for Everyone"). Critics, however, respond that such positive assessments of gentrification overstate the opportunities that the poor gain from a neighborhood's transformation while understating the pressures that drive displacement. Gentrification does little to improve the lives of poor residents who are forced to move from a neighborhood that is on an upward trajectory.

Globalization and gentrification point to the continuing evolution of the city. Of course, things in a city are in constant change. But local policies can help to determine just how a city responds to the pressures of globalization and gentrification. These processes raise important questions: Just whom do cities serve? Who has the "right" to the city?

Movers & Shakers

How Immigrants Are Reviving Neighborhoods Given up for Dead

JOEL KOTKIN

For decades the industrial area just east of downtown Los Angeles was an economic wreck, a 15-square-block area inhabited largely by pre–World War II derelict buildings. Yet now the area comes to life every morning, full of talk of toys in various South China dialects, in Vietnamese, in Korean, in Farsi, in Spanish, and in the myriad other commercial languages of the central city.

The district now known as Toytown represents a remarkable turnaround of the kind of archaic industrial area that has fallen into disuse all across the country. A combination of largely immigrant entrepreneurship and the fostering of a specialized commercial district has created a bustling marketplace that employs over 4,000 people, boasts revenues estimated at roughly $500 million a year, and controls the distribution of roughly 60 percent of the $12 billion in toys sold to American retailers.

"In December we have about the worst traffic problem in downtown," proudly asserts Charlie Woo, a 47-year-old immigrant who arrived in 1968 from Hong Kong and is widely considered the district's founding father. During the holiday season, thousands of retail customers, mostly Latino, come down to the district seeking cut-rate toys, dolls, and action figures, including dubious knockoffs of better-known brands. For much of the rest of the year, the district sustains itself as a global wholesale center for customers from Latin America and Mexico, which represent nearly half the area's shipments, as well as buyers from throughout the United States.

Few in L.A.'s business world, City Hall, or the Community Redevelopment Agency paid much attention when Woo started his family's first toy wholesaling business in 1979. "When Toytown started, the CRA didn't even know about it," recalls Don Spivack, now the agency's deputy administrator. "It happened on its own. It was a dead warehouse district."

How dead? Dave Zoraster, an appraiser at CB Richard Ellis, estimates that in the mid-1970s land values in the area—then known only as Central City East—stood at $2.75 a square foot, a fraction of the over $100 a square foot the same property commands today. Vacancy rates, now in the single digits, then

hovered at around 50 percent. For the most part, Spivack recalls, development officials saw the district as a convenient place to cluster the low-income, largely transient population a safe distance from the city's new sparkling high-rises nearby.

To Charlie Woo, then working on a Ph.D. in physics at UCLA, the low land costs in the area presented an enormous opportunity. Purchasing his first building for a mere $140,000, Woo saw the downtown location as a cheap central locale for wholesaling and distributing the billions of dollars in toys unpacked at the massive twin ports of Long Beach and Los Angeles, the nation's dominant hub for U.S.–Asia trade and the world's third-largest container port. Woo's *guanxi,* or connections, helped him establish close relationships with scores of toy manufacturers in Asia, where the vast majority of the nation's toys are produced. The large volume of toys he imported then allowed him to take a 20 percent margin, compared with the 40 to 50 percent margins sought by the traditional small toy wholesalers. Today Woo and his family own 10 buildings, with roughly 70 tenants, in the area; their distribution company, Megatoys, has annual sales in excess of $30 million.

Toytown's success also has contributed to a broader growth in toy-related activity in Southern California. The region—home to Mattel, the world's largest toy maker—has spawned hundreds of smaller toy-making firms, design firms, and distribution firms, some originally located in Toytown but now residing in sleek modern industrial parks just outside the central core. Other spin-offs, including a new toy design department at the Otis College of Art and Design in West Los Angeles and the Toy Association of Southern California, have worked to secure the region's role as a major industry hub.

Woo envisions Toytown as a retail center. But whatever its future, the district's continuing success stands as testament to the ability of immigrant entrepreneurs and specialized industrial districts to turn even the most destitute urban neighborhoods around. Woo notes: "The future of Toytown will be as a gathering point for anyone interested in toys. Designers and buyers will come to see what's selling, what the customer wants. The industry will grow all over, but this place will remain ground zero."

For much of the 19th and early 20th centuries, immigrants filled and often dominated American cities. With the curtailment of immigration in the 1920s, this flow was dramatically reduced, and urban areas began to suffer demographic stagnation, and in some places rapid decline. Only after 1965, when immigration laws were reformed, did newcomers return in large numbers, once again transforming many of the nation's cities.

This was critical, because despite the movement of young professionals and others into the urban core, native-born Americans continued, on balance, to flee the cities in the 1990s. Only two of the nation's 10 largest metropolitan areas, Houston and Dallas, gained domestic migrants in the decade. As over 2.5 million native-born Americans fled the nation's densest cities, over 2.3 million immigrants came in.

The impacts were greatest in five major cities: New York, Los Angeles, San Francisco, Miami, and Chicago. These cities received more than half of the estimated 20 million legal and 3 million to 5 million illegal immigrants who arrived over the past quarter century. Without these immigrants, probably all these cities would have suffered the sort of serious depopulation that has afflicted such cities as St. Louis, Baltimore, and Detroit, which until recently have attracted relatively few foreigners.

In this two-way population flow, America's major cities and their close suburbs have become ever more demographically distinct from the rest of the country. In 1930, one out of four residents of the top four "gateway" cities came from abroad, twice the national average; by the 1990s, one in three was foreign-born, five times the norm. Fully half of all new Hispanic residents in the country between 1990 and 1996 resided in the 10 largest cities. Asians are even more concentrated, with roughly two in five residing in just three areas: Los Angeles, New York, and San Francisco.

In places such as Southern California, immigration has transformed the economic landscape. Between 1992 and 1999, the number of Latino businesses in Los Angeles County more than doubled. Some of these businesses have grown in areas that previously had been considered fallow, such as Compton and South-Central Los Angeles. In these long-established "ghettos," both incomes and population have been on the rise largely because of Latino immigration, after decades of decline.

A similar immigrant-driven phenomenon has sparked recoveries in some of the nation's most distressed neighborhoods, from Washington, D.C., to Houston. Along Pitkin Avenue in Brooklyn's Brownsville section, Caribbean and African immigrants, who have a rate of self-employment 20 to 50 percent higher than that of native-born blacks, have propelled a modest but sustained economic expansion.

"Immigrants are hungrier and more optimistic," says Harvard's William Apgar. "Their presence is the difference between New York and Detroit."

The recovery of such once forlorn places stems largely from the culture of these new immigrants. Certainly Brooklyn's infrastructure and location remain the same as in its long decades of decline. Along with entrepreneurship, the newcomers from places such as the Caribbean have brought with them a strong family ethic, a system of mutual financial assistance called *susus,* and a more positive orientation to their new place. "Immigrants are hungrier and more optimistic," notes William Apgar of Harvard's Joint Center for Housing Studies. "Their upward mobility is a form of energy. Their presence is the difference between New York and Detroit."

It is possible that newcomers to America might even be able to revive those cities that have not yet fully felt the transformative power of immigration. A possible harbinger can be seen on the South Side of St. Louis, a city largely left out of the post-1970s immigrant wave. Once a thriving white working-class community, the area, like much of the rest of the city, had suffered massive depopulation and economic stagnation.

This began to change, however, in the late 1990s, with the movement into the area of an estimated 10,000 Bosnian refugees, along with other newcomers, including Somalis, Vietnamese, and Mexicans. Southern Commercial Bank loan officer Steve Hrdlicka, himself a native of the district, recalls: "Eight years ago, when we opened this branch, we sat on our hands most of the time. We used to sleep quite a lot. Then this place became a rallying place for Bosnians. They would come in and ask for a loan for furniture. Then it was a car. Then it was a house, for themselves, their cousins."

In 1998, largely because of the Bosnians, Hrdlicka's branch, located in a South St. Louis neighborhood called Bevo, opened more new accounts than any of the 108-year-old Southern Commercial's other six branches. Over the last two years of the 1990s, the newcomers, who have developed a reputation for hard work and thrift, helped push the number of accounts at the branch up nearly 80 percent, while deposits have nearly doubled to $40 million.

"Bosnians," says one immigrant, "don't care if they start by buying the smallest, ugliest house. At least they feel they have something."

A translator at the Bevo branch, 25-year-old Jasna Mruckovski, has even cashed in on the Bosnians' homebuying tendencies. Moonlighting as a real estate salesperson, she has helped sell 33 homes in the area over the past year, all but one to Bosnian buyers. In many cases, she notes, these homes were bought with wages pooled from several family members, including children. Mruckovski, a refugee from Banjo Luka who arrived in St. Louis in 1994, observes: "St. Louis is seen as a cheap place to live. People come from California, Chicago, and Florida, where it's more expensive. Bosnians don't care if they start by buying the smallest, ugliest house. At least they feel they have something. This feeling is what turns a place like this around."

Immigration also helps cities retain their preeminence in another traditional urban economic bastion: cross-cultural trade. Virtually all the great cities since antiquity derived much of their sustenance through the intense contact between differing peoples in various sorts of markets. As world economies have developed through the ages, exchanges between races and cultures have been critical to establishing the geographic importance of particular places. Historian Fernand Braudel suggests, "A world economy always has an urban center of gravity, a city, as the logistic heart of its activity. News, merchandise, capital, credit, people, instructions, correspondence all flow into and out of the city. Its powerful merchants lay down the law, sometimes becoming extraordinarily wealthy."

Repeatedly throughout history, it has been outsiders—immigrants—who have driven cross-cultural exchange. "Throughout the history of economics," observes social theorist Georg Simmel, "the stranger appears as the trader, or the trader as stranger." In ancient Greece, for example, it was *metics,* largely foreigners, who drove the marketplace economy disdained by most well-born Greeks. In Alexandria, Rome, Venice, and Amsterdam—as well as the Islamic Middle East—this pattern repeated itself, with "the stranger" serving the critical role as intermediary.

As in Renaissance Venice, the increasing ethnic diversity of America's cities plays a critical role in their domination of international trade.

As in Renaissance Venice and early modern Amsterdam or London, the increasing ethnic diversity of America's cities plays a critical role in their domination of international trade. Over the past 30 years, cities such as New York, Los Angeles, Houston, Chicago, and Miami have become ever more multi-ethnic, with many of the newcomers hailing from growing trade regions such as East Asia, the Caribbean, and Latin America. The large immigrant clusters in these cities help forge critical global economic ties, held together not only by commercial bonds but by the equally critical bonds of cultural exchange and kinship networks.

These newcomers have redefined some former backwaters into global trading centers. Miami's large Latino population—including 650,000 Cubans, 75,000 Nicaraguans, and 65,000 Colombians—has helped turn the one-time sun-and-fun capital into the dominant center for American trade and travel to South America and the Caribbean. Modesto Maidique, president of Florida International University, who is himself a Cuban émigré, observes: "If you take away international trade and cultural ties from Miami, we go back to being just a seasonal tourist destination. It's the imports, the exports, and the service trade that have catapulted us into the first rank of cities in the world."

Like the *souk* districts of the Middle East, diversified cities provide an ideal place for the creation of unique, globally oriented markets. These *souks,* which are fully operational to this day, are home mostly to small, specialized merchants. In most cases, the districts consisted of tiny unlighted shops raised two or three feet from street level. Stores are often grouped together by trade, allowing the consumer the widest selection and choice.

The emergence of the Western *souk* is perhaps most evident in Los Angeles, home to Toytown. Within a short distance of that bustling district are scores of other specialized districts—the downtown Fashion Mart, the Flower district, and the jewelry, food, and produce districts are crowded with shoppers, hustlers, and buyers of every possible description. These districts' vitality contrasts with the longstanding weakness of downtown L.A.'s office market, which has been losing companies and tenants to other parts of the city.

Similar trade-oriented districts have arisen in other cities, such as along Canal Street in New York, in the "Asia Trade District" along Dallas's Harry Hines Boulevard, and along the Harwin Corridor in the area outside the 610 Loop in Houston. Once a forlorn strip of office and warehouse buildings, the Harwin area has been transformed into a car-accessed *souk* for off-price goods for much of East Texas, featuring cut-rate furniture, novelties, luggage, car parts, and electronic goods.

These shops, owned largely by Chinese, Korean, and Indian merchants, have grown from roughly 40 a decade ago to more than 800, sparking a boom in a once-depressed real estate market. Over the decade, the value of commercial properties in the district has more than tripled, and vacancies have dropped from nearly 50 percent to single digits. "It's kind of an Asian frontier sprawl around here," comments David Wu, a prominent local store owner.

Indeed, few American cities have been more transformed by trade and immigration than Houston. With the collapse of energy prices in the early 1980s, the once booming Texas metropolis appeared to be on the road to economic oblivion. Yet the city has rebounded, in large part because of the very demographic and trade patterns seen in the other Sun Belt capitals. "The energy industry totally dominated Houston by the 1970s—after all, oil has been at the core of our economy since 1901," explains University of Houston economist Barton Smith. "Every boom leads people to forget other parts of the economy. After the bust, people saw the importance of the ports and trade."

Since 1986, tonnage through the 25-mile-long Port of Houston has grown by one-third, helping the city recover the jobs lost during the "oil bust" of the early 1980s. Today, Smith estimates, trade accounts for roughly 10 percent of regional employment and has played a critical role in the region's 1990s recovery. By 1999 a city once renowned for its plethora of "see-through" buildings ranked second in the nation in total office space absorption and third in rent increases.

Immigrants were the critical factor in this turnaround. Between 1985 and 1990, Houston, a traditional magnet for domestic migrants, suffered a net loss of over 140,000 native-born residents. But the immigrants kept coming—nearly 200,000 over the past decade, putting the Texas town among America's seven most popular immigrant destinations.

Among those coming to Houston during the 1970s boom was a Taiwan-born engineer named Don Wang, who in 1987 founded his own immigrant-oriented financial institution, Metrobank. Amid the hard times and demographic shifts, Wang and his clients—largely Asian, Latin, and African immigrants—saw an enormous opportunity to pick up real estate, buy homes, and start businesses. Minority-owned enterprises now account for nearly 30 percent of Houston's business community.

Says Wang: "In the 1980s everyone was giving up on Houston. But we stayed. It was cheap to start a business here and easy to find good labor. We considered this the best place to do business in the country, even if no one on the outside knows it. . . . When the oil crisis came, everything dropped, but it actually was our chance to become a new city again."

Increasingly, the focus of immigrants—and their enterprise—extends beyond the traditional *souk* economy to a broader part of the metropolitan geography. Most dramatic has been the movement to the older rings of suburbs, which are rapidly replacing the inner city as the predominant melting pots of American society. This trend can be seen across the nation, from the Chinese- and Latino-dominated suburbs east of Los Angeles to the new immigrant communities emerging in southern metropolitan areas such as Houston, Dallas, and Atlanta. This move marks a sharp contrast to the immediate postwar era, when these suburbs, like their high-tech workforces, remained highly segregated.

The demographic shift in the near suburbs started in the 1970s, when African-Americans began moving to them in large numbers. In the ensuing two decades, middle-class minorities and upwardly mobile recent immigrants have shown a marked tendency to replace whites in the suburbs, particularly in the inner ring, increasing their numbers far more rapidly than their Anglo counterparts. Today nearly 51 percent of Asians, 43 percent of Latinos, and 32 percent of African Americans live in the suburbs.

This development is particularly notable in those regions where immigration has been heaviest. Among the most heavily Asian counties in the nation are such places as Queens County in New York, Santa Clara and San Mateo counties in Northern California, and Orange County, south of Los Angeles. Queens and Fort Bend County, in suburban Houston, rank among the 10 most ethnically diverse counties in the nation.

Today these areas have become as ethnically distinctive as the traditional inner cities themselves, if not more so. Some, like Coral Gables, outside of Miami, have become both ethnic and global business centers. Coral Gables is home to the Latin American division headquarters of over 50 multinationals.

Other places, such as the San Gabriel Valley east of Los Angeles, have accommodated two distinct waves of ethnic settlement, Latino and Asian. Cities such as Monterey Park, Alhambra, and San Gabriel have become increasingly Asian in character; areas such as Whittier and La Puente have been transformed by Latino migration. Yet in both cases, the movement is predominantly by middle-class homeowners. "For us this isn't a dream, this is reality," notes Frank Corona, who moved to the area from East Los Angeles. "This is a quiet, nice, family-oriented community."

The melting pot has spilled into the suburbs. About 51 percent of Asians, 43 percent of Latinos, and 32 percent of African Americans live in the suburbs.

The reason the melting pot has spilled into the suburbs lies in the changing needs of immigrants. In contrast to the early 20th century, when proximity to inner-city services and infrastructure was critical, many of today's newcomers to a more dispersed, auto-oriented society find they need to stop only briefly, if at all, in the inner cities. Their immediate destination after arrival is as likely to be Fort Lee as Manhattan, the San Gabriel Valley as Chinatown or the East L.A. barrios. Notes Cal State Northridge demographer James Allen: "The immigrants often don't bother with the inner city anymore. Most Iranians don't ever go to the center city, and few Chinese ever touch Chinatown at all. Many of them want to get away from poor people as soon as possible."

As proof, Allen points to changes in his own community, the San Fernando Valley, which for a generation was seen as the epitome of the modern suburb. In the 1960s, the valley was roughly 90 percent white; three decades later it was already 44 percent minority, with Latinos representing nearly one-third the total population. By 1997, according to county estimates, Latinos were roughly 41 percent of the valley population, while Asians were another 9 percent.

Similarly dramatic changes have taken place outside of California. Twenty years ago, Queens County was New York's largest middle-class and working-class white bastion, the fictional locale of the small homeowner Archie Bunker. Today it is not Manhattan, the legendary immigrant center, but Queens that is easily the most diverse borough in New York, with thriving Asian, Latino, and middle-class African-American neighborhoods. Over 40 percent of the borough's businesses are now minority-owned, almost twice as high as the percentage in Manhattan.

This alteration in the suburban fabric is particularly marked in the American South, which largely lacks the infrastructure of established ethnic inner-city districts. Regions such as Atlanta experienced some of the most rapid growth in immigration in the last two decades of the millennium; between 1970 and 1990, for example, Georgia's immigrant population grew by 525 percent. By 1996, over 11.5 million Asians lived in the South. Yet since most Southern cities lacked the preexisting structure of an ethnic Asian or Latino community to embrace the newcomers, most new immigrants chose to cluster not in the central city but in the near suburbs.

"Well, we still have one fried-chicken place left somewhere around here," jokes Houston architect Chao-Chiung Lee over dim sum in one of the city's heavily Asian suburbs. "It's a kind of the last outpost of the native culture lost amid the new Chinatown."

Yet if the successes of immigrants represent the success of the melting pot, the demographic shift also presents some potential challenges. In addition to a swelling number of entrepreneurs and scientists, there has been a rapid expansion of a less-educated population. For example, Latinos, the fastest-growing group in Silicon Valley, account for 23 percent of that region's population but barely 7 percent of its high-tech work force. Part of the problem lies with education: Only 56 percent of Latinos graduate from high school, and less than one in five takes the classes necessary to get into college.

Indeed, as the economy becomes increasingly information-based, there are growing concerns among industry and political leaders that many of the new immigrants and, more important, their children may be unprepared for the kind of jobs that are opening up in the future. Immigrants may be willing to serve as bed changers, gardeners, and service workers for the digital elites, but there remains a serious question as to whether their children will accept long-term employment in such generally low-paid and low-status niches.

George Borjas, a leading critic of U.S. immigration policy and professor of public policy at Harvard's John F. Kennedy School of Government, suggests that recent immigration laws have tilted the pool of newcomers away from skilled workers toward those less skilled, seriously depleting the quality of the labor pool and perhaps threatening the social stability of the immigration centers. "The national economy is demanding more skilled workers," Borjas says, "and I don't see how bringing more unskilled workers is consistent with this trend. . . . When you have a very large group of unskilled workers, and children of unskilled workers, you risk the danger of creating a social underclass in the next [21st] century."

In the coming decades, this disconnect between the labor force and the economy in some areas could lead to an exodus of middle-class people and businesses to less troubled places, as happened previously in inner cities. Across the country, many aging suburbs, such as Upper Darby near Philadelphia and Harvey outside Chicago, are well on the way to becoming highly diverse suburban slums as businesses move farther out into the geographic periphery. Others—in regions including Boston, New Orleans, Cleveland, St. Louis, Dallas, and Indianapolis—now struggle to retain their attractiveness.

If unchecked, a broader ghettoization looms as a distinct possibility, particularly in some of the older areas filled with smaller houses and more mundane apartment buildings. These areas could become—as have some suburbs of Paris—dysfunctional, balkanized losers in the new digital geography. "It's a different place now. We can go either way," says Robert Scott, a former L.A. planning commissioner and leader of the San Fernando Valley's drive to secede from Los Angeles.

No longer "lily white" enclaves, suburbs must draw their strength, as the great cities before them did, from their increasingly diverse populations.

Scott grew up in the once all-white, now predominantly Latino community of Van Nuys. "The valley can become a storehouse of poverty and disenchantment," he says, "or it can become a series of neighborhoods with a sense of uniqueness and an investment in its future." As Scott suggests, for these new melting pots, the best course may be not so much to try clinging to their demographic past as to find a way to seize the advantages of their more diverse roles, both economically and demographically. No longer "lily white" enclaves, such communities increasingly must draw their strength, as the great cities before them did, from the energies, skills, and cultural offerings of their increasingly diverse populations.

Critical Thinking

1. How does the story of Charlie Woo and Toytown illustrate the often overlooked contributions that immigration makes to a city and its neighborhoods?
2. Which are the top five "gateway cities" in the United States? How did immigration to these cities help to prevent their descent into the spiral of deep decline apparent in cities like Detroit and St. Louis?
3. Why are immigrants today increasingly found in suburbia, as contrasted to the immigration of the early 20th century?

JOEL KOTKIN (jkotkin@pacbell.net) is a senior fellow with the Pepperdine University Institute for Public Policy and a research fellow of the Reason Public Policy Institute. Excerpted from the book *The New Geography: How the Digital Revolution Is Reshaping the American Landscape* by Joel Kotkin. Copyright © 2000 by Joel Kotkin. Reprinted by arrangement with Random House Trade Publishing, a division of Random House Inc.

From *Reason Magazine*, December 2000, pp. 40–46. Excerpted from *The New Geography: How the Digital Revolution Is Reshaping the American Landscape* (Random House 2000). Copyright © 2000 by Joel Kotkin. Reprinted by permission of the author.

Swoons Over Miami

A conversation with author Saskia Sassen, who coined the term "global city." As she tells *Foreign Policy*:
Don't focus only on London and New York. The rest of the world should want to be the next Miami.

CHRISTINA LARSON

In the 1970s and 80s, back when crime peaked in Manhattan and downtowns across the United States and talent and money were draining out to the suburbs, a young sociologist named Saskia Sassen had a hunch the emerging conventional wisdom about the death of the city was wrong.

Then a researcher in New York City, conversant in five languages, she spent her time trolling the small shops and businesses around Wall Street. Even as the city's local economy was struggling, she recognized the emergence of new ties to the world beyond New York—small, specialized financial and marketing firms with global links, immigrant communities with ties back home, museum curators drawing upon international networks. Sassen predicted that the Big Apple was not dead, but about to spring back to life, with more international clout than ever.

In 1991, when Sassen published her first book, *The Global City,* which popularized the term, many onlookers were skeptical. After all, the United States was then mired in recession, and urban planners weren't yet talking about how to reinvent downtown or attract a "creative class." Many thought that opportunities would flourish outside cities, and telecommuting might soon make the morning commute obsolete. But in the two decades since, history has proven Sassen right. Today, cities are increasingly important, both as places where people desire to live and as global nodes of commerce, culture, and ideas.

On the occasion of the publication of *Foreign Policy*'s *2010 Global Cities Index,* we caught up with Sassen to ask her to pick the next round of urban winners and losers for the 21st century. The most extraordinary success? The rise of Miami. Missed opportunity? Beirut.

Foreign Policy: What distinguishes a *global city?*

Saskia Sassen: A global city makes new norms. And two requirements for that happening are complexity and diversity. Quite often, in countries around the world, it's the most global city, especially New York, where new national and international norms are made.

FP: Is a global city always a megacity, and vice versa?

SS: I'm so glad you asked. Most global cities are really not megacities. Some are, but the question of size is a tricky one. Size is important for a global city because you need enormous diversity in very specialized sectors, a whole range of them. Some of the leading global cities are very large, like Tokyo or Shanghai. On the other hand, you have cities that are simply very large, like Mumbai or São Paulo. I don't think Lagos is a global city; it's just a huge city. You have a lot of very large cities that are not necessarily global cities.

FP: Can any city become a global city?

SS: No, I don't think that any city can.

FP: So what's the magic recipe?

SS: Many of today's global cities are old-world cities that reinvented themselves. Like London or Istanbul, they already had enormous complexity and diversity. On the other hand, there are old-world cities, like Venice, that are definitely not global cities today.

And then there's Miami. Never an old-world city, today Miami is certainly a global city—why? It's quite surprising. Where did its diversity and complexity come from? Let's go back to the history. Before the 1990s, Miami was sort of a dreadful little spot, frankly. There was lots of domestic tourism; it was cheap; it was rundown; it was seen as dominated by the Cubans. But several important things happened. One was the infrastructure of international trade that the Cubans in Miami developed. There was also real estate development, often spurred by wealthy individuals from South America.

All this coincided with the opening of Latin America. In the 1990s and early 2000s, firms from all over the world—the Taiwanese, Italians, Korean, French, all over—set up regional headquarters in Miami. In the 1990s, there was also deregulation, so Miami becomes the banking center for Central America. Then the art circuit, the designers' circuit, and other things began to come into the city. Large international corporations began to locate branches there, forging a strong bridge with Europe that doesn't run through New

York. That mix of cultures—in such a concentrated space, and covering so many different sectors—created remarkable diversity and complexity. Of course, the Miami case is rather exceptional.

FP: So what's the future Miami of Africa?

SS: You have probably two cities that people could think of as complex places in sub-Saharan Africa. One is Nairobi, Kenya, where some of the architecture still reflects British colonial history. The other one is Johannesburg, South Africa. In recent years, I would say Jo'burg is more dynamic, but Nairobi has lost ground.

FP: And the Miamis of Asia?

SS: In China, there are fast-growing cities like Shenzhen, which is also a port and a place where things come together. But Chinese cities are too controlled to be equivalent to Miami.

Two similar cases might be Singapore and Dubai. Both have constructed themselves arduously, with a lot of resources and government-driven projects, mind you. The market alone could not have done it in either Singapore or Dubai. In a sense, the whole city is a government-driven project—they have constructed themselves as global cities, and very significant ones.

Elsewhere? Quito, Ecuador; Bogotá, Colombia; Caracas, Venezuela—these are all cities with deep colonial histories; they were important nodes, part of a colonial empire, so there was a strong international connection already. They are cities to watch.

But Miami, a little outpost that suddenly explodes—that is still very rare. Dubai and Singapore are the only great similar examples.

FP: How do you explain them?

SS: Well, I think Dubai and Singapore are government-driven projects. It took a lot of hard work. In a way Singapore is surprising. Culturally it's not cosmopolitan; on the other hand, there was the obligation to learn several languages. Everybody had to study English.

FP: Are there any cities that missed, or are missing, their chance to be global cities?

SS: Beirut, if it had not had a civil war that destroyed it. Beirut had once been the global financial center and banking and commercial center for that whole region. The networks of the Lebanese are truly global and enormously sophisticated; they're everywhere. That keeps sustaining Beirut a bit, but really can't transform it. And I think that void in the region is partially what allowed Dubai to become a major trading center, and then a financial center and global city.

Dubai, you know, has it all supposedly—including skiing now, which is ridiculous, so that you can function there. Still, it's difficult to invest in real estate for the long term there. So many people who actually work in Mumbai prefer to live in Dubai. The flights that go from Dubai to Mumbai are HUGE! And the planes are full of business people! And I've flown that.

The first class is fantastic, and it's not that long between flights because there is a lot of traffic between those two cities now.

FP: Is old Europe then old news?

SS: Well, I think Copenhagen, in a way, is becoming the Dubai of Europe. I love that image. I just get so amused by these things. It used to be that London was the platform for Europe. The Japanese firms, the Dutch, German, Spanish, Italian, even the French firms—if they wanted to operate in Europe, they located in London.

But today, you don't need that single platform. So Copenhagen and Zurich are two cities that have become very attractive for all kinds of reasons to firms, whether European firms or firms from the rest of the world. And so they locate in Copenhagen, which is a very reasonable city: much cheaper, well organized, and it ranks as one of the top cities in terms of reliability, investors' protections, good on everything. And Zurich, I don't know if you have been to Zurich, but if you can live in Zurich, why live anywhere else in Europe? It's absolutely so stunning.

FP: Where did you grow up?

SS: Well I grew up, first of all, in five languages. And I lived in the Netherlands, Argentina, Italy, and then I studied in France, I came to the United States, and I went back to France, and so that kind of a life. I speak like a native from Buenos Aires, you know, a particular city.

FP: Can you speculate on what FP's Global Cities rankings might look like in 15 years?

SS: I think that many of today's top global cities are here to stay. Of course there'll be some shift in their relative influence. And trends like the ascendance of Dubai or of Copenhagen over the last few years. Or Singapore—15 years ago Singapore was radically different. Maybe it looked the same, but it was a different type of global city—it was not a global city, really.

Istanbul is going to be enormously significant. I mean, who are the top investors in Istanbul today? They are from both the West and the East. The East includes Kazakhstan, China, Russia, Bulgaria; it's just extraordinary.

The other thing that is happening is of course China. In the future, I think that China and Chinese cities will be even more significant.

FP: Will China's emerging megacities be global cities? By 2030, McKinsey and Co. projects there will be 221 cities in China with populations of more than 1 million.

SS: Not global cities in the same way—they will be *Chinese* global cities. What I mean is that Beijing will never be a global city *of* the world, but it will be a global city *in* the world. The distinction is that *of* the world means that you have to really become a bit de-nationalized, more ethnically and linguistically diverse. Beijing is still quite homogeneous. Same thing with Tokyo. Tokyo never became a global city *of* the world. It's not. But *in* the world, it's very powerful. In China, only Hong Kong is *of* the world, because it has been evolving global connections there for a hundred years.

FP: So there's no mainland Chinese Miami?

SS: Please tell me if you discover it.

Critical Thinking

1. What is globalization? Can you identify the various processes or aspects of globalization and how they affect cities?

2. What makes a Global City different from any other big or medium-sized city?

Christina Larson is a contributing editor at *Foreign Policy* and a fellow at the New America Foundation.

Saskia Sassen is Robert S. Lynd professor of sociology at Columbia University and Centennial visiting professor at the London School of Economics. She is the author, most recently, of *Territory, Authority, Rights: From Medieval to Global Assemblages,* among other works.

Reprinted in entirety by McGraw-Hill with permission from *Foreign Policy,* August 27, 2010. www.foreignpolicy.com. © 2010 Washingtonpost.Newsweek Interactive, LLC.

Outsourcing: Beyond Bangalore

Companies are increasingly sending IT work to hubs outside India. They're saving money but facing a whole new raft of challenges.

RACHAEL KING

After 10 months of working with software developers in Bangalore, India, Bill Wood was ready to call it quits. The local engineers would start a project, get a few months' experience, and then bolt for greener pastures, says the U.S.-based executive. Attrition rose to such a high level that year that Wood's company had to replace its entire staff, some positions more than once. "It did not work well at all," recalls Wood, vice-president of engineering at Ping Identity, a maker of Internet security software for corporations. Frustrated, Wood began searching for a partner outside India. He scoured 15 companies in 8 different countries, including Russia, Mexico, Argentina, and Vietnam.

That path is being trod by a lot of executives, eager for new sources of low-cost, high-tech talent outside India. Many are fed up with the outsourcing hub of Bangalore, where salaries for info tech staff are growing at 12% to 14% a year, turnover is increasing, and an influx of workers is straining city resources. Even Indian outsourcing pioneers Tata Consultancy Services, Wipro Technologies (WIT), and Infosys Technologies (INFY), which have helped foreign companies shift software development and other IT operations to Bangalore, are starting to expand into smaller Indian cities, as well as China (see BusinessWeek.com, 11/14/06, "Patience is a Virtue in China, India IT Learns"). "Overall, in terms of productivity and quality of life, beyond Bangalore is better," says Wipro Chief Information Officer Laxman Badiga. "Bangalore is getting more crowded, and the real infrastructure is getting stretched."

So companies are setting their sights on a slew of emerging hot spots for IT outsourcing. Need a multilingual workforce adept at developing security systems and testing software? *Buna ziua,* Bucharest. Want low-cost Linux developers? *Bienvenidos a* Buenos Aires, where many companies adopted open-source software after the devaluation of the peso in 2002 made licenses from abroad prohibitively expensive. Other cities on the list include Moscow and St. Petersburg in Russia and Prague in the Czech Republic, according to consulting firm neoIT. Other hot spots include Mexico City, São Paulo, and Santiago in Latin America; and within Asia, Dalian, China, and Ho Chi Minh City, Vietnam.

The Search for Lower Costs

Make no mistake: India remains an IT outsourcing powerhouse, with $17.7 billion in software and IT services exports in 2005, compared with $3.6 billion for China and $1 billion for Russia, according to trade organizations in each country. And India's outsourcing industry is still growing at a faster pace than that of Russia and other wannabe Bangalores.

Yet many companies can't resist the lure of cheaper labor. "Ninety percent of all outsourcing deals in the market today have been structured around cost improvement only," says Linda Cohen, vice-president of sourcing research at consulting firm Gartner (IT). By the third year of an outsourcing deal, after all the costs have been squeezed out, companies get antsy to find a new locale with an even lower overhead.

But moving IT operations into developing countries like Vietnam or China can also pose big risks, such as insurmountable language and cultural differences, geopolitical instability, and the risk of stolen intellectual property. "You keep following the money, but how often are you going to move people around?" asks Cohen. Even the routine day-to-day management of an offshore team can require significant project management expertise. "If you don't have experience and don't do it well, it can negate savings," says Barry Rubenstein, program manager of application outsourcing and offshore services at IDC.

Mix of Outsourcing Locations

Plenty of providers are ready to help clients overcome those obstacles. Companies including Accenture (ACN), EDS (EDS), IBM Global Services (IBM), and Genpact are building global networks, comprised of operations in a variety of cities, aimed at giving customers a mix of worker skills and labor costs. "We tailor where you want your people, based on the premium you want to pay," says Charlie Feld, executive vice-president of portfolio development at EDS.

Continental Airlines (CAL), for instance, uses an EDS center in India for development of some software that runs on mainframes, but the airline handles some finance work through an EDS office in Brazil. Accenture uses its global network of facilities in a similar fashion. "Today we are about 35% in high-cost locations, such as the U.S. and Britain; 20% in medium-cost locations like Spain, Ireland, and Canada; and about 45% in low-cost locations like the Philippines, India, China, and Eastern Europe," says Jimmy Harris, global managing director of infrastructure outsourcing at Accenture.

When Bob Gett, CEO of Boston systems integration firm Optaros, decided to hire an overseas outfit to handle development of some applications or programs designed to perform specific tasks, he scouted out six or seven countries in Eastern Europe. He finally settled on Akela, an outsourcing company in Bucharest, Romania. Gett found Romania attractive because of its good education system, multilingual population, and abundance of technical talent.

Benefiting from Geography

The move reduces costs by 60% to 75%, Gett figures, letting Optaros offer competitive pricing to customers. "We're going to where the most cost-effective talent is in the world, but it has to be feasible," he says. "It can't be where there are economic, time zone, or language barriers." In fact, Gett needs his application developers to interact directly with customers in the U.S. and Western Europe, so he appreciates that Akela workers speak English and French and are closer to the Optaros Geneva office than workers in India would be.

Companies such as Genpact, Accenture, Wipro, and Infosys are hoping Romania's expected admission to the European Union will make it even more appealing for companies from Western Europe to do business there.

Dalian, a seaport in northeast China, is also turning out to be an ideal center for outsourcing, in large part because of its geography and history. Located in the northeast corner of China, Dalian is close to both Korea and Japan and was, in the first half of the 20th century, occupied by Japan. So there's still a labor pool of Japanese speakers (see BusinessWeek.com, 3/28/05, "China: Golf, Sushi—and Cheap Engineers").

Intellectual Property Issues

Dalian's labor costs are lower than in Japan, so it's become a center for application development for Japanese companies. U.S. firms outsource some technology work there as well. General Electric (GE) and Nissan (NSANF) outsource work to Genpact's operations in Dalian. Genpact was the first outsourcing firm to locate in the city in June, 2000. Accenture and IBM Global Services have since moved in.

There are certainly challenges for companies that wish to outsource to China, including the potential theft of intellectual property. To combat this, Infosys Technologies has disabled USB drives on PCs to limit the ability of workers to take data out of the office. "We've taken extraordinary efforts to protect the intellectual property of our clients," says Stephen Pratt, CEO Infosys Consulting, a subsidiary of Infosys Technologies, which has operations in Shanghai.

For U.S. companies that need to collaborate closely with offshore workers, South America is an attractive option because

the time zones are similar and the infrastructure is strong (see BusinessWeek.com, 1/30/06, "Can Latin America Challenge India?").

Infrastructure Counts

Brazil boasts a mature software and IT industry, and the nation's providers such as Politec, Stefanini IT, and ActMinds are keen to do more offshore business. Stefanini, which has served clients such as Whirlpool (WHR) and Johnson & Johnson (JNJ), derives about 20% of its revenue from international operations, but the company would like to expand that to 50% by 2008.

Total Brazilian software and IT services revenue is $17.16 billion, while revenue from offshore software development is a much smaller $205.3 million, according to Brazil IT, an association of Brazilian IT services providers. "If we can get a client interested enough that they will go to Brazil, they will do business with us," says Eric Olsson, principal consultant with Politec, which has done work for clients such as insurer MetLife (MET), software colossus Microsoft (MSFT), and SAIC (SAI), a provider of a host of scientific and engineering services. Companies are drawn to Brazil's modern infrastructure, with airports and highways that are first world, says Olsson, whose company is the largest IT services provider in Brazil.

Good roads and the developers who drive on them don't come cheap, though. A software engineer in Brazil costs $20 to $35 per hour. That's lower than in the U.S. but pricier than in India.

Threat to U.S. Workers

And while a technically skilled global labor force is a boon to companies, the picture isn't so rosy for U.S. workers. Instead of competing with just India, now U.S. IT workers will need to go up against workers all over the world. In 2005, about 24% of North American companies used offshore providers to meet some of their software needs, according to Forrester Research (FORR). Over the next five years, spending on offshore IT services is set to increase at a compound annual growth rate of 18%, according to IDC.

The effect in the U.S. is that starting salaries in the engineering field—when adjusted for inflation—have stayed constant or decreased in the past five years or so, says Vivek Wadhwa, executive in residence at Duke University. "It doesn't make much sense to get into programming anymore," says Wadhwa, who worries that a lack of talent in certain industries, such as telecom, along with the outsourcing of research and development will erode U.S. competitiveness (see BusinessWeek.com, 11/7/06, "The Real Problem with Outsourcing"). But U.S. companies say that hiring programmers in India, who might make a fifth of what programmers do in the U.S., allows the companies to survive in a globally competitive economy.

After traveling the world, Ping Identity's Wood finally settled on Luxoft, an outsourcing provider based in Moscow that has served high-profile clients such as Boeing (BA), Citigroup's (C) Citibank, and Dell (DELL). While programmers are typically 20% more expensive in Moscow than in Bangalore, Wood found that there wasn't much difference in the hourly rate for the kind of work that he needed. "Indian companies are cheap until you ask for people with experience, and we wanted workers with eight years or more of experience," he says.

Russia's high-end software developers are drawing plenty of offshore business to Moscow and St. Petersburg, which together account for about 60% of the country's software development exports. Those exports have grown from $352 million in 2002 to nearly $1 billion in 2005, according to RUSSOFT, an association of software development firms from Russia, Belarus, and Ukraine (see BusinessWeek.com, 1/30/06, "From Russia with Technology?"). Providers EPAM and Luxoft are starting to gain some international recognition as well, both making Brown & Wilson's Top 50 Best Managed Global Outsourcing Vendors for the first time in 2006.

For Wood, the biggest benefit of working with Luxoft is a cultural one. "One of the reasons we're in Russia is that we found a common value set. Their work ethic is strong, and these people are very outspoken," says Wood. He says engineers in Moscow have no trouble proposing a different course of action when necessary. He says he found workers in Bangalore to be reticent. And since Russian developers stick around longer—turnover is now in the low teens—Wood has plenty of time to take those opinions to heart.

Critical Thinking

1. How does the digitalization of information create a world that, to use the words of Thomas Friedman, is "flat"? How has Bangalore come to symbolize all that a "flat world" represents?

2. As seen in the growth of Bangalore, how does a "flat world" affect the economic prospects of U.S. cities?

3. Are there limits to a "flat world" and global competition? Why don't all industries essentially leave the United States and shift more of their production overseas?

RACHAEL KING is a writer for *BusinessWeek.com* in San Francisco.

China Makes, the World Takes

A look inside the world's manufacturing center shows that America should welcome China's rise—for now.

JAMES FALLOWS

Half the time I have spent in China I have spent in factories. At least that's how it feels—and it's a feeling I sought. The factories where more than 100 million Chinese men and women toil, and from which cameras, clothes, and every other sort of ware flow out to the world, are to me the most startling and intense aspect of today's China. For now, they are also the most important.

They are startling above all in their scale. I was prepared for the skyline of Shanghai and its 240-mph Maglev train to the airport, and for the non-stop construction, dust, and bustle of Beijing. Every account of modern China mentions them. But I had no concept of the sweep of what has become the world's manufacturing center: the Pearl River Delta of Guangdong province (the old Canton region), just north of Hong Kong. That one province might have a manufacturing workforce larger than America's. Statistics from China are largely guesses, but Guangdong's population is around 90 million. If even one-fifth of its people hold manufacturing jobs, as seems likely in big cities, that would be 10 million—versus 14 million in the entire United States.

One facility in Guangdong province, the famous Foxconn works, sits in the middle of a conurbation just outside Shenzhen, where it occupies roughly as much space as a major airport. Some 240,000 people (the number I heard most often; estimates range between 200,000 and 300,000) work on its assembly lines, sleep in its dormitories, and eat in its company cafeterias. I was told that Foxconn's caterers kill 3,000 pigs each day to feed its employees. The number would make sense—it's one pig per 80 people, in a country where pigs are relatively small and pork is a staple meat (I heard no estimate for chickens). From the major ports serving the area, Hong Kong and Shenzhen harbors, cargo ships left last year carrying the equivalent of more than 40 million of the standard 20-foot-long metal containers that end up on trucks or railroad cars. That's one per second, round the clock and year-round—and it's less than half of China's export total. What's in the containers that come back from America? My guess was, "dollars"; in fact, the two leading ship-borne exports from the United States to China, by volume, are scrap paper and scrap metal, for recycling.

And the factories are important, for China and everyone else. Someday China may matter internationally mainly for the nature of its political system or for its strategic ambitions. Those are significant even now, of course, but China's success in manufacturing is what has determined its place in the world. Most of what has been good about China over the past generation has come directly or indirectly from its factories. The country has public money with which to build roads, houses, and schools—especially roads. The vast population in the countryside has what their forebears acutely lacked, and peasants elsewhere today still do: a chance at paying jobs, which means a chance to escape rural poverty. Americans complain about cheap junk pouring out of Chinese mills, but they rely on China for a lot that is not junk, and whose cheap price is important to American industrial and domestic life. Modern consumer culture rests on the assumption that the nicest, most advanced goods—computers, audio systems, wall-sized TVs—will get cheaper year by year. Moore's Law, which in one version says that the price of computing power will be cut in half every 18 months or so, is part of the reason, but China's factories are a big part too.

Much of what is threatening about today's China also comes from its factories. Many people inside China, and nearly everyone outside, can avoid the direct effects of the country's political controls. It is much harder to avoid its pollution. The air in Chinese cities is worse than I expected, and because the pollution affects so many people in such a wide range of places, it is more damaging than London's, Manchester's, or Pittsburgh's in their worst, rapidly industrializing days. The air pollution comes directly from the steel works, cement plants, and other heavy-industry facilities that are helping the country prosper, and indirectly from the electric power plants that keep everything running. (Plus more and more cars, though China still has barely one-thirtieth as many per capita as the United States.) The sheer speed and volume with which factories and power plants across China increase their output of soot and gases make the country's air-pollution problems the world's. The heightened competition for oil, ore, and other commodities to feed the factories affects other nations, as do slapdash standards of food purity and safety, which may have led to tainted worldwide supplies of animal food. The ultimate fear in the developed world, of course, is that as China creates millions of new factory jobs unknown millions will lose such jobs in America, Canada, Germany, even Japan.

But these factories are both surprising and important in a less obvious, though also fundamental, way. Almost nothing about the way they work corresponds to the way they are discussed in the United States. America's political debates about the "China opportunity" and, even more, the "China threat" seem distant, theoretical, and imprecise from the perspective of the factories where the outsourcing and exporting occur. The industrialists from the United States, Europe, or Japan who are deciding how much of their production to move to China talk about the process in very different terms from those used in American political discussion. One illustration: The artificially low value of Chinas currency, relative to the dollar, comes near the top of American complaints about Chinese trade policy. (The currency is the yuan renminbi—literally, "people's money"—or RMB). This is more like the eighth or tenth issue that comes up when business officials discuss the factories they are opening in one country and closing in another. And when it does come up, the context is usually whether the RMB's rise will force a company to put its next factory not in China's crowded coastal region but someplace with even lower costs, like the remote interior provinces, where salaries are lower and commercial space is cheaper—or perhaps Vietnam or Cambodia.

So too with complaints about Chinese government subsidies for exporting industries, widespread abuse of intellectual property, and even "slave labor" inside the vast factories. Some of these complaints are well-founded, others are not; but even if all were true, they would misdescribe and undervalue what is going on here. Talking about Chinese industrial growth, Americans are in the position of 19th-century Europeans who acted as if America's industrial rise could be explained simply by its vast natural resources and its exploitation of immigrant and slave labor, plus its very casual attitude toward copyright and patent laws protecting foreign, mainly British, books and inventions. (Today, Americans walk the streets of China and see their movies, music, software, and books sold everywhere in cheap pirate versions. A century and a half ago, Charles Dickens walked the streets of young America and fumed to see his novels in cheap pirate versions.) All those factors played their part, but they were not the full story of America's rise—nor do the corresponding aspects of modern China's behavior fully explain what China has achieved.

I can't pretend to know the complete story of China's industrial rise. But I can describe what I have seen, and the main way it has changed my mind.

Large-scale shifts in economic power have effects beyond the purely economic. Americans need not be hostile toward China's rise, but they should be wary about its eventual effects. The United States is the only nation with the scale and power to try to set the terms of its interaction with China rather than just succumb. So starting now, Americans need to consider the economic, environmental, political, and social goals they care about defending as Chinese influence grows.

America's political debates about the "China opportunity" and the "China threat" seem distant, theoretical, and imprecise from the perspective of the factories.

The consideration might best start from the point about which I've changed my mind: So far, America's economic relationship with China has been successful and beneficial—and beneficial for both sides. Free trade may not always be good for all participants, and in the long run trade with China may hold perils for the United States. But based on what I have seen in China, and contrary to what I expected before I came, so far it is working as advertised. Before thinking about what should be changed, Americans should appreciate what has gone right. A good place to begin that story is Shenzhen.

How it Works: The View from the Four Points

Each time I went to breakfast at the Sheraton Four Points in Shenzhen, I felt as if I were in a movie. I had a specific scene in mind: the moments aboard a U.S. aircraft carrier in a typical World War II movie when the flight crews gather in the wardroom to discuss the mission on which they're about to embark.

The morning crowd at the Four Points has that same sort of anticipatory buzz. Shenzhen, which is the part of China immediately north of Hong Kong and its "New Territories," did not exist as a city as recently as Ronald Reagan's time in the White House. It was a fishing town of 70,000 to 80,000 people, practically unnoticeable by Chinese standards. Today's other big coastal manufacturing centers, such as Xiamen, Guangzhou, Hangzhou, and Shanghai, were for centuries consequential Chinese cities. Not Shenzhen. Its population has grown at least a hundredfold in the past 25 years—rather than merely tripled or quadrupled, as in other cities. It is roughly as populous as New York, like many Chinese cities I keep coming across. Shenzhen has scores of skyscrapers and many, many hundreds of factories.

The story of Shenzhen's boom is in a sense the first chapter in modern China's industrialization. "During the founding period, Shenzhen people were bold and resolute in smashing the trammels of the old ideas," says the English version of the city's history, as recounted in Shenzhen's municipal museum in an odd, modern-Chinese combination of Maoist bombast and super-capitalist perspective. "With the market-oriented reforms as the breakthrough point, they shook off the yoke of the planned economy, and gradually built up new management systems."

What all this refers to is the establishment, in the late summer of 1980, of Shenzhen as a "special economic zone," where few limits or controls would apply and businesses from around the world would be invited to set up shop. Shenzhen was attractive as an experimental locale, not just because it was so close to Hong Kong, with its efficient harbor and airport, but also because it was so far from Beijing. If the experiment went wrong, the consequences could be more easily contained in this southern extremity of the country. Nearly every rule that might restrict business development was changed or removed in Shenzhen. Several free-trade processing zones were established, where materials and machinery coming in and exports going out would be exempt from the usual duties or taxes.

Modern Shenzhen has traits that Americans would associate with a booming Sun Belt city—transient, rough, unmannered, full of opportunity—and that characterized Manchester, Detroit, Chicago, Los Angeles at their times of fastest growth. Newspapers that cover Shenzhen are full of stories of drugs, crime, and vice in the most crowded tenement areas, where walls and sidewalks are covered with spray-painted phone numbers. Some are for prostitutes, but many are for vendors who can provide fake documents—health certificates, diplomas, residence credentials—for those seeking work.

The Sheraton Four Points is part of the process that keeps Shenzhen growing. It is one of the places foreigners go when they are ready to buy from China.

The foreigners in their 30s through 50s who come to Shanghai are often financiers, consultants, or lawyers. They tend to be lean, with good suits and haircuts. Those in Beijing are often diplomats, academics, or from foundations or NGOs. They look a little less polished. The scene in and around Shenzhen is different. It is an international group—Americans, Taiwanese, Europeans, Japanese—of a single class. Virtually all of them are designers, engineers, or buyers from foreign companies who have come to meet with Chinese factory owners. The Americans in the group tend to be beefier than the Shanghai-Beijing crowd, and more Midwestern-looking. Some wear company shirts or nylon jackets with their company's logo on the pocket.

When the Four Points restaurant opens at 6:30 in the morning, foreigners begin assembling for breakfast, the meal when people most crave their native cuisine. It is laid out for all comers on a huge buffet: for the Europeans, sliced meats and cheese, good breads, strong coffee, muesli and yogurt. For the Japanese, pickles, sushi, cold noodles, smoked eel over rice. For the Taiwanese and other Chinese, steamed buns, dim sum, hot congee cereal. For the Americans, the makings of a Denny's-style "Slam" breakfast: thick waffles, eggs, hash-brown potatoes, sausage and bacon and ham. My wife finally accused me of spending so much time in Shenzhen just for the breakfasts.

The room is noisy, as people discuss their plans for the day or meet the Chinese factory officials who will conduct them on their tours. The room empties dramatically by nine o'clock, as people go out to meet their drivers and vans, and the day's factory touring and contract signing begin. As best I could tell from chatting with fellow guests, in all my trips to the Four Points, I was the only person there not on a buying mission.

Nearly every morning one man, a 41-year-old Irish bachelor, sits at the same table at the Four Points. Very late in the evening, he is at that table for dinner too. The table is near the entrance, from which the rest of the room can be surveyed. On a typical night, the company he owns will have 10 to 15 rooms booked at the hotel, for foreign visitors coming to do business with him. Often a few will join him for dinner. When the waiters see this man coming, they bring the plain Western food—meat, potatoes—they know he's interested in. "Do you have the same thing every night?" I asked him when I saw the waiters' reflexive response to his arrival. "I didn't come here for the food," he replied.

This man has lived in an apartment at the Four Points for the last two years, and in other hotels around Shenzhen for the previous eight. He makes a point of telling people that he does not speak Chinese—most business visitors who try, he says, have to work so hard to cope with the language that they forget what they're negotiating about. But at useful points in meetings he drops in Chinese colloquialisms so that people must wonder whether in fact he has understood everything that has been said. (He tells me he hasn't.) His name is Liam Casey, and I have come to think of him as "Mr. China."

"Mr. China" is an established jokey honorific, like *People* magazine's "Sexiest Man Alive—2003." Since the days of Marco Polo, successive foreigners have competed informally for recognition as the person who *really* understands the country and can make things

happen here. The hilarious 2005 memoir *Mr. China,* by Tim Clissold, describes the heartbreak and frustration of a young British financier who thought he could figure out the secrets of success in China when it was first opening up to Western commerce.

Liam Casey has succeeded where Tim Clissold was frustrated, but he is careful not to sound overconfident. "Just when you think you know what's happening here, that's when you're in danger," he says. "You see some new product on the market, and you wonder where it was made—and it turns out to be a factory you drove by every day for five years and never knew what was going on inside! You can be here so long and know so little." But for my purposes he is Mr. China, because he is at the center of the overlapping flows of humanity bringing the world's work to China.

When not dining or sleeping at the Four Points, Casey runs a company he owns outright, with 800 employees (50 of them are from Ireland, America, or one of a dozen other nations; the rest are Chinese) and sales last year of about $125 million. He is of medium height and fit-seeming in a compact way, with thick dark hair and a long face that generally has an impish expression. He has a strong Irish accent and dresses informally. He walks, talks, and moves so fast that I was generally scrambling to keep up.

Casey grew up on a farm outside Cork, had no formal education after high school, and first worked as a salesman in garment shops in Cork and then Dublin. He got involved in buying garments from Europe, with a friend set up a Crate & Barrel–style store in Ireland, then decided to travel. At age 29 he arrived in Southern California and worked briefly for a trading company. He says he would be in America still—"Laguna, Newport Beach, ah, I luvved it"—but he could not get a green card or long-term work permit, and didn't want to try to stay there under the radar.

(I might as well say this in every article I write from overseas: The easier America makes it for talented foreigners to work and study there, the richer, more powerful, and more respected America will be. America's ability to absorb the world's talent is the crucial advantage no other culture can match—as long as America doesn't forfeit this advantage with visa rules written mainly out of fear.)

So in 1996, just after he turned 30, Casey went to Taipei for an electronics trade show. It was his first trip to Asia, and, he says, "I could see this is where the opportunity was." Within a year, he had set up operations in the Shenzhen area and started the company now known as PCH China Solutions. The initials stand for Pacific Coast Highway, in honor of his happy Southern California days.

What does this company do? The short answer is outsourcing, which in effect means matching foreign companies that want to sell products with Chinese suppliers who can make those products for them. Casey describes his mission as "helping innovators leverage the manufacturing supply chain here in China." To see how this works, consider the great human flows that now converge in southern China, which companies like Casey's help mediate.

One is the enormous flow of people, mainly young and unschooled, from China's farms and villages to Shenzhen and similar cities. Some arrive with a factory job already arranged by relatives or fixers; some come to the cities and then look for work. In the movie version of *Balzac and the Little Chinese Seamstress,* two teenaged men from the city befriend a young woman in the mountain village where they have been sent for rustication during the Cultural Revolution. One day the young woman unexpectedly leaves. She has gone to "try her luck in a big city," her grandfather tells them. "She said she wanted a new life." The new life is in Shenzhen.

Multiplied millions of times, and perhaps lacking the specific drama of the *Balzac* tale, this is the story of the factory towns. As in the novel, many of the migrants are young women. In the light-manufacturing operations I have seen in the Pearl River Delta and around Shanghai, the workforce is predominantly female. Signing on with a factory essentially means making your job your life. Workers who come to the big coastal factory centers either arrive, like the little seamstress, before they have a spouse or children, or leave their dependents at home with grandparents, aunts, or uncles. At the electronics and household-goods factories, including many I've seen, the pay is between 900 and 1,200 RMB per month, or about $115 to $155. In the villages the workers left, a farm family's cash earnings might be a few thousand RMB per year. Pay is generally lowest, and discipline toughest, at factories owned and managed by Taiwanese or mainland Chinese companies. The gigantic Foxconn (run by its founder, Terry Guo of Taiwan) is known for a militaristic organization and approach. Jobs with Western firms are the cushiest but are also rare, since the big European and American companies buy mainly from local subcontractors. Casey says that monthly pay in some factories he owns is several hundred RMB more than the local average. His goal is to retain workers for longer than the standard few-year stint, allowing them to develop greater skills and a sense of company spirit.

A factory work shift is typically 12 hours, usually with two breaks for meals (subsidized or free), six or seven days per week. Whenever the action lets up—if the assembly line is down for some reason, if a worker has spare time at a meal break—many people place their heads down on the table in front of them and appear to fall asleep instantly. Chinese law says that the standard workweek is 40 hours, so this means a lot of overtime, which is included in the pay rates above. Since their home village may be several days' travel by train and bus, workers from the hinterland usually go back only once a year. They all go at the same time—during the "Spring Festival," or Chinese New Year, when ports and factories effectively close for a week or so and the nation's transport system is choked. "The people here work hard," an American manager in a U.S.-owned plant told me. "They're young. They're quick. There's none of this 'I have to go pick up the kids' nonsense you get in the States."

At every electronics factory I've seen, each person on an assembly line has a bunch of documents posted by her workstation: her photo, name, and employee number, often the instructions she is to follow in both English and Chinese. Often too there's a visible sign of how well she's doing. For the production line as a whole there are hourly totals of target and actual production, plus allowable and actual defect levels. At several Taiwanese-owned factories I've seen, the indicator of individual performance is a childish outline drawing of a tree with leaves. After each day's shift one of the tree's leaves is filled in with a colored marker, either red or green. If the leaf is green, the worker has met her quota and caused no problems. If it's red, a defect has been traced back to her workstation. One red leaf per month is within tolerance; two is a problem.

As in all previous great waves of industrialization, many people end up staying in town; that's why Shenzhen has grown so large. But more than was the case during America's or England's booms in factory work, many rural people, especially the young women, work for two or three years and then go back to the country with their savings. In their village they open a shop, marry a local man and start a family, buy land, or use their earnings to help the relatives still at home.

Life in the factories is obviously hard, and in the heavy-industry works it is very dangerous. In the same week that 32 people were murdered at Virginia Tech, 32 Chinese workers at a steel plant in the north were scalded to death when a ladleful of molten steel was accidentally dumped on them. Even in Chinese papers, that story got less play than the U.S. shooting—and fatal coal-mine disasters are so common that they are reported as if they were traffic deaths. By comparison, the light industries that typify southern China are tedious but less overtly hazardous. As the foreman of a Taiwanese electronics factory put it to me when I asked him about rough working conditions, "Have you ever seen a Chinese farm?" An American industrial designer who works in China told me about a U.S. academic who toured his factory and was horrified to see young female workers chained to their stations. What she saw was actually the grounding wire that is mandatory in most electronics plants. Each person on the assembly line has a Velcro band around her wrist, which is connected to the worktable to avoid a static-electricity buildup that could destroy computer chips.

That so many people are in motion gives Shenzhen and surrounding areas a rootless, transient quality. The natural language of southern China is Cantonese, but in the factory cities the lingua franca is Mandarin, the language that people from different parts of China are likeliest to share. "I don't like it here," a Chinese manager originally from Beijing told me, three years into a work assignment to Shenzhen. "There are no roots or culture." "For the first few weeks I was here, I thought it was soulless," Liam Casey says of the town that has been his home for 10 years. "But like any fast-moving place, the activity is the character. It's like New York. You arrive at the airport and go downtown, and when you get out of that cab, no one knows where you came from. You could have been there one hour, you could have been there 10 years—no one can tell. It's similar here, which makes it exciting." Casey told me that, to him, Shanghai felt slow "and made for tourists." Indeed, I am regularly surprised to find that people stroll rather than stride along the sidewalks of Shanghai: It's a busy city with slow pedestrians. Or maybe Casey's outlook is contagious.

Another great flow into Shenzhen and similar cities is of entrepreneurs who have come and set up factories. The point of the Shenzhen liberalizations was less to foster any one industry than to make it easy for businesses in general to get a start.

Many entrepreneurs attracted by the offer came from Taiwan, whose economy is characterized by small, mainly family-owned firms like those that now abound in southern China. Overall, mainland China's development model is closer to Taiwan's than to Japan's or Korea's. In all these countries and throughout East Asia, governments use many tools to maximize industrial output: tax policy, trading rules, currency values, and so on. But Japanese and Korean policy has tended to emphasize the welfare of large, national-champion firms—Mitsubishi and Toyota, Lucky Gold Star and Samsung—whereas Taiwan's exporters have been thousands of small firms, a few of which grew large, China is, of course, vaster than the other countries combined, but its export-oriented companies are small. One reason for the atomization is pervasive mistrust and corruption, plus a shaky rule of law. Even Foxconn, China's largest exporter, was only No. 206 on last year's Fortune Global 500 list of the biggest companies in the world. When foreigners have trouble entering the Japanese or Korean markets, it is often because they run up against barriers protecting big, well-known local interests. The problem in China is typically the opposite: Foreigners don't know where to start or whom to deal with in the chaos of small, indistinguishable firms.

For me, the fragmented nature of the Chinese system is symbolized by yet another of the stunning sights in Shenzhen: the SEG Electronics Market, a seven-story downtown structure whose every inch is crammed with the sales booths of hundreds of mom-and-pop electronics dealers. "Chips that I couldn't dream of buying in the U.S., reels of rare ceramic capacitors that I only dream about at night!" Andrew "Bunnie" Huang, a Chinese-American electronics Ph.D. from MIT, wrote in his blog after a visit. "My senses tingle, my head spins. I can't suppress a smirk of anticipation as I walk around the next corner, to see shops stacked floor to ceiling with probably a hundred million resistors and capacitors." As he noted, "within an hour's drive north" were hundreds of factories that could "take any electronics ideas and pump them out by the literal boatload." The market is part permanent trade show, part supply stop for people who suddenly need some capacitors or connectors for a prototype or last-minute project, part swap meet where traders unload surplus components.

One last flow coining into Shenzhen, which makes the other flows possible, is represented by the people at the Four Points: buyers from high-wage countries who have decided that they want to take advantage of, rather than compete with, low-cost Chinese manufacturers. This is where our Mr. China, and others like him, fit in.

This is also where a veil falls. In decades of reporting on military matters, I have rarely encountered people as concerned about keeping secrets as the buyers and suppliers who meet in Shenzhen and similar cities. What information are they committed to protect? Names, places, and product numbers that would reveal which Western companies obtain which exact products from which Chinese suppliers. There are high- and low-road reasons for their concern.

The low-road reason is the "Nike problem." This is the buyers' wish to minimize their brands' association with outsourcing in general and Asian sweatshops in particular, named for Nike's PR problems because of its factories in Indonesia. By Chinese standards, the most successful exporting factories are tough rather than abusive, but those are not the standards Western customers might apply.

The high-road reason involves the crucial operational importance of the "supply chain." It is not easy to find the right factory, work out the right manufacturing system, ensure the right supply of parts and raw material, impose the right quality standards, and develop the right relationship of trust and reliability. Companies that have solved these problems don't want to tell their competitors how they did so. "Supply chain is intellectual property," is the way Liam Casey put it. Asking a Western company to specify its Chinese suppliers is like asking a reporter to hand over a list of his best sources.

Because keeping the supply chain confidential is so important to buyers, they try to impose confidentiality on their suppliers. When an outside company's reputation for design and quality is strong—Sony, Braun, Apple—many Chinese contractors like to drop hints that they are part of its supply chain. But the ones who really are part of it must be more discreet if they want to retain the buying company's trust (and business).

So I will withhold details, but ask you to take this leap: If you think of major U.S. or European brand names in the following businesses, odds are their products come from factories like those I'm about to describe. The businesses are: computers, including desktops, laptops, and servers; telecom equipment, from routers to mobile phones; audio equipment, including anything MP3-related, home stereo systems, most portable devices, and headsets; video equipment of all sorts, from cameras and camcorders to replay devices; personal-care items and high-end specialty-catalog goods; medical devices; sporting goods and exercise equipment; any kind of electronic goods or accessories; and, for that matter, just about anything else you can think of. Some of the examples I'll give come from sites in Shenzhen, but others are from facilities near Shanghai, Hangzhou, Guangzhou, Xiamen, and elsewhere.

"The people here work hard," an American manager in a U.S.-owned plant says. "They're young. They're quick. There's none of this 'I have to go pick up the kids' nonsense you get in the States."

Why does a foreign company come to our Mr. China? I asked Casey what he would tell me if I were in, say, some branch of the steel industry in Pittsburgh and was looking to cut costs. "Not interested," he said. "The product's too heavy, and you've probably already automated the process, so one person is pushing a button. It would cost you almost as much to have someone push the button in China."

But what is of intense interest to him, he said, is a company that has built up a brand name and relationships with retailers, and knows what it wants to promote and sell next—and needs to save time and money in manufacturing a product that requires a fair amount of assembly. "That is where we can help, because you will come here and see factories that are better than the ones you've been working with in America or Germany."

Here are a few examples, all based on real-world cases: You have announced a major new product, which has gotten great buzz in the press. But close to release time, you discover a design problem that must be fixed—and no U.S. factory can adjust its production process in time.

The Chinese factories can respond more quickly, and not simply because of 12-hour workdays. "Anyplace else, you'd have to import different raw materials and components," Casey told me. "Here, you've got nine different suppliers within a mile, and they can bring a sample over that afternoon. People think China is cheap, but really, it's *fast*." Moreover, the Chinese factories use more human labor, and fewer expensive robots or assembly machines, than their counterparts in rich countries. "People are the most adaptable machines," an American industrial designer who works in China told me. "Machines need to be reprogrammed. You can have people doing something entirely different next week."

Or: You are an American inventor with a product you think has "green" potential for household energy savings. But you need to get it to market fast, because you think big companies may be trying the same thing, and you need to meet a target retail price of $100. "No place but China to do this," Mr. China said, as he showed me the finished product.

Or: You are a very famous American company, and you worry that you've tied up too much capital keeping inventory for retail stores at several supply depots in America. With Mr. China's help, you start emphasizing direct retail sales on your Web site—and do all the shipping and fulfillment from one supply depot, run by young Chinese women in Shenzhen, who can ship directly to specific retail stores.

Over the course of repeated visits to Shenzhen—the breakfasts!—and visits to other manufacturing regions, I heard about many similar cases and saw some of the tools that have made it possible for Western countries to view China as their manufacturing heartland.

Some involve computerized knowledge, Casey's PCH has a Google Earth-like system that incorporates what he has learned in 10 years of dealing with Chinese subcontractors. You name a product you want to make—say, a new case or headset for a mobile phone. Casey clicks on the map and shows the companies that can produce the necessary components—and exactly how far they are from each other in travel time. This is hard-won knowledge in an area where city maps are out of date as soon as they are published and addresses are approximate. (Casey's are keyed in with GPS coordinates, discreetly read from his GPS-equipped mobile phone when he visits each factory.) If a factory looks promising, you click again and get interior and exterior photos, a rundown on the management, in some cases videos of the assembly line in action, plus spec sheets and engineering drawings for orders they have already filled. Similar programs allow Casey and his clients to see which ship, plane, or truck their products are on anywhere in the world, and the amount of stock on hand in any warehouse or depot. (How do they know? Each finished piece and almost every component has an individual bar code that is scanned practically every time it is touched.)

The factories whose workflow Casey monitors vary tremendously, though not in their looks. I've come to think that there is only one set of blueprints for factories in China: a big, boxy, warehouse-looking structure, usually made of concrete and usually five stories; white or gray outside; relatively large windows, which is how you can tell it from the workers' dormitories; high ceilings, to accommodate machines. But inside, some are highly automated while some are amazingly reliant on hand labor. I'm not even speaking of the bad, dangerous, and out-of-date factories frequently found in the north of China, where leftover Maoist-era heavy-industry hulks abound. Even some newly built facilities leave to human hands work that has been done in the West for many decades by machines. Imagine opening a consumer product—a mobile phone, an electric toothbrush, a wireless router—and finding a part that was snapped on or glued into place. It was probably put there by a young Chinese woman who did the same thing many times per minute throughout her 12-hour workday.

I could describe many installations, but I was fascinated by two. The first represents one extreme in automation. It is owned and operated by Inventec, one of five companies based in Taiwan that together produce the vast majority of laptop and notebook computers sold under any brand anywhere in the world. Everyone in America has heard of Dell, Sony, Compaq, HP, Lenovo-IBM Think-Pad, Apple, NEC, Gateway, Toshiba. Almost no one has heard of Quanta, Compal, Inventec, Wistron, Asustek. Yet nearly 90 percent of laptops and notebooks sold under the famous brand names are actually made by one of these five companies in their factories in mainland China. I have seen a factory with three "competing" brand names coming off the same line.

The Inventec installation I saw was in an export-processing zone in Shanghai specially created for the company, in which imported components for manufacturing and finished products for export were free of the usual duties or taxes. It turns out more than 30,000 notebook computers per day, under one of the brand names listed above. Each day, an Inventec plant on the same campus produces hundreds of large, famous-brand-name server computers to run Internet traffic.

This is today's rough counterpart to the Ford Motor Company's old River Rouge works. In the heyday of The Rouge, rubber, steel, and other raw materials would come into the plant, and finished autos would come out. Here, naked green circuit boards, capacitors, chip sets, and other components come in each day, and notebook computers come out. Some advanced components arrive already assembled: disk drives from Taiwan or Singapore, LCD screens from Korea or Japan, keyboards and power supplies from other plants in China.

The overall process looks the way you would expect a high-tech assembly line to. Conveyers and robots take the evolving computer from station to station; each unit arrives in front of a worker a split second after she has finished with the previous one. Before a component goes into a machine, its bar code is scanned to be sure it is the right part; after it is added, the machine is "check-weighed" to see that its new weight is correct. Hundreds of tiny transistors, chips, and other electronic parts are attached to each circuit board by "pick and place" robots, whose multiple arms move almost too fast to follow. The welds on the board are scanned with lasers for defects. Any with problems are set aside for women specialists, looking through huge magnifying glasses, to reweld. Why did this factory invest so much in robots and machine tools? I asked a supervisor from Taiwan. "People can't do it precisely enough," was his answer. These factories automate not what's too expensive but what's too delicate for human beings to perform.

Many of the notebook computers have been ordered online, and as they near completion each is "flavored" for its destination. The day I visited, one was going to Tokyo, with a Japanese keyboard installed and Japanese logos snapped into the right places on the case; the next one was headed for the United States. After display screens are installed, each computer rides on a kind of racetrack along the ceiling of the factory, where it runs for several hours to make sure that all components work. Then the conveyers carry it to the final flavoring step—the "burn in" of the operating system, which on my visit was Windows Vista, in many languages. One engineer pointed out that because Vista requires up to 10 times as much disk space as Windows XP, the assembly line had to be altered to allow a much longer, slower passage through the burn-in station.

The other facility that intrigued me, one of Liam Casey's in Shenzhen, handled online orders for a different well-known American company. I was there around dawn, which was crunch time. Because of the 12-hour time difference from the U.S. East Coast, orders Americans place in the late afternoon arrive in China in the dead of night. As I watched, a customer in Palatine, Illinois, perhaps shopping from his office, clicked on the American company's Web site to order two $25 accessories. A few seconds later, the order appeared on the screen 7,800 miles away in Shenzhen. It automatically generated a packing and address slip and several barcode labels. One young woman put the address label on a brown cardboard shipping box and the packing slip inside. The box moved down a conveyer belt to another woman working a "pick to light" system: She stood in front of a kind of cupboard with a separate open-fronted bin for each item customers might order from the Web site; a light turned on over each bin holding a part specified in the latest order. She picked the item out of that bin, ran it past a scanner that checked its number (and signaled the light to go off), and put it in the box. More check-weighing and rescanning followed, and when the box was sealed, young men added it to a shipping pallet.

By the time the night shift was ready to leave—8 A.M. China time, 7 P.M. in Palatine, 8 P.M. on the U.S. East Coast—the volume of orders from America was tapering off. More important, the FedEx pickup time was drawing near. At 9 A.M. couriers would arrive and rush the pallets to the Hong Kong airport. The FedEx flight to Anchorage would leave by 6 P.M., and when it got there, the goods on this company's pallets would be combined with other Chinese exports and re-sorted for destinations in America. Forty-eight hours after the man in Palatine clicked "Buy it now!" on his computer, the item showed up at his door. Its return address was a company warehouse in the United States; a small MADE IN CHINA label was on the bottom of the box.

At 8 A.M. in Shenzhen, the young women on the night shift got up from the assembly line, took off the hats and hairnets they had been wearing, and shook out their dark hair. They passed through the metal detector at the door to their workroom (they pass through it going in and coming out) and walked downstairs to the racks where they had left their bikes. They wore red company jackets, as part of their working uniform—and, as an informal uniform, virtually every one wore tight, low-rise blue jeans with embroidery or sequins on the seams. Most of them rode their bikes back to the dormitory; others walked, or walked their bikes, chatting with each other. That evening they would be back at work. Meanwhile, flocks of red-topped, blue-bottomed young women on the day shift filled the road, riding their bikes in.

Good For Us—For Now

What should we make of this? The evidence suggests what I hadn't expected: that the interaction has been good for most participants—so far. Has the factory boom been good for China? Of course it has. Yes, it creates environmental pressures that, if not controlled, could pollute China and the world out of existence. The national government's current Five Year Plan—the 11th, running through 2010—has as its central theme China's development as a "harmonious society," or *hexie shehui,* a phrase heard about as often from Chinas leadership as "global war on terror" has been heard from America's. In China, the phrase is code for attempting to deal with income inequalities, especially the hardships of farmers and millions of migrant laborers. But it is also code for at least talking about protecting the environment.

And, yes, throughout China's boom many people have been mistreated, oppressed, sometimes worked to death in factories. Even those not abused may be lonely and lost, with damaging effects on the country's social fabric. But this was also the story of Britain and America when they built their great industries, their great turbulent industrial cities, and ultimately their great industrial middle classes. For China, it is far from the worst social disruption the country has endured in the last 50 years. At least this upheaval, unlike the disastrous Great Leap Forward of the 1950s and Cultural Revolution of the '60s and early '70s, has some benefits for individuals and the nation.

Some Westerners may feel that even today's "normal" Chinese working conditions amount to slave labor—$100 a month, no life outside the factory, work shifts so long there's barely time to do more than try to sleep in a jam-packed dormitory. Here is an uncomfortable truth I'm waiting for some Chinese official to point out: The woman from the hinterland working in Shenzhen is arguably better off economically than an American in Chicago living on minimum wage. She can save most of what she makes and feel she is on the way up; the American can't and doesn't. Over the next two years, the minimum wage in the United States is expected to rise to $7.25 an hour. Assuming a 40-hour week, that's just under $1,200 per month, or about 10 times the Chinese factory wage. But that's before payroll deductions and the cost of food and housing, which are free or subsidized in China's factory towns.

Chinese spokesmen do make a different point about their economy, and they rattle it off so frequently that Western audiences are tempted to dismiss it. They say, "Whatever else we have done, we have brought hundreds of millions of people out of poverty." That is true, it is important, and the manufacturing export boom has been a significant part of how China has done it. This economic success obviously does not justify everything the regime has done, especially its crushing of any challenge to one-party rule. But the magnitude of the achievement can't be ignored. For all of the billions of dollars given in foreign aid and supervised by the World Bank, the greatest good for the greatest number of the world's previously impoverished people in at least the last half century has been achieved in China, thanks largely to the outsourcing boom.

Has the move to China been good for American companies? The answer would seemingly have to be yes—otherwise, why would they go there? It is conceivable that bad partnerships, stolen intellectual property, dilution of brand name, logistics nightmares, or other difficulties have given many companies a sour view of outsourcing; I have heard examples in each category from foreign executives. But the more interesting theme I have heard from them, which explains why they are willing to surmount the inconveniences, involves something called the "smiley curve."

The curve is named for the U-shaped are of the 1970s-era smiley-face icon, and it runs from the beginning to the end of a product's creation and sale. At the beginning is the company's brand: HP, Siemens, Dell, Nokia, Apple. Next comes the idea for the product: an iPod, a new computer, a camera phone. After that is high-level industrial design—the conceiving of how the product will look and work. Then the detailed engineering design for how it will be made. Then the necessary components. Then the actual manufacture and assembly. Then the shipping and distribution. Then retail sales. And, finally, service contracts and sales of parts and accessories.

The significance is that China's activity is in the middle stages—manufacturing, plus some component supply and engineering design—but America's is at the two ends, and those are where the money is. The smiley curve, which shows the profitability or value added at each stage, starts high for branding and product concept, swoops down for manufacturing, and rises again in the retail and servicing stages. The simple way to put this—that the real money is in brand name, plus retail—may sound obvious, but its implications are illuminating.

At each factory I visited, I asked managers to estimate how much of a product's sales price ended up in whose hands. The strength of the brand name was the most important variable. If a product is unusual enough and its brand name attractive enough, it could command so high a price that the retailer might keep half the revenue. (Think: an Armani suit, a Starbucks latte.) Most electronics products are now subject to much fiercer price competition, since it is so easy for shoppers to find bargains on the Internet. Therefore the generic Windows-style laptops I saw in one modern factory might go for around $1,000 in the United States, with the retailer keeping less than $50.

Where does the rest of the money go? The manager of that factory guessed that Intel and Microsoft together would collect about $300, and that the makers of the display screen, the disk-storage devices, and other electronic components might get $150 or so apiece. The keyboard makers would get $15 or $20; FedEx or UPS would get slightly less. When all other costs were accounted for, perhaps $30 to $40—3 to 4 percent of the total—would stay in China with the factory owners and the young women on the assembly lines.

Other examples: A carrying case for an audio device from a big-name Western company retails for just under $30. That company pays the Chinese supplier $6 per case, of which about half goes for materials. The other $24 stays with the big-name company. An earphone-like accessory for another U.S.-brand audio device also retails for about $30. Of this, I was told, $3 stayed in China. I saw a set of high-end Ethernet connecting cables. The cables are sold, with identical specifications but in three different kinds of packaging, in three forms in the United States: as a specially product, as a house brand in a nationwide office-supply store, and with no brand over eBay. The retail prices are $29.95 for the specialty brand, $19.95 in the chain store, and $15.95 on eBay. The Shenzhen-area company that makes them gets $2 apiece.

"Here, you've got nine different suppliers within a mile, and they can bring a sample over that afternoon," Casey told me. "People think China is cheap, but really, it's *fast*."

In case the point isn't clear: Chinese workers making $1,000 a year have been helping American designers, marketers, engineers, and retailers making $1,000 a week (and up) earn even more. Plus, they have helped shareholders of U.S.-based companies.

All this is apart from a phenomenon that will be the subject of a future article: China's conversion of its trade surpluses into a vast hoard of dollar-denominated reserves. Everyone understands that in the short run China's handling of its reserves has been a convenience to the United States. By placing more than $1 trillion in U.S. stock and bond markets, it has propped up the U.S. economy. Asset prices are higher than they would otherwise be; interest rates are lower, whether for American families taking out mortgages or for American taxpayers financing the ever-mounting federal debt. The dollar has also fallen less than it otherwise would have—which in the short run helps American consumers keep buying Chinese goods.

Everyone also understands that in the long run China must change this policy. Its own people need too many things—schools, hospitals, railroads—for it to keep sending its profits to America. It won't forever sink its savings into a currency, the dollar, virtually

guaranteed to keep falling against the RMB. This year the central government created a commission to consider the right long-term use for Chinas reserves. No one expects the recommendation to be: Keep buying dollars. How and when the change will occur, what it will be, and what consequences it will have, is what everyone would like to know.

One other aspect of Chinas development to date has helped American companies in their dealings with it. This is the fact that China, so far, has been different in crucial ways from America's previous great Asian challenger; Japan. Americans have come to view the Japanese economy as a kind of joke, mainly because the Tokyo Stock Exchange has been in a slump for nearly 20 years. Nonetheless, Japan remains the worlds second-largest economy. Toyota has overtaken General Motors to become the largest automaker; Japan's exporters have continually increased their sales of electronics and other high-value goods; and the long-standing logic of the Japanese system, in which consumers and investors suffer so that producers may thrive, remains intact.

Japan was already a rich and modern country, as China still is not, by the time trade friction intensified, in the 1980s. More important, its leading companies were often competing head-to-head with established high-value, high-tech companies in the United States: Fujitsu against IBM, Toshiba against Intel, Fuji against Kodak, Sony and Matsushita against Motorola, and on down the list. Gains for Japanese companies often meant direct losses for companies in America—whether those companies were seen as stodgy and noninnovative, like the Detroit firms, or technologically agile and advanced, like the semiconductor makers.

For the moment, Chinas situation is different. Its companies are numerous but small. Lenovo and Qingdao are its two globally recognized brand names. But Lenovo is known mainly because it bought the ThinkPad brand from IBM, and a quarter of Qingdao Beer is owned by Anheuser-Busch. Chinese exporters have done best when working for, rather than against, Western companies, as Foxconn (like numerous smaller firms) has in working with Apple. While the Chinese government obviously wants to strengthen the country's brands—for instance, with an aircraft company it hopes will compete with Boeing and Airbus—its "industrial planning" has mainly taken the form not of specific targeting but of general business promotion, as with the incentives that brought companies to Shenzhen.

China's economy, technically still socialist, has also been strangely more open than Japans. Through its first four decades of growth after World War II, Japan was essentially closed to foreign ownership and investment. (Texas Instruments and IBM were two highly publicized exceptions to the rule.) China's industrial boom, by contrast, is occurring during the age of the World Trade Organization, to which it was admitted in 2001. Under WTO rules, China is obliged to open itself to foreign investment and ownership at a much earlier stage of its development than Japan did. Its export boom has been led by foreign firms. China is rife with intellectual piracy, hidden trade barriers, and other impediments. But overall it is harder for foreign economies or foreign companies to claim damage from China's trade policies than from Japans.

When I was living in Japan through its boom of the late '80s, I argued in this magazine that its behavior illustrated some great historic truths that economic models cannot easily include. Sometimes societies pursue goals other than the one economists consider rational: the greatest possible growth of consumer well-being. This has been true of America mainly during wartime, but also when it has pursued martial-toned projects thought to be in the nation's interest: building interstate highways, sending men into space, perhaps someday developing alternative energy supplies. In a more consistent way, over decades, this has been true of Japan.

Chinese workers making, $1,000 a year have been helping American designers, marketers, engineers, and retailers making $1,000 a week (and up) earn even more.

For anyone who has taken Ec 101, the natural response would be: That's their problem! They're making high-quality products for everyone else, so what's not to like? But in the past decade, a growing number of respectable economists have argued that the situation is not that simple. If one nation deliberately promotes high-tech and high-value industries, it can end up with more of those industries, and more of the high-wage jobs that go with them, than it would have otherwise. This is not economically "rational"—European countries have paid heavily for each job they have created through Airbus. But Boeing sells fewer airplanes and employs fewer engineers than it presumably would without competition from Airbus. The United States does not have to emulate Europe's approach, or Japan's. But it needs to be aware of them, and of the possible consequences. (With different emphases, Paul Samuelson of MIT, Alan Blinder and William Baumol of Princeton, and Ralph Gomory, head of the Alfred P. Sloan Foundation, have advanced this argument.)

China's behavior, and that of its companies, is easier to match with standard economic theories than Japan's. So far, deals like those struck at the Sheraton Four Points have been mainly good for all parties. Chinese families have new opportunities in life. American customers have wider choices. American investors have better returns. But, of course, there are complications.

First is the social effect visible around the world, which in homage to China's Communist past we can call "intensifying the contradictions." Global trade involves one great contradiction: The lower the barriers to the flow of money, products, and ideas, the less it matters where people live. But because most people cannot move from one country to another, it will always matter where people live. In a world of frictionless, completely globalized trade, people on average would all be richer—but every society would include a wider range of class, comfort, and well-being than it now does. Those with the most marketable global talents would be richer, because they could sell to the largest possible market. Everyone else would be poorer, because of competition from a billions-strong labor pool. With no trade barriers, there would be no reason why the average person in, say, Holland would be better off than the average one in India. Each society would contain a cross section of the world's whole income distribution—yet its people would have to live within the same national borders.

We're nowhere near that point. But the increasing integration of the American and Chinese economies pushes both countries toward it. This is more or less all good for China, but not all good for America. It means economic benefits mainly for those who have already succeeded, a harder path up for those who are already at a disadvantage, and further strain on the already weakened sense of fellow feeling and shared opportunity that allows a society as diverse and unequal as America's to cohere.

A further problem is that China's business and governmental leaders are all too aware of how the smiley curve affects them. Yes, it's better to have jobs that pay $1,000 a year than none at all. But it would be better still to have jobs that pay many times as much and are at more desirable positions along the curve. If the United States were in China's position, it would be doing everything possible to bring more high-value work within its borders—and that, of course, is what China is trying to do. Everywhere you turn you see an illustration.

Just a few: In the far north of China, Intel has just agreed to build a major chip-fabrication plant, with high-end engineering and design jobs, not just seats on the assembly line. In Beijing, both Microsoft and Google have opened genuine research centers, not just offices to serve the local market. Down in Shenzhen, Liam Casey's company is creating industrial-design centers, where products will be conceived, not just snapped together. What was recently a factory zone in Shanghai is being gentrified; local authorities are pushing factories to relocate 10 miles away, so their buildings can be turned into white-collar engineering and design centers.

At the moment, most jobs I've seen the young women in the factories perform have not been "taken" from America, because in America these assembly-type tasks would be done by machines. But the Chinese goal is, of course, to build toward something more lucrative.

Many people I have spoken with say that the climb will be slow for Chinese industries, because they have so far to go in bringing their design, management, and branding efforts up to world standards. "Think about it—global companies are full of CEOs and executives from India, but very few Chinese," Dominic Barton, the chairman of McKinsey's Asia Pacific practice, told me. The main reason, he said, is Chinas limited pool of executives with adequate foreign-language skills and experience working abroad. Andy Switky, the managing director-Asia Pacific for the famed California design firm IDEO, described a frequent Chinese outlook toward quality control as "happy with crappy." This makes it hard for them to move beyond the local, low-value market. "Even now in China, most people don't have an iPod or a notebook computer," the manager of a Taiwanese-owned audio-device factory told me. "So it's harder for them to think up improvements, or even tell a good one from a bad one." These and other factors may slow China's progress. But that's a feeble basis for American hopes.

The measures Americans most often discuss for dealing with China are not much better as a long-term basis for hope. Yes, the RMB is now undervalued against the dollar. Yes, that makes Chinese exports cheaper than they would otherwise be. And yes, the RMB's value should rise—and it will. But at no conceivable level would it bring those Shenzhen jobs back to Ohio. At best it would make U.S. exports, from locomotives and high-tech medical equipment to wine and software, more attractive. Such commercial victories are important, but they are unlikely to be advanced by threats of retaliatory tariffs if China does not speed the RMB's climb. Also, the faster the dollar falls against the RMB, the faster Chinese authorities might move their assets out of dollars to stronger currencies.

This year the U.S. government imposed special tariffs, called countervailing duties, on imports of glossy paper from China. This is the kind of paper used to print magazines and catalogs, and Chinese exports of it to the United States rose tenfold from 2004 to 2006. The U.S. government said the duties were necessary to offset the export subsidies Chinese manufacturers receive via low-cost loans, tax breaks, and other benefits. Under WTO rules, export subsidies of all sorts are prohibited; U.S. officials, academics, and trade groups have prepared lists of de facto subsidies that cut the price of Chinese goods to U.S. consumers by 25 percent, 40 percent, and even more. (The Chinese—like the Europeans, Australians, and others—are quick to retort that the United States subsidizes many products too, especially exports from large-scale farms.)

This is obviously significant. But think again of those Ethernet connectors that retail for $29.95 and cost only $2 to make. Removing all imaginable subsidies might push the manufacturing cost to $3. Suppose it went to $4. That would have a big effect on decisions made by corporations that outsource to China—Can they raise the retail price? Must they just accept a lower margin? Should they build the next factory in Vietnam?—but it would not make anyone bring production back to the United States.

Government policy and favoritism may play a big role in China's huge road-building and land-development policies, but they seem to be secondary factors in the outsourcing boom. For instance, when I asked Mr. China which officials I should try to interview in the local Shenzhen government to understand how they worked with companies, he said he didn't know. He'd never met any.

American complaints about the RMB, about subsidies, and about other Chinese practices have this in common: They assume that the solution to long-term tensions in the trading relationship lies in changes on China's side. I think that assumption is naive. If the United States is unhappy with the effects of its interaction with China, that's America's problem, not China's. To imagine that the United States can stop China from pursuing its own economic ambitions through nagging, threats, or enticement is to fool ourselves. If a country does not like the terms of its business dealings

with the world, it needs to change its own policies, not expect the world to change. China has done just that, to its own benefit—and, up until now, to America's.

Are we uncomfortable with the America that is being shaped by global economic forces? The inequality? The sense of entitlement for some? Of stifled opportunity for others? The widespread tear that today's trends—borrowing, consuming, looking inward, using up infrastructure—will make it hard to stay ahead tomorrow, particularly in regard to China? If so, those trends themselves, and the American choices behind them, are what Americans can address. They're not China's problem, and they're not the fault of anyone in Shenzhen.

Critical Thinking

1. What is outsourcing? Use Fallows's description of the Sheraton Four Points hotel in Shenzhen to explain how the government of China seeks to attract manufacturing orders from overseas firms.

2. Why do numerous firms from the United States and other countries eventually decide to outsource production to China, even despite their initial reluctance to do so?

3. What are work conditions like in China's factories? How can the growth of these factories be criticized? How can the growth of these factories be defended?

4. What does Fallows mean when he refers to the "liberalization" of China's economic policy, as evident in Shenzhen?

JAMES FALLOWS is an *Atlantic* national correspondent.

From *The Atlantic*, July/August 2007, pp. 48–72. Copyright © 2007 by Atlantic Monthly Group. Reprinted by permission. Distributed by Tribune Media Services.

The Rise of the Creative Class

Why cities without gays and rock bands are losing the economic development race.

RICHARD FLORIDA

A s I walked across the campus of Pittsburgh's Carnegie Mellon University one delightful spring day, I came upon a table filled with young people chatting and enjoying the spectacular weather. Several had identical blue t-shirts with "Trilogy@CMU" written across them—Trilogy being an Austin, Texas-based software company with a reputation for recruiting our top students. I walked over to the table. "Are you guys here to recruit?" I asked. "No, absolutely not," they replied adamantly. "We're not recruiters. We're just hangin' out, playing a little Frisbee with our friends." How interesting, I thought. They've come to campus on a workday, all the way from Austin, just to hang out with some new friends.

I noticed one member of the group sitting slouched over on the grass, dressed in a tank top. This young man had spiked multi-colored hair, full-body tattoos, and multiple piercings in his ears. An obvious slacker, I thought, probably in a band. "So what is your story?" I asked. "Hey man, I just signed on with these guys." In fact, as I would later learn, he was a gifted student who had inked the highest-paying deal of any graduating student in the history of his department, right at that table on the grass, with the recruiters who do not "recruit."

What a change from my own college days, just a little more than 20 years ago, when students would put on their dressiest clothes and carefully hide any counterculture tendencies to prove that they could fit in with the company. Today, apparently, it's the company trying to fit in with the students. In fact, Trilogy had wined and dined him over margarita parties in Pittsburgh and flown him to Austin for private parties in hip nightspots and aboard company boats. When I called the people who had recruited him to ask why, they answered, "That's easy. We wanted him because he's a rock star."

While I was interested in the change in corporate recruiting strategy, something even bigger struck me. Here

was another example of a talented young person leaving Pittsburgh. Clearly, my adopted hometown has a huge number of assets. Carnegie Mellon is one of the world's leading centers for research in information technology. The University of Pittsburgh, right down the street from our campus, has a world-class medical center. Pittsburgh attracts hundreds of millions of dollars per year in university research funding and is the sixth-largest center for college and university students on a per capita basis in the country. Moreover, this is hardly a cultural backwater. The city is home to three major sports franchises, renowned museums and cultural venues, a spectacular network of urban parks, fantastic industrial-age architecture, and great urban neighborhoods with an abundance of charming yet affordable housing. It is a friendly city, defined by strong communities and a strong sense of pride. In the 1986 Rand McNally survey, Pittsburgh was ranked "America's Most Livable City," and has continued to score high on such lists ever since.

Yet Pittsburgh's economy continues to putter along in a middling flat-line pattern. Both the core city and the surrounding metropolitan area lost population in the 2000 census. And those bright young university people keep leaving. Most of Carnegie Mellon's prominent alumni of recent years—like Vinod Khosla, perhaps the best known of Silicon Valley's venture capitalists, and Rick Rashid, head of research and development at Microsoft—went elsewhere to make their marks. Pitt's vaunted medical center, where Jonas Salk created his polio vaccine and the world's premier organ-transplant program was started, has inspired only a handful of entrepreneurs to build biotech companies in Pittsburgh.

Over the years, I have seen the community try just about everything possible to remake itself so as to attract and retain talented young people, and I was personally involved in many of these efforts. Pittsburgh has launched a multitude

The Creativity Index

The key to economic growth lies not just in the ability to attract the creative class, but to translate that underlying advantage into creative economic outcomes in the form of new ideas, new high-tech businesses and regional growth. To better gauge these capabilities, I developed a new measure called the Creativity Index (column 1). The Creativity Index is a mix of four equally weighted factors: the creative class share of the workforce (column 2 shows the percentage; column 3 ranks cities accordingly); high-tech industry, using the Milken Institute's widely accepted Tech Pole Index, which I refer to as the High-Tech Index (column 4); innovation, measured as patents per capita (column 5); and diversity, measured by the Gay Index, a reasonable proxy for an area's openness to different kinds of people and ideas (column 6). This composite indicator is a better measure of a region's underlying creative capabilities than the simple measure of the creative class, because it reflects the joint effects of its concentration and of innovative economic outcomes. The Creativity Index is thus my baseline indicator of a region's overall standing in the creative economy and I offer it as a barometer of a region's longer run economic potential. The following tables present my creativity index ranking for the top 10 and bottom 10 metropolitan areas, grouped into three size categories (large, medium-sized and small cities/regions).

—Richard Florida

of programs to diversify the region's economy away from heavy industry into high technology. It has rebuilt its downtown virtually from scratch, invested in a new airport, and developed a massive new sports complex for the Pirates and the Steelers. But nothing, it seemed, could stem the tide of people and new companies leaving the region.

I asked the young man with the spiked hair why he was going to a smaller city in the middle of Texas, a place with a small airport and no professional sports teams, without a major symphony, ballet, opera, or art museum comparable to Pittsburgh's. The company is excellent, he told me. There are also terrific people and the work is challenging. But the clincher, he said, is that, "It's in Austin!" There are lots of young people, he went on to explain, and a tremendous amount to do: a thriving music scene, ethnic and cultural diversity, fabulous outdoor recreation, and great nightlife. Though he had several good job offers from Pittsburgh high-tech firms and knew the city well, he said he felt the city lacked the lifestyle options, cultural diversity, and tolerant attitude that would make it attractive to him. As he summed it up: "How would I fit in here?"

This young man and his lifestyle proclivities represent a profound new force in the economy and life of America. He is a member of what I call the creative class: a fast-growing, highly educated, and well-paid segment of the workforce on whose efforts corporate profits and economic growth increasingly depend. Members of the creative class do a wide variety of work in a wide variety of industries—from technology to entertainment, journalism to finance, high-end manufacturing to the arts. They do not consciously think of themselves as a class. Yet they share a common ethos that values creativity, individuality, difference, and merit.

More and more businesses understand that ethos and are making the adaptations necessary to attract and retain creative class employees—everything from relaxed dress codes, flexible schedules, and new work rules in the office to hiring recruiters who throw Frisbees. Most civic leaders, however, have failed to understand that what is true for corporations is also true for cities and regions: Places that succeed in attracting and retaining creative class people prosper; those that fail don't.

Stuck in old paradigms of economic development, cities like Buffalo, New Orleans, and Louisville struggled in the 1980s and 1990s to become the next "Silicon Somewhere" by building generic high-tech office parks or subsidizing professional sports teams. Yet they lost members of the creative class, and their economic dynamism, to places like Austin, Boston, Washington, D.C., and Seattle—places more tolerant, diverse, and open to creativity. Because of this migration of the creative class, a new social and economic geography is emerging in America, one that does not correspond to old categories like East Coast versus West Coast or Sunbelt versus Frostbelt. Rather, it is more like the class divisions that have increasingly separated Americans by income and neighborhood, extended into the realm of city and region.

The Creative Secretary

The distinguishing characteristic of the creative class is that its members engage in work whose function is to "create meaningful new forms." The super-creative core of this new class includes scientists and engineers, university professors, poets and novelists, artists, entertainers, actors, designers, and architects, as well as the "thought leadership" of modern society: nonfiction writers, editors, cultural figures, think-tank researchers, analysts, and other opinion-makers. Members of this super-creative core produce new forms or designs that are readily transferable and broadly useful—such as designing a product that can be widely made, sold and used; coming up with a theorem or strategy that can be applied in many cases; or composing music that can be performed again and again.

Beyond this core group, the creative class also includes "creative professionals" who work in a wide range of knowledge-intensive industries such as high-tech sectors, financial services, the legal and healthcare professions,

Table 1 Large Cities Creativity Rankings

Rankings of 49 metro areas reporting populations over 1 million in the 2000 Census

The Top Ten Cities	Creativity Index	% Creative Workers	Creative Rank	High-Tech Rank	Innovation Rank	Diversity Rank
1. San Francisco	1057	34.8%	5	1	2	1
2. Austin	1028	36.4%	4	11	3	16
3. San Diego	1015	32.1%	15	12	7	3
3. Boston	1015	38.0%	3	2	6	22
5. Seattle	1008	32.7%	9	3	12	8
6. Raleigh–Durham–Chapel Hill	996	38.2%	2	14	4	28
7. Houston	980	32.5%	10	16	16	10
8. Washington–Baltimore	964	38.4%	1	5	30	12
9. New York	962	32.3%	12	13	24	14
10. Dallas	960	30.2%	23	6	17	9
10. Minneapolis	960	33.9%	7	21	5	29
The Bottom Ten Cities	**Creativity Index**	**% Creative Workers**	**Creative Rank**	**High-Tech Rank**	**Innovation Rank**	**Diversity Rank**
49. Memphis	530	24.8%	47	48	42	41
48. Norfolk–Virginia Beach, VA	555	28.4%	36	35	49	47
47. Las Vegas	561	18.5%	49	42	47	5
46. Buffalo	609	28.9%	33	40	27	49
45. Louisville	622	26.5%	46	46	39	36
44. Grand Rapids, MI	639	24.3%	48	43	23	38
43. Oklahoma City	668	29.4%	29	41	43	39
42. New Orleans	668	27.5%	42	45	48	13
41. Greensboro–Winston-Salem	697	27.3%	44	33	35	35
40. Providence, RI	698	27.6%	41	44	34	33

and business management. These people engage in creative problem-solving, drawing on complex bodies of knowledge to solve specific problems. Doing so typically requires a high degree of formal education and thus a high level of human capital. People who do this kind of work may sometimes come up with methods or products that turn out to be widely useful, but it's not part of the basic job description. What they are required to do regularly is think on their own. They apply or combine standard approaches in unique ways to fit the situation, exercise a great deal of judgment, perhaps try something radically new from time to time.

Much the same is true of the growing number of technicians and others who apply complex bodies of knowledge to working with physical materials. In fields such as medicine and scientific research, technicians are taking on increased responsibility to interpret their work and make decisions, blurring the old distinction between white-collar work (done by decisionmakers) and blue-collar work (done by those who follow orders). They acquire their own arcane bodies of knowledge and develop their own unique ways of doing the job. Another example is the secretary in today's pared-down offices. In

many cases this person not only takes on a host of tasks once performed by a large secretarial staff, but becomes a true office manager—channeling flows of information, devising and setting up new systems, often making key decisions on the fly. These people contribute more than intelligence or computer skills. They add creative value. Everywhere we look, creativity is increasingly valued. Firms and organizations value it for the results that it can produce and individuals value it as a route to self-expression and job satisfaction. Bottom line: As creativity becomes more valued, the creative class grows.

The creative class now includes some 38.3 million Americans, roughly 30 percent of the entire U.S. workforce—up from just 10 percent at the turn of the 20th century and less than 20 percent as recently as 1980. The creative class has considerable economic power. In 1999, the average salary for a member of the creative class was nearly $50,000 ($48,752), compared to roughly $28,000 for a working-class member and $22,000 for a service-class worker.

Not surprisingly, regions that have large numbers of creative class members are also some of the most affluent and growing.

The New Geography of Class

Different classes of people have long sorted themselves into neighborhoods within a city or region. But now we find a large-scale re-sorting of people among cities and regions nationwide, with some regions becoming centers of the creative class while others are composed of larger shares of working-class or service-class people. To some extent this has always been true. For instance, there have always been artistic and cultural communities like Greenwich Village, college towns like Madison and Boulder, and manufacturing centers like Pittsburgh and Detroit. The news is that such sorting is becoming even more widespread and pronounced.

In the leading centers of this new class geography, the creative class makes up more than 35 percent of the workforce. This is already the case in the greater Washington, D.C. region, the Raleigh-Durham area, Boston, and Austin—all areas undergoing tremendous economic growth. Despite their considerable advantages, large regions have not cornered the market as creative class locations. In fact, a number of smaller regions have some of the highest creative-class concentrations in the nation—notably college towns like East Lansing, Mich. and Madison, Wisc. (See Table 3, "Small-size Cities Creativity Rankings.")

At the other end of the spectrum are regions that are being bypassed by the creative class. Among large regions, Las Vegas, Grand Rapids, and Memphis harbor the smallest concentrations of the creative class. Members of this class have nearly abandoned a wide range of smaller regions in the outskirts of the South and Midwest. In small metropolitan areas like Victoria, Texas, and Jackson, Tenn., the creative class comprises less than 15 percent of the workforce. The leading centers for the working class among large regions are Greensboro, N.C. and Memphis, Tenn., where the working class makes up more than 30 percent of the workforce. Several smaller regions in the South and Midwest are veritable working class enclaves with 40 to 50 percent or more of their workforce in the traditional industrial occupations.

These places have some of the most minuscule concentrations of the creative class in the nation. They are symptomatic of a general lack of overlap between the major creative-class centers and those of the working class. Of the 26 large cities where the working class comprises more than one-quarter of the population, only one, Houston, ranks among the top 10 destinations for the creative class.

Chicago, a bastion of working-class people that still ranks among the top 20 large creative centers, is interesting because it shows how the creative class and the traditional working class can coexist. But Chicago has an advantage in that it is a big city, with more than a million members of the creative class. The University of Chicago sociologist Terry Clark likes to say Chicago developed an innovative political and cultural solution to this issue. Under the second Mayor Daley, the city integrated the members of the creative class into the city's culture and politics by treating them essentially as just another "ethnic group" that needed sufficient space to express its identity.

Las Vegas has the highest concentration of the service class among large cities, 58 percent, while West Palm Beach, Orlando, and Miami also have around half. These regions rank near the bottom of the list for the creative class. The service class makes up more than half the workforce in nearly 50 small and medium-size regions across the country. Few of them boast any significant concentrations of the creative class, save vacationers, and offer little prospect for upward mobility. They include resort towns like Honolulu and Cape Cod. But they also include places like Shreveport, Lou. and Pittsfield, Mass. For these places that are not tourist destinations, the economic and social future is troubling to contemplate.

Plug-and-Play Communities

Why do some places become destinations for the creative while others don't? Economists speak of the importance of industries having "low entry barriers," so that new firms can easily enter and keep the industry vital. Similarly, I think it's important for a place to have low entry barriers for people—that is, to be a place where newcomers are accepted quickly into all sorts of social and economic arrangements. All else being equal, they are likely to attract greater numbers of talented and creative people—the sort of people who power innovation and growth. Places that thrive in today's world tend to be plug-and-play communities where anyone can fit in quickly. These are places where people can find opportunity, build support structures, be themselves, and not get stuck in any one identity. The plug-and-play community is one that somebody can move into and put together a life—or at least a facsimile of a life—in a week.

The plug-and-play community is one that somebody can move into and put together a life—or at least a facsimile of a life—in a week.

Creative centers also tend to be places with thick labor markets that can fulfill the employment needs of members of the creative class, who, by and large, are not looking

Table 2   Medium-Size Cities Creativity Rankings

Rankings of 32 metro areas reporting populations 500,000 to 1 million in the 2000 Census

The Top Ten Cities	Creativity Index	% Creative Workers	Creative Rank	High-Tech Rank	Innovation Rank	Diversity Rank
1. Albuquerque, NM	965	32.2%	2	1	7	1
2. Albany, NY	932	33.7%	1	12	2	4
3. Tuscon, AZ	853	28.4%	17	2	6	5
4. Allentown–Bethlehem, PA	801	28.7%	16	13	3	14
5. Dayton, OH	766	30.1%	8	8	5	24
6. Colorado Springs, CO	756	29.9%	10	5	1	30
7. Harrisburg, PA	751	29.8%	11	6	13	20
8. Little Rock, AR	740	30.8%	4	10	21	11
9. Birmingham, AL	722	30.7%	6	7	26	10
10. Tulsa, OK	721	28.7%	15	9	15	18
The Bottom Ten Cities	Creativity Index	% Creative Workers	Creative Rank	High-Tech Rank	Innovation Rank	Diversity Rank
32. Youngstown, OH	253	23.8%	32	32	24	32
31. Scranton–Wilkes-Barre, PA	400	24.7%	28	23	23	31
30. McAllen, TX	451	27.8%	18	31	32	9
29. Stockton–Lodi, CA	459	24.1%	30	29	28	7
28. El Paso, TX	464	27.0%	23	27	31	17
27. Fresno, CA	516	25.1%	27	24	30	2
26. Bakersfield, CA	531	27.8%	18	22	27	19
25. Fort Wayne, IN	569	25.4%	26	17	8	26
24. Springfield, MA	577	29.7%	13	30	20	22
23. Honolulu, HI	580	27.2%	21	14	29	6

just for "a job" but for places that offer many employment opportunities.

Cities and regions that attract lots of creative talent are also those with greater diversity and higher levels of quality of place. That's because location choices of the creative class are based to a large degree on their lifestyle interests, and these go well beyond the standard "quality-of-life" amenities that most experts think are important.

The list of the country's high-tech hot spots looks an awful lot like the list of the places with highest concentrations of gay people.

For instance, in 1998, I met Gary Gates, then a doctoral student at Carnegie Mellon. While I had been studying the location choices of high-tech industries and talented people, Gates had been exploring the location patterns of gay people. My list of the country's high-tech hot spots looked an awful lot like his list of the places with highest concentrations of gay people. When we compared these two lists with more statistical rigor, his Gay Index turned out to correlate very strongly to my own measures

of high-tech growth. Other measures I came up with, like the Bohemian Index—a measure of artists, writers, and performers—produced similar results.

Talented people seek an environment open to differences. Many highly creative people, regardless of ethnic background or sexual orientation, grew up feeling like outsiders, different in some way from most of their schoolmates. When they are sizing up a new company and community, acceptance of diversity and of gays in particular is a sign that reads "non-standard people welcome here."

The creative class people I study use the word "diversity" a lot, but not to press any political hot buttons. Diversity is simply something they value in all its manifestations. This is spoken of so often, and so matter-of-factly, that I take it to be a fundamental marker of creative class values. Creative-minded people enjoy a mix of influences. They want to hear different kinds of music and try different kinds of food. They want to meet and socialize with people unlike themselves, trade views and spar over issues.

As with employers, visible diversity serves as a signal that a community embraces the open meritocratic values of the creative age. The people I talked to also desired nightlife with a wide mix of options. The most highly

Table 3   Small-Size Cities Creativity Rankings

Rankings of 63 metro areas reporting populations 250,000 to 500,000 in the 2000 Census

The Top Ten Cities	Creativity Index	% Creative Workers	Creative Rank	High-Tech Rank	Innovation Rank	Diversity Rank
1. Madison, WI	925	32.8%	6	16	4	9
2. Des Moines, IA	862	32.1%	8	2	16	20
3. Santa Barbara, CA	856	28.3%	19	8	8	7
4. Melbourne, FL	855	35.5%	1	6	9	32
5. Boise City, ID	854	35.2%	3	1	1	46
6. Huntsville, AL	799	35.3%	2	5	18	40
7. Lansing–East Lansing, MI	739	34.3%	4	27	29	18
8. Binghamton, NY	731	30.8%	12	7	3	60
9. Lexington, KY	717	27.0%	28	24	10	12
10. New London, CT–Norwich, RI	715	28.1%	23	11	13	33
The Bottom Ten Cities	**Creativity Index**	**% Creative Workers**	**Creative Rank**	**High-Tech Rank**	**Innovation Rank**	**Diversity Rank**
63. Shreveport, LA	233	22.1%	55	32	59	57
62. Ocala, FL	263	16.4%	63	61	52	24
61. Visalia, CA	289	22.9%	52	63	60	11
60. Killeen, TX	302	24.6%	47	47	51	53
59. Fayetteville, NC	309	29.0%	16	62	62	49
58. York, PA	360	22.3%	54	54	26	52
57. Fayetteville, AR	366	21.1%	57	57	42	17
56. Beaumont, TX	372	27.8%	25	37	56	55
55. Lakeland–Winter Haven, FL	385	20.9%	59	56	53	5
54. Hickory, NC	393	19.4%	61	48	32	30

valued options were experiential ones—interesting music venues, neighborhood art galleries, performance spaces, and theaters. A vibrant, varied nightlife was viewed by many as another signal that a city "gets it," even by those who infrequently partake in nightlife. More than anything, the creative class craves real experiences in the real world.

They favor active, participatory recreation over passive, institutionalized forms. They prefer indigenous street-level culture—a teeming blend of cafes, sidewalk musicians, and small galleries and bistros, where it is hard to draw the line between performers and spectators. They crave stimulation, not escape. They want to pack their time full of dense, high-quality, multidimensional experiences. Seldom has one of my subjects expressed a desire to get away from it all. They want to get into it all, and do it with eyes wide open.

Creative class people value active outdoor recreation very highly. They are drawn to places and communities where many outdoor activities are prevalent—both because they enjoy these activities and because their presence is seen as a signal that the place is amenable to the broader creative lifestyle. The creative-class people in my studies are into a variety of active sports, from traditional ones like bicycling, jogging, and kayaking to newer, more extreme ones, like trail running and snowboarding.

Places are also valued for authenticity and uniqueness. Authenticity comes from several aspects of a community—historic buildings, established neighborhoods, a unique music scene, or specific cultural attributes. It comes from the mix—from urban grit alongside renovated buildings, from the commingling of young and old, long-time neighborhood characters and yuppies, fashion models and "bag ladies." An authentic place also offers unique and original experiences. Thus a place full of chain stores, chain restaurants, and nightclubs is not authentic. You could have the same experience anywhere.

Today, it seems, leading creative centers provide a solid mix of high-tech industry, plentiful outdoor amenities, and an older urban center whose rebirth has been fueled in part by a combination of creativity and innovative technology, as well as lifestyle amenities. These include places like the greater Boston area, which has the Route 128 suburban complex, Harvard and MIT, and several charming inner-city Boston neighborhoods. Seattle has suburban Bellevue and Redmond (where Microsoft is located), beautiful mountains and country, and a series of revitalized urban neighborhoods. The San Francisco Bay area has everything from posh inner-city neighborhoods to ultra-hip districts like SoMa (South of Market) and lifestyle enclaves like Marin County as well as the Silicon Valley. Even Austin includes traditional high-tech developments to the north, lifestyle centers for cycling and outdoor activities, and a revitalizing university/downtown community centered on vibrant Sixth Street, the warehouse district and the music scene—a critical element of a thriving creative center.

Institutional Sclerosis

Even as places like Austin and Seattle are thriving, much of the country is failing to adapt to the demands of the creative age. It is not that struggling cities like Pittsburgh do not want to grow or encourage high-tech industries. In most cases, their leaders are doing everything they think they can to spur innovation and high-tech growth. But most of the time, they are either unwilling or unable to do the things required to create an environment or habitat attractive to the creative class. They pay lip service to the need to "attract talent," but continue to pour resources into recruiting call centers, underwriting big-box retailers, subsidizing downtown malls, and squandering precious taxpayer dollars on extravagant stadium complexes. Or they try to create facsimiles of neighborhoods or retail districts, replacing the old and authentic with the new and generic—and in doing so drive the creative class away.

It is a telling commentary on our age that at a time when political will seems difficult to muster for virtually anything, city after city can generate the political capital to underwrite hundreds of millions of dollars of investments in professional sports stadiums. And you know what? They don't matter to the creative class. Not once during any of my focus groups and interviews did the members of the creative class mention professional sports as playing a role of any sort in their choice of where to live and work. What makes most cities unable to even imagine devoting those kinds of resources or political will to do the things that people say really matter to them?

The answer is simple. These cities are trapped by their past. Despite the lip service they might pay, they are unwilling or unable to do what it takes to attract the creative class. The late economist Mancur Olson long ago noted that the decline of nations and regions is a product of an organizational and cultural hardening of the arteries he called "institutional sclerosis." Places that grow up and prosper in one era, Olson argued, find it difficult and often times impossible to adopt new organizational and cultural patterns, regardless of how beneficial they might be. Consequently, innovation and growth shift to new places, which can adapt to and harness these shifts for their benefit. This phenomenon, he contends, is how England got trapped and how the U.S. became the world's great economic power. It also accounts for the shift in economic activity from the old industrial cities to newer cities in the South and West, according to Olson.

Olson's analysis presciently identifies why so many cities across the nation remain trapped in the culture and attitudes of the bygone organizational age, unable or unwilling to adapt to current trends. Cities like Detroit, Cleveland, and my current hometown of Pittsburgh were at the forefront of the organizational age. The cultural and attitudinal norms of that age became so powerfully ingrained in these places that they did not allow the new norms and attitudes associated with the creative age to grow up, diffuse and become generally accepted. This process, in turn, stamped out much of the creative impulse, causing talented and creative people to seek out new places where they could more readily plug in and make a go of it.

Most experts and scholars have not even begun to think in terms of a creative community. Instead, they tend to try to emulate the Silicon Valley model which author Joel Kotkin has dubbed the "nerdistan." But the nerdistan is a limited economic development model, which misunderstands the role played by creativity in generating innovation and economic growth. Nerdistans are bland, uninteresting places with acre upon acre of identical office complexes, row after row of asphalt parking lots, freeways clogged with cars, cookie-cutter housing developments, and strip-malls sprawling in every direction. Many of these places have fallen victim to the very kinds of problems they were supposed to avoid. The comfort and security of places like Silicon Valley have gradually given way to sprawl, pollution, and paralyzing traffic jams. As one technology executive told *The Wall Street Journal,* "I really didn't want to live in San Jose. Every time I went up there, the concrete jungle got me down." His company eventually settled on a more urban Southern California location in downtown Pasadena close to the CalTech campus.

Kotkin finds that the lack of lifestyle amenities is causing significant problems in attracting top creative people to places like the North Carolina Research Triangle. He quotes a major real estate developer as saying, "Ask anyone where downtown is and nobody can tell you. There's not much of a sense of place here. . . . The people I am selling space to are screaming about cultural issues." The Research Triangle lacks the hip urban lifestyle found in places like San Francisco, Seattle, New York, and Chicago, laments a University of North Carolina researcher: "In Raleigh-Durham, we can always visit the hog farms."

The Kids Are All Right

How do you build a truly creative community—one that can survive and prosper in this emerging age? The key can no longer be found in the usual strategies. Recruiting

64

more companies won't do it; neither will trying to become the next Silicon Valley. While it certainly remains important to have a solid business climate, having an effective people climate is even more essential. By this I mean a general strategy aimed at attracting and retaining people—especially, but not limited to, creative people. This entails remaining open to diversity and actively working to cultivate it, and investing in the lifestyle amenities that people really want and use often, as opposed to using financial incentives to attract companies, build professional sports stadiums, or develop retail complexes.

The benefits of this kind of strategy are obvious. Whereas companies—or sports teams, for that matter—that get financial incentives can pull up and leave at virtually a moment's notice, investments in amenities like urban parks, for example, last for generations. Other amenities—like bike lanes or off-road trails for running, cycling, rollerblading, or just walking your dog—benefit a wide swath of the population.

There is no one-size-fits-all model for a successful people climate. The members of the creative class are diverse across the dimensions of age, ethnicity and race, marital status, and sexual preference. An effective people climate needs to emphasize openness and diversity, and to help reinforce low barriers to entry. Thus, it cannot be restrictive or monolithic.

Openness to immigration is particularly important for smaller cities and regions, while the ability to attract so-called bohemians is key for larger cities and regions. For cities and regions to attract these groups, they need to develop the kinds of people climates that appeal to them and meet their needs.

Yet if you ask most community leaders what kinds of people they'd most want to attract, they'd likely say successful married couples in their 30s and 40s—people with good middle-to-upper-income jobs and stable family lives. I certainly think it is important for cities and communities to be good for children and families. But less than a quarter of all American households consist of traditional nuclear families, and focusing solely on their needs has been a losing strategy, one that neglects a critical engine of economic growth: young people.

Young workers have typically been thought of as transients who contribute little to a city's bottom line. But in the creative age, they matter for two reasons. First, they are workhorses. They are able to work longer and harder, and are more prone to take risks, precisely because they are young and childless. In rapidly changing industries, it's often the most recent graduates who have the most up-to-date skills. Second, people are staying single longer. The average age of marriage for both men and women has risen some five years over the past generation. College-educated people postpone marriage longer than the national averages. Among this group, one of the fastest growing categories is the never-been-married. To prosper in the creative age, regions have to offer a people climate that satisfies this group's social interests and lifestyle needs, as well as address those of other groups.

Furthermore, a climate oriented to young people is also attractive to the creative class more broadly. Creative-class people do not lose their lifestyle preferences as they age. They don't stop bicycling or running, for instance, just because they have children. When they put their children in child seats or jogging strollers, amenities like traffic-free bike paths become more important than ever. They also continue to value diversity and tolerance. The middle-aged and older people I speak with may no longer hang around in nightspots until 4 A.M., but they enjoy stimulating, dynamic places with high levels of cultural interplay. And if they have children, that's the kind of environment in which they want them to grow up.

My adopted hometown of Pittsburgh has been slow to realize this. City leaders continue to promote Pittsburgh as a place that is good for families, seemingly unaware of the demographic changes that have made young people, singles, new immigrants, and gays critical to the emerging social fabric. People in focus groups I have conducted feel that Pittsburgh is not open to minority groups, new immigrants, or gays. Young women feel there are substantial barriers to their advancement. Talented members of racial and ethnic minorities, as well as professional women, express their desire to leave the city at a rate far greater than their white male counterparts. So do creative people from all walks of life.

Is there hope for Pittsburgh? Of course there is. First, although the region's economy is not dynamic, neither is it the basket case it could easily have become. Twenty years ago there were no significant venture capital firms in the area; now there are many, and thriving high-tech firms continue to form and make their mark. There are signs of life in the social and cultural milieu as well. The region's immigrant population has begun to tick upward, fed by students and professors at the universities and employees in the medical and technology sectors. Major suburbs to the east of the city now have Hindu temples and a growing Indian-American population. The area's gay community, while not large, has become more active and visible. Pittsburgh's increasing status in the gay world is reflected in the fact that it is the "location" for Showtime's "Queer as Folk" series.

Many of Pittsburgh's creative class have proven to be relentless cultural builders. The Andy Warhol Museum and the Mattress Factory, a museum/workspace devoted to large-scale installation art, have achieved worldwide recognition. Street-level culture has a growing foothold in Pittsburgh, too, as main street corridors in several older working-class districts have been transformed. Political leaders are in some cases open to new models of development. Pittsburgh Mayor Tom Murphy has been an ardent promoter of biking and foot trails, among other things. The city's absolutely first-rate architecture and urban design community has become much more vocal about the need to preserve historic buildings, invest in neighborhoods, and institute tough design standards. It would be very hard today (dare I say nearly impossible) to knock down historic buildings and dismember vibrant urban neighborhoods as was done in the past. As these new groups and efforts reach critical mass, the norms and attitudes that have long prevailed in the city are being challenged.

For what it's worth, I'll put my money—and a lot of my effort—into Pittsburgh's making it. If Pittsburgh, with all of its assets and its emerging human creativity, somehow can't make it in the creative age, I fear the future does not bode well for other older industrial communities and established cities, and the lamentable new class segregation among cities will continue to worsen.

Critical Thinking

1. Who are the "creative class"?
2. What should a city do if it wishes to attract the creative class and creative industries?

RICHARD FLORIDA is a professor of regional economic development at Carnegie Mellon University and a columnist for *Information Week*. This article was adapted from his forthcoming book, *The Rise of the Creative Class: and How It's Transforming Work, Leisure, Community and Everyday Life* (Basic Books).

Studies: Gentrification a Boost for Everyone

Everyone knows gentrification uproots the urban poor with higher rents, higher taxes and $4 lattes. It's the lament of community organizers, the theme of the 2004 film *Barbershop 2* and the guilty assumption of the yuppies moving in.

RICK HAMPSON

But everyone may be wrong, according to Lance Freeman, an assistant professor of urban planning at Columbia University.

In an article last month in *Urban Affairs Review*, Freeman reports the results of his national study of gentrification—the movement of upscale (mostly white) settlers into rundown (mostly minority) neighborhoods.

His conclusion: Gentrification drives comparatively few low-income residents from their homes. Although some are forced to move by rising costs, there isn't much more displacement in gentrifying neighborhoods than in non-gentrifying ones.

In a separate study of New York City published last year, Freeman and a colleague concluded that living in a gentrifying neighborhood there actually made it less likely a poor resident would move—a finding similar to that of a 2001 study of Boston by Duke University economist Jacob Vigdor.

Freeman and Vigdor say that although higher costs sometimes force poor residents to leave gentrifying neighborhoods, other changes—more jobs, safer streets, better trash pickup—encourage them to stay. But to others, gentrification remains a dirty word.

"All you have to do is talk to people around here," says James Lewis, a tenant organizer in Harlem, New York's most famous black neighborhood. "Everybody with money is moving into Harlem, and the people who are here are being displaced."

Even residents who have survived gentrification tend to believe it forces people out.

Maria Marquez, 37, has slept on the sofa for 12 years to give her mother and son the two bedrooms in their apartment in Chicago's gentrifying Logan Square area. But eventually, she says, "we're gonna get kicked out. It's a matter of time."

Kathe Newman, assistant professor of public policy at Rutgers University, argues that Freeman's research in New York understates the extent of displacement. But she says he has raised a good question: How, in the face of relentlessly higher living costs, do so many poor people stay put?

A Hot-Button Issue

Gentrification has spawned emotional disputes in cities around the nation:

- In northwest Fort Lauderdale, where streets are named for the district's prominent old African-American families, three of four new home buyers are white, according to a survey by the *Sun-Sentinel*. City Commissioner Carlton Moore told the newspaper his largely black constituency fears displacement, even though he says it won't happen.
- In the predominantly Latino working class barrio of East Austin, the new Pedernales Lofts condominiums have raised adjacent land values more than 50% since 2003. Last fall, someone hung signs from power lines outside the lofts saying, "Stop gentrifying the East Side" and "Will U give jobs to longtime residents of this neighborhood?"
- In Charlotte, a City Council committee voted in December to remove language from a city planning department report that downplayed gentrification's threat to neighborhoods. Development could uproot some people, councilman John Tabor told the *Charlotte Observer*, "If there are people in these neighborhoods who have to move because they can't afford their taxes, that's who I want to help," he said.
- In Boston's North End, the destruction of the noisy Central Artery elevated highway promises to attract younger, more affluent new residents and dilute the traditional Italian immigrant culture.

In the two decades after World War II, government urban renewal schemes tore down whole neighborhoods and scattered residents.

Gentrification, which appeared in the 1970s, was something else. Motivated by high gasoline prices, suburban sprawl and a new taste for old architecture, some middle class whites began moving into neighborhoods that had gone out of fashion a generation or two earlier.

Here's how it works: A dilapidated and depopulated but essentially attractive neighborhood—solid housing stock, well laid-out streets, proximity to the city center—is discovered by artists, graduate students and other bohemians.

Block by block, the neighborhood changes. The newcomers fix up old buildings. Galleries and cafes open, and mom 'n' pop groceries close. City services improve. Finally, the bohemians are joined by lawyers, stockbrokers and dentists. Property values rise, followed by property taxes and rents.

To some urban planners, gentrification is a solution to racial segregation, a shrinking tax base and other problems. To others, it *is* a problem: Poor blacks and Hispanics, who've held on through hard times and sometimes started the neighborhood's comeback, are ousted by their own success.

Jose Sanchez, an urban planning expert at Long Island University in Brooklyn, says some changing neighborhoods stabilize with a mixture of people. But he says the poor—and the bohemian pioneers—can also be "washed out" by scheming landlords or government policies such as rezoning and urban renewal.

The Poor Stay Put

Freeman and Vigdor say gentrification has gotten a bad rap. When they studied New York City and Boston, respectively, they found that poor and less educated residents of gentrifying neighborhoods actually moved less often than people in other neighborhoods—20% less in New York.

For his national study published this year, Freeman found only a slight connection between gentrification and displacement. A poor resident's chances of being forced to move out of a gentrifying neighborhood are only 0.5% greater than in a non-gentrifying one.

So how do some neighborhoods change so dramatically? Freeman says it's mostly the result of what he calls "succession": Poor people in gentrifying neighborhoods who move from their homes—for whatever reason—usually are replaced by people who have more income and education.

Freeman and Vigdor say skeptics who view gentrification merely as "hood snatching" should remember three things:

- Many older neighborhoods have high turnover, whether they gentrify or not. Vigdor says that over five years, about half of all urban residents move.

- Such neighborhoods often have so much vacant or abandoned housing that there's no need to drive anyone out to accommodate people who want to move in. A quarter of the housing in one section of Boston's South End was vacant in 1970; the population had dropped by more than 50% over 20 years. Today, the population has increased more than 50%, and the vacancy rate is less than 2%.

- Rising housing costs in gentrifying districts may ensure that poor residents who do move leave the neighborhood, rather than settle elsewhere in it. Since

their places usually are taken by more affluent, better educated people, the neighborhood's character and demographics change.

Vigdor argues that hatred of gentrification is largely irrational: "We were angry when the middle class moved out of the city," he says. "Now we're angry when they move back."

He asks whether Detroit, which in 50 years has lost half its population and most of its middle class, would not have been better off with gentrification than it has been without it.

A Housing Shortage

Gentrification is a symptom of a bigger problem: Metro areas don't create enough housing, Vigdor says. When prices in the suburbs get high enough, home buyers start looking at "undervalued" urban housing. If it's close to downtown and has some period charm, so much the better.

But critics insist gentrification does real harm to real people. Lewis, the Harlem organizer, says he can't get statements from people who were forced out because he doesn't know where they went.

A surprising number of poor people, however, manage to hold on. Some explanations:

- **Homeownership.** Homeowners face rising property taxes, but unlike renters they also stand to gain from rising values. Idida Perez, 46, complains that taxes and escrow payments on her two-family house near Logan Square in Chicago have jumped $300 a month over the past few years. But the house, which she and her husband bought for $200,000 in 1990, is now worth $400,000.

- **Rent control.** Samuel Ragland, 82, pays $115 a month for his one-room rent-controlled apartment on fast-gentrifying West 120th Street in Harlem. His building is being converted into condos, but under New York law, his landlord can't move him out unless he's given a comparable apartment at a comparable rent in the same area.

- **Government subsidies.** Carole Singleton, 52, had to retire from her job as a hospital administrator after she got cancer. But she's been able to stay in Harlem because she pays only $300 of the $971 rent for her apartment; a federal housing subsidy covers the rest.

- **Doubling (or tripling) up.** After the rent on Ofelia Sanchez's one-bedroom apartment in the Logan Square area went from $500 to $600, she and her two kids moved into a three-bedroom with Sanchez's mother and her sister's family. The apartment houses 10 people. Sanchez and her son share a bed, and her daughter sleeps on the floor. But Sanchez won't move; she works as a tutor at the local elementary school, and her mother babysits while she takes classes at Chicago State University. "This is home," she says of the neighborhood where she's lived for 26 of her 27 years. "I don't know anyone anywhere else."

- **Landlord-tenant understandings.** In return for $595 monthly rent for a two-bedroom apartment, tenant Maria Marquez rakes the leaves and shovels the front walk. She lays floor tile, repairs holes in the porch and changes light fixtures. It enables her, her son and her mother to stay in an area of Chicago where two-bedrooms rent for $1,000.

- **More income devoted to rent.** Poor New York households in gentrifying neighborhoods spent 61% of their income on housing, compared with 52% for the poor in non-gentrifying ones, Freeman found. Klare Allen, who is in her mid-40s, has been able to keep her three-bedroom apartment in Roxbury, a black neighborhood close to downtown Boston. But she has to pay $1,400 a month—75% of her monthly income.

- **Prayer.** Alma Feliciano, 46, of Boston asked God for an affordable apartment that would allow her and her four children to stay in Roxbury and continue to attend her church, Holy Tabernacle. Her prayers were granted—a unit in a federally subsidized complex. Otherwise, she says, she would have had to leave the city.

One reason poor families make such heroic efforts to stay is because the quality of life is improving—partly thanks to gentrification.

In the Logan Square area, Marquez says, an influx of higher-income newcomers has coincided with what seems like more aggressive policing.

"The gang bangers are not around as much, and you don't see the prostitutes on the corners like you used to," she says.

Idida Perez hates the rising prices but admits, "There are a lot more small cafes owned by people from the neighborhood, and I am a big coffee drinker." And new businesses mean new jobs: Someone has to pour those lattes.

Critical Thinking

1. Why do cities pursue gentrification?
2. What criticisms are often made of gentrification?
3. Are there benefits that gentrification can bring to poorer residents of an inner-city neighborhood that is undergoing upgrading?
4. How do critics attack the more positive assessment of gentrification presented in this article?

From *USA Today,* April 19, 2005. Copyright © 2005 by *USA Today,* a division of Gannett Satellite Information Network, Inc. Reprinted by permission via Rightslink.

UNIT 4

Competitive Pressures and Economic Development

Unit Selections

Learning Outcomes

After reading this unit, you should be able to:

- Understand why many economists often do not consider public subsidies for sports arenas to be a good investment for a city.

- Explain why city and state officials continue to give extensive subsidies for new sports stadiums and arenas despite evidence that casts doubts as to the cost-effectiveness of such investments.

- Propose the terms of a "good" deal for a city when it comes to subsidizing the construction of sports stadiums and arenas; How does a "good" deal for the city differ from the many "bad" deals that cities have signed in their efforts to retain sports franchises?

- Define a city's "growth coalition" (also called a "growth machine") and identify the various members who constitute a city's "growth coalition."

- Defend a city's use of eminent domain powers to "take" private property for local economic development.

- Criticize a city's use of eminent domain powers to "take" private property for local economic development.

- Detail what the U.S. Supreme Court said in its ruling on eminent domain in its *Kelo* decision.

- Evaluate what the states have done in defining local eminent domain powers in the years immediately following the *Kelo* decision.

- Differentiate between a "megapolitan area" and a "metropolitan area."

- Come to your own conclusion regarding the desirability of public investment in high-speed rail (HSR) systems.

Student Website

www.mhhe.com/cls

Internet References

American Public Transportation Association, Center for High-Speed Rail
   www.highspeedrailonline.com

Californians for High-Speed Rail
   www.ca4hsr.org

Field of Schemes
   www.fieldofschemes.com

Legislative Analyst's Office (LAO), State of California
   www.lao.ca.gov/reports/2011/trns/high_speed_rail/high_speed_
   rail_051011.pdf

Midwest High-Speed Rail Association
   www.midwesthsr.org

The Railist: High-Speed Rail News, a Project of Planetizen
   www.therailist.com

Reason Foundation
   www.reason.org

U.S. Conference of Mayors. 2010 Report on the Economic Impact of High-Speed Rail on U.S. Cities
   www.usmayors.org/highspeedrail

U.S. High-Speed Rail Association
   www.ushsra.com

As Paul Peterson observed in his influential book *City Limits,* a city must be able to attract and retain businesses for its economic well-being. Cities need both the jobs and the tax base that businesses provide. But while a city needs businesses, a major business firm often has a fairly wide choice of communities in which it can locate its headquarters and production facilities. As a result, U.S. cities often wind up offering tax breaks (often referred to as tax abatements) and various other costly incentives in their efforts to attract desirable businesses and to prevent existing firms from relocating elsewhere. Cities often pay for expensive infrastructure improvements, including strengthened roadways to support heavy trucks, upgraded sewer facilities to accommodate the wastewater needs of manufacturing plants, and new fiber-optic networks and other state-of-the-art improvements in telecommunications capacity.

Of course, all of these tax abatements and improvements have a cost. They require a city to raise taxes on residents and other businesses. Or a city may pay for promised concessions by diverting revenues away from the public schools and other important public services.

Just when is it wise for a city to offer such concessions to businesses? When are such concessions unnecessary and a waste of taxpayer money?

In each city, the highly influential members of the city's growth coalition advocate the continued award of development subsidies. Downtown business owners, real estate interests, property developers, and organized labor all stand to gain financial benefits from development projects that they argue are crucial to a city's future competitiveness and prosperity. Members of the growth coalition, for instance, may argue that the construction of a new stadium is essential if a city is to maintain a sports franchise and the city's "major league" image. They point out that Indianapolis used just such a strategy, investing in a number of new sports facilities, to shake off the city's "Indiana-no-place" image and to become the amateur sports capital of the United States. San Diego similarly used the construction of Petco Field for the Padres baseball team to kick-start new development in a large downtown area, christened Ballpark Village, lying just beyond the stadium fences.

Yet, not all stadium and convention center projects wind up being a "good deal" for the city. Across the United States, cities have continued to provide generous support for new sports arenas even though numerous studies have pointed to the rather minor overall economic benefits that a city gains from extensive public investment in a new stadium (Article 15, "Stop the Subsidy-Sucking Sports Stadiums"). The analyses provided by the growth coalition often underpredict the costs and overstate the revenues that a city will receive from a new sports facility, convention center, or other growth project. When deals result in financial shortfalls, it is almost always the taxpayer who is obligated to pick up the additional costs.

Heywood Sanders (Article 16, "A Lot of Hooey") similarly questions whether extensive municipal investment in a new convention center really makes sense for most cities. In city after city, the growth coalition has hired expert financial consultants who deliver elaborate presentations loaded with graphs and

Glow Images

statistics that persuade decision makers of the extensive benefits that a new convention center will bring to a city. These studies often argue that a new facility will generate so much activity that it will pay for itself over time. But Sanders points out that there are just too few good-paying conventions to fill meeting halls built in so many cities. In most cities, instead of paying for itself, a convention center will require a never-ending stream of operating subsidies from taxpayers.

One of the most explosive contemporary controversies in the field of local economic development revolves around the use of eminent domain powers, the ability of the government to take private land for public use, paying the owners fair compensation (Article 17, "Eminent Domain Revisited"). The power of eminent domain is actually mentioned in the United States Constitution, where the Fifth Amendment permits "private property [to] be taken for public use," but only if the government pays the owners "just compensation."

But what constitutes a public use sufficient to justify an eminent domain taking? Most Americans have no objection when the government takes a private parcel of land, compensating the owner, in order to construct a new publicly owned road, bridge, airport, or a university campus. But can a local government seize the property of one private owner in order to give it to a new private owner who intends to build an upscale housing project, shopping center, or other structure that promises to bring new jobs and tax revenues to an ailing city?

New London, Connecticut, used its eminent domain powers to assemble the land for a project that included new offices, residences, shopping malls, and a resort hotel. But a few holdout property owners sued, and the controversy worked its way up to the U.S. Supreme Court. In its *Kelo* decision, the Court ruled on behalf of the local government, that New London did indeed have the right to take private property for economic development. For a city that was suffering extensive economic ills, actions intended to create jobs did constitute a public purpose that justified an eminent domain taking.

But the Court did not give its whole-hearted endorsement to such property takings. In its *Kelo* decision, the Court also observed that, as cities are not mentioned in the U.S. Constitution but are strictly speaking the administrative creations of subunits of the state, each state may limit the powers—including the eminent domain powers—that it gives to local governments. As the public outcry over eminent domain continued (fueled, in part, by conservative talk-radio hosts who exaggerated the threat to individual homeowners and church property), state after state enacted new restrictions that narrowed local eminent domain authority. The new laws give greater protection to individual property rights but at the price of making it more difficult for local governments to undertake actions that will commence a community's economic rebirth.

In an age of capital mobility, economists have come to recognize that competition is not so much city versus city but region versus region. Corporate leaders look at an entire region, not at an individual community, in determining whether or not a specific location has the access to resources, markets, talented labor, and the modern infrastructure that a firm requires. As business executives examine the economic potential of an entire region, communities in a region that collaborate to meet various needs of a business stand the best chances of being chosen as the site for an important new development.

Robert Lang and Christina Nicholas observe that the real border of a metropolitan region extend beyond the borders of any single community and even beyond the borders of a metropolitan area as they have been conventionally and narrowly defined (Article 18, "From Metropolitans to Megapolitans"). The commuting shed that defines the talent pool of a megapolitan region, extends beyond the borders of an individual metropolitan area. Clusters of cities in a region and even households in portions of seemingly remote exurban areas are now linked with one another via modern highways and Web-based telecommunications and transportation systems.

Lang and Nicholas argue for the investment in high-speed rail (HSR) to tie communities in an economic region even more closely together. High-speed trains can help make all of the cities in a region more attractive to major firms, enabling managers and researchers living across the region to meet more frequently and to visit facilities throughout the region as needed. Japan, France, China, and Spain are among the countries that have invested in "bullet trains" to tie their cities together, opening sites in previous hard-to-reach communities to new development. Lang and Nicholas argue that the United States needs to make a similar investment in high-speed rail or else will find that its communities will lose businesses to more economically integrated regions overseas.

Critics of high-speed rail, however, argue that HSR in the United States is not likely to work all that well, that few Americans will leave the comforts of the automobile for the train. HSR systems are expensive to build and will require steep taxpayer subsidies to operate. The initial California HSR line, as proposed, does not extend into the downtowns of either Los Angeles or San Francisco. The first phase of construction will stretch only from Bakersfield to Modesto, with future terminuses planned only to reach the far outskirts of San Francisco and L.A. Such truncated HSR routes represent a compromise by the system's designers who sought to reduce the project's costs and to lessen the opposition of suburban homeowners who feared the disruption to their lives that would accompany HSR routes that cut through densely populated suburban areas on their way to the downtowns of the state's two major cities (Article 19, "What California Can Learn from Spain's High-Speed Rail").

Stop the Subsidy-Sucking Sports Stadiums

NEIL DEMAUSE

On a busy streetcorner in downtown Brooklyn, the steel girders are starting to rise. After a decade of protests by residents (including local celebrities like Steve Buscemi, Jennifer Egan and Jonathan Lethem) and innumerable lawsuits, developer Bruce Ratner's vision of a new arena to bring the New Jersey Nets basketball team to Brooklyn—with the aid of about $500 million in city and state subsidies—is taking root, with a scheduled opening in September 2012.

Yet Atlantic Yards, as Ratner has dubbed his twenty-two-acre development project on the edge of the bustling neighborhood of Prospect Heights, won't look much like the image he first unveiled in 2003. The "Miss Brooklyn" office tower, which was supposed to bring jobs to the community, is gone, a victim of the virtual collapse of New York's commercial real estate market. Meanwhile, the condo towers that were supposed to provide more than 2,250 units of affordable housing are unlikely to be built anytime soon, if at all. (The latest plan involves a "modular" building, akin to stacking shipping containers thirty-four stories high.) The Nets, meanwhile, are spending two seasons playing in Newark's Prudential Center, another heavily subsidized building ($200 million fronted by taxpayers) that was supposed to revitalize its surrounding neighborhood but that still rests among the same discount stores and fast-food joints that lined Market Street before the arena opened in 2007.

It's a story that could have been told in almost any American city over the past two decades. Owners of teams in the "big four" sports leagues—the NFL, MLB, NBA and NHL—have reaped nearly $20 billion in taxpayer subsidies for new homes since 1990. And for just as long, fans, urban planners and economists have argued that building facilities for private sports teams is a massive waste of public money. As University of Chicago economist Allen Sanderson memorably put it, "If you want to inject money into the local economy, it would be better to drop it from a helicopter than invest it in a new ballpark."

Studies demonstrating pro sports stadiums' slight economic impact go back to 1984, the year Lake Forest College economist Robert Baade examined thirty cities that had recently constructed new facilities. His finding: in twenty-seven of them, there had been no measurable economic impact; in the other three, economic activity appeared to have decreased. Dozens of economists have replicated Baade's findings, and revealed similar results for what the sports industry calls "mega-events": Olympics, Super Bowls, NCAA tournaments and the like. (In one study of six Super Bowls, University of South Florida economist Phil Porter found "no measurable impact on spending," which he attributed to the "crowding out" effect of non-football tourists steering clear of town during game week.)

Meanwhile, numerous cities are littered with "downtown catalysts" that have failed to catalyze, from the St. Louis "Ballpark Village," which was left a muddy vacant lot for years after the neighboring ballpark opened, to the Newark hockey arena sited in the midst of a wasteland of half-shuttered stores.

"Public subsidies for stadiums are a great deal for team owners, league executives, developers, bond attorneys, construction firms, politicians and everyone in the stadium food chain, but a really terrible deal for everyone else," concludes Frank Rashid, a lifelong Detroit Tigers fan and college English professor. Rashid co-founded the Tiger Stadium Fan Club in 1987, and for the next twelve years he fought an unsuccessful battle against Michigan's plans to spend $145 million in public funds to replace that historic ballpark. "The case is so clear against this being a top priority for cities to be doing with their resources, I would have thought that wisdom would have prevailed by now."

Yet the amount of public money being spent on sports facilities continues to rise. According to Harvard urban planner Judith Grant Long, cities, states and counties spent a record $6.5 billion on stadiums and arenas in the 1990s, then shattered that mark the following decade with an additional $10.1 billion—a 31 percent increase after accounting for inflation. And that's not counting hidden subsidies like lease breaks, property tax exemptions and the use of tax-exempt government bonds, which Long estimates have added at least another 10 percent to the public's tab.

Why do new sports facilities have such a hold on local elected officials? The simplest explanation is fear: because team owners can choose new cities but cities can't choose new teams—thanks to the leagues' government-sanctioned monopolies over franchise placement—mayors feel they must offer owners anything they want. "Politicians continue to believe that it would be political disaster to lose a team on their watch," Baade says.

Actually losing a team, though, is extremely rare. Most team owners prefer to keep plugging for new stadiums in their hometowns even after their bluff has been called. Florida Marlins president David Samson first declared in 2004 that a new stadium bill "has to happen in the next week. And if not, we'll move on." He repeated similar threats for four years, until the city of Miami and Miami-Dade County finally agreed to kick in more than $478 million for a new stadium with a retractable roof.

Similarly, after successfully using relocation threats to get the city of Pittsburgh to help fund a new hockey arena, Penguins owner and NHL legend Mario Lemieux admitted, "Our goal was to remain here in Pittsburgh all the way. Those trips to Kansas City and Vegas and other cities was just to go, and have a nice dinner and come back. . . . That was just a way for us to put more pressure, and we knew it would work at the end of the day." (It's also worth noting that even in those few cities where teams have moved, no local elected official has yet been voted out of office as a result. A Wisconsin state senator who cast the deciding vote for a new Brewers stadium in 1995 did, however, become his state's first legislator to be recalled by voters.)

There are other theories that explain local officials' enduring love for sports facilities. The "edifice complex" predisposes them to build big, shiny structures—which can display a plaque bearing your name more easily than, say, reduced kindergarten class sizes. Then there are the perks that accrue to those who befriend team owners, like getting to throw the first pitch or entertain donors in your own luxury box.

For politicians eager to embrace sports deals, it's easy to find consulting firms willing to produce glowing "economic impact studies"—even though sports economists nearly unanimously dismiss them as hogwash. For example: Economic Research Associates told the city of Arlington, Texas, that spending $325 million on a new stadium for billionaire oil baron Jerry Jones's Dallas Cowboys would generate $238 million a year in economic activity. Critics immediately pointed out that this merely totaled up all spending that would take place in and around the stadium. Hidden deep in the report was the more meaningful estimate that Arlington would see just $1.8 million a year in new tax revenues while spending $20 million a year on stadium subsidies.

Jeanette Mott Oxford, who was an antisubsidy activist before being elected a Missouri state representative, says it's easy for her colleagues to be distracted with flashy claims. "Unfortunately, it doesn't appear that elected officials are much into evidence-based decision-making," she explains. "Folks believe the threat that jobs will be lost, that somehow the team will move. Then there's the civic pride element around the status of having a team. I think that too often, those motivate people no matter what the evidence says."

Outright manipulation also plays a role. As Kevin Delaney and Rick Eckstein discovered while researching their book *Public Dollars, Private Stadiums,* cities were far more likely to approve subsidy deals if they had strong "growth coalitions" of local political and business leaders spearheading campaigns on the owners' behalf. Explains Delaney, "That can then keep the team owner more in the background, so they're not getting so smacked with the idea that this is some kind of corporate welfare."

Business leaders have also been known to donate to local political campaigns, of course. Yet even stadium critics in local government say that the sway provided by corporate pressure is not simply a matter of buying votes. For my book *Field of Schemes,* I asked Minnesota State Senator John Marty about how the Twins ownership had persuaded the state legislature to approve about $387 million in public stadium funds after more than ten years of repeated rejections. "One of the lobbying efforts that's very effective is, 'The only way this issue will ever go away is if we pass it,' " explained Marty. But more than that, he noted, the ubiquitous presence of lobbyists helped legislators dismiss polls that consistently showed two-thirds of Minnesotans opposed stadium subsidies. "Because of lobbying, most legislators don't believe that: 'This may be true statewide, but not in my district.' " The main impact of the lobbying, insisted Marty, was less to change minds than to provide political cover. "It warps our perspective of what's going on in the world," he said.

Even where elected officials have gotten smarter about rejecting subsidies, the sports industry is increasingly outmaneuvering them. Twenty years ago, most sports subsidies came in the form of straight cash giveaways for construction costs. Today, they are more likely to arrive via tax breaks, free land, government-subsidized tax-free loans, or discounts to offset operating and maintenance costs. When Long looked at these hidden subsidies, she found that they added an average of 40 percent to sports facilities' public sticker price. The most notable examples are the new stadiums for the Yankees and Mets, which opened in New York City in 2009. The team owners promised to pay all $1.7 billion in construction costs—but it was later revealed that they were collecting a combined $1.8 billion in lease and tax breaks against the outlays.

Jim Nagourney, who spent three decades negotiating stadium deals on behalf of government agencies and team owners, describes how he helped snooker city officials as a consultant to the Los Angeles Rams, who were then negotiating a move to a new stadium in St. Louis. "We had a whiteboard, and we're putting stuff down" to demand in a stadium lease, he recalls. "I said, 'Guys, some of this is crazy.' And John Shaw, who was president of the Rams at the time—brilliant, brilliant guy—said, 'They can always say no. Let's ask for it.' " The result, which Nagourney calls "probably the most scandalous deal in the country," included a clause requiring the new stadium to remain "state-of-the-art," or else the team could break its lease and leave. "The city was poorly represented—the city is always poorly represented. . . . We put in all of these ridiculous things, and the city didn't have the sense to say no to any of them."

The reason this dynamic recurs is simple, Nagourney says: cities rely on in-house legal teams to negotiate stadium deals. "A city attorney is not going to know where the money really is. They're not going to understand advertising, they're not going to understand concessions—just a whole range of issues that the team officials intimately understand. They know where the dollars are, and the municipal attorneys do not."

Despite recession-strapped state budgets and the fact that most teams occupy homes that are less than twenty years old, there appears to be no end in sight to the stadium-subsidy game. Teams that have recently received new stadiums have begun to go around to the back of the line for still newer ones. Latest on the list are the Atlanta Falcons (housed in the Georgia Dome, built in 1992 for $214 million in state money) and the St. Louis Rams (in the Edward Jones Dome, opened in 1995 for $280 million). The Rams are threatening to use Shaw's "state-of-the-art" clause to move if they don't get their way.

For Baade, the only answer is for local elected officials to start standing up and saying no to all demands for sports subsidies. "I think cities need to band together and say, look, we've got some countervailing power, we're simply not going to compete with one another for a professional sports presence." (A bill briefly proposed by US Representative David Minge in the late 1990s would have forced localities to end the "economic war among the states," as a Minneapolis Federal Reserve vice president called it, by slapping an excise tax on any subsidies designed to benefit individual corporations; the legislation died without a whimper.) "If they do that, then pro sports leagues that hold the ultimate negotiating card—'We're going to leave if you don't give us what we want'—will have no place to go."

But, he admits, "I think that's a long way off."

Critical Thinking

1. Local political and business leaders often argue for public subsidies for a new sports stadium to the city or regional economy. Yet, studies by economists reveal that public subsidies for sports stadiums do not tend to bring impressive economic benefits. What factors, according to the economists, diminish the economic impact of a new sports arena?

2. Are the threats of franchise owners to relocate always credible?

3. Why do local officials' vote for subsidies for new sports arenas continue to rise, despite studies that indicate that such subsidies are not a good use of taxpayer money?

4. What is a local "growth coalition"? Who makes up the local growth coalition? How does the existence of a local growth coalition explain the willingness of local and state governments to continue to provide generous subsidies for sports stadiums?

NEIL DEMAUSE, a journalist based in Brooklyn, New York, is a contributing editor to *City Limits,* a senior editor for *Baseball Prospectus* and the co-author, with Joanna Cagan, of *Field of Schemes.*

"A Lot of Hooey"

Heywood Sanders on Convention Center Economics

Neil deMause

Heywood Sanders of the University of Texas–San Antonio is undoubtedly the best-known (and best informed) independent critic of publicly financed convention centers, a multi-billion-dollar business that is starting to rival sports stadiums in its ubiquity and cost to taxpayers. In late July 2004, Neil deMause spoke with Sanders about the convention-center game for fieldofschemes.com; an edited transcript follows.

It seems that from an economic development standpoint, convention centers should be a better deal than other development, because it's all fresh blood, right?

That's what always intrigued me about it. The argument is that, compared to a stadium or arena that would simply be moving around existing dollars, the logic of the convention center is that it's bringing in people from out of town. So it's effectively importing new dollars. Compared to other big economic investments, that should be a big plus.

That's the theory, at least. And to the extent that it does that in practice, it should be a boon to the community. It just doesn't happen.

Have there been a lot of studies of economic impact of convention centers?

There are comparable to the stadium side, which you've seen and talked about in *Field of Schemes*, and which *Public Dollars, Private Stadiums* talks about. Almost every center and/or expansion comes with a consultant feasibility study that says so many new people will come, and those people will stay multiple days in local hotels, and will spend hundreds of dollars every one of those days, and will yield ultimately hundreds of thousands in new direct spending multiplied by some inappropriate multiplier, generating massive economic impact numbers. I have an office and a house filled with such studies.

I've tried to look at it in the terms that the impact studies have, and that is: If you build it, do they come, in what volume, for how long? And how has that evolved over time? Because we're looking at a situation that is subject to a whole series of larger cyclical and systemic market changes over time. When [New York's] Javits [Convention Center] was first proposed in the early '80s and ultimately built, the situation changed as the national economy expanded and evolved during the '90s, and today its situation is remarkably different.

Among other things, we've seen a massive increase in the last ten or 15 years in the availability of convention center exhibit space. In the period since Javits opened, there are new centers in Washington, in Boston—which just opened in June—in Philadelphia. There is a new center that will open up in 2005 in downtown Hartford. There is a center that opened after Javits in Providence. The state of New York has Buffalo sitting on a host of studies for a new convention center, Albany doing likewise, with the state legislature having just approved the creation of a convention center authority in Albany. We have folks in Syracuse looking at the development of a new headquarters hotel to serve their convention center, and the possibility of an expansion of their center. We have Pittsburgh just having opened their center about a year and a half ago. And that's just in the region!

This amounts to about a 50% increase in space—and lots more space coming on line. Another half million square feet in Chicago, another half million in New Orleans.

So while the logic of the convention center is that it's bringing people from out of town, you have to flip that logic on its head. Because to some extent the stadium's market is guaranteed: Local as it is, some number of people will go to a game—even to a Jets game. But in a market where dozens and dozens of cities are building new or expanded convention centers, the likelihood of any one city, including New York, substantially gaining market share . . .

Is there any evidence, either in terms of broad studies or specific anecdotal evidence, of how different centers have done when they expanded?

Sure. They either don't gain business or they lose it.

Let me give a tiny bit of background. The newest fillip of this is the contention by the standard industry consultants that a large headquarters hotel is essential to the convention center business. That is, in fact, part of the argument with the Javits.

In an article *Government Finance Review* published in June, I looked into how many of those hotels these days are publicly owned. What I call "hotel socialism" is alive and well and spreading, and cities around the country are literally getting into the hotel business in situations where private capital can't or won't take on the risk.

The idea being that a hotel is necessary in order to book the convention space?

That's right. So this article looks at four of these cases, to see how that actually works: Once you have the hotel, what happens, both to the hotel and to the convention center? In perhaps the most intriguing case, the city of St. Louis largely bankrolled, in part using a $98 million federal empowerment zone bond, with some private equity investment, a new 1081-room Marriott Renaissance Hotel. It opened in 2003. It was supposed to do 62% occupancy; it has done under 50%. It has run in the red since it opened. It has only made its payments on that $98 million bond by going into credit reserves. Moody's downgraded the bond in September from the bottom investment grade to a speculative grade. They have subsequently put it on their watch list, because it looks like it's going even further under, and the thing is burning money. *[Editor's note: Moody's further downgraded the bonds last month, adding: "Unless the local convention business improves significantly, we expect continued credit deterioration absent third-party financial support of the hotel."]*

It was built with the argument that St. Louis had, circa '98 or '99, 33 major convention events a year. The CDB director argued that with the hotel, they'd get 50. A spokesman for the hotel developer argued that they'd get 56. So what did they do last year? *Twenty-four.*

We are simply looking at a market that, by all accounts, is enormously overbuilt. Cities around the country are discounting convention center rates, and in a number of cases, literally giving away the space for free.

That was the other thing I was going to ask you about. Obviously it's not just a question of how many conventions you hold, but whether or not they pay full rate.

Well, increasingly nobody pays full rate. I'm finishing up a piece for Brookings looking at precisely this phenomenon, and tracing the recent performance of 15 or 20 major centers around the country. What folks have not much noticed buried in the Price Waterhouse Coopers feasibility study is that Javits has seen a significant decrease in its business, from about 1.4 million annual attendance to 1 million.

I'm sure that they would argue that that's because it's too small to book the larger conventions.

They'll never get larger conventions. Even the convention centers that have expanded—Las Vegas, for example, expanded its public convention center, adding a million square feet to a million-square-foot center. So with double the space, as of January 2002, what happened to the attendance at the Las Vegas Convention Center in 2002? It went down. And what happened in 2003? It went down again.

So this is the question everyone always asks me about stadiums, but: If it's such a terrible deal, why is everyone rushing to do this?

Because this has nothing to do with the ostensible public argument or economic discourse about job creation and importing spending, and everything to do with the politics of land development. A fact that is, in the case of Javits, all the more obvious, for the enormous impact on adjacent private development that Javits has had in the years since it's been opened—and that is to say, essentially, nothing. You can't get a hotel room nearby. You can barely get anything to eat nearby. If all of these people are coming, with all of this money to spend, why have they not generated much new private development?

The answer in the case of Javits is they're really not coming, and they're really not spending. In fact, the Javits center is notable because it has about the lowest yield of hotel room nights to attendance of any center in the country. The argument typically goes that all of the attendees are coming from some distant place, staying lots of nights at hotel rooms, and leaving lots of cash behind. But a great many of the events that happen at convention centers, particularly in the case of Javits, are trade show events, not professional meetings, in which you come in, do a turn or two around the exhibit at the center, and leave. In that case, particularly given Manhattan's hotel rates, it's easy to get into Javits, spend a day or two, and go.

At the same time, many of the events at Javits attract folks who are already in the metropolitan area. Those folks might invest in subway fare, or take a PATH train across the Hudson. But what they're not doing is spending lots of money staying over.

So do you have a sense of why this has such political support?

These things have enormous political support in lots of places. If you go online and rummage a little bit, you're going to get some numbers on how the new Boston center is doing. They were supposed to do over 300,000 attendees this year; they'll actually do something on the order of 50,000. Four events this year. They now have about 50 booked through 2010, of which half are events that were already in Boston.

That's important to understand: If you have a bigger center, you give George Little and Reed Exhibitions and the other folks in the business more space to sell. It's great for them. But you don't necessarily draw more people. The assumption, which I take apart in some detail in the piece I'm doing for Brookings, that the business is constantly expanding so you need to keep up, is a lot of hooey. It stopped expanding a while ago, and it's not clear there's anything to keep up with.

So how do the consultants justify projecting huge growth?

It depends on which consultant, and which city, and what they're arguing. I just had a conversation with one of my former students who's now a news reporter here in San Antonio, which is talking about substantial public funding for a 1000-room headquarters hotel. And the consultant turned in a report on how San Antonio lacks a major headquarters hotel. Now, there's a 1001-room Marriott directly across the street. And they termed that not a "headquarters hotel" but a "primary hotel." It turns out, however, that in two previous studies, one in Denver, one in Fort Worth, by the same consulting firm, in a table constructed in exactly the same way, that hotel is listed as a: headquarters hotel!

Have you seen anywhere that a city has put money into a convention center, and it's actually been money well spent?

There are two places that have historically done well in expanding their convention business: that's Las Vegas and Orlando. And historically, they have managed to grow their business with great regularity. New Orleans for a long time in the 1990s seemed to be successful. Anaheim and San Diego may, but because of a lack of available information that I've been able to get my hands on, it's not entirely clear.

But there's something in common certainly about the first two of them, and to some extent, about the other three, that's worth noting.

You also did say that Las Vegas just doubled their space, though—

And there I would argue that in fact the historical performance clearly is no real guide to the current market environment.

So would you say that we've really tapped out the need for convention center space? Is there any need for anybody to build anything, or is there enough room for everybody to rattle around at this point?

Let me put it this way. If we're talking about large centers seeing attendance declines on the order of 40 or 50% or more, the question becomes: Even if the economy has turned around, even if people do start traveling more regularly, even if the convention and trade show business has not seen substantial erosion by the changes in various economic sectors, changes in the popular desire to travel, changes in technology and communication, it's going to take a while of double-digit growth to get those cities back to where they were four or five years ago. And once they're back there, assuming they get there, there are two other things. First, between now and then, we know there's more space coming on the market. That's in the works—the bonds have been sold, that steelwork is up.

Secondly, even if you get back to where you were, you still have to compete with everybody else who has space. And again, centers are engaged in a price war. The internet brings every day news of a center that's offering its space for free. If a place like Dallas is offering rebates on hotel rooms, where does that leave the most expensive destination in the continental U.S.?

Critical Thinking

1. City after city has built or modernized convention centers, yet few cities find that such centers are profitable. Why is it that convention centers are so seldom self-sustainable—that so few actually make money?
2. Who are the members of a city's "growth coalition"? Why do the members of a growth coalition support continued investment in new convention centers?
3. What role do consultant studies play in justifying the construction of new convention centers? Why do convention centers, after they are built, seldom generate the economic impact that the expert studies predicted would occur?

Eminent Domain Revisited

MARK BERKEY-GERARD

Joy Chatel fears she will lose the house that has been her life for decades.

The four-story brick building on Duffield Street in Brooklyn serves as her home, a classroom where she home schools her seven grandchildren, and a business where she operates a hair salon.

Under the city's plan to rezone and develop downtown Brooklyn, approximately 130 residences and 100 businesses, including Chatel's, would be condemned. The city says the plan to replace them is a key element in a larger strategy to retain jobs that are leaving for New Jersey and elsewhere—and that it will ultimately benefit the residents of Brooklyn and the entire city.

Chatel argues there is more at stake than her private property. She and several other building owners in the area say that their houses are historic treasures where slaves found sanctuary as part of the "underground railroad," a claim the city disputes.

"Oral history is all we have to prove there was an underground railroad," she told the Daily News. "It's not like they have a neon sign outside."

In New York City, the government's power to take over private property—eminent domain—is a factor in so many pending development projects that the one involving Joy Chatel's home is actually among the least-known current battles.

In Prospect Heights, Brooklyn, the real estate developer Forest City Ratner Companies has a proposal to take over private homes and businesses and replace them with the Atlantic Yards project, a basketball arena, thousands of condos, and 16 towers.

In upper Manhattan, Columbia University is considering eminent domain as an option in its efforts to expand its campus.

And in Willets Point, Queens, the city is looking to replace a 13-block area that is home to scrap metal yards and auto shops with a waterfront shopping district to complement a new stadium for the New York Mets.

New York City's landscape has been remade over and over again, and in the process hundreds of thousands of New Yorkers have lost their private property so that the government can build roads, bridges, public housing, parks, playgrounds, and hospitals.

The concept of eminent domain—and debate surrounding the practice—dates back to the founding of the nation.

"Eminent domain means the power of the crown over his or her domain," said Dwight Merriam, author of the book *Eminent Domain Use and Abuse.* "The theory is that the government really owns all of the property and can take it back whenever it wants."

The nation's founders tried to address the issue in the Fifth Amendment to the U.S. Constitution, which guarantees citizens "just compensation" when private property is taken for "public use."

But what exactly is a "public use"?

Until the case of *Berman vs. Parker* in 1954, the Supreme Court ruled that it was for such clearly public physical structures as bridges, highways, schools, and train tracks.

Today, in an era when government and private developers often work closely with one another, the term "public use" is used for sports stadiums, corporate headquarters, office buildings, museums, and even shopping malls.

New York's Eminent Domain Powers

In New York State, eminent domain can be used to remove areas of "blight"—which means deteriorating, vacant, or obsolete buildings or even oddly shaped parcels of land. Historically, the courts and lawmakers have used the term "blight" rather liberally.

For 40 years, "master builder" Robert Moses, made use of the power to level entire neighborhoods for projects like the West Side highway, Lincoln Center, and the Triborough Bridge.

An entire downtown neighborhood, including a string of small electronics shops known as "Radio Row," was demolished to make way for the World Trade Center.

In the 1980s, the city and state condemned property in Times Square to rid the area of sex shops and other abandoned buildings. Currently, on 43rd Street, the New York Times is building a new headquarters on a property obtained through eminent domain.

In 2001, the state took over several buildings on Wall Street in order to make way for an expansion of the New York Stock Exchange, an idea which never became a reality.

And recently in Harlem, a dozen businesses were demolished to make way for a Home Depot.

The *Kelo vs. New London* Case

The issue of eminent domain gained a new level of attention last summer when the United States Supreme Court ruled that the government could use eminent domain to take away private property and then sell it to a private developer.

In the case, known as *Kelo vs. New London,* the court ruled in a 5 to 4 vote that the city of New London, Connecticut, could take the property of 15 homeowners for the purpose of economic development. The city plans to transfer the property to developers who will build office space, a hotel, housing, and a riverfront esplanade.

The Kelo case has sparked new debate among legal and planning experts.

Some say that while eminent domain is appropriate to build schools or hospitals, it should not benefit private developers, because it can too easily abused.

"We never hear that eminent domain should be used to take a Hyatt and build mixed-income housing," said Susan Fainstein, a professor of urban studies at Columbia University. "It is always about taking property away from poor people and give it to someone who is much better off."

Others say that if a project produces tax revenue and jobs, economic development can be considered legitimate "public purpose."

"We shouldn't think that these projects are 'bad' just because they are the work of private developers," said Jerilyn Perine, who served as housing commissioner under Mayor Michael Bloomberg.

Backlash against Eminent Domain

Concern over the *Kelo* case has also inspired a flurry of legislation at the national and local level.

In Congress, a bill, dubbed the "Private Property Rights Protection Act of 2005, has already passed the House and is awaiting a vote in the Senate. It would withhold federal aid from states that Congress believes abuse eminent domain.

In New York, there are several bills being considered in Albany, including a package of legislation drafted by Assembly member Richard Brodsky which would slow down local eminent domain proceedings, create an ombudsman to oversee the use of the law, and require 150 percent of market value be paid for private property that the government takes over. This week, the New York City Council will hold hearings on the subject.

And recently opponents of eminent domain claimed victory when the U.S. Court of Appeals ruled that the city of Port Chester, New York, failed to properly alert a businessman of his right to challenge an eminent domain decision before the government seized his four buildings to make way for a convenience store. The court's decision, some said, was a warning to local governments who may be tempted to take private property without properly notifying the people who own it.

Three Current Eminent Domain Projects in New York City

While the experts debate how eminent domain should be used, residents and businesses in neighborhoods where it is being considered struggle to preserve the future of their communities.

Atlantic Yards and Prospect Heights, Brooklyn

In December 2003, developer Bruce Ratner, along with Mayor Michael Bloomberg and Governor George Pataki, unveiled plans for a massive project in downtown Brooklyn, known as the "Atlantic Yards." The latest version of the plan would build a Frank Gehry designed basketball arena for the New Jersey Nets and 16 skyscrapers with office space and 7,300 apartments.

In order to acquire the 22 acres of land needed for the project, New York's Empire State Development Corporation is planning to use the government's power of eminent domain to condemn two parcels of land.

Opponents of eminent domain say that the state would take over approximately 53 properties. Local groups, which oppose the plan, say more than 330 residents, 33 businesses with 235 employees, and a 400 person homeless shelter will be displaced by the project.

And Daniel Goldstein, who works for the group Develop Don't Destroy and lives in the area of the proposed development, warns that the definition of "blight" could apply to any neighborhood in the city.

"On any six square block in this city you will find a property that might be 'dilapidated' or 'structurally unsound' or 'vacant,' and all throughout the city nearly every property could be considered 'economically underutilized,'" said Goldstein.

However some in the area, including many local officials, have praised the development, in particular for the "community benefits agreement" with neighborhood representatives that promises that 50 percent of the 4,500 rental apartments will go to low and middle-income residents, with 10 percent of these set aside for seniors. The project also sets aside 35 percent of the jobs for minority workers and another 10 percent for women.

But even some supporters of the project, like Assembly member Roger Green, question the use of eminent domain.

"Under the definition of blight, as related to poverty or environmental degradation, this definition is not related to Prospect Heights," Green said at recent state hearing.

Columbia University Expansion, Manhattanville

Last summer, Anne Whitman, who runs a moving company out of her building on Broadway and 129th Street, received a letter from Columbia University informing her that the institution planned to build a biotech research center where her business stands.

Columbia offered to help Whitman find a single-floor building outside of Manhattan; she rejected the offer.

"Since then," Whitman said, "it has been all out war."

Columbia University plans to spend $5 billion over the next 25 years to build a new campus in upper Manhattan. The 18-acre complex would stretch from West 125th Street to West 133rd Street between 12th Avenue and Broadway and would house biotech research facilities, a building for its art school, student and faculty housing, and administrative buildings.

The university says the campus will create 14,500 permanent jobs in the area.

Columbia hopes to convince area residents and businesses that there is a mutually acceptable resolution. Failing that, it has suggested that the state could use eminent domain to transfer control of these properties.

However, local businesses, community board members, and students at Columbia University oppose the plan and criticize its approach to the negotiations with the community.

For some of the area's landowners, the talk of eminent domain has poisoned negotiations.

"They say 'deal with us now or deal with the state later,'" said Whitman, who also sits on Community Board Nine. "It's like having a gun to your head."

Willets Point, Queens

For decades, city planners have had their eye on Willets Point, a 13-block area on a peninsula on the Flushing River that is home to scrap metal yards and auto shops.

In the 1960s, Robert Moses attempted to force out the local business owners to make way for the World's Fair. In the 1990s, the New York Mets wanted to build a new stadium on the land. Recently, some have proposed a new stadium for the New York Jets football team or facilities for the now-defunct 2012 Olympic bid on the grounds. All of these plans failed.

Now, the city is determined to transform the area to include an attractive waterfront shopping and residential enclave, which would complement another proposed stadium for the New York Mets.

Although the city will not discuss the details of its plans at the current time, scrap metal yard owners fear that eminent domain may be used to move them out.

"Sounds to me like they're going to pull a sneak attack," said Richard Musick, president of the Willets Point Business Association.

There is little doubt that the area—which is riddled with large potholes and abandoned cars, and even lacks plumbing in some areas—will meet the definition of "blight." And some local officials, like Councilmember John Liu expresses confidence that the owners "will be given fair compensation, and relocated, if necessary."

But the scrap metal and auto shop owners say that it will be nearly impossible to find other neighborhoods that would welcome their businesses.

Critical Thinking

1. What is eminent domain? Is it constitutional or is it against the U.S. Constitution? What exactly does the U.S. Constitution say about eminent domain?
2. How is the present-day controversy over eminent domain really a controversy over what constitutes "public use"? How do local governments today use eminent domain powers for more than the taking of property necessary to build a road or a university campus?
3. What did the Supreme Court in its *Kelo* decision rule about the local use of eminent domain by local governments for economic development—is it allowable or not?
4. New York has been more moderate than other states in its reaction to the *Kelo* decision. How have the states generally responded in the wake of the Court's *Kelo* ruling?

From Metropolitans to Megapolitans

ROBERT LANG AND CHRISTINA NICHOLAS

In a space as large as France, the Netherlands and Belguim combined, America's megapolitans house more than 2.5 times as many people. In fact, they are more densely settled than Europe as a whole and, by some estimates, will house two-thirds of the U.S. population by 2040.

Yet, the United States is often referred to as the land of wide-open spaces with low population density. And, at times, the nostalgia for how America once was is used to influence and validate public policy. For instance, some policy experts firmly believe that the U.S. cannot support European-style passenger rail.

It is true the average population density in the U.S.—about 100 persons per square mile—is roughly half that of Western European countries. But the comparison is misguided. The U.S. has a significant amount of densely settled urban areas scattered throughout. While megapolitans occupy only 17 percent of the contiguous 48 states' land base, America's megapolitan clusters, as a group, form the world's third most populous country, behind China and India.

Metropolitan regions are the large areas spanning cities and counties that are connected through commuting patterns and economic exchanges. However, as these regions continue to grow, they form even more complex and extensive linkages. Megapolitans, as they are often referred to, are strings of metropolitan areas connected by shared transportation networks, labor markets and culture. The megapolitan clusters are metropolitan regions networked either by commuting, trucking, or commuter airlines and separated by less than 550 miles. Thus far, metropolitans view nearby regions as competitors rather than partners. In fact, only one metropolitan area has a regionally elected governing body: the Metro Council of Portland, Oregon, created in the 1980s. No other region has followed suit.

However, a less formal, self-organizing, voluntary form of regionalism is beginning to emerge. At times this regionalism is created by business interests, as is the case with Phoenix and Tucson. These two cities are marketed together as a collaborative region in an economic development initiative *"Arizona Sun Corridor: Open for Business."*

Other megapolitan areas exist in the public conscious. Any traveler on the Pacific Coast Highway can distinguish between Northern California and Southern California. The differences are part environment, part mood. "Southland," or the area between Santa Barbara and San Diego, exists in the public mind as a place completely separate from Northern California. Or, as the Dallas-Fort Worth area highlights, two cities can have a mutual distaste for one another that evolves into acceptance and celebration of metropolitan integration. This transformation was prompted by the federal aid formula which placed a single airport between them.

A sense of shared identity, whether occurring formally or organically, does not guarantee good planning results, but it does enable public acceptance of the idea that an extensive area crossing jurisdictional boundaries can form one distinct region. There are many benefits to this.

Metropolitan partnerships can help secure a region's vitality in the global economy. Phoenix and Tucson, for instance, can pool their collective assets and markets to produce a global gateway known as the Sun Corridor. Phoenix is a large-scale region with an international airport and global links. Tucson received the state's original land grant university, and is home to the University of Arizona, which has strong research capacity in space science and optics and contains the main branch of Arizona's medical school. Roughly speaking, Phoenix has the global access and Tucson has the technology. Local elected officials and business leaders in Orlando and Tampa are following suit to create the Florida Corridor—its goal to combine Orlando's tourist economy and global connectivity with Tampa's major port and industries tied to logistics.

Cooperation among megapolitans such as Seattle-Portland or Chicago-Detroit-Cleveland-Pittsburgh becomes increasingly important as the federal government must ensure that taxpayer money spent on infrastructure improvements and resource-land management is not wasted. Our past proves a lack of planning at a broad level can produce inefficient outcomes, as is the case with several transportation infrastructure projects. Failure to coordinate at a broad level has also led to infighting among cities and states. Case in point is Atlanta's ongoing feud with Alabama and Florida over water rights.

While our cities and counties increasingly get on board with regional collaboration, this process requires a shift in the way we traditionally think about the many cities and counties that surround us. For instance, despite the strong objections by local officials and business leaders, Florida Gov. Rick Scott killed high speed rail between Tampa and Orlando. We can recognize his rationale was tied political discourse rather than disdain for regional collaboration. Nonetheless, his actions dampened the chances for regional integration between Tampa and Orlando and stifled their ability to compete against other megapolitans which have pooled their metropolitans' talent and resources to create a single unified region.

The sooner we recognize that the United States is evolving into a nation of densely settled economic engines and act accordingly, the better able we are to sustain long-term economic development to the mid-21st century and beyond.

Critical Thinking

1. How does the concept of a megapolitan area force us to rethink popular conceptions of where we live, of what is our local community?

2. How does a megapolitan area differ from the more commonly used concept of a metropolitan area?

3. How do Lang and Nicholas argue that a high-speed rail (HSR) system, including the proposed Tampa-Orlando HSR route, increase the economic capacity and global competitiveness of a megapolitan region?

4. Contrary to Lang and Nicholas, what criticisms can be made against public investment in HSR systems?

ROBERT E. LANG is co-author, with Arthur C. Nelson, of the new book *Megapolitan America: A New Vision for Understanding America's Metropolitan Geography* (American Planning Association, 2011). **CHRISTINA NICHOLAS** is a PhD student who works with him.

What California Can Learn from Spain's High-Speed Rail

Tim Sheehan

I t's 8 A.M. at the Puerto de Atocha train station in central Madrid. Business travelers armed with cellphones and laptops, and pleasure travelers toting cameras and carry-on bags, make their way through security to board the high-speed trains that connect Spain's capital to cities across the nation.

The sprawling station, which dates to the 1890s, serves not only the AVE, or Alta Velocidad Española, high-speed trains, but also the city's metro subway and commuter trains. It sits amid a bustling district of offices, hotels, restaurants, museums and other businesses.

This is the vision shared by backers of California's proposed, but controversial, high-speed rail system. And there are lessons—from both successes and mistakes—that California can learn from Spain's 20-year history with high-speed trains.

Top among them is just how hard it is to be self-sufficient, even when conditions seem ideal, as they have in Spain.

Despite popular and political support from the very beginning, the AVE rail system faces a tougher future in the midst of Europe's financial crisis.

Already, service between some smaller cities has been cut because too few people ride the trains. Some wonder if it is anything more than a luxury commuter service.

Among the growing fraternity of nations with high-speed trains, Spain is considered the best geographic and cultural analogy to California and its train plans. The long-distance AVE trains and their regional cousins Avant and Alvia, which share the high-speed tracks, connect major urban centers but pass through smaller cities and stretches of rural farmland, just like what is planned for California.

They've gotten people out of their cars and off airplanes, sliced travel times and attracted millions of riders a year—just what California rail boosters hope will happen here.

Since the late 1980s, Spain has spent about $60 billion to build and equip its high-speed network.

President Barack Obama touted Spain's system as a model for American high-speed rail plans when he announced billions of dollars in federal investments in April 2009.

And Transportation Secretary Ray LaHood voiced admiration for the Spanish network when he visited Spain last summer.

"We know that you are the experts. We know that you have developed a state-of-the-art system here," he said. "It's not lost on anyone that when President Obama proposed this high-speed rail plan, he specifically called out Spain as an example for America to emulate."

Spain's system, however, was launched in conditions *much different from what California is experiencing today.* Political unity, a thriving economy and the spotlight of international events—a world exposition in Seville and the Olympic Games in Barcelona—all provided an impetus for Spain to embark on its high-speed journey.

About the only major point of contention was where the first line from Madrid should go (Seville won over Barcelona), not whether it should happen at all.

While Spain continues to build and expand its system through both good and bad economic times, cost is a key concern in cash-strapped California. Planners are wrestling with a price tag that has doubled over the past two years and grappling with the thorny issue of where to get the money to build it when both state and federal budgets are under strain.

Unlike in California, Spain's high-speed rail effort has not been a public or political punching bag. It's rapidly expanded to become Europe's most extensive high-speed network—and third only to China and Japan's worldwide—while facing remarkably little of the NIMBYism, farm opposition or politics fermenting throughout California.

The people who ride the AVE trains love them. Merchants who do business near the stations in rail-connected cities such as Barcelona, Seville and Cordova say they generally believe the trains are good for their cities, good for business and good for the country. The project has been supported by both conservative- and Socialist-led governments.

But with Spain and the rest of Europe mired in a lingering economic crisis, those attitudes may slowly be changing.

Economists and engineers acknowledge that the system is well engineered, well built and state of the art and that the service is top notch, comfortable, safe and punctual.

Despite assurances from the Spanish government that the long-distance AVE trains operate without a public subsidy, academics and analysts don't believe that even the busiest high-speed route—between Madrid and Barcelona—musters enough riders to cover its operating costs, much less the billions of euros invested to build the build the infrastructure over the past 20 years.

On an overcast November morning, rain clouds hang low in the sky over the olive orchards of Castile-La Mancha, the territory of central Spain. As the 10 A.M. AVE train from Madrid to Seville races gracefully on its steel tracks, trees and structures flash past the window—the only tangible indication to passengers that they are moving at more than 180 mph.

In a car, the roughly 300-mile drive to Seville, in the southwestern region of Andalusia, would take about five to six hours. This eight-car, French-built Alstom Class 100 train can hold up to 332 passengers and cross the distance in less than 2½ hours.

Inside the passenger cars, the ride is smooth and quiet. The seats have plenty of legroom and a power outlet for electronics. Attendants give earbuds to passengers so they can listen to music or watch movies. About the only convenience lacking is Wi-Fi Internet access.

Fewer than half of the seats on this train—one of 21 daily high-speed AVE or Alvia trains to Seville—are occupied, so there is plenty of room to spread out, even in tourist class.

Tourist-class tickets on the Madrid-Seville train run between $56 and $112, depending on the departure time.

At one of four small tables in the car, a young woman from Madrid taps away at her laptop keyboard, occasionally pausing to answer her cellphone to field a call from work.

Esther San Felipe, a pharmaceutical representative, says she enjoys taking the AVE train, riding it to Seville about once a month for business.

"It's a luxury; it's so comfortable," she says.

She breaks off to answer her insistent phone. "And you can work when you're on the train," she continues after hanging up.

There are certainly cheaper ways to get around the country. A bus ticket from Madrid to Seville costs about $27, but takes between 6½ and 8 hours. Airline flights are faster to cover the distance and can be about the same price or less.

"But you have to get to the airport one or two hours early, find a place to park, go through security and then wait at the airport at the other end," San Felipe added. "For just a little bit more money, you can have something much better."

The Ridership Challenge

San Felipe is hardly alone in her enthusiasm for the high-speed trains.

The Madrid-to-Seville line became Spain's first high-speed train route when it opened in early 1992, coinciding with Seville hosting Expo 1992.

Renfe, the Spanish government-owned company that operates all passenger trains in the country—including the AVE, Avant and Alvia high-speed trains—under the umbrella of the Ministry of Public Works and Transport, reports that by the end of 1993, the first full year of high-speed service, AVE trains accounted for more than half of all passenger travel between Madrid and Seville. Automobile traffic, in the meantime, fell from 60 percent of the volume to about 34 percent.

For more than a decade, Madrid-Seville was Spain's only operating high-speed line, and ridership grew modestly, reaching about 4.8 million by 2002. New lines to Lleida, Zaragoza and Huesca opened in 2003 and to Tarragona, Valladolid and Malaga in 2006 and 2007, but they didn't drive much growth.

It wasn't until high-speed tracks opened to Barcelona, Spain's second-largest city, four years ago that ridership experienced a real growth spurt.

Total high-speed ridership on the long-distance and regional trains peaked at nearly 17 million in 2009.

Ridership has since tapered off as Spain, like the rest of Europe and much of the world, copes with economic troubles.

Spain now has nearly 1,740 miles of high-speed tracks, lines that serve as spokes with Madrid as the hub. By 2015, the nation plans to nearly double the miles of track.

Over the next decade, the Spanish government plans to spend up to $77 billion more to expand and improve its high-speed lines, said Juan Ignacio Campo Jori, director of international projects for ADIF, another government-owned company that manages and operates Spain's railway infrastructure.

But with no sign of Europe's financial crisis letting up, some say the government needs to slow its spending.

In the early years of developing high-speed trains, Spain was "in kind of a booming situation," said Andreu Ulied, director of a noted engineering and consulting firm in Barcelona. "Now the situation is completely different."

In recent years, the European Union funneled about $17 billion in grants and billions more in low-interest loans to Spain to improve its high-speed rail.

But Ulied said that will end in a couple of years, leaving Spain to bear the entire cost of its ambitious expansion plans.

Ulied and Germá Bel, a professor of political economics at the University of Barcelona, agree that none of the Spanish high-speed rail routes has enough riders to make the system financially sustainable.

"There is no question whether it can cover its costs. It cannot," Bel said. "It actually has not recovered one single euro from the infrastructure investment. The government claims they are recovering the operating costs, but the numbers are not clear."

The busiest high-speed lines in the world are capable of making money, Bel said, including between Paris and Lyon, where about 25 million people ride the French TGV trains each year, and the Japanese Shinkansen trains between Tokyo and Osaka, which draw about 130 million riders a year.

"But this is not the case with any single line in Spain," Bel said. "The most crowded operation is Madrid–Barcelona, and it has not even had 6 million people in a year."

Ulied said Spain's efforts have been based not on serious economic analysis, but on political desires to connect the rest of the nation to Madrid. "We had the money, we had the ability to do so, so we did it," he said. "The engineering was very good. The quality of the service is excellent. And everything is nice, very nice. The problem is that it is luxurious. Maybe it is too good for us."

"The question is maybe the whole thing was partially a mistake," Ulied said of lines to smaller cities with fewer riders. "We didn't need all these lines, actually."

The Newest Route

The latest high-speed line to open in Spain is the 243-mile route between Madrid and Valencia, on the Mediterranean coast. The AVE trains have sliced the travel time between the two cities from about 3½ hours by car to just more than 1½ hours by train.

Valencia's new Joaquin Sorolla train station sits near the old Estació del Nord that serves regional commuter trains and the city's subway. Just a few blocks away is the Carrer de Cristóbal Colón, the main street of a bustling shopping district of department stores, boutiques and restaurants.

Maria Jose Martin, who manages the nearby C&A clothing store, said the company typically sends people on the train for business trips because it's cheaper than flying.

"I think it's good," she said through an interpreter. "It brings Madrid and Valencia closer together and allows for more flow of people between the two cities."

And, she added, the trains are good for Valencia's business community because they bring more tourists on day trips.

But Martin acknowledged that "the ticket price is still pretty high" for families on holiday.

On a rainy morning, Jacinto Calvillo is among the passengers waiting at the station to board the train for a business trip. "I have a car for work, but I like to take the train," Calvillo said through an interpreter.

Calvillo said he believes high-speed rail has been a good investment for the nation "to bring together or connect the big cities in Spain, but not necessarily covering the smaller distances."

"The main disadvantage is that they haven't prioritized which lines are most important, so a lot of money has been spent on lines that aren't as important," he said. "But it has created greater movement of business, more connections and more commerce."

The train station in Valencia, like stations in other cities, plays host to various retail stores and restaurants that serve travelers—including the ubiquitous golden arches of McDonald's. It looks and smells like any other McDonald's—kids tugging on their parents' sleeves asking for a Happy Meal and people munching on burgers and fries.

A few hours later, aboard an afternoon train back to Madrid, a visit to the operator's cab offers a rare driver's-eye view of the high-speed ride. It's quiet in the passenger cars, but on the way to the cockpit, there is a deafening roar in the locomotive that houses the powerful electric motors.

Jose Jimenez, a 30-year train operator for Renfe, sits at the driver's console of the Spanish-built Talgo AVE Class 112 train, which can carry up to 365 passengers. Jimenez occasionally flips on the windshield wipers to clear the raindrops, giving a clear view of just how fast the train is moving.

The train's speed increases steadily as Jimenez nudges a small joystick throttle with his left thumb and forefinger: 155 mph, then 160, 165, 175. The power lines flash overhead, and the concrete ties of the railroad tracks fly under the train at a dizzying clip if you stare too long.

Now the speed is 180, 183, 184, 185. Finally, Jimenez looks over his shoulder, smiling broadly, and nods with pride as his electronic display flashes 302 kilometers per hour—187 mph.

Where to Begin?

The Talgo trains—nicknamed Pato ("Duck" in English) because of their streamlined, elongated noses—are capable of doing 205 mph, but the maximum operating speed is supposed to be 186 mph.

No doubt that technicians for both Renfe and ADIF, sitting in front of computer consoles in Madrid, knew exactly when and where Jimenez bent the speed limit. Sensors embedded along the rail line and GPS sensors aboard the trains feed a constant stream of real-time information back to the control centers.

Large screens on the walls of Renfe's control center at the Puerto de Atocha station show operators the exact location and speed of each train in the system, duplicating the information on the smaller computer monitors. Video screens also show trains as they enter and leave stations.

The Atocha center monitors more than 90 train trips daily to cities in eastern and southern Spain, said José Espada Rodelgo, manager of Renfe's operations coordination center. With that many trains coming and going, the real-time data is crucial to managing schedules and making sure the trains are running on time, he said.

Renfe managers prize customer satisfaction and on-time performance for their trains. On the Madrid–Seville route, for instance, the company promises to refund passengers their full fare if the train arrives at its destination more than five minutes late.

But at least one scheduled train could not be saved. Earlier this year, Renfe shut down its direct once-daily AVE train between Cuenca, Albacete and Toledo, bypassing Madrid. That lone train attracted only a handful of passengers a day—not nearly enough to justify keeping the service alive.

"These are small cities, so it is not possible to run a train for only 7 or 10 passengers," said Jose Domingo Carreño López, Renfe's manager of technical standards.

While they acknowledge that high-speed rail is an expensive undertaking, officials with Renfe, the train operating company, and ADIF, which manages the infrastructure and tracks, say the system has helped Spain boost its technological capacity, improve its manufacturing efficiency and export its expertise to other countries.

"Our Spanish technology has increased because of the high-speed," said Campo Jori, ADIF's international projects manager. "We started by learning from the French, the Germans and the Japanese, but now we have our own technology. Our companies are benefiting from 1992 to now because of high-speed."

Led by Renfe and ADIF, a consortium of more than a dozen Spanish technology and construction companies recently won the contract to build and operate Saudi Arabia's first high-speed train line from Medina to Mecca. "We have companies that do extensive engineering, telecom, signaling, rolling stock, construction and management," Campo Jori said.

And Spain is among the high-speed nations that hope to participate in construction of California's proposed 520-mile line between San Francisco and Los Angeles.

California officials, armed with about $3 billion in federal stimulus and transportation funds from the Obama administration and $3 billion in money from Proposition 1A—a 2008 bond measure—want to start construction this year on a 120-mile stretch from north of Fresno to Bakersfield.

Future sections would extend toward San Francisco or Los Angeles if more money becomes available. But no high-speed trains would operate on the line until it extends to the Bay Area or the Los Angeles basin.

Backers in California tout the potential environmental benefits—reduced air pollution and less freeway congestion—of getting people out of gasoline- and diesel-fueled automobiles and onto electric-powered trains.

Even the enthusiastic Spanish officials, however, are curious about the logic of starting in the sparsely populated middle of California. The environmental benefits won't be realized, they said, if the cities along the first line don't have enough people to generate ridership.

"You need to have either Los Angeles or San Francisco," said Pedro Pérez del Campo, environmental policy director for ADIF. "They should build it where it will have an impact so that people will support it."

Building the system in the first place has significant disruptive effects before any benefits can be realized, Pérez del Campo said.

"It can be a failure or a fiasco if it starts in two cities that aren't as well populated or if there isn't as much attraction," he said. "The lesson is to do it right the first time, or extending it will not be possible because the public won't be in agreement. The people here have been in agreement."

Critical Thinking

1. Can high-speed rail (HSR) systems attract sufficient ridership to make them economically viable? What are the key design factors of Spain's HSR system that help attract ridership?

2. What mistakes should California and other states avoid in their efforts to establish an HSR system?

3. What would you consider to be the essential features of a desirable HSR system? What, in your mind, would be an undesirable HSR system?

UNIT 5
Citizen Participation

Unit Selections

Learning Outcomes

After reading this unit, you should be able to:

- Recognize Jane Jacobs's contribution to cities and how her writings changed the nature of urban planning.

- Identify the characteristics that, according to Jane Jacobs, help to make good cities and good neighborhoods.

- Explain the concepts of "eyes on the street" and "social capital" and how mid-twentieth-century "slum clearance," "urban renewal," and highway construction programs destroyed these assets in many inner-city neighborhoods.

- Differentiate between participatory mechanisms that effectively empower citizens as opposed to those more limited processes that offer citizens a real opportunity to help shape the decisions that have a direct influence on their lives.

- Define a "community development corporation" (CDC).

- Explain how "partnerships" are a key part of the approach of CDCs as they seek to improve conditions in troubled inner-city communities.

- Identify the assistance that CDCs can provide as cities tackle the problems of vacant properties.

Student Website
www.mhhe.com/cls

Internet References

CommunityWealth.Org
http://community-wealth.org/strategies/panel/cdcs/articles.html
E-Governance Institute: Citizen Participation
http://andromeda.rutgers.edu/~egovinst/Website/citizenspg.htm
National Civic Review
www.ncl.org/publications/ncr
Shelterforce
www.shelterforce.org

Citizen participation is based on the democratic notion that people should have a say in the making of decisions that affect their lives. In cities, citizen participation represents an attempt to open up decision-making processes that were once largely the preserve of growth coalition interests and members of the city bureaucracy.

Over the past half century, cities have witnessed a citizen participation revolution. The roots of participatory programs lie in the 1950s and 1960s, when citizens began to confront urban renewal and highway construction programs that tore apart urban neighborhoods and displaced thousands from their homes (Article 20, "Jane Jacobs' Radical Legacy"). Public officials came to recognize the dangers inherent in top-down decision making, introducing new bottom-up processes to ensure the engagement of persons whose lives were directly affected by the decisions being made. Just like a private business, local government has come to see the virtues of responding to "customer" concerns. Computerization and the Internet are also creating new opportunities for the notifications of citizens and for e-democracy.

But citizen participation is often very difficult to bring about. Residents are often disinterested in municipal affairs or too busy to participate. Poor, inner-city residents remain skeptical of structured participatory processes, having been disappointed by one governmental program after another that promised to change their neighborhoods for the better but wound up doing very little. A city's bureaucratic officialdom may also be less than willing to listen to the perspectives of citizens who lack professional knowledge and training. Even officials who value citizen engagement will be willing, at times, to cut participatory processes short in order to put an end to delays in order to "get things done."

But citizen participation does not have to be oppositional or obstructionist in tone. One piece of good news concerning U.S. cities has been the emergence over the past decades of a new style of citizen participation, as embodied in the mushrooming numbers of community development corporations (CDCs). Community development corporations are neighborhood-based groups that seek to create partnerships that will build new units of affordable housing, neighborhood health centers, and other important facilities in low-income communities. CDCs also seek

Blend Images/Hill Street Studios/Getty Images

to run housing, job training, and after-school programs of value to the residents of poorer communities. CDCs operate via a bridge-building approach, working in collaboration with governmental officials, bankers, business leaders, and the heads of nonprofit organizations in order to piece together the finances necessary for housing rehabilitation and new construction and the operation of essential community facilities.

But in recent years partners for community projects have become increasingly difficult to find, a consequence of an underperforming economy that has led to tight municipal and nonprofit budgets. In numerous cities, CDCs also find that they must operate within the parameters of a city policy that gives new priority to tearing down excessive housing stock, not to rehabilitating or constructing new affordable dwelling units (Article 21, "Where Do We Fit in?"). Yet, CDCs can be a valuable resource in local efforts to "repurpose" vacant lands and to stabilize neighborhoods threatened by the specter of property abandonment and decline.

Jane Jacobs' Radical Legacy

Sometimes a book can change history. Books often influence ideas, but only rarely do they catalyze activism.

PETER DREIER

In the 1960s, a handful of books triggered movements for reform. These include Michael Harrington's *The Other America* (1962), which inspired the war on poverty; Rachel Carson's *Silent Spring* (1962), which helped galvanize the environmental movement; Betty Friedan's *The Feminine Mystique* (1963), the manifesto of modern feminism; Ralph Nader's *Unsafe at Any Speed* (1965), which made its author a household name and precipitated the rise of the consumer movement; and Charles Hamilton and Stokely Carmichael's *Black Power* (1967), which signaled the civil rights movement's transformation toward black separatism.

Jane Jacobs' 1961 book, *The Death and Life of Great American Cities,* belongs in this pantheon. Perhaps more than anyone else during the past half century, Jacobs changed the way we think about livable cities. Indeed, it is a mark of her impact that many people influenced by her ideas have never heard of her. Her views have become part of the conventional wisdom, if not always part of the continuing practice, of city planning.

The 1950s was the heyday of urban renewal, the federal program that sought to wipe out urban "blight" with the bulldozer. Its advocates were typically downtown businesses, developers, banks, major daily newspapers, big-city mayors and construction unions—what John Mollenkopf would later call the "growth coalition" and Harvey Molotch would label the "growth machine." Most planners and architects at the time joined the urban renewal chorus. It was, after all, their bread and butter. Moreover, they convinced themselves that big development projects would "revitalize" downtown business districts, stem the exodus of middle-class families to suburbs and improve the quality of public spaces.

Jacobs, a journalist, was self-taught. She had no college degree. This may have been liberating, because she was unencumbered by planning orthodoxy, although she carefully read and thoroughly critiqued the major thinkers in the field. Had she studied architecture or urban planning when she was college age (in the 1930s and 1940s), she would have been taught the value of top-down planning and modernist mega-projects. Instead, she learned about cities by observing and doing. In the 1950s, she wrote a series of articles in *Fortune* magazine (later

the basis for *The Death and Life of Great American Cities*) that said, essentially, cities are for people.

When Robert Moses, New York's planning czar and perhaps the most powerful unelected city official of the 20th century, proposed building a highway bisecting Jacobs' Greenwich Village neighborhood, she sprung into action, mobilizing her neighbors to challenge and confront the bulldozer bully in the name of human-scale, livable communities. She was no armchair liberal. She was fully engaged in her community and in the battle to save it. For her efforts, she was arrested and jailed. Her courageous efforts helped catalyze a broader grassroots movement against the urban renewal bulldozer, first in New York and then around the country.

She persisted even as Moses and other powerful figures tried to vilify her. Eventually, her dissenting ideas found a wider audience. In 1969, Mayor John Lindsay killed Moses' expressway plan. In other cities, mayors and planning agencies began to rethink the bulldozer approach to urban renaissance. In 1974, President Nixon canceled the urban renewal program.

Jacobs' book became required reading in planning and urban studies programs. She was hailed for her visionary writing and activism. But she refused to accept sainthood, turning down honorary degrees from more than 30 institutions. She always gave credit to the ordinary people on the front lines of the battle over the future of their cities.

Jacobs was a thinker and a doer who had a profound influence on two distinct, but overlapping, groups: city planners and community organizers. She is best known for her impact on city planning. She was among the most articulate voices against "slum clearance," high-rise development, highways carved through urban neighborhoods and big commercial projects.

Cities, she believed, should be untidy, complex and full of surprises. Good cities encourage social interaction at the street level. They are pedestrian friendly. They favor walking, biking and public transit over cars. They get people talking to each other. Residential buildings should be low-rise and should have stoops and porches. Sidewalks and parks should have benches. Streets should be short and wind around neighborhoods. Livable neighborhoods require mixed-use buildings—especially first-floor retail and housing above. She saw how "eyes on the street" could make neighborhoods safe as well as supportive, prefiguring an idea that later got the name "social capital." She favored corner stores over big chains. She liked newsstands and pocket parks where people can meet casually. Cities, she believed, should foster a mosaic of architectural styles and heights. And they should allow people from different income, ethnic, and racial groups to live in close proximity.

Although many developers and elected officials still favor the top-down approach, most planners and architects have absorbed Jacobs' lessons. Advocates of "smart growth" and "new urbanism" claim Jacobs' mantle, although she would no doubt dispute some of their ideas, particularly the failure of these approaches to make room for poor and working class folks. In later writings, Jacobs touted the role of cities as the engines of economic prosperity. In doing so, she anticipated arguments against unfettered suburban sprawl, recent debates about the reliance of suburbs on healthy cities, and the new wave of thinking about regionalism.

More importantly, perhaps, Jacobs paved the way for what became known as "advocacy planning." Starting in the 1960s, a handful of urban planners chose to side with residents of low-income urban neighborhoods against the power of city redevelopment agencies that pushed for highways, luxury housing, expansion of institutions such as hospitals and universities, corporate-sponsored mega projects, and government subsidies for sports complexes and convention centers.

Based in universities or in small nonprofit firms, advocate planners played an important role in battles over development in most major cities. They provided technical skills (and sometimes political advice) for community groups engaged in trench warfare against displacement and gentrification. At first isolated within the profession, advocate planners soon moved from the margins to the mainstream—or at least became enough of a force to have a serious impact on urban planning education. These activist planners worked for advocacy consulting firms (such as Urban Planning Aid), community groups and university planning departments (such as Pratt Institute's Center for Community and Environmental Development), and as oppositional "guerillas" inside municipal planning agencies or even, as recounted in Norm Krumholz and Pierre Clavel's book, *Reinventing Cities: Equity Planners Tell Their Stories* (1994) for progressive neighborhood-oriented mayors.

Often overlooked is Jacobs' influence on community organizing. Most histories of community organizing trace its origins and evolution to the settlement houses of the Progressive Era, to Saul Alinsky's efforts (starting in the late 1930s in Chicago), to adapt labor organizing strategies to community problems, and to the tactical creativity of the civil rights movement. But Jacobs' activist work showed people around the country that they could fight the urban renewal bulldozer—and win.

The upsurge of neighborhood organizing that emerged in the 1960s and 1970s was triggered by the initial battles against urban renewal, or what some critics called "Negro removal." By leading the fight in New York City, the nation's largest city and media center, Jacobs inspired people in New York and other cities to organize to stop the destruction of their communities

and to find more community-friendly ways to achieve such goals as improving housing. They won some battles and lost others, but many of them persisted to gain increasing influence over plans by city governments and private developers for their neighborhoods. Out of this cauldron emerged new leaders, new organizations and new issues—such as the fight over bank redlining, tenants rights and rent control, neighborhood crime, environmental racism and underfunded schools. Some groups that were founded to protest against top-down plans began thinking about what they were for. Hundreds of community development corporations (CDCs) emerged out of these efforts. National networks of community organizations, such as ACORN, the Industrial Areas Foundation, PICO and National Peoples Action, and thousands of other independent community organizing groups, unwittingly built on Jacobs' efforts.

In 1981, Harry Boyte chronicled this revival of grassroots activism in his book, *The Backyard Revolution.* Even though it, and many subsequent books about community organizing, don't acknowledge (and may even be unaware of) Jacobs' influence, these activists were (and still are) standing on her shoulders as well as those of Jane Addams, Saul Alinsky and Ella Baker. Jacobs is mentioned once, in passing, in Peter Medoff and Holly Sklar's fascinating book, *Streets of Hope,* about the Dudley Street Neighborhood Initiative, that brought together residents of Boston's Roxbury ghetto, along with local churches, social agencies and other institutions, to rebuild their community as an "urban village" from the bottom up, starting in the 1980s. Few if any of DSNI's leaders, or foundation allies, had ever heard of her. But it is unlikely that Medoff, DSNI's first director, who graduated from Columbia's urban planning program, had not been influenced—directly (by reading her book) or indirectly (by studying with professors familiar with Jacobs' writing and activism)—by the activist author of *The Death and Life of Great American Cities.*

A fierce critic of Moses' efforts to decimate New York neighborhoods, Jacobs was equally opposed to President Johnson's plans to destroy Vietnamese villages. Always an activist, she marched in anti-war rallies. In 1968, Jacobs moved with her husband and children from New York City to Toronto, triggered by her anti-war sentiments. She didn't want their two draft-age sons to have to go to Vietnam.

She had a profound influence on city planning and community activism in her adopted country. There, too, she did battle with powerful forces who pushed for highways over public transit, and large scale projects over people-oriented neighborhoods. As she did in the U.S., she helped lead the fight to preserve neighborhoods and stop expressways, including the proposed Spadina Expressway that would have cut right through the heart of her own Annex neighborhood (where she lived until her death in a three-story brick building) as well as parts of downtown. Soon after moving to Toronto, she wrote a newspaper article critical of city planners for their plans to "Los Angelize" Toronto, which she described as "the most hopeful and healthy city in North America, still unmangled, still with options." It is difficult to know how much of Canada's success in creating more humane cities is due to Jacobs' influence, but many Canadian politicians, planners and advocates give her credit.

One unfortunate side effect of the battle against urban renewal in the United States was a knee-jerk opposition to government efforts to improve cities, a sentiment that lingers on. We see this in the growing antagonism to the use of eminent domain. Rather than see it as a tool that could be wielded for good or evil—depending on whether a city regime is progressive, liberal or conservative—many people in the U.S. view the tool itself as the enemy.

Canadians, too, battled against their country's version of urban renewal. But they, like Jacobs, did not view elected officials or government actions with the same degree of suspicion, as mean-spirited and heartless. They oppose government officials when they are in the pockets of private developers and businesses or refuse to listen to the voices of ordinary people. During Jacobs' years in Canada, municipal and provincial governments were often controlled by the Liberal Party and the progressive New Democratic Party—both to the left of the liberal wing of the Democratic Party in the U.S. The two Canadian parties had close ties to labor unions, environmentalists, women's rights advocates and community activists.

Canada has a similar economy and distribution of wealth to the U.S., but it provides a much wider and generous array of government-sponsored social insurance and safety net provisions to cushion the harshness of poverty. The U.S.'s stingy social programs have only a minor impact in reducing the poverty rate, while programs in Canada have a dramatic impact in lifting children, low-wage workers and the elderly out of poverty. Not surprisingly, compared with the U.S., Canada has a much smaller poverty rate, a higher proportion of subsidized housing, more mixed-income neighborhoods, less economic segregation and fewer homeless people. It also has safer cities, greater reliance on public transit, lower levels of pollution and traffic congestion and stronger downtown and neighborhood commercial districts.

Jacobs was a true "public intellectual," who put her ideas into practice. She loved cities and urban neighborhoods. She was fearless and feisty. She was a moralist, who believed that people had a responsibility to the greater good, and that societies and cities existed to bring out the best in people.

Critical Thinking

1. How did Jane Jacobs view major urban projects, including slum clearance and urban renewal programs?
2. According to Jacobs, what makes a city livable? Do major urban rebuilding projects enhance or destroy the characteristics of a good city?
3. What is advocacy planning? How does it differ from top-down planning?

PETER DREIER, an NHI board member, is E.P. Clapp Distinguished Professor of Politics and director of the Urban & Environmental Policy program at Occidental College in Los Angeles. He is coauthor of *Place Matters: Metropolitics for the 21st Century* and several other books.

Where Do We Fit in? CDCs and the Emerging Shrinking City Movement

As some cities begin to admit they are shrinking, CDCs in high-abandonment neighborhoods are rethinking their traditional roles, and even their missions.

ALAN MALLACH

There's nothing new about shrinking cities. Many American cities have been losing population steadily since the 1950s and 1960s, as suburbanization, deindustrialization, and migration to the Sun Belt have all taken their toll. Detroit has lost a million people since 1950, a decline of 54 percent, and vast areas of open land where pheasants strut through the underbrush have replaced houses, stores, and factories. Other cities, including Youngstown, Cleveland, Dayton, and Buffalo, are in the same boat.

What is new is that more and more cities are coming out and admitting that they are shrinking. In the early 1990s, when Detroit's city ombudsman, Marie Farrell-Donaldson, a respected African-American civic leader, called for the city to recognize that it was shrinking and begin to act accordingly, the response was a mixture of anger and ridicule. Today, Detroit Mayor Dave Bing has embraced shrinkage and set a planning process in motion that explicitly recognizes that the future Detroit will be a smaller, greener city than it once was.

Planning for a shrinking city is tough. Cities like Detroit, Cleveland, and Youngstown have begun to recognize that they have far more houses and apartments than they will ever need in the future. They have large areas that have lost most of their population, where most of the houses have been demolished, and where few if any prospective homeowners want to buy. At the same time, many other seemingly healthy neighborhoods are at risk. As Detroit's Karla Henderson says, "Even some of our stronger neighborhoods are at a tipping point with vacancy."

With rents and sales prices at rock bottom, with vacant units in the thousands, and demand not enough to keep houses even in the cities' stronger neighborhoods occupied, cities face a series of tough choices. Building more new housing, particularly affordable housing, means (with rare exceptions) that even more older homes will be abandoned. Disproportionately poor populations and high unemployment mean that these cities need to find new engines to drive their local economy or face a future as little more than bankrupt wards of a fraying welfare

state. At the same time, with cities facing massive deficits, the pressure to cut back on services and infrastructure in largely depopulated areas is strong. Many of these strategies can be controversial, stirring up memories of discredited practices like urban renewal and redlining.

Roles for CDCs

Community development corporations (CDCs) in cities like Detroit and Cleveland have been working for years to rebuild neighborhoods, and they find themselves challenged by this new movement.

Detroit's CDCs, led by their association, Community Development Advocates of Detroit (CDAD), have embraced the challenge head-on. At the end of 2008, well before Mayor Bing was elected, CDAD pulled together a task force to take a serious look at Detroit's future. As CDAD's chair, Southwest Housing Solutions Executive Director Tim Thorland, says, "It is only when we understand the conditions and strategies necessary for the entire city that we can begin to make decisions about specific neighborhoods."

The task force report, published in February 2010, was not a master plan, but was designed to be a strategic framework for revitalizing the city's neighborhoods. The task force identified 11 different types of area in Detroit, ranging from older, viable neighborhoods they dubbed "traditional residential sectors" to "urban homestead sectors" and "naturescapes," largely vacant areas that CDAD suggests should be seen as future natural landscapes. CDAD did not attempt to map the different types of area they identified, leaving that effort for the next—and probably more difficult—phase of their work.

Cleveland, which has lost half a million in population since 1950, a decline of 55 percent, is also looking at reimagining itself as smaller place. As Senior Vice President Bobbi Reichtell of Neighborhood Progress, Inc., a foundation-funded local intermediary, describes it, "In the summer of 2007, we started the conversation, and were awarded a grant from the Surdna

Foundation to engage the Kent State Urban Design Collaborative in a citywide planning process to look at repurposing vacant land, making it more productive, adding value in neighborhoods." (Getting city buy-in required promising to avoid using the term "shrinking," but with that promise, the city government has been a strong supporter.) This conversation turned into the Re-Imagining a More Sustainable Cleveland initiative. Reichtell lists the kinds of ideas that came up for using vacant land: "brownfields remediation techniques, capture storm water, native plantings. A few categories rose to the top. High interest in local food made urban agriculture one of them."

Once the plan had been approved by the city's Planning Commission, in 2009, Neighborhood Progress invited CDCs and others to submit proposals for a series of pilot projects to use vacant land based on the ideas of the Urban Design Collaborative. Fifty-six small grants of $20,000 or less (most under $10,000) were awarded for projects such as market gardens, orchards, pocket parks, and phytoremediation of brownfield sites. A number of CDCs competed for the grants, including Mount Pleasant NOW Development Corporation, Fairfax Renaissance Development Corporation, and Slavic Village CDC.

The focus on what can be done by communities with lots of vacant land lessens the sting of Cleveland's decision to focus its housing development and rehab resources in a couple targeted neighborhoods, says Reichtell. "Rather than saying 'Oh you're a second class citizen, we're not going to do anything in your neighborhood,' we are sending resources for projects that can in some cases create as much vibrancy as if you'd rehabbed a house."

Cleveland has a robust CDC infrastructure. Youngstown, a city which has lost nearly two-thirds of its population, lacked strong CDCs, and the local Raymond John Wean Foundation took the lead to create one, funding the Youngstown Neighborhood Development Corporation (YNDC) in 2009 and helping to recruit Presley Gillespie, a highly-skilled veteran of banking and urban real estate, as the group's executive director. As Gillespie puts it, "Before, there were organizations that were doing low-income housing, those sorts of things. Our approach is comprehensive. We want to transform the image, the confidence, the physical conditions, and the market demand for our neighborhoods."

YNDC's mission is actually to concentrate on the stronger neighborhoods, with, as he puts it, "the most chance for success." Gillespie says, though, that their target neighborhoods "are distressed, have seen disinvestment, decline and vacancy. It's not like we're going to places that are fine." Realistically, there are few places inside Youngstown's borders that don't need serious help.

Meanwhile, Detroit's CDCs have not been idle. Once the CDAD report came out, its members turned to the tough task of figuring out how to bring the framework down to the ground. During the past year, a CDAD working group led by Sam Butler, former executive director of Creekside CDC on Detroit's East Side and now part of the Detroit Vacant Properties Campaign, partnered with Data-Driven Detroit (D3) to develop indicators of neighborhood conditions that could be used by CDCs and neighborhood groups to evaluate their own conditions. "We're trying to make information accessible," says Butler. "We need to give residents a way to talk about their neighborhoods, to empower them to think strategically."

Armed with the indicators, Detroit's CDCs have kicked off two pilot efforts to translate the strategic framework into specific neighborhood plans. Half a dozen CDCs have come together in a collaborative effort in the city's lower East Side. During 2011, they will be working with a 125-member resident advisory group to come up with strategies for a large area that includes a lot of vacant land, but also two pockets of stable housing. The other pilot, led by Urban Neighborhood Initiatives, will address a smaller area in the city's Southwest corridor.

Changing the Equation

Shrinking cities challenge the basic equation that most CDCs have followed from their inception. That equation had two features. The first was that the neighborhood where the CDC was working—and by inference all neighborhoods—could be "saved," revitalized, and turned into a thriving community. The second was that development, particularly new housing, was a central part of the process of revitalization.

In a city that has and will have for the foreseeable future a far smaller population than it once had, not every neighborhood is a candidate for revitalization. Neighborhoods that may have been vital communities 30 or 40 years ago, but which have lost 70 or 80 percent of their population, and where occupied houses are fewer than vacant ones and both are rarer than vacant lots, are not likely to come back as vibrant urban neighborhoods. Given the limited demand for housing in such cities as a whole, any new homes built in such an area would at best draw demand from somewhere else, undermining some other part of the city. More likely, they would sit vacant.

This goes directly to the second part of the equation. Many, perhaps most, CDCs identify themselves with what they build—after all, that's why they're called community development corporations. What does a CDC do if there's no need to build any more houses or apartments in their neighborhood, and where decent quality private housing is available at the same or lower rent than a tax-credit project? That's not just a question of mission; for many CDCs it may be a question of survival, since many have come to rely on developer fees as a major source of funds to cover their operating budgets.

The fact is, however, that there are many ways a CDC can add value and strengthen a neighborhood without building any new housing. Youngstown Neighborhood Development Corporation's flagship project in the Idora neighborhood is a program they call Lots of Green. Idora is a viable neighborhood with many nice houses, but with too much scattered vacant land. So, Gillespie says, "we decided to take over about 150 vacant lots, and clean, repurpose, and reactivate those lots into neighborhood assets. We turn lots into urban agriculture, pocket parks, green space, and a side lot program for adjacent homeowners. Our urban ag site has community gardens, fruit orchards, rain gardens, green space." YNDC is working with Ohio State to use vacant land in the area to reduce stormwater runoff.

At the same time, YNDC is focusing on strengthening Idora's housing market by helping people make home repairs, providing incentives for people to buy homes in the neighborhood, and using NSP funds for selective rehab of key vacant structures that are important to the neighborhood's fabric.

One of the most valuable features of the CDAD strategic framework is that, after identifying the 11 different types of area, it goes on to offer a menu of suggestions for CDCs working in each type of area. Some of the things it suggests CDCs could take on in traditional residential sectors include:

- Code enforcement and blight reduction
- Strategies to catalyze private market housing activity
- Weatherization and greening assistance
- Planning for use of vacant lots
- Fostering community engagement for land use planning and resident cohesion

In naturescapes, on the other hand, the framework suggests that CDCs could help create a land conservancy, facilitate resident relocation, partner with others to encourage deconstruction (taking buildings down in such a way as to be able to reuse building materials and fixtures, as opposed to demolition) of existing vacant buildings, and support community policing.

Many CDCs, and not only those in shrinking cities, have begun to reevaluate their mission and think about neighborhood revitalization more comprehensively, often in ways more sensitive to market constraints and opportunities. Some have always had a comprehensive approach, such as Detroit's Warren/Conner Development Coalition, which is now playing a leading role in the lower East Side pilot project.

Many other CDCs are still grappling with these issues, as did Detroit's CDCs as they went through a nearly yearlong process of rethinking; as the CDAD report notes, "We must also hold up a mirror to ourselves. We must be willing to restructure, realign and even merge when necessary."

Still to Be Answered

Even once CDCs in shrinking cities embrace a new role suited to their context, two big question marks remain that are not within the control of individual CDCs or even CDCs as a group or industry.

First is how to pay the bills. CDCs trying to reinvent themselves around new models of community building that do not involve housing development struggle with the question of how to pay for the new activities that new strategies demand and how to replace developer fees with other sources of revenue, particularly at a time when both public and private funds are in short supply. Warren/Conner's effective Rebuilding Communities Initiative, which focused on small-scale community-building efforts in conjunction with residents, block clubs, and civic associations, was forced to close in 2008 as a result of funding cuts. This problem will not be easy to solve.

The second problem is perhaps even more fundamental. A successful revitalization strategy for a shrinking city demands, as the CDAD report states, a "citywide, realistic and collaborative strategy." The realities of shrinking population, limited

housing demand, and limited resources cry out for targeted strategies, where people look at the city as a whole and start making thoughtful decisions about what is going on where, and what makes sense in different places: where new housing might be built, where low-density quasi-suburban neighborhoods might emerge, and where land should be set aside for urban farms or habitat restoration. It is hard, if not impossible, for a CDC to mount an effective neighborhood effort built around shrinkage without being part of a larger citywide strategy.

Most CDCs recognize how important city government is and how closely tied their respective efforts are. The view from the other side is mixed. Cleveland has a long tradition of city–CDC collaboration, and in this area, as NPI's Reichtell put it, "The city and CDCs have close to a consensus over which neighborhoods should have housing and which demolition." Elsewhere, the picture is less clear. In Detroit, some people are concerned that the city may see CDC initiatives as competition, rather than collaborators, in the city's Detroit Works Project, an ambitious and multifaceted effort to rethink the city's future. In Buffalo, N.Y., the city's reluctance to acknowledge that it has become a smaller city has stymied the emergence of realistic, collaborative strategies.

This is unfortunate. A handful of one-shot community meetings or charrettes cannot substitute for the sustained effort of a strong CDC. Many CDCs can provide on-the-ground capacity and engagement with specific neighborhoods and communities that cannot be replicated by city government or replaced by any other public or private entity. Bringing this capacity and engagement to bear is critical if tough decisions about resources, priorities and directions are going to be made and turned into realistic strategies. As a growing number of cities recognize their new reality as shrinking cities and begin planning for that reality, CDCs will have to make sure that they have a seat at the table.

Critical Thinking

1. In what service areas have community development corporations (CDCs) enjoyed their greatest success? What are the achievements of CDCs in working in disadvantaged neighborhoods?

2. How does the "shrinking cities" movement constrain the operations of CDCs?

3. How have CDCs adapted? What roles can CDCs play in more troubled cities where extensive vacant properties and new economic realities mitigate against building new units of affordable housing?

ALAN MALLACH, senior fellow of the National Housing Institute, is the author of many works on housing and planning, including *Bringing Buildings Back and Building a Better Urban Future: New Directions for Housing Policies in Weak Market Cities.* He served as director of housing and economic development for Trenton, N.J. from 1990 to 1999. He is also a fellow at the Center for Community Progress and The Brookings Institution.

UNIT 6

School Choice and School Reform

Unit Selections

Learning Outcomes

After reading this unit, you should be able to:

- Identify the variety of "school choice" strategies for educational reform.

- Distinguish between a voucher school, a charter school, and a regular public school or neighborhood school.

- Identify the most ardent backers and the most ardent opponents of charter schools and other school choice programs.

- Evaluate the evidence concerning the successes, limitations, and criticisms of charter schools.

- Assess the degree to which the establishment of charter schools can help alleviate the racial isolation of public school classrooms.

- Explain how a program of tax credits can be used to promote school choice.

- Point to the special risks of using tax credits as a tool for promoting school choice.

- Assess the evidence on the racial isolation of public school classrooms: Does the data show that U.S. school systems are making continued progress toward racial segregation or that the progress made in the past is beginning to slip away?

- Summarize the most important U.S. Supreme Court decisions since the 1970s regarding local efforts at school desegregation.

- Debate the desirability of various strategies that are aimed at improving the racial balance of public school classrooms.

Student Website

www.mhhe.com/cls

Internet References

The Brookings Institution
www.brookings.edu/topics/school-choice.aspx

Carnegie Foundation for the Advancement of Teaching
www.carnegiefoundation.org

Center for Education Reform
www.edreform.com

Center for Research on Educational Outcomes (CREDO), Stanford University
www.credo.stanford.edu/research-reports.html

Center for School Reform at the Heartland Institute
http://heartland.org/issues/education

Civil Rights Project, UCLA
www.civilrightsproject.ucla.edu

Friedman Foundation for Educational Choice
www.edchoice.org

National Alliance for Public Charter Schools
www.publiccharters.org

National Center on School Choice, Vanderbilt University
www.vanderbilt.edu/schoolchoice/research-home.html

National Education Association (NEA)
www.nea.org

School Choice, Wisconsin
www.schoolchoiceinfo.org

Thomas B. Fordham Institute

For many city and suburban residents, "the schools" are the focal point of their involvement in local government, the service of greatest importance to them. Study after study, however, underscores that American public schools are not performing particularly well. Students in the United States lag behind children of other countries in math and science education and in other important competencies. Increasingly pessimistic about the future of public education, critics of the public schools have begun to search for alternatives.

One set of reform measures embraces the idea of choice, where parents and children are given new options, decreasing their reliance on underperforming public schools. A program of school vouchers, for instance, gives each participating family a certificate that can be used when deciding just which public school or private academy their child will attend.

But the concept of "choice" in education is more complicated than it may initially appear to be. The details and eligibility requirements of a choice program determine just which children are helped and which are effectively bypassed. A program that awards vouchers of substantial dollar value will enable large numbers of students to gain access to private and parochial (i.e., church-affiliated) schools. But such voucher programs are expensive and are likely to require a reduction in the public funding of traditional public schools, diminishing the quality of programs available to their schoolchildren. If the dollar value of a voucher is more limited, the program becomes more affordable; but private school tuition will remain beyond the reach of most lower- and working-class families, leaving their children with no real option but to attend the usual public schools.

Advocates argue that vouchers and other choice programs empower parents to find a school that matches their child's needs. Critics respond that such school choice programs are, in fact, quite dangerous, that they will exacerbate urban inequality by draining resources from the public schools. In programs where add-ons are permitted, that is where parents are allowed to add their own funds to supplement the value of a voucher, the potential for class and racial segregation is particularly severe: better-off students will use voucher support to leave the public

© SW Productions / Getty Images

schools, which will become under resourced dumping grounds of hopelessness for children who are left behind.

A system of tax credits can also help spur educational choice. A parent can choose to enroll a student in a private school, pay tuition, and then use the amount paid in tuition to calculate a reduction in the taxes that the family would normally pay the government at the end of the year. Such a system promotes choice but suffers obvious dangers. A conventional tax credit offers financial assistance to a family that can afford to pay private school tuition and then wait for partial reimbursement when filing taxes later in the year. A tax credit is of no real value to poor families who cannot afford private tuitions and who have no, or only a very small, tax liability.

The creation of charter schools offers a more popular and pragmatic alternative to the more far-reaching voucher and tax credit systems. A charter academy is a special or innovative school established under state auspices (i.e., given a state charter). Charter schools are public schools that are freed from numerous state rules and regulations in order to allow them greater flexibility in curriculum design, hiring, teaching, and school administrative practices. In many ways, charter schools are expected to show the flexibility and innovative teaching practices of private schools. As public schools, charter schools cannot charge tuition and hence suffer a lesser risk of class and racial segregation as compared to other school choice programs.

Charter schools are popular, and their numbers are growing. By 2012, forty states allowed the creation of charter schools; an estimated 2 million children attend more than 5,000 charter schools across the United States (figures provided by the National Alliance for Charter Schools). New York, Chicago, and a great many other cities have expanded the number of innovative charter schools. New Orleans turned to charter schools as the backbone of its efforts to restructure public education as part of the city's post–Katrina rebuilding.

Charters schools, like vouchers and tax credits, seek to create an environment of competition that will spur already-existing public schools to better performance. As a loss of enrollment to charter schools could lead to a reduction of funds and teaching positions, the creation of charter schools may even lead a city's more conventional public schools to respond with a new sense of urgency to the concerns voiced by students and parents.

But do choice programs deliver the educational gains and extensive benefits that their enthusiasts promise? According to critics, choice schools seldom produce dramatic increases in student achievement. Oftentimes, students in voucher and charter schools exhibit test scores that differ only little, if at all, from the scores of equivalent students in conventional public schools.

Gail Robinson (Article 22, "Charter Schools") surveys the new popularity of charter schools in New York City and seeks to assess where they have met their goals and where they have failed to live up to their promise. John Witte et al. similarly compare the educational outcomes in charter schools and more traditional public schools in Wisconsin, a state with a strong history of offering choice programs. Witte et al. find generally positive, but not overwhelmingly or uniformly positive, results for charter schools (Article 23, "The Performance of Charter Schools in Wisconsin"). While charter schools show some gains in working with at-risk students, the charter approach by itself provides no "magic bullet" or overall cure for the ills of public education.

One much-debated consequence of school choice programs concern their potential impact on racial integration. Advocates claim that choice programs will lead to greater school integration, that parents will be willing to send their children to racially-mixed classrooms when students share an interest and when a school offers a quality program and enthusiastic classroom instruction. Critics respond that choice programs provide yet one more opportunity for white flight, that is for whites (and others) to leave integrated classrooms, undermining the gains in classroom diversity that have been achieved over the years. In New York City, the existence of numerous single-race charter schools shows that charter academies cannot always be counted on to improve racial integration (Article 24, "Why Don't We Have Any White Kids?").

Inner-city school children are not always the primary beneficiaries of choice programs. Poor children clearly *do* receive benefits when program eligibility is clearly targeted on the poor, as are the Cleveland and Milwaukee voucher programs. But other school children—not the inner-city poor—receive much of the benefits when choice programs are not targeted but are more universal and allow the participation of large numbers of middle-class and even more affluent families. In Georgia, tax credits for the creation of scholarships has done relatively little to increase the educational choices of needy students. Instead, the program has largely provided financial assistance to parents whose children are already enrolled in private academies or to families who wish to have their children attend religious-oriented schools (Article 25, "Public Money Finds Back Door to Private Schools").

The existence of single-race charter schools in New York City and other cities points to an increasingly perplexing problem, the rising resegregation of public school classrooms. Resegregation, of course, is not confined to charter schools. As soon as the Supreme Court decisions permitted, localities across the United States terminated school bussing and other desegregation efforts. The courts have even allowed local schools to end school integration efforts in cases where localities have yet to produce substantial racial integration (Article 26, "Here Comes the Neighborhood").

The Supreme Court has even acted to limit the ability of local school districts to initiate voluntary programs to increase racial diversity in the classroom. In 2007, a sharply divided Court struck down the efforts by Seattle and Louisville to use specialized magnet schools to promote racial integration. The Court ruled that the school systems unconstitutionally gave too much emphasis to an applicant's race in deciding just which students would gain entrance to the city's specialized schools (Article 27, "Schools Seek New Diversity Answers after Court Rejects Race as Tiebreaker"). The five-member Court majority saw the classification of people by their race, even for the purpose of promoting racial diversity, as an impermissible discrimination that denied white school applicants the "equal protection of the law" under the 14th Amendment.

Civil rights groups argue that, in such rulings, the Court has stood the meaning of the 14th Amendment, which had been enacted after the Civil War, on its head and had set back the struggle for racial equality. But civil rights advocates argue that the Justices did not close the door to all local programs aimed at ending the racial isolation of public school classrooms. Local authorities can still plan school locations and draw school attendance zones to promote integration. School districts may even establish magnet schools and other diversity programs that will survive the Court's scrutiny, just as long as the programs are "narrowly tailored" and meet a variety of educational objectives (Article 28, "Integrating Suburban Schools: How to Benefit from Growing Diversity and Avoid Segregation").

Charter Schools

GAIL ROBINSON

The school playground is cramped, the day is bleak and chilly, but the kindergarten students are having fun, and one boy in particular resists going back inside. "You haven't made good choices," two teachers tell him. To his more cooperative classmates, the teachers say, "*You* have made good choices."

The use of the phrase "good choices" is no accident. "We believe in creating a democratic society where our children feel they have a choice," said school leader Rita Danis.

But "choice" holds another meaning at UFT Charter Elementary, a new school in the East New York section of Brooklyn run by the teachers union. It is a charter school. As such it is key to Mayor Michael Bloomberg and Chancellor Joel Klein's campaign to give city parents more choices about where to send their children to school.

While Bloomberg has set more requirements for public schools, he has, in an apparent contradiction, sought to encourage charter schools, which function outside of those rules. He hopes to more than double the number of charter schools in the city, from 47 to 100. "It's time to clear away the barriers to the creation of charter schools," Bloomberg said in a recent speech.

But charter schools, such as One World in Astoria and Carl Icahn in the Bronx, educate only about one percent of city public school students and only four percent in the nation as a whole. So why have they attracted so much attention? And why do some people think they can help solve New York City's education problems?

The Appeal of Charters

Charter schools receive public money but are independently and privately run. Though they must comply with certain state regulations and health and safety rules, they do not have to operate under union contracts, and they exist largely outside the Department of Education bureaucracy.

The charter school movement began in the 1970s, the brainchild of Ray Budde, a professor of education at the University of Massachusetts. He suggested that individual teachers could be given contracts, which he dubbed charters, to explore new approaches. United Federation of Teachers president Albert Shanker then expanded the idea to call for granting entire schools charters (with union approval). The first charter school in the U.S. opened in St. Paul, Minnesota, in 1992. Today about 580,000 students in the country attend 2,400 charter schools.

But New York was slow to embrace charter schools. The legislature finally approved them in 1998 as part of a political deal. Governor George Pataki agreed to support a legislative pay raise if the lawmakers approved charters. The bill included a rigorous application process for charter schools and a ceiling on the number of new charter schools.

As Pataki hailed the bill's passage, he noted that dozens of state schools were considered to be failing. "We're telling the parents in those neighborhoods, you have no choice but to send your child to a school that we know fails. Well, now they're going to have an option," Pataki said, "and I think all the schools are going to be better because of that."

Seven years later, New York City's 47 charter schools have a total of about 12,000 students—compared with about 1.1 million in conventional public schools. (Charter schools are considered public schools too.) Fifteen of the 47, including the UFT school, opened this fall. The vast majority are elementary schools and many are small, with fewer than 200 pupils.

A Choice or a Drain?

While much of the adamant opposition to charters has faded, conflicts remain over their performance and how they should be controlled and regulated. In many ways, these disputes come down to a battle over who should control education, what some have likened to a "power struggle."

Charter schools offer parents choice, particularly in poorer neighborhoods. But they also provide a counterweight to the so-called "educrats" and unions, often derided by Bloomberg and others. The lack of the union and of longtime school administrators holds particular appeal for many on the political right. It is no coincidence that one of the leading academic proponents of charter schools is the Goldwater Institute in Arizona—named for the founder of the modern American conservative moment.

"I see charter schools as, first, a source of needed education options for disadvantaged kids otherwise stuck in failing district schools and unable to afford private schools; second, a source of important external pressure on traditional school systems (and private schools); and, third, a preview of things to come for public education as a whole," as the big bureaucracies lose much of their power said Chester Finn, a charter school advocate.

Charter schools also benefit from being contrasted with vouchers, which give parents money to spend on their children's education as they see fit. "Instead of pushing private school vouchers that funnel scarce dollars away from the public schools, we will support public school choice, including charter schools and magnet schools that meet the same high standards as other schools," said the Democratic Party platform for 2004.

"The educational establishment has been willing to allow charters in some states just to forestall vouchers," Clint Bolick of the Alliance for School Choice told *The New York Times.*

Those who remain opposed argue that charter schools drain energy and resources from the public schools, while only educating a tiny percentage of kids. As evidence, some point to Albany, where the public school system has lost more than 1,000 students and must spend about $10 million a year on charters.

Instead of moving to create a new parallel school system, "parents are interested in improving the schools that they have," said David Ernst, spokesman for the state Schools Board Association.

Do Charters Work?

Most New York City charter schools have existed for only a few years, if that, and so information about their performance remains sketchy.

In general, the results appear promising. For example, on eighth grade tests, where the city's regular public school students tend to stumble, charter school students did better, according to figures compiled by the Center for Charter School Excellence.

But nationally the statistics are murkier. The first study comparing students in regular schools with those in charters, released in August 2004, found that charter school students often did not perform as well as students in regular public schools. Finn called the results "dismayingly low" and called for those overseeing charters to be more demanding.

On the most recent National Assessment of Education Progress test, charter school students did not do as well as public school students. They did, however, narrow the gap between the two types of schools. This prompted a pro charter group, the National Alliance for Public Charter Schools, to say the scores showed "real progress for charter schools," while the American Federation of Teachers declared that charters "continue to lag behind regular public schools."

What Parents Want

To many New York City parents, such arguments are academic. They are dissatisfied with their local public school and want something better for their child but cannot afford private school.

The city's charter schools are concentrated in poorer neighborhoods. Ninety percent of their students are black or Latino, and almost three quarters come from families poor enough that they qualify for a free school lunch. But the students are less likely than their regular school counterparts to need special education services, according to a state report.

Parents of students at the UFT school only have to look to I.S. 292, the public junior high school that resides in the same building as the charter school, to see what they are up against. Although a new principal has reportedly tried to turn the school around, in 2004, 28 percent of its eighth graders failed to meet even minimum state standards in reading.

And some charters offer services that go far beyond what public schools provide. At Harlem Day Charter, for example, students can stay at school until 5:30 P.M. at no charge. Some of that time is devoted to a program where artists supervise students in projects such as a felt mural showing how to count in Swahili. A fourth grade classroom boasts a bank of new computers, and a room set aside for parents offers computers as well as books that might be of interest. And the school takes advantage of a foundation program where students go to a local Barnes and Noble and get to spend $50 each on books of their own choosing.

Charter schools can adjust their programs to meet the wishes of parents in the community. And so many of the city charter schools stress academic basics, feature strict disciplinary codes and require uniforms. Some are single sex schools. Seth Andrew, who has applied to launch a charter school called *Democracy Prep* first looked at lots of other charter schools. He was particularly impressed by those that set "incredibly high expectations with plans for college for all kids"—expectations that extend to behavior as well as academics.

To parents such an approach seems to have appeal. The charters select students by lottery and most, if not all, have more applicants than they can accept.

How Do They Do It?

Harlem Day receives slightly over $9,000 per student from the Department of Education, less than the public schools receive for each child. But, many say, money goes further in charter schools.

For one, new charter schools do not have to be unionized. "The big Kahuna is the union contract," said Peter Murphy, director of policy for the New York State Charter School Association. "The contract dictates things beyond wages and salaries" and takes away the school leader's ability to manage.

And charter school teachers may make less than their public school counterparts or work longer hours.

It seems clear that the UFT launched its charter school partly to rebut the contention that a UFT contract hampers education. Instead, union officials blame the school bureaucracy for excess costs. They say that administrative expenses take up 11 percent of most schools' budgets; at the UFT school, that figure is four percent.

But cost savings are only part of the story. Most charter schools raise money to supplement what they get from the city. Educating a student at the Harlem Day costs $3,400 to $4,000 more than the school receives from the city, said its director, Keith Meacham. But real estate developer Benjamin Lambert founded the school, and he and his brother Henry Lambert have helped it find space and money. And the Carl Icahn School in the South Bronx got a $3 million facility from the businessman for whom it is named.

Flexibility contributes to the success of charter schools, according to Paula Gavin, executive director of the city Center for Charter School Excellence. But, in addition, she said, the schools benefit from having a clear mission and a drive to fulfill that mission. They are small, Gavin said—"not just class size, but the overall school is smaller. The size of the school allows individual attention." And,

she said, charters must be accountable for what they do and do not do.

Spreading Reform

New York City and state do more than many other cities and states to promote charter schools. The city provides some schools with space in Department of Education buildings and recently launched a $250 million program to help other charters build their own homes. It has also established the New York City Center for Charter School Excellence in partnership with several foundations to help charter applicants and to assist existing schools.

Charter school advocates praise many things about New York state's charter law. But they do not like the cap, which limits the number of new charter schools in the entire state to 100, with 50 for the city. As of last month, some 42 schools were competing for the remaining 16 spots left for charters statewide.

The original rationale for the cap was that the state should be sure charter schools would work before launching too many of them. But now that charters have a track record, charter proponents say, the cap has outlived any use it might have once had.

Bloomberg wants the state to eliminate the cap entirely and give him the authority to create charter schools without going to the state. Others call for doubling the cap to 200.

Supporters of charter schools would also like to see the government boost its allocation for each child in a charter school. "At the end of the day, they're all our children," said Mimi Corcoran, executive director of Beginning with Children Foundation, an early sponsor of charters.

But, while every child's future is important, won't spending money for charters still leave behind the vast majority of students who remain in regular public schools?

Supporters say no, contending that competition from charter schools may spur public schools to do better. Charters can, the argument goes, function as laboratories, developing techniques public schools can adopt. For example, said Corcoran, charters developed the idea of lead teachers, paying senior teachers extra money to remain in the classrooms rather than go into administration. Now that concept has been incorporated into the new union contract.

But many of the approaches used in charter schools, such as smaller class size, have already proved successful. Public schools simply don't have the money or the freedom to implement them.

"Our members envy the autonomy charter schools have," said Ernst of the school boards association. While the state frees charter schools from many regulations, he said, it subjects public schools to requirements that are "costly, onerous, time consuming and not always in line with good educational process."

Similarly, while Bloomberg and Klein encourage charters to be independent, they have imposed a uniform curriculum on most regular public schools, increased standardized testing and, critics charged, micromanaged teachers and principals.

Brian Ferguson, the principal of One World, is reluctant to set up a conflict between charters and more conventional public schools. "I'm sort of always leery to say that we're doing it and the public schools aren't doing it, because that's not the case," he said. "I think that we're both trying to get from each other what the best practices are for educating our children."

Critical Thinking

1. What arguments can be made in favor of charter schools?
2. What possible criticisms can be made against charter schools? How can critics argue that school choice programs, including charter schools, may have undesirable impacts?
3. Do charter schools work? What does the evidence from New York show? What do national statistics show?
4. How do inner-city parents, especially African-American and Latino parents, generally feel about charter schools?
5. How do charter schools save money? Should their approach to cost savings be applauded or criticized?

The Performance of Charter Schools in Wisconsin

JOHN WITTE ET AL.

Research on school choice has exploded since its modest beginning less than two decades ago. In addition to producing general works on the benefits or pathologies of a competitive marketplace for education, scholars have devoted substantial attention to two other questions: First, does the academic performance of students who exercise choice improve? Second, does school choice improve the performance and accountability of the traditional public system overall?

School choice takes four forms: intra-district choice, which allows students to go to any traditional public school of their choosing; inter-district choice, which extends that choice across district boundaries; charter schools; and voucher schools. Much scholarly interest has focused on the most controversial form, voucher schools, in which parents receive public money to send their children to private schools. Though few public voucher programs operate, a large number of studies assess their impact. These studies have produced little consensus.

School choice based on charter schools has been less politically controversial. Charter schools are public schools that operate under a management contract. A charter school submits to the requirements of a contract with its authorizing agency in exchange for exemptions from many of the rules and regulations that govern traditional public schools. In theory, if a school does not meet the obligations of its charter, then the authorizing agency will revoke the contract and close the school. If choice and competition work, then poor quality schools will not be tolerated. Most advocates of charter schools see improved educational performance as the primary goal, although others cite the importance of additional goals, such as competition. Regardless, charter schools have gained advocates across the political spectrum. Both the Republican and Democratic parties called for more charter schools across the country in 2000 and in 2004. And,

as of September 2006, more than 3,900 charter schools were open in 41 states and the District of Columbia.

Research on the relative effectiveness of charter over traditional schools has not been without controversy, however. National-level studies have reported advantages, disadvantages, and mixed results. At times, the debate among researchers has spilled to the pages of *The New York Times* and been described as a "dustup". State-level studies offer conflicting assessments for Michigan, North Carolina, and California. Two unpublished studies that consider Wisconsin in the context of national studies based on National Assessment of Educational Progress data suggest some advantages for charters.

We assess the performance of charter schools in Wisconsin at both the individual student and school levels. Our data come from two sources: first, data on individual students in Milwaukee in charter and traditional schools for the academic years 1998–99 through 2001–02; second, school-level state data on standardized tests in the fourth and eighth grades for two academic years, 2000–01 and 2001–02. For the school-level data, we apply a statistical analysis that harnesses the plethora of publicly available aggregated data generated by the No Child Left Behind law. We believe this method will help scholars improve their analyses of schools, especially when performance data on individual students are not available.

We find generally positive results for the effects of charter schools relative to traditional schools.

We find generally positive results for the effects of charter schools relative to traditional schools, although not uniformly so. Both individual-student and school-level analyses show this relative advantage for charter schools, although for one year, eighth-grade results favor traditional public schools. Our school-level analyses suggest that charter schools attain their advantage primarily by moving poorly performing students to proficiency rather than moving proficient students to advanced levels.

Our analyses suggest that charter schools attain their advantage primarily by moving poorly performing students to proficiency rather than moving proficient students to advanced levels.

Charter Schools in Wisconsin

Despite Wisconsin's leadership in school choice initiatives, including the nation's first voucher program, laws facilitating charter schools developed slowly. The initial authorization in 1993 allowed only 20 schools statewide. Subsequent laws removed this restriction and, more importantly, allowed several universities, the City of Milwaukee, a technical college, and school districts to issue charters. By the 2002–03 school year, the number of charter schools had risen to 130, with more than 19,000 enrolled students, approximately 2 percent of all public school students in Wisconsin. Charter schools in Milwaukee, Wisconsin's largest city, enroll minority students at approximately the same rate as traditional schools, while charter schools elsewhere in the state tend to enroll somewhat higher percentages of minorities. Charter schools in Milwaukee have about one-quarter fewer free-lunch qualified students than traditional schools. This trend is consistent with the tendency of charter schools to use the free-lunch program less than traditional schools. In addition, high schools make up a disproportionately large share of charter schools, and high school students in general are less likely to participate in the free-lunch program. A 2005 study of California charters found that those created by conversion of existing traditional schools to charter status were more effective than newly created charters, and that those with a higher proportion of instruction in traditional classroom settings were more effective. As more than two-thirds of Wisconsin charter schools are startups rather than conversions, they should be somewhat disadvantaged. Although our data do not allow us to assess in detail the method of instruction in charters, we were able to estimate that about half of Wisconsin charter schools were directed primarily toward at-risk students. In all of the 19 charter schools we visited throughout the state during the course of the study, school personnel sought to improve the achievement of at-risk students, often outside of traditional classroom settings. Consequently, the deck seems stacked against finding an advantage for Wisconsin charters relative to traditional schools.

Assessing Charter School Performance

Analyzing performance of charter schools presents numerous challenges. First, as with all studies of performance at the elementary level, very few quantitative measures exist other than standardized test scores. Attendance varies little in any setting. Small children go to school, and when they do not, it usually relates to illness. Behavioral measures also vary little and unpredictably, based on school-level philosophies. Increasingly, students are not graded until the higher elementary grades. Thus, we have to rely on standardized tests as indicators of student performance. Other measures, such as parental involvement and satisfaction, were not available for this study and have rarely been available in other studies.

At the middle school level, measures other than test scores begin to be useful, although they are also very limited. Students increasingly are given "at-risk" placements in specialty schools. We control for those schools in our estimates of achievement. However, we judge that behavioral data (suspension rates), attendance, and other measures of dysfunctional school action are still very sporadic and come under the purview of the principal. Thus, at the middle school level, we believe a control on the type of school (as at-risk or not) will measure some level of disadvantage. We question the reliability of other measures of performance beyond test results.

We are not as confident about using test data to measure the success of students in charter high schools, most of which provided specialized education for at-risk students, many of whom are severely at-risk. For example, several charter schools, in Milwaukee and outside, were "last chance" schools for students who were in legal custody, rehab programs, or had been expelled from other schools. Often these schools were, in the words of one administrator, "schools to teach kids how to go to school." The preparation of students to return to more traditional schools usually had minor academic components and much more emphasis on "life skills," self-discipline, and avoidance of adverse behaviors. Outside of Milwaukee, all charter high schools had some at-risk component, and, therefore, less emphasis on academics. That was not true of Milwaukee, so we included 9th- and 10th-graders in our individual student-level analyses. Because of the high percentage of at-risk charter high schools across the state, we limit the statewide school-level analysis to 4th and 8th grade.

Student-Level Performance of Charter and Non-charter Schools in Milwaukee

We obtained individual student test data for the Milwaukee school district, including students in its charter schools. With these data, we performed conventional statistical analyses, using administratively available data to control for student characteristics, and various value-added specifications that take advantage of repeated test data for each student.

Results confirm that charter school students in most grades appear to be performing better than students in traditional schools.

Results

Overall, the results confirm that charter school students in most grades appear to be performing better than students in traditional schools. These effects are quite robust across all races, with very positive effects for whites and Hispanics. With the exception of some black students, being in a charter school produces positive effects relative to students in traditional schools in Milwaukee, with Hispanics and whites showing the largest gains.

The test data and our analysis suggest that the largest advantages of charter schools lie in gains for math. We are not certain why this occurs, but case studies in Milwaukee indicate that a number of the charter schools emphasized science, math, or technology. In breaking down test results by grade, we find that charter schools students do modestly less well in grades 3, 4, and 10, compared to students in traditional, non-charter schools. The explanation for grades 3 and 4 may be that students have spent less time in charters in those grades and so do not begin to realize the benefits of being in charter schools until they reach grade 5. For 10th-graders, the explanation may be that charter high schools are more likely to be for at-risk students, and so their curricula do not focus as much on academic subjects.

School-Level Performance of Charter and Non-Charter Schools

Analyzing school performance in terms of levels of proficiency offers several advantages. First, policy-makers seem to be enamored with judging schools, not necessarily students. The No Child Left Behind law, the standards movement, and most charter laws are clear examples. In view of this, we must get better at school-level analyses. Second, privacy laws increasingly impede access to student-level data for evaluations, even if sanitized of student identity, unless political authorities (states, school boards) agree to release such data. Third, the standards movement has affected data and testing; students and schools must meet certifiable levels of performance against clearly stated standards for grades and subjects. These performance standards do not necessarily have to adhere to population "norms" based simply on the distribution of test scores across comparable populations, which puts students up against other students. Rather, performance standards serve as the goal and the club to assure that students achieve appropriate levels of proficiency.

Wisconsin has changed the testing protocol to adhere to federal law that stipulates that schools must be judged against state standards. Therefore, we apply a technique to estimate a school-level model based on performance criteria. Because these types of performance criteria have national scope, we think the method we demonstrate has utility beyond the assessment of charter schools. As the method considers differences along the performance spectrum rather than just central tendencies, it offers more nuanced assessments of school performance.

For each school, the Wisconsin Department of Instruction reports for five subject areas the proportions of fourth- and eighth-graders who achieve four levels of performance: minimal, basic, proficient, and advanced. Our analysis of these data takes into account variation in school characteristics such as a specialized pedagogical approach, pupil-teacher ratios, or differences in the student body.

Results

The fourth-grade results show that charter schools had lower proportions of students performing at the minimal and basic levels for all subjects in 2000–01 and 2001–02. The results differed, however, for the advanced category. In four subjects in 2000–01, non-charter schools had higher proportions of students in the advanced category. There appeared to be no clear differences with respect to the advanced category between types of schools in 2001–02.

School control variables had the expected effects. The higher the percentage of black, free-lunch, and disabled students in a school, the greater the number of students who tested at the minimal or basic categories. The percentage of disabled students had a greater effect than the percentage of poor or black students.

Results for eighth graders were very different in 2000–01, with non-charter schools doing better than charters. For language arts, this included every performance category. Non-charter schools had fewer students in minimal and basic, and more in advanced. The situation dramatically reversed in 2001–02. The results favored charter schools, except for social studies. As with the fourth-grade results, charter schools seemed to do better at getting students out of the minimal and basic categories, rather than pushing them into advanced (although that occurred for language arts and social studies).

What happened in the two very different eighth grade years? The answer comes from looking very carefully at the schools in each year. First, in the first year (2000–01), when traditional schools outperformed charter schools, only 12 charter schools reporting test data. Five other charter schools did not. Two of these schools were charters in 2000–01 but did not begin eighth grade until the next year. Two others had too few students tested either overall or in subcategories of students. The other, for unknown reasons, reported only national percentile rankings in 2000–01. When we look at these five "missing schools" in the next year, they had better scores than the reporting schools in 2000–01 by well over 3 national percentile rankings on all the tests but one. Second, and more important, the schools tested in both years simply improved on their prior years' scores. This does not indicate that eighth graders are doing uniformly better in charter schools, but it explains the deviations and suggests further tracking is required.

We find that traditional schools had a greater proportion of students in the advanced level than did charter schools. This means that charter schools seem to be making their inroads by bringing students out of the minimal and basic levels in proportions higher than we would expect based on school characteristics; traditional schools seem to hold an advantage in bringing students up to the advance level in proportions higher than we would expect based on school characteristics. In view of the aggregate student populations served by charter versus traditional students, this pattern should be expected and applauded.

One could reasonably argue that controlling for school-level demographics does not adequately control for unmeasured selection bias. One possible way to get at this using our method would be to analyze aggregate results for different races or for poor or non-poor students

as determined by free-lunch status. In Wisconsin, with its small school sizes and small populations of minority students in many schools, attempts to do this dropped out too many schools. However, because No Child Left Behind requires publishing these breakdown aggregates, we recommend this kind of analysis when possible.

Conclusions

Charter schools clearly provide additional options for students and families not only in Wisconsin's one large city, Milwaukee, but also in a number of other medium-sized cities and towns throughout the state. In many districts, charters offer the major alternative to the traditional systems that are in place and operating quite satisfactorily for many families. It is also clear that charter schools offer options to students who do not match the overall demographic makeup of the districts in which they reside. This creates more diverse student populations in these schools.

With the exception of one eighth-grade cohort, we believe that, subject to the cautions already raised, the achievement test results for schools in Wisconsin should be interpreted as favoring charter schools. In Milwaukee, charter school students consistently outperformed traditional students. The effects were largest for Hispanic and white students, larger in math, and most pronounced in grades 5 through 9. Analysis of statewide data that control for school characteristics indicates that charter schools did better than traditional public schools at ensuring that students achieve at the proficient level of performance. Finally, our finding are generally consistent with other studies using National Assessment of Educational Progress aggregated data, in which Wisconsin charter school students did very well, and better than charter schools in all but one other state.

Why might this be the case? We offer two reasons. First, local school boards authorize most charter schools in Wisconsin—and all of them in our study. According to a 2005 National Center for Education Statistics study, district-authorized charters perform better than schools authorized by state boards, colleges, or other entities. Further, charter schools authorized by school boards, with no controls for differing school populations, were slightly better than all other public schools.

Second, we offer a qualitative reason. In most of the apparently successful charter schools we visited, strong leadership was evident. Not only did local superintendents enthusiastically support the school, but so did school boards and other district officials. Within these successful schools, two forms of leadership were apparent—often not by the same person. One person, or a small group of people, was inspirational and instrumental in starting the school and shaping its initial vision. Equally important was a competent, day-to-day administrator. Certainly other reasons exist, but future research on charter schools is necessary for us to understand what is in the black box and whether these explanations also fit the experiences of schools in other states.

Critical Thinking

1. What exactly is a charter school? How does a charter school differ from a normal public school?
2. How do charter schools differ from the more controversial program of school vouchers?
3. What does the evidence show about the educational impact of charter schools in Wisconsin? Do charter schools lead to better student learning and higher scores on achievement tests?

JOHN WITTE and DAVID WEIMER are professors of public affairs and political science at the La Follette School of Public Affairs at the University of Wisconsin–Madison, where PAUL SCHLOMER is a doctoral candidate in political science. ARNOLD SHOBER is an assistant professor of political science at Lawrence University. The authors thank Martin Carnoy for helpful advice and the U.S. Department of Education for financial support. The findings and conclusions reported are the sole responsibility of the authors. A longer, more detailed version of this article appears in the summer 2007 issue of the Journal of *Policy Analysis and Management,* volume 26, no. 3.

'Why Don't We Have Any White Kids?'

N. R. KLEINFIELD

In seventh-grade English class, sun leaked in through the windows. Horns bleated outside. The assignment was for the arrayed students to identify a turning point in their lives. Was it positive or negative? They hunched over and wrote fervidly.

Floriande Augustin, a first-year teacher at the school, invited students to share their choices. Hands waved for attention. One girl said it was when she got a cat, though she was unsure why. Another selected a car crash. A third brought up the time when her cousin got shot and "it was positive because he felt his life was crazy and he went to college so he couldn't get shot anymore."

The lesson detoured into Martin Luther King Jr. and his turning points. Ms. Augustin listed things like how his father took him shopping for shoes and they were made to wait in the back. How a bus driver told him to relinquish his seat to a white passenger and stand in the rear. How he wasn't allowed to play with his white friends once he started school, because he went to a black school and his white friends went to a white school.

The students scribbled notes. Unmentioned was a ticklish incongruity that hung glaringly obvious in the air. This classroom at Explore Charter School in Flatbush, Brooklyn, was full of black students in a school almost entirely full of black students. As Ms. Augustin, who is also black, later reflected, "There was something about, 'Huh, here we are talking about that and look at us—we're all the same.'"

In the broad resegregation of the nation's schools that has transpired over recent decades, New York's public-school system looms as one of the most segregated. While the city's public-school population looks diverse—40.3 percent Hispanic, 32 percent black, 14.9 percent white and 13.7 percent Asian—many of its schools are nothing of the sort.

About 650 of the nearly 1,700 schools in the system have populations that are 70 percent a single race, a *New York Times* analysis of schools data for the 2009–10 school year found; more than half the city's schools are at least 90 percent black and Hispanic. Explore Charter is one of them: of the school's 502 students from kindergarten through eighth grade this school year, 92.7 percent are black, 5.7 percent are Hispanic, and a scattering are of mixed race. None are white or Asian. There is a good deal of cultural diversity, with students, for instance, of Haitian, Guyanese and Nigerian heritage. But not of class.

Nearly 80 percent of the students qualify for subsidized lunch, a mark of poverty. The school's makeup is in line with charter schools nationally, which are overall less integrated than traditional public schools.

At Explore, as at many schools in New York City, children trundle from segregated neighborhoods to segregated schools, living a hermetic reality.

The school's enrollment is even more racially lopsided than its catchment area. Students are chosen by lottery, with preference given to District 17, its community school district, which encompasses neighborhoods like Flatbush, East Flatbush, Crown Heights and Farragut. Census data for District 17 put the kindergarten-through-eighth-grade population at 75 percent black, 13 percent Hispanic, 12 percent white and 1 percent Asian. But the white students go elsewhere—many to yeshivas or other private schools.

Tim Thomas, a fund-raiser who is white and lives in Flatbush, writes a blog called The Q at Parkside, about the neighborhood. He has spoken to white parents trying to comprehend why the local schools aren't more integrated, even as white people move in. "They say things like they don't want to be guinea pigs," he said. "The other day, one said, 'I don't want to be the only drop of cream in the coffee.'"

Decades of academic studies point to the corroding effects of segregation on students, especially minorities, both in diminished academic performance and in the failure to equip them for the interracial world that awaits them.

"The preponderance of evidence shows that attending schools that are diverse has positive effects on children throughout the grades, and it grows over time," said Roslyn Mickelson, a professor of sociology and public policy at the University of North Carolina at Charlotte, who has reviewed hundreds of studies of integrated schooling. "To put it another way, the problems of segregation are accentuated over time," she said.

Even if a segregated school provides a solid education, studies suggest, students are at a disadvantage. "What is a good education?" Dr. Mickelson said. "That you scored well on a test?"

One way race presents itself at Explore is in the makeup of the teaching staff. It is 61 percent white and 35 percent black, a sensitive subject among many students and parents who would prefer more black teachers. Most of the administration and central staff members—including the school's founder, the current principal, the upper-school's academic head and the lower-school's academic head, as well as the high school counselor and social worker—are white.

As Ms. Augustin said: "When I came here and started to talk about myself, the students were shocked that I was here. I started to wonder, did they really have role models?"

After school one Tuesday, 10 students assembled in a classroom to talk about the school and race. The school paid for snacks: Doritos and Oreo cookies, Coke and 7Up.

What did they think of the absence of racial diversity?

"It doesn't really prepare us for the real world," said Tori Williams, an eighth grader. "You see one race, and you're going to be accustomed to one race."

Jahmir Duran-Abreu, another eighth grader, said: "It seems it's black kids and white teachers. Like one time we were talking and I said I like listening to Eminem and my teacher said this was ghetto. She was white. I was pretty upset. I was wondering why she would say something like that. She apologized, but it sticks with me."

Jahmir, one of Explore's few Hispanic students, is its first student to get into Stuyvesant High School, one of the city's premier schools. He was also admitted to Dalton, an elite private school, where he intends to go. He wants someday to become an actor.

Shakeare Cobham, in sixth grade, offered a different view: "It's more comfortable to be with people of your own race than to be with a lot of different races."

Tori came back: "I disagree. It doesn't prepare us."

Yata Pierre, in eighth grade, said, "It doesn't really matter as long as your teachers are good teachers."

Trevon Roberts-Walker, a sixth grader, responded, "When we are in high school and college, it's not going to be all one race."

Jahmir: "Yeah, in my high school there will be predominantly white kids, and I think this school will be so much better if it were more diverse."

Kenny Wright, in eighth grade, piped in, "You could have more discussion instead of all the same thoughts."

Ashira Mayers, in seventh grade, said: "We'd like to hear from other races. How do they feel? What's happening with them?"

Later on, Ashira elaborated: "We will sometimes talk about why don't we have any white kids? We wonder what their schools are like. We see them on TV, with the soccer fields and the biology labs and all that cool stuff. Sometimes I feel I have to work harder because I don't have all that they have. A lot of us think that way."

Explore's founder, Morty Ballen, 42, grew up in the Philadelphia suburbs, where his father ran several delis. A product of Teach for America, he taught English in a high school in Baton Rouge, La., that went from being all white to half-black. The white teachers would tell racist jokes in the faculty lounge, he said. He taught at an all-black school in South Africa started by a white woman, then at a largely black-and-Hispanic middle school on the Lower East Side. The experiences soaked in.

"I'm very cognizant of my whiteness, and that I have power," he said. "I need to incorporate this reality in my leadership."

He is also gay and knows about feeling different in school. "The only people who were like me were two kids who went to drugs," he said. "One died in high school, and the other died recently."

Mr. Ballen founded Explore in 2002, resolute that a public school could deliver a good education to disadvantaged students. He now leads a Brooklyn charter network. (His fourth school is scheduled to open in September.) The school began in Downtown Brooklyn. In 2004, it relocated to a former bakery factory in Flatbush, where most classrooms were windowless. In August, the Education Department moved it to 655 Parkside Avenue, squeezing it into the fourth floor and portions of the third in a building occupied by Middle School 2 and Public School K141, a special-education school.

The shared building is relatively new and in good shape, but the library is half the size of a classroom, the space so tight that a few thousand books must be kept in storage. The cafeteria, auditorium, gym and playground are shared. Instead of a computer lab, the school has a rolling computer cart of laptops, used mostly for math classes. There is no playground equipment for the younger grades. There are a limited number of musical instruments, so the school has no band, or much in the way of after-school athletics. There are no accelerated classes for high-performing students.

Explore students wear uniforms and have a longer school day and year than the students in the other schools in the building, schools with which they have a difficult relationship. A great deal of teaching is done to the state tests, the all-important metric by which schools are largely judged. In the hallway this spring, before the tests, a calendar counted down the days remaining until the next round.

Explore's academic performance has been inconsistent. Last year, the school got its charter renewed for another five years, and this year, for the first time, three students, including Jahmir, got into specialized high schools. Yet, on Explore's progress report for the 2010–11 school year, the Education Department gave it a C (after a B the previous year). In student progress, it rated a D.

"We weren't doing right by our students," Mr. Ballen said.

In response, a new literacy curriculum was introduced and greater emphasis was put on applauding academic achievement. School walls are emblazoned with motivational signs: "Getting the knowledge to go to college"; "When we graduate . . . we are going to be doctors." Teachers are encouraged to refer to students as "scholars."

Convinced that student unruliness was impeding learning, the school installed a rigid discipline system. Infractions—for transgressions like calling out without permission, frowning after being given a demerit, being off task—lead to detention for upper-school students. On some days, 50 students land in detention, a quarter of the upper school.

Positive behavior does bring rewards, like making the Respect Corps, which allows a student to wear an honorary T-shirt. Winning an attendance contest can lead to treats for the class or the freedom to wear jeans.

Still, some students have taken to referring to Explore as "the prison school."

Out of uniform and barefoot, Amiyah Young was getting her books in order for homework. She was at home, two blocks from school, in an apartment she shares with her grandparents, mother and 2-year-old brother. She is in sixth grade, willowy, with watchful eyes, a dexterous thinker, one of the school's top students. She hopes to go to a university like Princeton and become a veterinarian, because she has noticed lots of people own animals.

She blithely showed her snug room, a converted dining nook containing her bed, her books, her stuffed animals, her cluster of snow globes. She said that some of her friends slept with their mothers or siblings, or on the couch.

Her mother, Shonette Kingston, 36, calm with an outreaching smile, works as an operating-room technician and attends nursing school. She separated from Amiyah's father when the girl was born. He is unemployed, and lives elsewhere in Brooklyn, but remains involved in her life.

"It's a bit weird," Amiyah said of the school's racial composition. "All my friends are predominantly black, and all the teachers are predominantly white. I think white kids go to different schools. I don't know. I haven't seen many white people in a big space before."

Would it be better if it were integrated?

"I think they would stop calling me white girl if there were white kids," she said. "Because my skin is a little lighter and I can't dance, they call me that. Some of them can't dance, either."

What else?

"I could talk the way I talk."

Other students speak street slang that she repudiates: "They will say to me, 'You are so white.' I tell them, I have two black parents. Do I look white?"

She had been having trouble making friends. This year, her mother noticed a speech change. "She's slacking off more to fit in," Ms. Kingston said. "She's saying: 'I been there.' 'I done that.'"

Amiyah confirmed this: "I speak a bit more freelance with my friends. Not full sentences. I don't use big words. They hate it when I do that."

She said she had become more popular.

Other students also relate the use of parlance linked to skin color. Shakeare Cobham, one of Amiyah's friends, said: "If you're darker, they'll call them burnt. Light-skinned ones get called white."

Zierra Page, who is in eighth grade, said: "The lighter-skinned girls think they're prettier. They'll say: 'She's mad dark. Look at me, I'm much prettier.'"

Amiyah's parents are bothered by the abundance of white teachers. Her mother said: "What do they know of our lives? They may be good teachers, but what do they know? You're coming from Milwaukee. You went to Harvard. Her dad complains about this all the time—what can they bring to these African-American kids? I'm trying to keep an open mind. I'm happy with the education."

Amiyah said, "The white teachers can't relate as much to us no matter how hard they try—and they really try."

To extract her from the synthetic isolation of her environment, Amiyah's parents have enrolled her in programs with more racial diversity like an acting class in Manhattan.

She is curious about better-off white children. "I'd like to see how they would react in the classroom when we have dance parties," she said. "I'd like to see how they would react to a birthday party. And to being around so many of us. I'd like to see what they would think of some of the girls in our school who have big hair and those big earrings."

Anything else?

She mulled that a moment, and said, "I wonder if it's fun."

Explore's administration neither encourages nor discourages discussion of race. Rarely is it openly examined.

A diversity task force was patched together over a year ago to look into things like how to bridge the divide among staff and students and their parents, and what the makeup of the staff should be. The group is preparing some recommendations.

Race, and its attendant baggage, of course, is a tricky subject. Teachers are of different minds about what to do with it.

Marc Engel, a former investment banker turned librarian and media coordinator at Explore, is 53 and white. He frets about power differentials and how to transcend race, how to steer the students' inner compass. "I worry so much about their role models," he said. "The rap stars. The fashion models. The basketball players."

He has his way of trying to fit in. "I call every kid brother and sister," he said. "I say, hey, brother; hey, sister. One kid once asked me, 'Are you my uncle?'"

Other staff members also wonder about the isolation of the students. Adunni Clarke, 34, who is black and is the lead intervention teacher who helps students and teachers who need extra support, said: "I don't know that our kids get their placement in the world. I don't know that they realize that they're competing against all these other cultures."

Talking about race "could be a Pandora's box to some extent," said Corey Gray, 27, who is white and in his first year at Explore as an eighth-grade language-arts teacher. "Is there a proper effective way to bring it in? There probably is. Do I know the way? No, I don't."

Many of the teachers are young, from different backgrounds, and there is steady turnover—from 25 percent to 35 percent in each of the past three years, a persistent issue at charter and high-poverty schools.

Tracy Rebe, the principal, is leaving this year. Her replacement, the fourth in the school's short history, will be the first black principal, though not by design.

Early in the year, Mauricia Gardiner, 30, who teaches fifth-grade math and is of mixed race, was listening as students read a story about a black teenager who tried to rob a woman. Instead of reporting him, the woman took him home and tried to set him straight. The woman's race wasn't mentioned.

Ms. Gardiner asked the class what race they imagined the woman to be. They said black, that no white woman would do that. Why? she asked.

"They would be scared of us," a student said.

"It's frustrating," Ms. Gardiner said. "We don't have a forum to address this. You can get all the education in the world. But you have to function in the world."

Darren Nielsen, 25, white, from Salt Lake City, is in his second year teaching, assigned to third grade. Last year, when he taught fourth grade, a student got miffed at him and said, "Oh, this white guy." He later spoke to the student about singling out someone in a negative way because of his or her race. He overheard students call one another "light-skinned crackers" and "dark-skinned crackers."

"We had discussions about that being inappropriate," Mr. Nielsen said. "I even said: I'm the lightest-skinned one of all. What does that make me?"

The discussion was quick. "I probably should have done more," he said. "It was hard on me as a first-year teacher and not knowing what to do."

He added: "I realize most of these kids are going to go to segregated schools until college. I wonder, am I preparing these kids for what goes on in college?"

Karen Hicks, 41, a former businesswoman who is now in her first year teaching fifth-grade math and science and is black, used to have a son in the school. "I would have put him in an integrated school if I had that option," she said.

Ms. Hicks recalled her first conference as a parent, with a white teacher, now gone: "The teacher said, 'Oh, you're so involved.' It felt patronizing. That should have been the expectation."

If anyone can relate to the students, it is James McDonald. Mr. McDonald, 41, black, the beloved gym teacher, has been with Explore since it opened. He grew up on the Lower East Side, where his father ran a liquor store and left home when Mr. McDonald was 9. He went to predominantly black and Latino schools, and says he didn't learn what he needed to learn.

In high school, he showed a college application essay to a scholarship committee member, who told him, "If you want to go to college, you better learn how to spell it." He had written "colledge." He realized the holes in his education. "It deflated me," he said.

He thinks Explore students are getting a much better education than he did. Still, he is concerned.

"Outside the school the kids are being reminded of what their race is," he said. "When they come to school, it's as if they are asked to ignore who they are."

"I don't see that a lot of them have aspirations to do great things," he added. "Some of them say, yeah, I want to be a doctor. But some, you ask them and they don't have an answer. I'd like to know how many actually believe they can do whatever they can."

The sixth-grade social studies students swept into Alexis Rubin's classroom. She slapped them five, bid them good afternoon. To settle them down, Ms. Rubin said, "Students are earning demerits in one . . . two. . . ."

She handed out a test on Colonial Williamsburg. She said, "Every scholar in this room will get a sheet of loose-leaf paper for your short response."

Of Explore's teachers, Ms. Rubin, 31, is perhaps the keenest about openly addressing race. She is in her third year at the school, is white and grew up on the Upper West Side.

Outside school, she is the co-chairperson of Border Crossers, an 11-year-old organization troubled by New York's segregated system that instructs elementary-school teachers how to talk about race in the classrooms.

As Jaime-Jin Lewis, the organization's executive director, puts it: "You don't want kids learning about sex on the playground. You don't want them to learn about race and class and power on the playground."

Ms. Rubin does Border Crossers exercises with her students like MeMaps, in which both students and teachers list characteristics about themselves, then create a "diversity flower," with petals listing each participant's unique traits.

During Ms. Rubin's first year at Explore, a parent called her up, screaming that she ignored her son and called only on the white students. Ms. Rubin pointed out that there actually weren't any white students to call on.

She said schools needed to "unpack" the issue of race and dismantle stereotypes.

"The beginning is naming it," she said.

A gauzy night in early spring, and the PTA meeting in the auditorium drew about three dozen parents. Details were given about picture day, about students needing to show up for preparation for the state tests, about neighborhood ne'er-do-wells who tried to rob some students, [with MetroCards and hats as their targets.]

Lakisha Adams, 35, who has three children in the school, spoke brightly of a Harlem mentoring program: "It teaches about how to shake someone's hand, how to walk without your pants dragging down. This is all black. We put our kids in a lot of programs with kids that don't look like us. Our kids don't relate to Great Neck."

Parents say they like Explore overall and the education it offers. To many, that is enough.

Sheryl Davis, 57, the PTA president, grew up in Brooklyn, and when she was in sixth grade, was bused out of her mostly black East New York school to a "lily-white school."

"I do remember the hate from the white students," she said. The next year, she was back in her former school.

"As I got older, I didn't really see that I gained from that experience," she said.

"I don't know that segregation is this horrible thing," Ms. Adams said. "The problem with segregation is the assumption that black is bad and white is good. Black can be great. That's what I instill my kids with."

Would she prefer an integrated school? "I can't say that I would."

Families often disagree among themselves. Calandra Maijeh, 38, and her husband, Ife Maijeh, 43, were at the school one evening with their four children, all Explore students.

"Color for me is not an issue," Ms. Maijeh said. "As long as the learning is up to par."

Mr. Maijeh said: "My thoughts are very different from my wife. I agree that everybody deserves an education. But I want white and black to be together as one."

Jean McCauley, 47, is a single mother with two sons by different fathers, both gone from her life. When her older son, now 26, began school, his father had a friend in TriBeCa, and they used his address to get him into Public School 234, a well-regarded, largely white school. "I feel so grateful for my son being in that environment," she said. "Expectations were so high. That school had everything. It was a world apart."

He graduated from college and works at a real estate agency.

For her younger son, Brandon Worrell, she didn't have that option. He is in sixth grade at Explore. She considers it a good school, but fears he doesn't learn racial tolerance. "At Explore he can't compare to anything," she said. "He won't know how to communicate with other races. He won't know there is a difference. I think color will always be the first thing he sees."

She added, "I speak to Brandon about race. But he doesn't get it. It's abstract."

A week wound up. Education was occurring. In kindergarten, they were reading "Sheep Take a Hike," while in first grade, students wrote about a small moment that happened to them. A girl wrote: "This morning my mom pulled out my tooth. Ow. Ow. Ow."

In sixth-grade math, they were reviewing order of operations, and in fifth-grade science they were learning about chyme. In third grade, they were writing a response to: How does Jimmy feel about raising goats? Use at least two details in your answer.

A student was told: "You have the right to be mad. You don't have the right to kick things."

Mr. Engel, teaching library, went around the room with the first graders and had them fill in the blank of "America is...."

The answers shot back: "America is ... my mommy."

"Pie."

"Whipped cream."

"Burger King"

"Our life."

Critical Thinking

1. According to school choice advocates, how can charter schools aid the racial integration of public schools?

2. What is the record of charter schools when it comes to racial integration?

3. Why, in cities like New York, have charter schools failed to produce the class and racial integration of public classrooms, as the backers of school choice had predicted?

4. Should cities continue to turn to public schools even in cases where they help to reinforce the racial isolation of public education?

Public Money Finds Back Door to Private Schools

Stephanie Saul

When the Georgia legislature passed a private school scholarship program in 2008, lawmakers promoted it as a way to give poor children the same education choices as the wealthy.

The program would be supported by donations to nonprofit scholarship groups, and Georgians who contributed would receive dollar-for-dollar tax credits, up to $2,500 a couple. The intent was that money otherwise due to the Georgia treasury—about $50 million a year—would be used instead to help needy students escape struggling public schools.

That was the idea, at least. But parents meeting at Gwinnett Christian Academy got a completely different story last year.

"A very small percentage of that money will be set aside for a needs-based scholarship fund," Wyatt Bozeman, an administrator at the school near Atlanta, said during an informational session. "The rest of the money will be channeled to the family that raised it."

A handout circulated at the meeting instructed families to donate, qualify for a tax credit and then apply for a scholarship for their own children, many of whom were already attending the school.

"If a student has friends, relatives or even corporations that pay Georgia income tax, all of those people can make a donation to that child's school," added an official with a scholarship group working with the school.

The exchange at Gwinnett Christian Academy, a recording of which was obtained by *The New York Times,* is just one example of how scholarship programs have been twisted to benefit private schools at the expense of the neediest children.

Spreading at a time of deep cutbacks in public schools, the programs are operating in eight states and represent one of the fastest-growing components of the school choice movement.

This school year alone, the programs redirected nearly $350 million that would have gone into public budgets to pay for private school scholarships for 129,000 students, according to the Alliance for School Choice, an advocacy organization. Legislators in at least nine other states are considering the programs.

While the scholarship programs have helped many children whose parents would have to scrimp or work several jobs to send them to private schools, the money has also been used to attract star football players, expand the payrolls of the nonprofit scholarship groups and spread the theology of creationism, interviews and documents show. Even some private school parents and administrators have questioned whether the programs are a charade.

Most of the private schools are religious. Nearly a quarter of the participating schools in Georgia require families to make a profession of religious faith, according to their websites. Many of those schools adhere to a fundamentalist brand of Christianity. A commonly used sixth-grade science text retells the creation story contained in Genesis, omitting any other explanation. An economics book used in some high schools holds that the Antichrist—a world ruler predicted in the New Testament—will one day control what is bought and sold.

The programs are insulated from provisions requiring church-state separation because the donations are collected and distributed by the nonprofit scholarship groups.

A cottage industry of these groups has sprung up, in some cases collecting hundreds of thousands of dollars in administrative fees, according to tax filings. The groups often work in concert with private schools like Gwinnett Christian Academy to solicit donations and determine who will get the scholarships—in effect limiting school choice for the students themselves. In most states, students who withdraw from the schools cannot take the scholarship money with them.

Public school officials view the tax credits as poorly disguised state subsidies, part of an expanding agenda to shift tax dollars away from traditional public schools. "Our position is that this is a shell game," said Chris Thomas, general counsel for the Arizona School Boards Association.

Some of the programs have also become enmeshed in politics, including in Pennsylvania, where more than 200 organizations distribute more than $40 million a year donated by corporations. Two of the state's largest scholarship organizations are controlled by lobbyists, and they frequently ask lawmakers to help decide which schools get the money, according to interviews. The arrangement provides a potential opportunity for corporate donors seeking to influence legislators and also gives the lobbying firms access to both lawmakers and potential new clients.

The programs differ from state to state, with varying tax benefits for donors and varying rules on who may receive the scholarships. Arizona's largest program permits donors to recommend students who already attend private schools. Pennsylvania's program lets them get scholarships and also lets scholarship organizations retain up to 20 percent in administrative fees.

Some states have moved to tighten restrictions after receiving complaints. In Florida, where the scholarships are strictly controlled to make sure they go to poor families, only corporations are eligible for the tax credits, eliminating the chance of parents donating for their own benefit. Also, all scholarships are handled by one nonprofit organization, and its fees are limited to 3 percent of donations. Florida also permits the scholarships to move with the students if they elect to change schools.

David Figlio, a professor at Northwestern University who has studied Florida's program, said it was an important alternative to public schools for some families. "They're doing it because they're feeling stuck," Dr. Figlio said. "Their kids are doing poorly in the classroom, and they don't know why."

In Georgia, the scholarship program was criticized for widespread abuses in a report last year by the Southern Education Foundation, a nonprofit group based in Atlanta that works to improve education.

State Representative Earl Ehrhart, a Republican who helped write the Georgia law, called that report "sophistry" and said that any abuses in the program were anomalies. "I can't tell you about the difference it makes in the lives of these kids," Mr. Ehrhart said.

The report found that from 2007, the year before the program was enacted, through 2009, private school enrollment increased by only one-third of one percent in the metropolitan counties that included most of the private schools in the scholarship program.

The logical conclusion was that most of the students receiving the scholarships had not come from public schools.

"The law was passed under a certain promise," said Steve Suitts, vice president of the foundation. "There is no evidence it's going to those purposes. The kids who were supposed to benefit are not benefiting."

'Fiendishly Clever'

The scholarship programs represent the expansion of a mission that began more than 10 years ago, when the school choice movement ran into headwinds over the use of vouchers.

Vouchers, which directly use public money to finance private school educations, were unpopular among many voters and legislators, and several state courts had found them unconstitutional.

Proponents decided to reposition themselves, and in 1997, Arizona's Legislature adopted the first tax-credit scholarship program.

For school choice advocates, the genius of the program was that the money would never go into public accounts, making

it less susceptible to court challenges. Representative Trent Franks, an Arizona Republican and former state lawmaker, is credited with the idea of routing the donations through nonprofit organizations. "The teachers' union called it fiendishly clever," Mr. Franks said during a recent interview.

"The difficulty of getting at this thing from a constitutional point of view is that there are private dollars coming from a private individual and going to a private foundation. It drives the N.E.A. completely off the wall because they can't say this is government funding," Mr. Franks said, referring to the National Education Association.

Kevin Welner, a professor of education at the University of Colorado, Boulder, who wrote a book on the tax-credit programs, dubbed them "neovouchers."

As predicted, tax credits have thus far withstood legal challenges, most recently when the Supreme Court upheld Arizona's program last year. It had been challenged on the grounds that it violated the Establishment Clause of the First Amendment, which prohibits government endorsement of religion.

A national network of school choice advocates has been promoting the programs with financing from conservative activists and foundations. The advocacy groups do everything from financing political advertising to lobbying state legislatures. One group, the American Federation for Children in Washington, D.C., has not shied from the rough-and-tumble of state politics.

In Florida's 2010 election, the federation supplied $255,000 to finance an organization that paid for advertising against Dan Gelber, who was running for attorney general and had opposed state financing for private schools.

The ads, mailed to Jewish neighborhoods, called Mr. Gelber "toxic to Jewish education." His staff found out about them from his 11-year-old daughter, who called the office in tears after finding an ad in their mailbox.

One big proponent of the tax-credit programs is the American Legislative Exchange Council, a coalition of conservative lawmakers and corporations that strongly influences many state legislatures. The council became a flash point in the Trayvon Martin case because it had championed the controversial Stand Your Ground gun laws.

"ALEC is a huge player in pushing forward a conservative agenda based on the premise that the free market and private sectors address social problems better than the government," said Julie Underwood, dean of the school of education at the University of Wisconsin, Madison, who has been critical of ALEC's education agenda.

Scholarship legislation was approved in Virginia this year and is gaining traction in other states, including New Hampshire and New Jersey, according to Malcom Glenn, a spokesman for the American Federation for Children. Schools participating in the programs range from elite private academies to small, inexpensive programs operating in church education wings. The New Jersey proposal would establish a five-year pilot program in several school districts, including Lakewood, a community with a number of Yeshivas.

"It's spreading," said Mr. Ehrhart, the Georgia lawmaker. "It's clearly a reaction to parents' concern about the educational experiences of their kids."

Enrolling for Dollars

After Georgia's scholarship program was adopted, parents of children in private schools began flooding public school offices to officially "enroll" their children.

Their plan was to fill out the paperwork even though they had no intention of ever sending their children to public schools. According to the way the law was interpreted, the enrollments would make them eligible for scholarships. Some public schools balked.

"I recently contacted you about having some trouble enrolling/registering my child in a public school while he is going to a private school," one parent wrote to a scholarship organization last year in an e-mail obtained by *The Times*. "A principal told us he cannot attend two schools at the same time, which is simply not true because public and private schools have nothing to do with each other. But we need to have my child enrolled in a public school in order to qualify for the student scholarship program."

The idea, based on a technical interpretation of the word "enroll," was promoted by State Representative David Casas, a Republican and co-sponsor of the scholarship legislation in Georgia. In meetings with parents, he had explained that the bill's wording was intentional—using the word "enrolled" rather than "attending"—to enable the scholarships' use by students already in private schools.

Parents questioned the idea. "Aren't people going to say that's a scam?" asked one father during a presentation by Mr. Casas that was posted on YouTube. "You've been going here for nine years. Now you're enrolling in public school? You're enrolled in two schools?"

Mr. Casas, the president of a seminary, assured him it was not a scam. "Feel fine about it," Mr. Casas said.

"Some people felt a little weird about that, felt it was dishonest that they would take their child, enroll them in a public school and not have them actually attend, but all of a sudden they actually qualified for a scholarship," Mr. Casas said at another meeting, where he called the program "too good to be true." A transcript of the comments was contained in the Southern Education Foundation report. Mr. Casas did not respond to inquiries seeking comment.

The Georgia Department of Education endorsed the interpretation.

Some scholarship programs rejected the idea, including one whose focus is on low-income students. "We actually checked that out and called the Department of Education," said Derek Monjure, who runs a scholarship organization called Arete Scholars Fund. "They agreed with it, but we didn't feel right with it and didn't do it. It was confusing to be told by the state organization that it's right."

Georgia's largest scholarship organization, the Georgia Goal Scholarship Program, said it interpreted the law to require that students must have attended public school for one semester, unless they are beginning school. The program has also established income guidelines for its recipients.

Some states collect little information on the scholarship organizations. When asked how many students switched from public to private schools, Linda Dunn, policy analyst for the Georgia Department of Education, said: "We don't collect that data. We don't regulate them in any fashion."

The fact that children already attending private schools can receive scholarships from some organizations means that Georgia's private schools have a ready source of donations—parents and families of existing students. While the law was advertised as a way to help needy students, it contained no income limits for eligible recipients. And although it prohibits donations designated for a specific student, some students are benefiting from the donations of relatives and friends.

Hanaiya Hassan, whose daughter attends Hamzah Academy in Alpharetta, Ga., said she had saved $5,000 by asking four friends to donate to a scholarship organization with money earmarked for her daughter's school. "If you collect four people for $2,500, then one of your children is free," she said.

The friends were awarded a tax credit. Depending on their tax bracket, some donors could actually come out ahead by filing for a federal charitable deduction as well as the state credit.

The Christian Heritage School in Dalton, Ga., circulated a flier for the 2011–12 school year titled "TUITION BREAKS FOR CURRENT FAMILIES!" It stated, "The scholarship tax credit is so vital to CHS that the school is encouraging all parents to participate in the program and enlist at least two others to do the same." Participating families would get a 10 percent tuition rebate and a $250 bonus. The rebates would be doubled or tripled depending on overall participation.

The school has discontinued the rebate program, its controller said.

At Gwinnett Christian Academy, Mr. Bozeman, who was recorded saying that donations would be funneled to the family that raised them, did not respond to requests for comment. He has been promoted to headmaster.

Similar deals, some nicknamed "swaps," in which parents donated for each other's children, have cropped up in Arizona as well, according to Mr. Thomas, the school board association general counsel there.

After news reports in 2009 about scholarships in Arizona being awarded based on the recommendations of donors, the state enacted a series of changes, including a prohibition on "swaps." Mr. Thomas, however, said he believed they were continuing.

Johnathan Arnold, headmaster of Covenant Christian Academy in Cumming, Ga., said he viewed using the program to discount tuition for existing students as unethical.

"We, as a Christian school, felt that wasn't the right approach," he said. "You're giving money out of the goodness of your heart with the intent to receive nothing in return. When you give it for the purpose of getting it back or actually make money on that, to me that doesn't qualify for the spirit of the law."

Getting in on the Act

When the gas drilling company XTO Energy made generous donations for private school scholarships in Pennsylvania, the corporate largess was hailed in ceremonies across the state. As the cameras flashed at one event in Punxsutawney, Sam Smith, the speaker of the Pennsylvania House and a local native, stood with an oversize cardboard check for area private schools.

The media events began in 2010 and have generated a burst of good will for XTO at a time when the controversy over the hydraulic fracturing drilling method has been growing in Pennsylvania. One state official remarked that the company, which donated $650,000 over the past three years, had gone "above and beyond" its duty. In reality, as much as 90 percent of XTO's donation was underwritten by taxpayers.

Also in attendance in Punxsutawney was Peter Gleason, chairman of the Bridge Educational Foundation, the middleman organization that arranged XTO's donations. Mr. Gleason congratulated the voters of Punxsutawney for having the wisdom to send Mr. Smith to Harrisburg. In addition to serving as chairman of Bridge, Mr. Gleason is a lobbyist in Harrisburg. Two other lobbyists, who have represented XTO, serve on Bridge's advisory board, as does the chief of staff to Mr. Smith. XTO was acquired in 2010 by Exxon Mobil.

While a spokesman for XTO said the company donated to provide additional educational opportunities to Pennsylvania schoolchildren, such arrangements appear to benefit all involved—donors with business before the legislature, lawmakers and lobbyists.

The Rev. Theodore Clater, a Pennsylvania advocate for school choice, said that Bridge and a similar Pennsylvania organization, Bravo Foundation, frequently asked lawmakers for advice when deciding where the money should go. Mr. Clater said he was not aware of any illegality, but nevertheless questioned that practice.

"You could get into all kinds of political games, favoritism," he said, emphasizing that his own scholarship organization tried to distribute its money without influence.

Mr. Smith said he saw no evidence that the program was politicized. Instead, he said, companies "have a certain amount of money they're going to put in charitable contributions anyway, and they now see 'I can get a tax credit and give back to education.'"

Bridge's director, Natalie Nutt, whose husband ran the campaign of Gov. Tom Corbett, a Republican, said all of the group's board members were selected for their devotion to school choice.

Between them, Bridge and Bravo control about $3 million in scholarship funds a year, putting them in the top 10 of more than 200 scholarship organizations in the state.

Among Bridge's founders in 2005 was John O'Connell, a lobbyist who had been a partner at Bravo.

In 2006, Mr. O'Connell pleaded guilty to federal charges of embezzling more than $200,000 from another nonprofit organization, Pennsylvania Law Watch, whose mission was to promote tort reform. Mr. O'Connell argued for a reduced sentence, citing his charitable work through Bridge and Bravo.

The federal government disagreed. "As a lobbyist, O'Connell's involvement in the Bravo Education Foundation and later in the Bridge Foundation was very beneficial to him in a business sense in that it afforded him excellent opportunities to cultivate new corporate clients and relationships with legislative leaders," prosecutors wrote.

Even some lawmakers have started their own scholarship organizations. Mr. Ehrhart, the legislative sponsor of the Georgia scholarship program, is also the unpaid chief executive of a scholarship organization, the Georgia Christian Schools Scholarship Fund.

In Arizona, one of the largest of more than 50 scholarship organizations, the Arizona Christian School Tuition Organization, is controlled by State Senator Steve Yarbrough, a Republican and chairman of the Senate Finance Committee. In an interview, Mr. Yarbrough pointed out that he was running the organization before he was elected to the Legislature. The organization paid Mr. Yarbrough $48,000 in 2010 and disbursed $313,000 to a company he partly owns to process scholarship applications.

Uneven Playing Fields

In Georgia, where the world revolves around high school football, the scholarships have driven a wedge between public and private schools.

Over the past few years, coaches at public high schools have complained about the defections of a number of players from large public schools who have left for small private academies. At Savannah Christian Preparatory School alone, four starting players migrated from nearby public schools and helped the team become last fall's Class A champions.

Coaches at the public schools have suspected that scholarships were given to their players by Savannah Christian and other private schools to build athletic programs. Athletic scholarships are banned in the state's high schools.

The coaches have not been able to prove their suspicions, but the growing dominance of private schools in Class A prompted the public schools last year to threaten to withdraw from the Georgia High School Association.

"This money just makes the playing field completely unlevel," said Larry Campbell, a coach in Lincoln County, Ga., who is known for his winning record. "The private schools are thriving, and they've got the money to go out and recruit the great athlete."

One star athlete, Keyante Green, went to Eagle's Landing Christian Academy in McDonough, Ga., in the ninth grade after his stunning performance in an annual championship game sponsored by an Atlanta radio personality. Keyante, then 14 and an eighth grader at a public school, was named most valuable player. His youth coach at the time, Dan Curl, predicted that Keyante would one day be heading to the N.F.L.

Within months, Mr. Curl had enrolled his son in high school at Eagle's Landing, he said, and had agreed to become a part-time middle school coach. He said he also told the school about Keyante.

"I told them I had a kid who is a good athlete, a stud athlete," Mr. Curl recalled recently. "They had already seen the highlight video. They said, 'Man, bring him over.'"

Mr. Curl said Keyante's family could not afford the approximately $10,000-a-year tuition at Eagle's Landing. He said he had helped fill out an application to the GOAL scholarship program for Keyante that first year and in the two subsequent years. The scholarship paid only part of his expenses, so Eagle's Landing's coaches sought donations to pay Keyante's remaining expenses, said Mr. Curl, who is no longer employed at the school. As a freshman in 2009, Keyante stole the show at a state playoff game with four touchdowns and 292 yards. The head coach at another school compared him to the Georgia legend Herschel Walker.

Neither Keyante, who will graduate in 2013, nor his family responded to requests for comment. Questioned about the scholarships, the Eagle's Landing assistant head of school, Chuck Gilliam, said in an e-mail that two of the school's 29 scholarship recipients played football. But he said the scholarships had "not been used to enhance the football program."

GOAL's director, Lisa Kelly, said in an e-mail that the organization adopted a written policy in 2009 prohibiting the use of scholarships to "recruit and provide aid to students for athletic purposes."

At Savannah Christian, Coach Donald Chumley, whose Raiders includes four recipients of GOAL scholarships, said: "I'm not going to say to you that some didn't say 'I want to go to college, and I want to play football.' But we don't select them on athletic ability. We select them on need."

Under a compromise, the public schools did not withdraw from the high school association. Instead, for the first time, the public and private schools in Class A will hold separate playoffs next fall.

A Boon for Creationists

The scholarships have amounted to a lifeline for many religious schools. One Catholic grade school in Berwick, Pa., regained its health through $87,000 in scholarship donations, according to the Rev. Edward Quinlan, the education secretary for the Diocese of Harrisburg, where nearly 20 percent of students receive scholarships. In Fort Lauderdale, Fla., 100 of the 160 students enrolled in Mount Bethel Christian Academy receive tax-credit scholarships, according to the school's headmaster.

In the Arizona case that went before the Supreme Court, the National School Boards Association joined local school officials and teachers in arguing that the program was skewed toward religious schools, openly selecting students for scholarships based on their religion.

Many religiously affiliated schools across the country are known for turning out well-educated students and teaching core subjects without a sectarian bias. But some schools financed by the tax-credit programs teach a fundamentalist dogma holding that the world was literally created in six days. Some of the schools use textbooks produced by Bob Jones University Press and A Beka Book, a Christian publisher in Pensacola, Fla.

The books became an issue in 2005 when the University of California system said it would not honor some credits of students who attended schools that use them.

In an ensuing lawsuit filed against the university by Christian schools, Donald Kennedy, a biologist who is a former president of Stanford, said in court papers that the science texts made statements that were "flatly wrong" and "plainly contrary to the scientific facts" when hewing to creationist theory. The case was ultimately decided in favor of the university.

"It's a Christian curriculum, and some parts of it are controversial," said Jon East, vice president for policy at Step Up For Students, the organization that runs the Florida scholarship program. The books are also used in some schools in Georgia and Pennsylvania.

An A Beka high school science text concluded that "much variety within the human race has developed from the eight people who left the Ark." Another text, used in sixth grade, makes repeated references to Noah and the flood, which it calls the reason for both the world's petroleum reserves and the development of fossils.

History and economics texts are also infused with fundamentalist theology and an unabashedly conservative viewpoint. The Great Depression, one says, was exaggerated to move the country toward socialism, and it described "The Grapes of Wrath" as propaganda.

Frances Paterson, a professor at Valdosta State University in Georgia who has studied the books, said they "frequently resemble partisan, political literature more than they do the traditional textbooks used in public schools."

Mr. Arnold, the headmaster of the Covenant Christian Academy in Cumming, Ga., confirmed that his school used those texts but said they were part of a larger curriculum.

"You have to keep in mind that the curriculum goes beyond the textbook," Mr. Arnold said. "Not only do we teach the students that creation is the way the world was created and that God is in control and he made all things, we also teach them what the false theories of the world are, such as the Big Bang theory and Darwinism. We teach those as fallacies."

Critical Thinking

1. How can a program of tax credits be used to spur student and parental choice in education?

2. What criticisms can be made of the Georgia program that serves to spur the creation of scholarships to enhance student choice in public education?

3. How do you think the shortcomings of the Georgia program can be corrected? Can you design a tax credit program for education that would have fewer of the shortcomings that the critics see in the Georgia program?

Here Comes the Neighborhood

Charlotte and the resegregation of America's public schools.

DAMIEN JACKSON

Darius Swann remembers the blazing cross that illuminated the night sky outside his window at Johnson C. Smith University in Charlotte. The year was 1966, and Swann, an African-American theology professor, had recently initiated a lawsuit against the Charlotte-Mecklenburg school system after his 6-year-old son was denied admission to a nearby elementary because he was black. "There's always a certain amount of danger whenever you take a stand," says the Presbyterian minister.

Around that time, Swann recalls, the homes of several of the city's African-American leaders were firebombed. "It drove home the point that such issues were deeply embedded in the psyche of the community," he says. "People were willing to resort to extreme measures."

Swann was willing to go pretty far himself. For more than a decade, Swann pursued his case in the courts. The lawsuit that bore his name, *Swann v. Charlotte-Mecklenburg Board of Education,* concluded successfully when a U.S. District Court judge ordered the creation of a more racially diverse school district. Later affirmed by the Supreme Court in 1971, Swann is commonly recognized as the case that "put the teeth" in the earlier *Brown v. Board of Education* decision by instituting timely and practical ways of combating separate and unequal education, such as busing and race-conscious student assignments. The case changed the face of American education in the 20th century, as the nation's school districts followed its lead toward increasing integration.

More than two decades later, that face is changing back. A recent study by Gary Orfield of the Civil Rights Project at Harvard University shows that more than 70 percent of the nation's African-American students currently attend predominantly minority schools, or schools where more than half the students are minority. (Close to 76 percent of Latinos attend schools with non-white majorities.) Though this growing trend can be attributed, in part, to declining public school enrollment by whites, the study reveals that the typical white public school student is educated in an institution that is 80 percent white.

Since 1995, 45 school districts across the country have been declared "unitary"—that is, sufficiently desegregated—and had their federal desegregation orders rescinded by the courts. Challenges by critics of court-ordered desegregation have sparked recent or ongoing court battles in school districts in a majority of states, including Alabama, Florida, Massachusetts, Michigan and Pennsylvania.

The trend toward resegregation is particularly pronounced in the South, a region where most of the *Swann*-based remedies for integrating schools were focused. Between 1988 and 1998, the percentage of blacks in majority white schools dropped from 43.5 to 32.7 percent. "There's something really bad happening," Orfield told a recent national conference on school resegregation at the University of North Carolina in Chapel Hill. "It's related to race. And it's getting worse."

Charlotte, which less than two decades ago boasted one of the most integrated school systems in the country, is rapidly heading toward resegregation. In 1999, the *Swann* decision was overturned by U.S. District Court Judge Robert Potter, a busing critic, who declared the Charlotte-Mecklenburg school district to be unitary.

The ruling resulted from a lawsuit brought by white advocates of "neighborhood schools"—an assignment model that prioritizes attendance in a student's own neighborhood. Given that neighborhoods in and around Charlotte, like elsewhere, are largely divided along racial and ethnic lines, neighborhood school models make it virtually impossible for districts to avoid resegregation.

"There's absolutely nothing wrong with integrated schools," says Paul Haisley, a Charlotte accountant and outspoken advocate of neighborhood schools. "But if it means a kid is going to leave his own neighborhood to spend an hour on a school bus each day, is it really worth it? I don't think so."

A majority of the Charlotte-Mecklenburg School Board was opposed to Potter's ruling—including all four African-American members—and it crafted a plan that tried to stem resegregation. The "school choice" plan allows parents to pick from a number of area schools within their "choice zone," with transportation provided. If they desire a school outside of their zone, they are responsible for their own transportation.

The plan prioritizes school choice for students whose home schools have high concentrations of poor students, and gives more funds to such schools. "Parents were leaving the system," contends Haisley, referring to the "white flight" commonly associated with increasing minority enrollment in a school district. "This plan was the best way of empowering parents and ensuring they had a choice."

Many African-Americans are less optimistic. "No community in America has ever been able to achieve separate but equal," says Arthur Griffin, a member of the school board who opposed the plan and Potter's ruling. Even with the new plan and a commitment from Charlotte's education, political and business leadership to equalize funding in majority-black city schools, Griffin believes school resegregation, along with its associated disparities, is just a matter of time. In the year since the plan has been in place, the number of elementary schools with more than 90 percent minority enrollment has already increased from 9 to 16.

Orfield's study provides a broader interpretation. Not unlike the disparities that produced the *Brown* decision a half-century ago, the nation's majority-minority schools are commonly "isolated by race and poverty" while offering "vastly unequal educational opportunities" than their majority-white counterparts. This stark reality—based largely in historically segregated housing patterns, white flight and an inequitable reliance on local property taxes for school funding—provides an unhealthy prognosis for a large-scale return to neighborhood schools in African-American communities across the country.

"Philosophically, I support the concept of neighborhood schools," says Griffin, who feels all students should have quality schools close to home. "Unfortunately, all neighborhoods are not created equal."

They never were. For a decade after the *Brown* decision in 1954, widespread southern resistance to integration by local school boards kept the vast majority of African-American students in the South in segregated schools. The passage of the 1964 Civil Rights Act stepped up the federal enforcement of desegregation orders and, by 1968, transformed the region into one where a quarter of all southern black students attended majority white schools.

After taking office in 1968, however, President Richard Nixon largely abandoned the enforcement of desegregation requirements, appointing four Supreme Court justices known for their pro-segregation leanings. The court issued a number of key decisions substantially limiting the scope and impact of school desegregation. *Keyes v. Denver* (1973) hampered plaintiffs in de facto segregated systems by requiring proof of "intentionally segregative school board actions in a meaningful portion of a school system." *Milliken v. Bradley* (1974) forbade such inter-district remedies to segregation as transferring students between predominantly black inner-cities and predominantly white suburbs.

Even so, earlier federal and local commitments, combined with the *Swann* decision, continued the trend toward integration. By 1988, the percentage of African-American students attending majority-white schools in the South peaked near 44 percent.

But this peak also marked a sharp turning point. The number of integrated southern schools steadily declined as a result of strong opposition to desegregation policy from the Reagan administration, which repealed federal desegregation assistance programs and advocated the end of relevant court orders. By the '90s, Supreme Court appointments by Reagan and George Bush Sr. had created a judicial majority committed to doing just that. In a number of key cases—including *Board of Education of Oklahoma City v. Dowell* and *Freeman v. Pitts*—the high court elected to end existing desegregation orders by making it easier to declare school systems unitary. It was irrelevant, the court further ruled, if the termination of such orders led to the resegregation of these school systems.

While capitalizing on an increasing political backlash to busing (yet not necessarily to integration), critics have often characterized school desegregation as a failed policy. Sociologist Roslyn Mickelson offers evidence to the contrary. The UNC-Charlotte professor, who spent years examining the academic impact of desegregation and related policies on students in Charlotte-Mecklenburg's public schools, found that "the more time both black and white students spent in desegregated elementary schools, the greater their academic achievement."

Her study highlights the positive effects of a desegregated setting on such current indicators of achievement as high school advanced placements and standardized test scores. It also reveals that "the higher the percent of blacks in a school, the lower the percent of the school's teachers who are fully credentialed, are experienced, and who possess master's degrees."

Mickelson concludes that the likely resegregation of the Charlotte-Mecklenburg schools "does not bode well for black children's education prospects." As the district returns to segregated neighborhood schools, she writes, "we can anticipate that racial antagonisms and racial gaps in achievement and attainment will grow."

While most black Charlotte residents say they should have access to good schools in their own neighborhoods, and some of them insist the burden of busing was placed disproportionately on their black children, most are quick to clarify that such sentiment does not reflect abandonment of the ideals of desegregation. "The customary line has been that we need to keep diversity in our schools," says Blanche Penn, a parent leader and the director of the West Charlotte Community Center. "I haven't heard anyone say otherwise."

Apparently, Charlotte residents are still largely committed to the concepts of integration and equity in funding. Griffin and other pro-desegregation African-Americans were recently re-elected to the school board by substantial margins over white advocates of neighborhood schools.

Even so, says Stoney Sellers, a prominent Charlotte businessman and community activist, it's ultimately a question of limited resources in a rapidly growing city. "At some point, as the growth continues, will the community choose school equity first, or will the money follow the development of all the new schools we're building?" Sellers asks. "Seven to 10 years down the road, how will our communities look then?"

"I am more concerned that a child is succeeding rather than if that child is in a diverse setting or not," says Lindalyn Kakadelis, a former school board member and teacher in Charlotte, who argues that diversity is an imprecise term "since we're almost at a point in America where white is a minority." Kakadelis says "the bottom line is student achievement," and she's "so tired of people making excuses" for low achievers and acting like "victims" of poverty and other social ills. "What I'm for," she adds, is "pushing everybody to succeed in their own schools."

"We know it's not just about integration or sitting in the same classrooms with whites," Sellers counters. His concerns are educational quality, the distribution of resources and academic achievement. "School desegregation wouldn't have meant much if there had been no impact on educational achievement."

"If we had the money, the certified teachers and everything we needed in our neighborhood schools, then I wouldn't have a problem with segregated schools," Penn says. "But we know that's not going to happen. The resources follow the folks with the money."

For Penn, it's back to the future. "Putting kids back in neighborhood schools brings back memories," she says, recalling her own experiences as a teen-age student at all-black West Charlotte High. "We got all the old, leftover books." She quickly adds that the African-American community "doesn't want leftovers."

Swann, who no longer lives in Charlotte, acknowledges the irony of his desire 30 years ago for his son to attend a white school in his own neighborhood. He contends that, for African-Americans, neighborhood schools are less significant because neighborhoods now reflect "proximity as opposed to a real community. A lot of people don't even know their neighbors."

Even so, without solutions to the current trend, African-Americans could find themselves with leftovers again. But despite the increasingly conservative tone of the country and its judicial system, new attempts at maintaining diversity in the public schools are afoot. A number of systems—including North Carolina's Wake County Schools, which includes Raleigh, the capital—are considering socioeconomic status in school assignments. In San Francisco, schools are using a "diversity index" that accounts for economic status, parental education levels and the number of languages spoken at a student's home. Similar approaches are being tried in Manchester, Connecticut, and La Crosse, Wisconsin.

But for some there's a bottom line. "Integrated neighborhoods produce integrated schools," says Steve Johnston, executive director of the Charlotte-based Swann Fellowship. The nonprofit organization, named for Swann and his wife Vera, was formed in 1997 to advance the value of diversity in public education.

Johnston contends that until white people and the institutions they control pay equitable wages to people of color and allow for the kind of educational institutions that can produce economic parity, the onus will always be on whites to make neighborhoods and schools integrated. "Economic diversity in housing patterns will create diverse schools," he says.

To Johnston, the solution is simple. "We can wait until we're all brown, or we can work at living together."

Swann adds: "I believe that the public school is the most important element in the transformation of a society. If the schools can change, then so can it."

Critical Thinking

1. How did the U.S. Supreme Court in its 1971 *Swann v. Charlotte-Mecklenburg Board of Education* decision make the city of Charlotte a symbol in the fight for school integration? What exactly did the Court rule in *Swann*?

2. What does the more recent statistical evidence reveal about Charlotte's schools? Are Charlotte's schools and other schools in the south becoming increasingly integrated or resegregated?

3. How have more recent court decisions affected the racial integration efforts started as a result of *Swann*?

4. How did the Supreme Court's 1974 *Millikin v. Bradley* decision and 1990s decision in *Board of Education of Oklahoma City v. Dowell* affect the prospects for school integration?

DAMIEN JACKSON is a writer in North Carolina. This story was produced under the George Washington Williams Fellowship for Journalists of Color, a project sponsored by the Independent Press Association.

Schools Seek New Diversity Answers after Court Rejects Race as Tiebreaker

Jessica Blanchard and Christine Frey

More magnet schools. More money to underperforming schools or ones that are largely segregated. Weighing whether a student comes from a poor or wealthy family.

These will likely be among the next batch of solutions the Seattle School District turns to as it attempts to foster diversity and create equally strong schools citywide.

With the racial tiebreaker portion of its school assignment plan shot down Thursday by the U.S. Supreme Court, Seattle district officials vowed to find another way to promote diversity in a city where schools and neighborhoods are still fairly segregated.

Wary of a potential court ruling against it, the Seattle School District has not been using the racial tiebreaker system.

"We have had a racially neutral student assignment system for the past five years, and our fears of having schools become more segregated have become fulfilled," said Gary Ikeda, the district's general counsel.

The high court's 5–4 decision, which struck down racial aspects of student assignment plans in Seattle and Louisville, Ky., brought to a close the lengthy legal battle that has been called the most crucial public education case since the landmark 1954 *Brown v. Board of Education* school desegregation decision.

Because the Seattle district has not used the racial tiebreaker since 2001 and next year's school assignments have already been set, the ruling won't have an immediate impact here.

It could, however, jeopardize similar voluntary desegregation plans in hundreds of districts nationwide. And it will force the Seattle district to come up with alternative methods to encourage racial diversity as it revamps its student assignment plan this summer.

To do so, however, the district will have to rethink and likely expand its idea of diversity. Perhaps when determining school assignments, the district could instead consider a student's economic background, or whether they're a recent immigrant or a special-needs student, for example.

"This ruling leaves us open to pursue diverse schools as a goal," said School Board member Michael DeBell. "And we'll be looking to define diversity more broadly."

How that goal is achieved, however, makes a difference. In his majority opinion, Chief Justice John Roberts wrote that classifying students by race only perpetuated the unequal treatment that the *Brown* ruling sought to extinguish.

"The way to stop discrimination on the basis of race is to stop discriminating on the basis of race," Roberts wrote.

The ruling applies to school districts that aren't under a court order to remove the vestiges of past discrimination.

Justice Anthony Kennedy sided with the court's four most conservative members in rejecting the Louisville and Seattle plans, but in a concurring opinion suggested race may be used as part of a district's broader plan to diversify schools.

Justice Stephen Breyer and the three more liberal members of the court strongly disagreed. In a sharp dissent, Breyer wrote that the ruling would "threaten the promise" of *Brown* and warned, "this is a decision that the court and the nation will come to regret."

Federal appeals courts had upheld the Seattle and Louisville plans after some parents sued. The Bush administration took the parents' side, arguing that racial diversity is a noble goal but can be sought only through race-neutral means.

The tiebreaker was part of a School Board decision in 1997 to allow the district's 46,000 students to attend a school of their choice. That assignment plan was intended to replace the district's widely unpopular mandatory busing program and return to a neighborhood schools assignment plan, so students could attend school closer to home.

School officials considered a student's race as one of several tiebreakers at popular schools; their race was a factor if the student's attendance would help bring the high school closer to the districtwide average of about 40 percent white students. The tiebreaker helped some minority students get into predominately white high schools, and vice versa.

A student with a sibling at a school got first priority; a student's race was the second tiebreaker, followed by the distance a student lived from the school.

But the plan had critics, including those parents whose students were denied seats at the high school of their choice based on their race. They formed Parents Involved in Community Schools and sued the district in 2000, claiming the racial tiebreaker policy was unfair and violated students' civil rights.

Kathleen Brose, the group's president, fought back tears Thursday as she discussed her victory.

"It's been seven years. A lot of people have moved on, but I don't want another parent to go through what I did—what we did," she said at a news conference.

Her daughter Elisabeth, now 22, wanted to attend Ballard High School, the closest high school to their Magnolia home. But she wasn't able to get a seat there, nor at her second or third choices. She finally ended up at Ingraham High, and later transferred to The Center School when it opened at the Seattle Center. The move was upsetting to the girl, who missed attending high school with her middle school friends, Brose said.

The school district's policy also affected students of color, said Seattle attorney Harry Korrell, who represented the parents. Some who wanted to attend Franklin High, their neighborhood school, were turned away because the district gave those seats to white students in an attempt to balance the school's racial mix.

The lawsuit challenged only the use of the racial tiebreaker for high school assignments, but the district in 2002 suspended the use of the tiebreaker for all schools while the case worked its way through the courts.

Seattle district officials, who have long maintained the racial tiebreaker is necessary and that racial diversity is a laudable goal within public schools, did not waver in that stance Thursday.

At an otherwise somber press conference, they portrayed the ruling as an endorsement of the importance of diversity in public schools.

"I don't believe it's a matter of winning or losing," outgoing Seattle Superintendent Raj Manhas said. "The high court affirmed that diversity matters. . . . That's fundamental."

Enrollment records show the racial makeup at some Seattle high schools has changed since the district suspended the use of the racial tiebreaker. Ballard High's student population has become whiter, for example, while Cleveland High has seen a jump in the percentage of black students.

Seattleites have long recognized that "the opportunity to learn with friends and peers from other races and backgrounds is a valuable part of the American educational experience," Manhas said. "We will be looking at all options available to us."

The idea of a socioeconomic tiebreaker has gained momentum in recent months, with some parents arguing it's a fairer way to determine which students need extra academic support and resources, and that poverty and race are often intertwined.

Still, it will be a challenge to integrate schools without being able to consider a student's race, said Mark Long, an assistant professor of public affairs at the University of Washington.

"Nothing correlates with race like race," he said. "Anytime you try to use some proxy indicator for race to lead to more diversity for a group of students, you're going to have more difficulty doing that."

Sharon Rodgers, president of the Seattle Council PTSA, said the goal should be to work to make all Seattle schools strong.

"Until we get all our schools to be top performing, whether we use one tiebreaker or another, we're just changing the particular population of students that are assigned to low performing schools," she said.

Key Dates

- **July 2000:** A group of Seattle parents called Parents Involved in Community Schools sues the Seattle school district for using race as a tiebreaker in assigning students to high schools.
- **Spring 2001:** The Seattle district halts the use of the tiebreaker while the case works its way through the courts.
- **April 6, 2001:** U.S. District Court Judge Barbara Rothstein says the policy doesn't violate the U.S. Constitution or anti-affirmative action Initiative 200.
- **April 16, 2002:** The 9th U.S. Circuit Court of Appeals says the policy is illegal under I-200 and the district must stop using it.
- **April 2002:** Ballard Principal David Engle announces his resignation to protest the ruling, saying it will "further intensify the racial divide in this city."
- **June 17, 2002:** The federal court withdraws its own decision and asks the state Supreme Court to consider the issue first.
- **June 26, 2003:** The state Supreme Court upholds the use of race as a tiebreaker.
- **Oct. 20, 2005:** The full 9th Circuit upholds the district's use of race as a tiebreaker.
- **Dec. 4, 2006:** The Seattle case and a similar case from Kentucky are argued before the U.S. Supreme Court.
- **June 28, 2007:** The U.S. Supreme Court rules against Seattle's use of race to determine school assignment.

Critical Thinking

1. What is a magnet school? Why have so many school districts turned to magnet schools as opposed to school busing and other programs for racial integration?
2. What exactly did the U.S. Supreme Court rule in its decision concerning the use of magnet schools as part of a program intended to produce voluntary integration?

Integrating Suburban Schools:

How to Benefit from Growing Diversity and Avoid Segregation

Brief History of Suburban Schools

Migration to suburbs began in the early 1900s and boomed in the post–World War II decades of the 50s and 60s. It was during the time of accelerated suburban development that the legal struggle to end racial segregation was at its height. The development of suburbs, therefore, began under overtly discriminatory policies, including the Federal Housing Administration's denial of mortgages in racially integrated communities. In 1954, however, the Supreme Court decided in *Brown vs. Board of Education* that "separate but equal" was a violation of the U.S. Constitution. In 1968, Congress passed the Fair Housing Act, which sought to curb housing discrimination and required affirmative actions to further residential integration by communities.

The *Brown* decision was pivotal to the advancement of racially integrated schools, along with other enforcement and funding efforts by the federal government, such as the Emergency School Aid Act passed in the 1970s that provided financial assistance for communities with integrated schools. Yet, discriminatory housing policies persisted and white migration to the suburbs resulted in many urban communities witnessing resegregation. More recently, despite such earlier resegregation trends in urban communities, little has been done in suburban communities to prevent a similar problem from occurring, even with clear evidence from both school statistics and housing transactions that minority families were becoming increasingly concentrated and segregated in the suburbs. Thus the failure to create policies promoting racially integrated suburbs is leading not only to the segregation of some suburban neighborhoods but also is often associated with the segregation of their schools.

By the mid 1970s, the Supreme Court slowly began limiting what it required in school desegregation cases. In one of the most significant cases of this era, *Milliken v. Bradley* (1974), the Court concluded that lower courts could not order "interdistrict" desegregation that encompasses urban as well as suburban school districts without first showing that the suburban district (or the state) was liable for the segregation across district boundaries. The practical impact of this decision was a serious blow to school desegregation remedies. In effect, a line was established between city and suburban school systems, which could not be crossed in designing desegregation plans. Whites, who for decades had tried to avoid the desegregation of their schools, finally had a place to go—the suburbs—where they could successfully do so.

Racial Transformation of Suburban Schools & the Spread of Segregation

According to the U.S. Census Bureau, the population of people of color in the U.S. will continue to rise. By 2050, for example, the number of Latinos and Asians is expected to triple, and the number of African Americans is projected to grow nearly two percent. The number of whites, on the other hand, is the only racial group expected to see a decline, from 66 percent to 46 percent. This trend toward an increasingly diverse population is even more evident among our nation's children. By 2050, the number of students of color in the U.S. will jump from 44 percent to 62 percent.

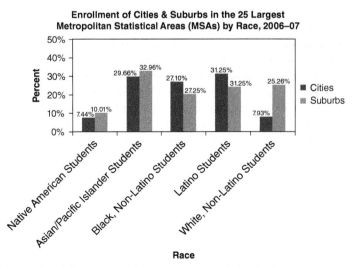

Enrollment of Cities & Suburbs in the 25 Largest Metropolitan Statistical Areas (MSAs) by Race, 2006–07

Source: Calculations from NCES Common Core of Data, 2006–07

While African American and Latino students continue to make up a significant percentage of students in schools located in cities, the migration of middle-class families of color to the suburbs has been steadily increasing since the 1970s. In fact, in 2006–07, a slightly lower percentage of African American and Latino students in the 25 largest metropolitan statistical areas (MSAs) were in the suburbs than in the cities. Within that context, higher shares of Latino students were in the suburbs of the large metropolitan areas in 2006–07 than was the case for African American students. Indeed, the percentage of Latino students enrolled in large suburban schools was nearly equal to the percentage of white students in the suburbs of the 25 largest MSAs. Of all racial groups, Asians were the largest percentage of students in the suburbs of the 25 largest MSAs. Nearly one in three Asian students in the public schools lived in large suburban areas. (Graph 1 illustrates these trends.)

The public schools in our largest two regions of the country, the West and South, already have non-white majorities. The Civil Rights Project's analysis of census data also finds that the percentage of white suburban residents in the largest 25 metropolitan areas fell from 81 percent to 72 percent in the 1990s, while each minority group living in the suburbs increased during this same period, most notably among Latinos. Furthermore, the suburban population grew in the largest 25 MSAs by approximately 17 percent, with nearly 20 million new residents. Given all of these trends, the suburbs, which have long been seen as overwhelmingly white, are not only more diverse today than ever before, but will be increasingly diverse in the future.

The problem, however, is that as diversity in suburban schools rises, the extent of racial isolation and segregation is rising as well. In 2006, for example, the majority of white suburban students (54 percent) attended schools that were more than half white, while a majority of African American and Latino students (67 and 75 percent, respectively) attended suburban schools with a non-white majority. Remarkably, nearly 30 percent of African American and Latino *suburban* students are in hyper-segregated suburban schools with 0–10 percent white students. Asian students, on the other hand, are made up of both a highly privileged and substantially disadvantaged group of students, with 20 percent of Asian suburban students in schools with majority white students and 43 percent in majority non-white schools.

These trends suggest that the racial segregation often associated with schools in the cities—of separate and often unequal schools with many students of color attending overcrowded and under resourced schools—is now spreading into parts of suburbia. And while educational policies continue to try to solve the problem of segregated schools by focusing on solutions within districts, the vast majority of racial/ethnic segregation in U.S. public schools occurs between and not within school districts. Due in part to the *Milliken v. Bradley* case, the fact is that the majority of segregation occurs between city school systems and suburban systems, and also between different suburban school systems.

The deepening segregation of suburban schools in the U.S. is an alarming trend that can be addressed as long as there is a thorough understanding of the serious problems associated with segregation and the curative need for integrated schools.

The Legal Landscape Governing School Integration

. . . A generation ago, the most common desegregation policies were those adopted to comply with court orders or negotiated agreements with federal agencies. Such policies were most frequently implemented in the south where many school districts had formerly operated separate schools for African American and white students. The Supreme Court's *Brown v. Board of Education* decision in 1954 declared such laws to be "inherently unequal" and therefore violated the U.S. Constitution. The *Brown* decision was followed in the late 1960s and early 1970s by subsequent Supreme Court decisions clarifying what was required in order to thoroughly desegregate and to eliminate segregation "root and branch." During the 1960s, the executive and legislative branches of the federal government also increased pressure on school districts to implement desegregation plans. By 1970, the South was the most integrated region of the country for African American students. In 1973, the Supreme Court, for the first time, also acknowledged the right of Latinos to desegregate.

In the 1970s, as desegregation cases came from outside the south, the Supreme Court began to limit the extent of desegregation efforts required to fully demonstrate that segregation had been eradicated. In 1974, the Court first limited desegregation in its *Milliken* decision, which effectively ended most city–suburban desegregation remedies. During the 1990s, a series of three decisions lessened considerably the burden districts had to meet to be declared "unitary" or released from federal court oversight. In the aftermath of these decisions, dozens of districts were declared unitary, and many have ended more far-reaching efforts to desegregate.

Some suburbs may still be under court order or bound by an Office for Civil Rights (OCR) agreement to desegregate their schools, and as such, must continue to abide by their commitments, seeking ways to make desegregation work most effectively and agreeing to modifications when necessary. Districts that have already been declared unitary may also be subject to another court order if new violations are found. And though many suburban communities, particularly in the northern and western regions of the country, were never placed under court supervision, the possibility for legal action still exists under a 1973 ruling in *Keyes v. Denver School District No. 1. Keyes* held that district policies intentionally segregating students—including siting new schools in racially isolated neighborhoods or drawing attendance zones in an isolating manner—were illegal. Today, racially transitioning and expanding suburbs are likely to confront decisions about constructing new schools and redistricting, and any policy decisions that serve to increase and deepen segregation are subject to scrutiny.

A number of districts continue to pursue integration voluntarily after they were declared unitary—and still others adopted integration policies even though they never had any remedial obligation to implement desegregation plans. These districts have chosen to voluntarily pursue integration, valuing its importance in helping to achieve their district's goals. Yet, as alluded to, just as the courts affected the desegregation efforts of districts a generation ago, so too are these newer plans also subject to compliance with relevant legal precedents.

On June 28, 2007, the Supreme Court weighed in on voluntary integration policies, issuing its own complicated decision in two cases at the same time. *Parents Involved in Community Schools v. Seattle School District* and *Meredith v. Jefferson County Board of Education* challenged the voluntary integration plans in Seattle, Washington and Louisville, Kentucky, respectively. (From now on, we'll refer to the Court's decision as the "*Seattle/Louisville* decision."). A majority of the Justices recognized the important goals of diversity and avoiding racial isolation in K–12 public schools, but the Court struck down particular aspects of the Seattle and Louisville student assignment plans because, in the Court's view, they were not carefully designed to achieve those goals. And, while the Court placed limits on the ability of school districts to consider race in student assignment plans, it did not—as some commentators have sometimes reported—rule out any and all considerations of race. In fact, a majority of the Justices explicitly left the door open for school districts to utilize race-conscious measures that promote diversity and avoid racial isolation in schools.

It is important to understand the historical context and legal implications of this decision before beginning to develop or modify the student assignment plan in your district, but this is not a simple task. As noted above, the Supreme Court issued a deeply divided and complex 185-page ruling that did not provide a clear and certain path about what you and your school district can do to promote diversity and avoid racial isolation in your schools. While the specific plans in Seattle and Louisville were struck down as unconstitutional, many of the policies and strategies that school districts commonly use to promote school diversity were not directly addressed or confronted by the Court. The purpose of this chapter is to provide you with as much guidance as we can offer.

An initial word of encouragement: the *Seattle/Louisville* decision does not, and should not, signal an end to efforts that bring children in communities together across lines of difference or that fight the inequities children almost inevitably encounter in racially isolated, under-resourced schools. What it does mean is that each school district must be careful as it explores the development and adoption of a comprehensive set of integrative school policies. Absent due caution, a voluntary school integration plan may be vulnerable to legal challenges by those who are dissatisfied with their children's assignment or who oppose racial integration on principle. Indeed, the Seattle/Louisville cases arose out of those very situations. . . .

Case Background

In order to fully describe the contours of the current legal landscape governing student assignment plans, we describe in detail the two plans under scrutiny in the *Seattle/Louisville* decision.

The Seattle and Louisville Student Assignment Plans

The Seattle and Louisville school districts, along with school districts throughout the country, voluntarily adopted modest measures to achieve racial diversity in their schools. Both the Seattle and Louisville districts sought to preserve educational choice for parents and students and considered race as a factor in student assignment only when schools were racially isolated or predominantly one race. Both districts' student assignment plans relied on the choices of students and parents to attend or transfer to integrated schools or to attend their neighborhood schools. In both districts, the plans provided that the percentage of white/non-white (Seattle) or African American/other (Louisville) students attending each school should roughly reflect the proportions of those students in the district as a whole.

The Seattle/Louisville *Decision*

The Justices were deeply divided in their views and issued five separate opinions. Chief Justice Roberts wrote the plurality opinion (an opinion written by a group of justices when no single opinion received the support of the majority of the court), which Justice Kennedy joined in part. But Justice Kennedy did not join significant portions of the plurality opinion, which means that those portions of the opinion do not carry a majority of the Court, and are not the law of the land. Put another way, the parts of the plurality opinion joined by Justice Kennedy—and only those parts—carried a majority of the Justices and constitute the opinion of the Court. [From now on, we'll refer to the portions of Chief Justice Robert's opinion that Justice Kennedy did not join (i.e., where only four justices signed on) as the plurality opinion; and the portions of the opinion where Justice Kennedy did sign on (i.e., where Justice Kennedy's additional vote constitutes a five-vote majority) as the opinion of the Court.]

Justice Kennedy wrote his own separate opinion, which we will focus upon in discussing the impact of the decision. We look to Justice Kennedy's opinion because in those areas where he disagreed with Chief Justice Roberts' opinion, he, together with the four dissenting Justices, formed a different majority (we'll call it the "Kennedy majority").

The Kennedy majority explicitly recognized that school districts have a "compelling interest" in promoting diversity and in avoiding racial isolation in schools. This opinion left the window open for school districts to continue to use race-conscious measures to achieve these interests, as long as individual students are not classified *solely* by their race. Before we discuss which race-conscious measures were given safe harbor by the Kennedy majority, we lay out the legal standard courts generally apply when school districts take account of race in student assignment.

The "Strict Scrutiny" Standard

Federal courts generally apply a legal standard called "strict scrutiny" whenever a governmental body, such as a public school board, explicitly considers or takes account of race. In the *Seattle/Louisville* decision, the Court held that school districts must meet the strict scrutiny standard when *individual* students are classified by their race (when race is considered more broadly, such as in the drawing of attendance boundaries, a lesser standard might apply. The application of strict scrutiny, however, does not automatically mean a court will find the use of race illegal. To assume so is a common misinterpretation of the law. But when a school district does take account of the race of individual students and its actions are challenged in court, the district needs to satisfy two distinct requirements under the strict scrutiny test. First, the individual racial classification must serve a *compelling interest*. Second, the racial classification must be *narrowly tailored* to further that compelling interest. In short-hand, these two requirements are referred to as the *compelling interest* prong and the *narrowly tailored* prong of the strict scrutiny test. The Supreme Court established the strict scrutiny test many years ago because it believed that the Equal Protection Clause of the Fourteenth Amendment to the U.S. Constitution was adopted to affirm the equality among citizens and therefore requires skepticism of any distinctions based on race or ethnicity.

If the school district fails to meet either of these two prongs, a court will find the challenged race-based policy illegal and order the district to stop using it. On the other hand, if the school district has designed its policy or plan to satisfy both of the requirements of strict scrutiny, then the district may continue using it as a method of fostering diversity and avoiding racial isolation in its schools.

Therefore, in the *Seattle/Louisville* decision, the Supreme Court only applied strict scrutiny to individual racial classifications, but indicated that a lesser standard might apply when race is considered more broadly, as in the drawing of school attendance boundaries or in the recruitment of certain students or faculty by race. As an example, taking account of the racial composition of the neighborhood where a student resides, instead of the race of that individual student, would not trigger strict scrutiny. Instead a lesser standard would apply, and the school district would only need to demonstrate that the use of race is rationally related to a legitimate interest.

Compelling Interest Prong

A compelling interest is simply legalese for "a really good, legally acceptable reason." When a school district uses or considers race in any way, such as in the assignment of students to schools, the law requires it to state a very good reason why it is conscious of race. Courts demand this justification to make sure that the district is not engaging in unconstitutional racial discrimination or simply pandering to racial politics.

Promoting diversity and avoiding racial isolation in schools. Since *Brown,* the courts have frequently discussed—and the public is aware of—the importance and value of diverse learning environments in K–12 public schools. Integration can result

in documented educational and social benefits, both short- and long-term, to students of all racial backgrounds. Integrated schools can also have a positive impact on the health of and public support for the school system itself, and on the success of our broader community and democratic society.

In the *Seattle/Louisville* decision, a majority of Justices recognized—for the first time—compelling interests in promoting student diversity and avoiding racial isolation in K–12 public schools (in the *Grutter v. Bollinger* decision of 2003, a Court majority had already acknowledged a compelling interest in diversity for higher education institutions). As Justice Kennedy noted,

> *"This Nation has a moral and ethical obligation to fulfill its historic commitment to creating an integrated society that ensures equal opportunity for all of its children. A compelling interest exists in avoiding racial isolation, an interest that a school district, in its discretion and expertise, may choose to pursue. Likewise, a district may consider it a compelling interest to achieve a diverse student population."*

This means that school districts can, and should, continue to take steps to pursue diversity and/or avoid racial isolation in schools.

Other related compelling interests. School systems that adopt voluntary school integration plans do so for a variety of reasons, not all of which may be explained by simply saying that there are educational benefits from attending diverse schools or potential harmful effects of attending racially isolated ones. Some of these other reasons—such as increased school safety, improved or equitable community and parental support, the countering of segregative residential patterns, or the maintenance of stability within the school system—are as, or even more, compelling. The Court appears to have combined or folded in each of these ancillary reasons with the interests in promoting diversity and avoiding racial isolation in schools, and so for efficiency's sake, we too will not independently address them here.

In the *Seattle/Louisville* decision, the Court reaffirmed two other compelling interests, but concluded that they did not apply in the context of K–12 voluntary integration efforts. The first of these two interests—in remedying the effects of past discrimination and segregation—is well established in the law. The remedial interest, as it is often called, was commonly recognized in the era of court-ordered desegregation. For the most part, the remedial interest can only be asserted when there has already been a judicial finding of overt racial discrimination, such as the maintenance of segregative student assignment policies. In a unitary school district, or one that has been released from its court order to desegregate, it is difficult to prove that any present-day racial segregation in schools is caused by intentional discrimination or the lingering effects of prior segregation. Thus, in most of the recent voluntary integration cases, including the *Seattle/Louisville* decision, courts have failed to adopt the remediation argument.

Narrow Tailoring Prong

The second part of the strict scrutiny test insists that individual racial classifications be narrowly tailored to their stated compelling interest. This requirement is little more than a legal means–ends analysis. A key to meeting the strict scrutiny standard is to ensure that the race-conscious method being employed (the means) is closely and narrowly tied to your stated goals (the ends). As it applies to voluntary school integration plans, it demands that a school system use individual racial classifications to achieve its stated goals that are no more or less intrusive than they need to be.

The Seattle and Louisville plans were struck down because the Court concluded that they were not narrowly tailored. To be narrowly tailored to achieve the compelling interest in diversity, a race-conscious admissions program must meet the following four requirements: (1) holistic, individualized review of each applicant where race is used in a flexible, non-mechanical way; (2) serious and good faith consideration of race-neutral alternatives; (3) no undue burden on non-minority applicants, and (4) periodic review of the program's continued necessity.

The Court identified three major problems with the consideration of race in the respective open choice and transfer provisions of the Seattle and Louisville student assignment plans. First, the Court objected to the binary (white/non-white or African American/non-African American) system of racial classifications, because it drew a crude racial distinction that did not promote diversity along its many racial and ethnic dimensions. Second, the Court held that neither Seattle nor Louisville had presented sufficient evidence to demonstrate that they had seriously considered race-neutral alternatives. Third, the Court determined that the race-conscious provisions of the Seattle and Louisville plans did not affect enough students to be deemed "necessary" to achieve racial integration.

In the *Seattle/Louisville* decision, a majority of the Justices recognized a different set of compelling interests that school districts can pursue, but still applied some of the narrow tailoring factors from the *Grutter* decision. *Grutter v. Bollinger* and *Gratz v. Bollinger* were two companion cases heard by the Supreme Court in 2003 challenging the consideration of race in college and university admissions. In *Grutter,* the Court affirmed the consideration of race as a factor in the individualized, holistic evaluation of applicants to the University of Michigan Law School. In *Gratz,* the Court struck down the admission policy of the University of Michigan's undergraduate school, because a certain number of points were automatically awarded to applicants from underrepresented minority groups. In the *Seattle/Louisville* decision, Justice Kennedy noted that school districts that take account of race as a component in student assignment should do so as part of a "nuanced, individual evaluation of school needs and school characteristics" informed by *Grutter.*

Permissible Race-Conscious Measures

So how can race be considered in assigning students to your schools after the *Seattle/Louisville* decision? First, Justice

Kennedy explicitly endorsed the following race-conscious methods, providing safe harbor to school districts to use and consider race in employing any and all of these strategies. These include:

- Strategic site selection of new schools
- Drawing attendance zones with general recognition of the racial demographics of neighborhoods
- Allocating resources for special programs
- Recruiting students and faculty in a targeted manner
- Tracking enrollments, performance and other statistics by race

Second, Justice Kennedy noted that race could be a component of other assignment methods as long as they reflect a "more nuanced, individual evaluation of school needs and student characteristics." Justice Kennedy did not provide particular examples, so it is not altogether clear what is included here. We do, however, have some guidance. We know that the racial tiebreaker in Seattle and the consideration of race in the evaluation of transfers in Louisville did not meet this "nuanced, individual evaluation" standard, and we also know that Justice Kennedy specifically provided that the consideration of race as a component in student assignment should be informed by the Supreme Court's decision in *Grutter v. Bollinger,* with the added adjustment that "the criteria relevant to student placement" in K–12 schools "would differ based on the age of the students, the needs of parents, and the role of the schools." Third, while Justice Kennedy clearly disfavored the use of individual racial classifications, he indicated that they could be used as a last resort.

What Kinds of Assignment Plans Are Considered Narrowly Tailored?

In practice, given the unique relationship between each school system and its student assignment methods, uncertainty remains about what would satisfy the narrow tailoring inquiry. But, in light of the Court's decision, below are some of the kinds of questions that you should expect courts to ask in determining whether a particular plan is sufficiently narrowly tailored.

Does the plan consider race in a sufficiently nuanced and context-appropriate way?

The Court was expressly concerned about the use of binary racial categories to assign students: white/non-white in Seattle and African American/non-African American in Louisville. The Court held that the Seattle school district considered students' race in a manner that was too crude to truly achieve racial diversity or reduce isolation. In particular, the classification of students as either "white" or "non-white" was a "blunt distinction" that the Court believed could not advance integration of a student population with significant numbers of African Americans, Asian Americans, Latinos, and Native

Fact Sheet
State of Segregation

Public school enrollment has undergone a dramatic transformation since the Civil Rights Era and is multiracial.

- Latino students are now the largest group of minority students in the public schools (19 percent); Latino students comprise over a third of students in the west (36 percent).
- Black students are 17 percent of all public school students and are more than a quarter of students in the south.
- The west now has a minority of white students (47 percent) and the south soon will (50 percent).

Students in the largest three racial groups typically attend schools in which less than half the students are from other races than themselves.

- White students are more isolated than students from any other racial/ethnic background. They go to schools, on average, where only one out of five students are from different racial groups. This gives white students very little opportunity to reap the benefits of integrated schools.
- Asian students are the most integrated group of students, although some subgroups of Asian students experience high levels of segregation.

Black students in the South for decades were more integrated than black students in any region of the country, although segregation levels for black students in the South have been rising rapidly since the late 1980s.

High—and growing—percentages of black and Latino students attend schools with high percentages of minority students.

- Nearly three-quarters of black and Latino students (73 percent and 77 percent, respectively) attend predominantly minority schools, or schools where more than half of students are nonwhite.
- Almost 40 percent of black and Latino students (38 percent and 39 percent, respectively) attended racially isolated minority schools in which less than 10 percent of students are white. Research shows that such schools are also very likely to be schools where more than half of students come from low-income families and have difficulty retaining highly qualified teachers.
- The percentage of black and Latino students attending both types of segregated schools has increased in the last fifteen years. Segregation levels are highest in the Northeast.

Why should we care about segregated schools? A great deal of social science evidence regarding the benefits of integrated schools and the harms of segregated schools is summarized in an amicus brief filed with the Supreme Court in October 2006; see "Brief of 553 American Social Scientists" at www.civilrightsproject. ucla.edu/research/deseg/amicus_parents_v_seattle.pdf.

For further information, please visit The Civil Rights Project website at www.civilrightsproject.ucla.edu. Statistics taken from "Racial Transformation and the Changing Nature of Segregation" by Gary Orfield and Chungmei Lee. Data analyzed is from the U.S. Department of Education's Common Core of Data, 2003–04.

Americans. Justice Kennedy concluded that: "[f]ar from being narrowly tailored to its purposes, the [Seattle] system threatens to defeat its own ends, and the school district has provided no convincing explanation for its design." Louisville was similarly condemned for employing a "limited notion of diversity," by viewing race exclusively in terms of "African American/other." Most important, this reasoning suggests that more nuanced and pluralistic considerations of race will be more likely to pass the Court's narrow-tailoring inquiry.

Were "race neutral" alternatives considered?

Given the long history of racial discrimination and oppression in America, courts tend to sanction using race-conscious policies—even for laudable purposes—only as a last resort.

Therefore, as part of the narrow-tailoring analysis, courts look to see if school districts might be able to achieve their compelling interests in ways that rely on racial considerations to a lesser extent, or not at all. In the Seattle and Louisville cases, the Court concluded that the districts did not present sufficient evidence that they had seriously considered race-neutral alternatives: Seattle, because it quickly rejected several race-neutral proposals and Louisville, because it had not presented evidence of its consideration of race-neutral strategies.

Consideration of these alternatives is crucial in implementing a successful and legal plan, even though research and the experience of certain school districts suggests that, depending on a district's geography and demography, race-neutral proposals may only be minimally effective in reducing racial isolation and promoting diversity. Nor do courts require that school districts exhaust every possible race-neutral possibility before adopting a race-conscious plan. Rather, they simply need evidence that the school district made a good-faith effort to explore other alternatives.

Is the use of race necessary to achieve stated goals?

The Court noted that the use of race had minimal effects on student assignments in both Seattle and Louisville. In the Court's view, the racial tiebreaker in Seattle had "ultimately affected" only 52 students, and in Louisville, the racial guidelines only impacted 3 percent of assignments. While the Court did not believe that a greater use of race would be preferable, it concluded that "the minimal impact of the [Seattle and Louisville's] racial classifications on school enrollment casts doubt on the necessity of using racial classifications." The bottom line is that if you are able to achieve your stated goals without using racial classifications, you should do so.

Is the use of race closely tied to stated goals?

A key to meeting the strict scrutiny standard is to ensure that the race-conscious method being employed (the means) is closely and narrowly tied to stated goals (the ends).

Critical Thinking

1. How did the Supreme Court's 1974 *Millikin v. Bradley* make it impossible for most big cities to effectively desegregate their schools?

2. How can it be argued that contemporary Supreme Court decisions mark a return to "separate but equal" education, a system that the Court had seemingly struck down in its famous 1954 *Brown v. Board of Education* decision?

3. What does the statistical evidence on the racial composition of public school classrooms reveal? Are U.S. schools moving along the road to racial integration? Or has progress been reversed?

4. What sort of desegregation steps can local school officials continue to take in the wake of Supreme Court rulings that have put limits on the use of magnet schools and other desegregation remedies?

5. What does the Civil Rights Project mean when it argues that the Court's rulings still permit local school districts to undertake desegregation measures that are "narrowly tailored"?

From *Civil Rights Project*, 2011. Copyright © 2011 by Civil Rights Project / Proyecto Derechos Civiles. Reprinted by permission.

UNIT 7
Policing and Crime

Unit Selections

Learning Outcomes

After reading this unit, you should be able to:

- Differentiate between the "law enforcement" and "order maintenance" jobs of the police.

- Propose the various steps that law enforcement agencies can take to reduce citizens' fear of crime and to increase the support that the public extends to the police.

- Explain how the broken-windows approach to policing differs from more traditional policing approaches.

- Understand why critics are often quite skeptical of the claims made by enthusiasts of broken-window policing.

- Explain why activists in minority communities are sometimes outspoken in their criticisms of broken-windows policing.

- Contrast the novel gang reduction strategies implemented by cities in southern California with more commonplace actions that law enforcement agencies have often taken in response to the problem of gang violence.

Student Website
www.mhhe.com/cls

Internet Reference

California Cities Gang Prevention Network
 www.ccgpn.org
Gang Reduction, City of Los Angeles
 http://mayor.lacity.org/issues/gangreduction/index.htm
National Forum on Youth Violence Prevention
 www.findyouthinfo.gov
Prof. Wesley G. Skogan Home Page: Community Policing; Crime and Disorder
 www.skogan.org
The Urban Institute, Policing and Crime Prevention
 www.urban.org/center/jpc/projects/Policing-and-Crime-Prevention.cfm

For a community to thrive, residents must enjoy a reasonable level of public safety. Businesses, too, are attracted to safe environments. But just how does a city reduce crime? There are no easy answers to this difficult social problem.

One fairly innovative approach contends that law enforcement officials should not devote the energies solely to pursuing drug "king pins," violent offenders, and the heads of organized crime syndicates. Instead, James Q. Wilson and George L. Kelling argue that major gains are made when police departments also focus on the many small violations of law and public order. According to the theory of broken-windows policing (Article 29, "Broken Windows"), the police and other members of the community send the wrong message by tolerating seemingly minor infractions (such as "tag artists" who spray-paint graffiti on walls and subway cars, turnstile jumpers who refuse to pay the subway fare, and "squeegee" window washers who demand a dollar for running a rag across the windshield of an automobile stopped at a red light). By tolerating such petty offenses, the community inadvertently communicates that disobedience of the law is acceptable, a message that serves to accelerate "urban decay" as potential offenders begin to think that they can "get away" with all sorts of incidents of law-breaking. In contrast, when law enforcement officials crack down on the "small stuff," they send a clear message that respect for the law and community norms is demanded. The broken-windows approach has an additional advantage: When officers stop and hold a person on a minor infraction, they often find that the violator is also wanted for more serious offenses.

The broken-windows approach was one of the tools that New York Mayor Rudy Giuliani and police chiefs William Bratton and Raymond Kelly used to turn around the image of late-twentieth-century New York as a wild place where the streets were out of control. Giuliani and his backers claim that the broken-windows approach led to a dramatic reduction in crime, producing gains in the city's livability that improved the city's business climate and poured the foundation for the city's economic renewal (Article 30, "How an Idea Drew People Back to Urban Life").

Critics, however, argue that the broken-windows approach receives too much credit for the drop in crime that was reported. Crime fell nationwide as the crack-cocaine epidemic receded. Crime fell in communities across the nation, even in those that had not adopted the broken-windows approach. Other critics worried about the extent to which such an aggressive law enforcement approach would violate individual freedoms and civil rights.

Another innovative approach to law enforcement, community policing, stems from the recognition that the police, acting by themselves, cannot successfully stop crime. Effective law enforcement requires the cooperation of citizens who will report infractions and business owners who will install locks and alarm systems, turn on outdoor lights at night, and direct the police to areas of illegal activity. Community policing seeks to build a partnership between law enforcement officers and neighborhood residents who meet with officers in "beat meetings" to discuss neighborhood problems. While many officers recognize the importance of establishing a strong partnership with the community, more "old guard" officers dismiss

© David R. Frazier Photolibrary, Inc.

community meetings as "social work" and a diversion from serious law enforcement activities.

Partnership building is part of the multi-pronged approach that defines the fairly successful gang reduction and prevention strategies implemented by communities in southern California (Article 31, "California Cities Gang Prevention Network: Promising Developments for Sustainability of Local Efforts"). The approaches taken by these cities share a common philosophical base: A city can effectively reduce gang problems by creating sufficient youth opportunities so that fewer young people will choose to join gangs. In gang-ridden neighborhoods, police officers not only walk the streets. Officers also meet with the kids in community centers and help supervise youth recreational activities. Law enforcement officials also work in partnership with private and nonprofit institutions to offer internships and youth literacy and education programs that further give young people constructive alternatives to gang membership. Social service workers, too, provide additional assistance, as they seek to involve, and build on the strength of, families.

The Police and Neighborhood Safety

Broken Windows

JAMES Q. WILSON AND GEORGE L. KELLING

I n the mid-1970s, the state of New Jersey announced a "Safe and Clean Neighborhoods Program," designed to improve the quality of community life in twenty-eight cities. As part of that program, the state provided money to help cities take police officers out of their patrol cars and assign them to walking beats. The governor and other state officials were enthusiastic about using foot patrol as a way of cutting crime, but many police chiefs were skeptical. Foot patrol, in their eyes, had been pretty much discredited. It reduced the mobility of the police, who thus had difficulty responding to citizen calls for service, and it weakened headquarter's control over patrol officers.

Many police officers also disliked foot patrol, but for different reasons: it was hard work, it kept them outside on cold, rainy nights, and it reduced their chances for making a "good pinch." In some departments, assigning officers to foot patrol had been used as a form of punishment. And academic experts on policing doubted that foot patrol would have any impact on crime rates; it was, in the opinion of most, little more than a sop to public opinion. But since the state was paying for it, the local authorities were willing to go along.

Five years after the program started, the Police Foundation, in Washington, D.C., published an evaluation of the foot-patrol project. Based on its analysis of a carefully controlled experiment carried out chiefly in Newark, the foundation concluded, to the surprise of hardly anyone, that foot patrol had not reduced crime rates. But residents of the foot-patrolled neighborhoods seemed to feel more secure than persons in other areas, tended to believe that crime had been reduced, and seemed to take fewer steps to protect themselves from crime (staying at home with the doors locked, for example). Moreover, citizens in the foot-patrol areas had a more favorable opinion of the police than did those living elsewhere. And officers walking beats had higher morale, greater job satisfaction, and a more favorable attitude toward citizens in their neighborhoods than did officers assigned to patrol cars.

These findings may be taken as evidence that the skeptics were right—foot patrol has no effect on crime; it merely fools the citizens into thinking that they are safer. But in our view, and in the view of the authors of the Police Foundation study (of whom Kelling was one), the citizens of Newark were not fooled at all. They knew what the foot-patrol officers were doing, they knew it was different from what motorized officers do, and they knew that having officers walk beats did in fact make their neighborhoods safer.

But how can a neighborhood be "safer" when the crime rate has not gone down—in fact, may have gone up? Finding the answer requires first that we understand what most often frightens people in public places. Many citizens, of course, are primarily frightened by crime, especially crime involving a sudden, violent attack by a stranger. This risk is very real, in Newark as in many large cities. But we tend to overlook or forget another source of fear—the fear of being bothered by disorderly people. Not violent people, nor, necessarily, criminals, but disreputable or obstreperous or unpredictable people: panhandlers, drunks, addicts, rowdy teenagers, prostitutes, loiterers, the mentally disturbed.

What foot-patrol officers did was to elevate, to the extent they could, the level of public order in these neighborhoods. Though the neighborhoods were predominantly black and the foot patrolmen were mostly white, this "order-maintenance" function of the police was performed to the general satisfaction of both parties.

One of us (Kelling) spent many hours walking with Newark foot-patrol officers to see how they defined "order" and what they did to maintain it. One beat was typical: a busy but dilapidated area in the heart of Newark, with many abandoned buildings, marginal shops (several of which prominently displayed knives and straight-edged razors in their windows), one large department store, and, most important, a train station and several major bus stops. Though the area was run-down, its streets were filled with people, because it was a major transportation center. The good order of this area was important not only to those who lived and worked there but also to many others, who had to move through it on their way home, to supermarkets, or to factories.

The people on the street were primarily black; the officer who walked the street was white. The people were made up of "regulars" and "strangers." Regulars included both "decent folk" and some drunks and derelicts who were always there but who "knew their place." Strangers were, well, strangers, and viewed suspiciously, sometimes apprehensively. The officer—call him Kelly—knew who the regulars were, and they knew him. As he saw his job, he was to keep an eye on strangers, and make certain that the disreputable regulars observed some informal but widely understood rules. Drunks and addicts could sit on the stoops, but could not lie down. People could drink on side streets, but not at the main intersection. Bottles had to be in paper bags. Talking to, bothering, or begging from people waiting at the bus stop was strictly forbidden. If a dispute erupted between a businessman and a customer, the businessman was assumed to be right, especially if the customer was a stranger. If a stranger loitered, Kelly would ask him if he had any means of support and what his business was; if he gave unsatisfactory answers, he was sent on his way. Persons who broke the informal rules, especially those who bothered people waiting at bus stops, were arrested for vagrancy. Noisy teenagers were told to keep quiet.

These rules were defined and enforced in collaboration with the "regulars" on the street. Another neighborhood might have different rules, but these, everybody understood, were the rules for *this* neighborhood. If someone violated them, the regulars not only turned to Kelly for help but also ridiculed the violator. Sometimes what Kelly did could be described as "enforcing the law," but just as often it involved taking informal or extralegal steps to help protect what the neighborhood had decided was the appropriate level of public order. Some of the things he did probably would not withstand a legal challenge.

A determined skeptic might acknowledge that a skilled foot-patrol officer can maintain order but still insist that this sort of "order" has little to do with the real sources of community fear—that is, with violent crime. To a degree, that is true. But two things must be borne in mind. First, outside observers should not assume that they know how much of the anxiety now endemic in many big-city neighborhoods stems from a fear of "real" crime and how

much from a sense that the street is disorderly, a source of distasteful, worrisome encounters. The people of Newark, to judge from their behavior and their remarks to interviewers, apparently assign a high value to public order, and feel relieved and reassured when the police help them maintain that order.

Second, at the community level, disorder and crime are usually inextricably linked, in a kind of developmental sequence. Social psychologists and police officers tend to agree that if a window in a building is broken *and is left unrepaired,* all the rest of the windows will soon be broken. This is as true in nice neighborhoods as in run-down ones. Window-breaking does not necessarily occur on a large scale because some areas are inhabited by determined window-breakers whereas others are populated by window-lovers; rather, one unrepaired broken window is a signal that no one cares, and so breaking more windows costs nothing. (It has always been fun.)

Philip Zimbardo, a Stanford psychologist, reported in 1969 on some experiments testing the broken-window theory. He arranged to have an automobile without license plates parked with its hood up on a street in the Bronx and a comparable automobile on a street in Palo Alto, California. The car in the Bronx was attacked by "vandals" within ten minutes of its "abandonment." The first to arrive were a family—father, mother, and young son—who removed the radiator and battery. Within twenty-four hours, virtually everything of value had been removed. Then random destruction began—windows were smashed, parts torn off, upholstery ripped. Children began to use the car as a playground. Most of the adult "vandals" were well-dressed, apparently clean-cut whites. The car in Palo Alto sat untouched for more than a week. Then Zimbardo smashed part of it with a sledgehammer. Soon, passersby were joining in. Within a few hours, the car had been turned upside down and utterly destroyed. Again, the "vandals" appeared to be primarily respectable whites.

Untended property becomes fair game for people out for fun or plunder, and even for people who ordinarily would not dream of doing such things and who probably consider themselves law-abiding. Because of the nature of community life in the Bronx—its anonymity, the frequency with which cars are abandoned and things are stolen or broken, the past experience of "no one caring"— vandalism begins much more quickly than it does in staid Palo Alto, where people have come to believe that private possessions are cared for, and that mischievous behavior is costly. But vandalism can occur anywhere once communal barriers—the sense of mutual regard and the obligations of civility—are lowered by actions that seem to signal that "no one cares."

We suggest that "untended" behavior also leads to the breakdown of community controls. A stable neighborhood of families who care for their homes, mind each other's children, and confidently frown on unwanted intruders can change, in a few years or even a few months, to an inhospitable and frightening jungle. A piece of property is abandoned, weeds grow up, a window is smashed. Adults stop scolding rowdy children; the children, emboldened, become more rowdy. Families move out, unattached adults move in. Teenagers gather in front of the corner store. The merchant asks them to move; they refuse. Fights occur. Litter accumulates. People start drinking in front of the grocery; in time, an inebriate slumps to the sidewalk and is allowed to sleep it off. Pedestrians are approached by panhandlers.

At this point it is not inevitable that serious crime will flourish or violent attacks on strangers will occur. But many residents will think that crime, especially violent crime, is on the rise, and they will modify their behavior accordingly. They will use the streets less often, and when on the streets will stay apart from their fellows, moving with averted eyes, silent lips, and hurried steps. "Don't get involved." For some residents, this growing atomization will matter little, because the neighborhood is not their "home" but "the place where they live." Their interests are elsewhere; they are cosmopolitans. But it will matter greatly to other people, whose lives derive meaning and satisfaction from local attachments rather than worldly involvement; for them, the neighborhood will cease to exist except for a few reliable friends whom they arrange to meet.

Such an area is vulnerable to criminal invasion. Though it is not inevitable, it is more likely that here, rather than in places where people are confident they can regulate public behavior by informal controls, drugs will change hands, prostitutes will solicit, and cars will be stripped. That the drunks will be robbed by boys who do it as a lark, and the prostitutes' customers will be robbed by men who do it purposefully and perhaps violently. That muggings will occur.

Among those who often find it difficult to move away from this are the elderly. Surveys of citizens suggest that the elderly are much less likely to be the victims of crime than younger persons, and some have inferred from this that the well-known fear of crime voiced by the elderly is an exaggeration: perhaps we ought not to design special programs to protect older persons; perhaps we should even try to talk them out of their mistaken fears. This argument misses the point. The prospect of a confrontation with an obstreperous teenager or a drunken

panhandler can be as fear-inducing for defenseless persons as the prospect of meeting an actual robber; indeed, to a defenseless person, the two kinds of confrontation are often indistinguishable. Moreover, the lower rate at which the elderly are victimized is a measure of the steps they have already taken—chiefly, staying behind locked doors—to minimize the risks they face. Young men are more frequently attacked than older women, not because they are easier or more lucrative targets but because they are on the streets more.

Nor is the connection between disorderliness and fear made only by the elderly. Susan Estrich, of the Harvard Law School, has recently gathered together a number of surveys on the sources of public fear. One, done in Portland, Oregon, indicated that three fourths of the adults interviewed cross to the other side of a street when they see a gang of teenagers; another survey, in Baltimore, discovered that nearly half would cross the street to avoid even a single strange youth. When an interviewer asked people in a housing project where the most dangerous spot was, they mentioned a place where young persons gathered to drink and play music, despite the fact that not a single crime had occurred there. In Boston public housing projects, the greatest fear was expressed by persons living in the buildings where disorderliness and incivility, not crime, were the greatest. Knowing this helps one understand the significance of such otherwise harmless displays as subway graffiti. As Nathan Glazer has written, the proliferation of graffiti, even when not obscene, confronts the subway rider with the "inescapable knowledge that the environment he must endure for an hour or more a day is uncontrolled and uncontrollable, and that anyone can invade it to do whatever damage and mischief the mind suggests."

In response to fear, people avoid one another, weakening controls. Sometimes they call the police. Patrol cars arrive, an occasional arrest occurs, but crime continues and disorder is not abated. Citizens complain to the police chief, but he explains that his department is low on personnel and that the courts do not punish petty or first-time offenders. To the residents, the police who arrive in squad cars are either ineffective or uncaring; to the police, the residents are animals who deserve each other. The citizens may soon stop calling the police, because "they can't do anything."

The process we call urban decay has occurred for centuries in every city. But what is happening today is different in at least two important respects. First, in the period before, say World War II, city dwellers—because of money costs, transportation difficulties, familial and church connections—could rarely move away from neighborhood problems. When movement did occur, it tended to be along public-transit routes. Now mobility has become exceptionally easy for all but the poorest or those who are blocked by racial prejudice. Earlier crime waves had a kind of built-in self-correcting mechanism: the determination of a neighborhood or community to reassert control over its turf. Areas in Chicago, New York, and Boston would experience crime and gang wars, and then normalcy would return, as the families for whom no alternative residences were possible reclaimed their authority over the streets.

Second, the police in this earlier period assisted in that reassertion of authority by acting, sometimes violently, on behalf of the community. Young toughs were roughed up, people were arrested "on suspicion" or for vagrancy, and prostitutes and petty thieves were routed. "Rights" were something enjoyed by decent folk, and perhaps also by the serious professional criminal, who avoided violence and could afford a lawyer.

This pattern of policing was not an aberration or the result of occasional excess. From the earliest days of the nation, the police function was seen primarily as that of a night watchman: to maintain order against the chief threats to order—fire, wild animals, and disreputable behavior. Solving crimes was viewed not as a police responsibility but as a private one. In the March, 1969, *Atlantic,* one of us (Wilson) wrote a brief account of how the police role had slowly changed from maintaining order to fighting crimes. The change began with the creation of private detectives (often ex-criminals), who worked on a contingency-fee basis for individuals who had suffered losses. In time, the detectives were absorbed into municipal police agencies and paid a regular salary; simultaneously, the responsibility for prosecuting thieves was shifted from the aggrieved private citizen to the professional prosecutor. This process was not complete in most places until the twentieth century.

In the 1960s, when urban riots were a major problem, social scientists began to explore carefully the order-maintenance function of the police, and to suggest ways of improving it—not to make streets safer (its original function) but to reduce the incidence of mass violence. Order-maintenance became, to a degree, coterminous with "community relations." But, as the crime wave that began in the early 1960s continued without abatement throughout the decade and into the 1970s, attention shifted to the role of the police as crime-fighters. Studies of police behavior ceased, by and large, to be accounts of the order-maintenance function and became, instead, efforts to propose and test ways whereby the police could solve more crimes, make more arrests, and gather better evidence. If these things could be done, social scientists assumed, citizens would be less fearful.

A great deal was accomplished during this transition, as both police chiefs and outside experts emphasized the crime-fighting function in their plans, in the allocation of resources, and in deployment of personnel. The police may well have become better crime-fighters as a result. And doubtless they remained aware of their responsibility for order. But the link between order-maintenance and crime-prevention, so obvious to earlier generations, was forgotten.

That link is similar to the process whereby one broken window becomes many. The citizen who fears the ill-smelling drunk, the rowdy teenager, or the importuning beggar is not merely expressing his distaste for unseemly behavior; he is also giving voice to a bit of folk wisdom that happens to be a correct generalization—namely, that serious street crime flourishes in areas in which disorderly behavior goes unchecked. The unchecked panhandler is, in effect, the first broken window. Muggers and robbers, whether opportunistic or professional, believe they reduce their chances of being caught or even identified if they operate on streets where potential victims are already intimated by prevailing conditions. If the neighborhood cannot keep a bothersome panhandler from annoying passersby, the thief may reason, it is even less likely to call the police to identify a potential mugger or to interfere if the mugging actually takes place.

Some police administrators concede that this process occurs, but argue that motorized-patrol officers can deal with it as effectively as foot-patrol officers. We are not so sure. In theory, an officer in a squad car can observe as much as an officer on foot; in theory, the former can talk to as many people as the latter. But the reality of police–citizen encounters is powerfully altered by the automobile. An officer on foot cannot separate himself from the street people; if he is approached, only his uniform and his personality can help him manage whatever is about to happen. And he can never be certain what that will be—a request for directions, a plea for help, an angry denunciation, a teasing remark, a confused babble, a threatening gesture.

In a car, an officer is more likely to deal with street people by rolling down the window and looking at them. The door and the window exclude the approaching citizen; they are a barrier. Some officers take advantage of this barrier, perhaps unconsciously, by acting differently if in the car than they would on foot. We have seen this countless times. The police car pulls up to a corner where teenagers are gathered. The window is rolled down. The officer stares at the youths. They stare back. The officer says to one, "C'mere." He saunters over, conveying to his friends by his elaborately casual style the idea that he is not intimidated by authority. "What's your name?"

"Chuck." "Chuck who?" "Chuck Jones." "What you doing, Chuck?" "Nothin." "Got a P.O. [parole officer]?" "Nah." "Sure?" "Yeah." "Stay out of trouble, Chuckie." Meanwhile, the other boys laugh and exchange comments among themselves, probably at the officer's expense. The officer stares harder. He cannot be certain what is being said, nor can he join in and, by displaying his own skill at street banter, prove that he cannot be "put down." In the process, the officer has learned almost nothing, and the boys have decided the officer is an alien force who can safely be disregarded, even mocked.

Our experience is that most citizens like to talk to a police officer. Such exchanges give them a sense of importance, provide them with the basis for gossip, and allow them to explain to the authorities what is worrying them (whereby they gain a modest but significant sense of having "done something" about the problem). You approach a person on foot more easily, and talk to him more readily, than you do a person in a car. Moreover, you can more easily retain some anonymity if you draw an officer aside for a private chat. Suppose you want to pass on a tip about who is stealing handbags, or who offered to sell you a stolen TV. In the inner city, the culprit, in all likelihood, lives nearby. To walk up to a marked patrol car and lean in the window is to convey a visible signal that you are a "fink."

The essence of the police role in maintaining order is to reinforce the informal control mechanisms of the community itself. The police cannot, without committing extraordinary resources, provide a substitute for that informal control, on the other hand, to reinforce those natural forces the police must accommodate them. And therein lies the problem.

Should police activity on the street be shaped, in important ways, by the standards of the neighborhood rather than by the rules of the state? Over the past two decades, the shift of police from order-maintenance to law-enforcement has brought them increasingly under the influence of legal restrictions, provoked by media complaints and enforced by court decisions and departmental orders. As a consequence, the order-maintenance functions of the police are now governed by rules developed to control police relations with suspected criminals. This is, we think, an entirely new development. For centuries, the role of the police as watchmen was judged primarily not in terms of its compliance with appropriate procedures but rather in terms of its attaining a desired objective. The objective was order, an inherently ambiguous term but a condition that people in a given community recognized when they saw it. The means were the same as those the community itself would employ, if

its members were sufficiently determined, courageous, and authoritative. Detecting and apprehending criminals, by contrast, was a means to an end, not an end in itself; a judicial determination of guilt or innocence was the hoped-for result of the law-enforcement mode. From the first, the police were expected to follow rules defining that process, though states differed in how stringent the rules should be. The criminal-apprehension process was always understood to involve individual rights, the violation of which was unacceptable because it meant that the violating officer would be acting as a judge and jury—and that was not his job. Guilt or innocence was to be determined by universal standards under special procedures.

Ordinarily, no judge or jury ever sees the persons caught up in a dispute over the appropriate level of neighborhood order. That is true not only because most cases are handled informally on the street but also because no universal standards are available to settle arguments over disorder, and thus a judge may not be any wiser or more effective than a police officer. Until quite recently in many states, and even today in some places, the police make arrests on such charges as "suspicious person" or "vagrancy" or "public drunkenness"—charges with scarcely any legal meaning. These charges exist not because society wants judges to punish vagrants or drunks but because it wants an officer to have the legal tools to remove undesirable persons from a neighborhood when informal efforts to preserve order in the streets have failed.

Once we begin to think of all aspects of police work as involving the application of universal rules under special procedures, we inevitably ask what constitutes an "undesirable person" and why we should "criminalize" vagrancy or drunkenness. A strong and commendable desire to see that people are treated fairly makes us worry about allowing the police to rout persons who are undesirable by some vague or parochial standard. A growing and not-so-commendable utilitarianism leads us to doubt that any behavior that does not "hurt" another person should be made illegal. And thus many of us who watch over the police are reluctant to allow them to perform, in the only way they can, a function that every neighborhood desperately wants them to perform.

This wish to "decriminalize" disreputable behavior that "harms no one"—and thus remove the ultimate sanction the police can employ to maintain neighborhood order—is, we think, a mistake. Arresting a single drunk or a single vagrant who has harmed no identifiable person seems unjust, and in a sense it is. But failing to do anything about a score of drunks or a hundred vagrants may destroy an entire community. A particular rule that seems to make sense in the individual case makes no sense when it is made a universal rule and applied to all cases. It makes no sense because it fails to take into account the connection between one broken window left untended and a thousand broken windows. Of course, agencies other than the police could attend to the problems posed by drunks or the mentally ill, but in most communities—especially where the "deinstitutionalization" movement has been strong—they do not.

The concern about equity is more serious. We might agree that certain behavior makes one person more undesirable than another, but how do we ensure that age or skin color or national origin or harmless mannerisms will not also become the basis for distinguishing the undesirable from the desirable? How do we ensure, in short, that the police do not become the agents of neighborhood bigotry?

We can offer no wholly satisfactory answer to this important question. We are not confident that there *is* a satisfactory answer, except to hope that by their selection, training, and supervision, the police will be inculcated with a clear sense of the outer limit of their discretionary authority. That limit, roughly, is this—the police exist to help regular behavior, not to maintain the racial or ethnic purity of a neighborhood.

Consider the case of the Robert Taylor Homes in Chicago, one of the largest public-housing projects in the country. It is home for nearly 20,000 people, all black, and extends over ninety-two acres along South State Street. It was named after a distinguished black who had been, during the 1940s, chairman of the Chicago Housing Authority. Not long after it opened, in 1962, relations between project residents and the police deteriorated badly. The citizens felt that the police were insensitive or brutal; the police, in turn, complained of unprovoked attacks on them. Some Chicago officers tell of times when they were afraid to enter the Homes. Crime rates soared.

Today, the atmosphere has changed. Police–citizen relations have improved—apparently, both sides learned something from the earlier experience. Recently, a boy stole a purse and ran off. Several young persons who saw the theft voluntarily passed along to the police information on the identity and residence of the thief, and they did this publicly, with friends and neighbors looking on. But problems persist, chief among them the presence of youth gangs that terrorize residents and recruit members in the project. The people expect the police to "do something" about this, and the police are determined to do just that.

But do what? Though the police can obviously make arrests whenever a gang member breaks the law, a gang can form, recruit, and congregate without breaking the law. And only a tiny fraction of gang-related crimes can be solved by an arrest; thus, if an arrest is the only recourse

for the police, the residents' fears will go unassuaged. The police will soon feel helpless, and the residents will again believe that the police "do nothing." What the police in fact do is to chase known gang members out of the project. In the words of one officer, "We kick ass." Project residents both know and approve of this. The tacit police–citizen alliance in the project is reinforced by the police view that the cops and the gangs are the two rival sources of power in the area, and that the gangs are not going to win.

None of this is easily reconciled with any conception of due process or fair treatment. Since both residents and gang members are black, race is not a factor. But it could be. Suppose a white project confronted a black gang, or vice versa. We would be apprehensive about the police taking sides. But the substantive problem remains the same: how can the police strengthen the informal social-control mechanisms of natural communities in order to minimize fear in public places? Law enforcement, per se, is no answer. A gang can weaken or destroy a community by standing about in a menacing fashion and speaking rudely to passersby without the law.

We have difficulty thinking such matters, not simply because the ethical and legal issues are so complex but because we have become accustomed to thinking of the law in essentially individualistic terms. The law defines *my* rights, punishes *his* behavior, and is applied by *that* officer because of *this* harm. We assume, in thinking this way, that what is good for the individual will be good for the community, and what doesn't matter when it happens to one person won't matter if it happens to many. Ordinarily, those are plausible assumptions. But in cases where behavior that is tolerable to one person is intolerable to many others, the reactions of the others—fear, withdrawal, flight—may ultimately make matters worse for everyone, including the individual who first professed his indifference.

It may be their greater sensitivity to communal as opposed to individual needs that helps explain why the residents of small communities are more satisfied with their police than are the residents of similar neighborhoods in big cities. Elinor Ostrom and her co-workers at Indiana University compared the perception of police services in two poor, all-black Illinois towns—Phoenix and East Chicago Heights—with those of three comparable all-black neighborhoods in Chicago. The level of criminal victimization and the quality of police–community relations appeared to be about the same in the towns and the Chicago neighborhoods. But the citizens living in their own villages were much more likely than those living in the Chicago neighborhoods to say that they do not stay at home for fear of crime, to agree that the local police have "the right to take any action necessary" to deal with problems, and to agree that the police "look out for the needs of the average citizen." It is possible that the residents and the police of the small towns saw themselves as engaged in a collaborative effort to maintain a certain standard of communal life, whereas those of the big city felt themselves to be simply requesting and supplying particular services on an individual basis.

If this is true, how should a wise police chief deploy his meager forces? The first answer is that nobody knows for certain, and the most prudent course of action would be to try further variations on the Newark experiment, to see more precisely what works in what kinds of neighborhoods. The second answer is also a hedge—many aspects of order-maintenance in neighborhoods can probably best be handled in ways that involve the police minimally, if at all. A busy, bustling shopping center and a quiet, well-tended suburb may need almost no visible police presence. In both cases, the ratio of respectable to disreputable people is ordinarily so high as to make informal social control effective.

Even in areas that are in jeopardy from disorderly elements, citizen action without substantial police involvement may be sufficient. Meetings between teenagers who like to hang out on a particular corner and adults who want to use that corner might well lead to an amicable agreement on a set of rules about how many people can be allowed to congregate, where, and when.

Where no understanding is possible—or if possible, not observed—citizen patrols may be a sufficient response. There are two traditions of communal involvement in maintaining order. One, that of the "community watchmen," is as old as the first settlement of the New World. Until well into the nineteenth century, volunteer watchmen, not policemen, patrolled their communities to keep order. They did so, by and large, without taking the law into their own hands—without, that is, punishing persons or using force. Their presence deterred disorder or alerted the community to disorder that could not be deterred. There are hundreds of such efforts today in communities all across the nation. Perhaps the best known is that of the Guardian Angels, a group of unarmed young persons in distinctive berets and T-shirts, who first came to public attention when they began patrolling the New York City subways but who claim now to have chapters in more than thirty American cities. Unfortunately, we have little information about the effect of these groups on crime. It is possible, however, that whatever their effect on crime, citizens find their presence reassuring, and that they thus contribute to maintaining a sense of order and civility.

The second tradition is that of the "vigilante." Rarely a feature of the settled communities of the East, it was primarily to be found in those frontier towns that grew up in advance of the reach of government. More than 350 vigilante groups are known to have existed; their distinctive feature was that their members did take the law into their own hands, by acting as judge, jury, and often executioner as well as policeman. Today, the vigilante movement is conspicuous by its rarity, despite the great fear expressed by citizens that the older cities are becoming "urban frontiers." But some community-watchmen groups have skirted the line, and others may cross it in the future. An ambiguous case, reported in *The Wall Street Journal*, involved a citizens' patrol in the Silver Lake area of Belleville, New Jersey. A leader told the reporter, "We look for outsiders." If a few teenagers from outside the neighborhood enter it, "we ask them their business," he said. "If they say they're going down the street to see Mrs. Jones, fine, we let them pass. But then we follow them down the block to make sure they're really going to see Mrs. Jones."

Though citizens can do a great deal, the police are plainly the key to order-maintenance. For one thing, many communities, such as the Robert Taylor Homes, cannot do the job by themselves. For another, no citizen in a neighborhood, even an organized one, is likely to feel the sense of responsibility that wearing a badge confers. Psychologists have done many studies on why people fail to go to the aid of persons being attacked or seeking help, and they have learned that the cause is not "apathy" or "selfishness" but the absence of some plausible grounds for feeling that one must personally accept responsibility. Ironically, avoiding responsibility is easier when a lot of people are standing about. On streets and in public places, where order is so important, many people are likely to be "around," a fact that reduces the chance of any one person acting as the agent of the community. The police officer's uniform singles him out as a person who must accept responsibility if asked. In addition, officers, more easily than their fellow citizens, can be expected to distinguish between what is necessary to protect the safety of the street and what merely protects its ethnic purity.

But the police forces of America are losing, not gaining, members. Some cities have suffered substantial cuts in the number of officers available for duty. These cuts are not likely to be reversed in the near future. Therefore, each department must assign its existing officers with great care.

Some neighborhoods are so demoralized and crime-ridden as to make foot patrol useless; the best the police can do with limited resources is respond to the enormous number of calls for service. Other neighborhoods are so stable and serene as to make foot patrol unnecessary. The key is to identify neighborhoods at the tipping point—where the public order is deteriorating but not unreclaimable, where the streets are used frequently but by apprehensive people, where a window is likely to be broken at any time, and must quickly be fixed if all are not to be shattered.

Most police departments do not have ways of systematically identifying such areas and assigning officers to them. Officers are assigned on the basis of crime rates (meaning that marginally threatened areas are often stripped so that police can investigate crimes in areas where the situation is hopeless) or on the basis of calls for service (despite the fact that most citizens do not call the police when they are merely frightened or annoyed). To allocate patrol wisely, the department must look at the neighborhoods and decide, from first-hand evidence, where an additional officer will make the greatest difference in promoting a sense of safety.

One way to stretch limited police resources is being tried in some public-housing projects. Tenant organizations hire off-duty police officers for patrol work in their buildings. The costs are not high (at least not per resident), the officer likes the additional income, and the residents feel safer. Such arrangements are probably more successful than hiring private watchmen, and the Newark experiment helps us understand why. A private security guard may deter crime or misconduct by his presence, and he may go to the aid of persons needing help, but he may well not intervene—that is, control or drive away—someone challenging community standards. Being a sworn officer—a "real cop"—seems to give one the confidence, the sense of duty, and the aura of authority necessary to perform this difficult task.

Patrol officers might be encouraged to go to and from duty stations on public transportation and, while on the bus or subway car, enforce rules about smoking, drinking, disorderly conduct, and the like. The enforcement need involve nothing more than ejecting the offender (the offense, after all, is not one with which a booking officer or a judge wishes to be bothered). Perhaps the random but relentless maintenance of standards on buses would lead to conditions on buses that approximate the level of civility we now take for granted on airplanes.

But the most important requirement is to think that to maintain order in precarious situations is a vital job. The police know this is one of their functions, and they also believe, correctly, that it cannot be done to the exclusion of criminal investigation and responding to calls. We may have encouraged them to suppose, however, on the basis of our oft-repeated concerns about serious, violent crime, that they will be judged exclusively on their capacity as crime-fighters. To the extent that this is the case, police administrators will continue to concentrate police personnel in the highest-crime areas (though not necessarily in the areas most vulnerable to criminal invasion), emphasize their training in the law and criminal apprehension (and not their training in managing street life), and join too quickly in campaigns to decriminalize "harmless" behavior (though public drunkenness, street prostitution, and pornographic displays can destroy a community more quickly than any team of professional burglars).

Above all, we must return to our long-abandoned view that the police ought to protect communities as well as individuals. Our crime statistics and victimization surveys measure individual losses, but they do not measure communal losses. Just as physicians now recognize the importance of fostering health rather than simply treating illness, so the police—and the rest of us—ought to recognize the importance of maintaining, intact, communities without broken windows.

Critical Thinking

1. What are the consequences of a broken window that is left unrepaired? How does an "untended" broken window lead to more serious neighborhood problems?
2. How can the broken-windows metaphor be applied to policing? On what sort of activities should police focus if they wish to increase order maintenance in a neighborhood?
3. How does the broken-windows emphasis on order maintenance in a community differ from more traditional policing approaches?

JAMES Q. WILSON is Shattuck Professor of Government at Harvard and author of *Thinking About Crime*. **GEORGE L. KELLING,** formerly director of the evaluation field staff of the Police Foundation, is currently a research fellow at the John F. Kennedy School of Government at Harvard.

How an Idea Drew People Back to Urban Life

Twenty years after 'Broken Windows,' James Q. Wilson assesses the theory.

JAMES Q. WILSON

Two decades ago, George Kelling and I published an article in the *Atlantic Monthly* entitled "Broken Windows: The Police and Neighborhood Safety." Maybe it was the catchy title, maybe it was the argument, but for some reason the phrase and maybe the idea spread throughout American policing, and now is being taken up by the police in many other countries. Today, I sometimes hear a police official explain to me that they have adopted the "broken windows" strategy as if I had never heard of it.

The idea was simple. Citizens want public order as much as they want crime reduced, and so the police ought to worry about public disorder as much as they worry about catching crooks. Disorder arises from minor offenses such as aggressive panhandling, graffiti sprayed on the outside of buildings, alcoholics wandering the streets, and hostile teenagers hanging around bus stops and delicatessens.

Even though chasing away or arresting people who did these things may not do much to reduce crime immediately and in any event would constitute at best a minor pinch that police officers rarely took seriously and that courts were likely to ignore, recreating public order would do two things: Convince decent citizens that they and not some hostile force were entitled to use the streets and (perhaps) reduce crime over time by inducing good people and discouraging bad ones from using the streets.

The idea arose from Mr. Kelling's study of the effects of foot patrol on crime and public attitudes in New Jersey. He worked for the Police Foundation as it carried out a rigorous evaluation of foot patrol in Newark when Hubert Williams was the police chief. The neighborhoods where the experiment took place were largely inhabited by blacks and the officers who did the patrolling were largely white. The theory was that foot patrol would make the streets safer.

By and large, police chiefs did not believe this; after all, an officer on foot could not do much to chase a burglar in a car, and besides thieves could easily avoid the streets where foot patrol officers were walking. Police officers did not much care for foot patrol either. Standing outside on a cold or rainy night in Newark was a lot less pleasant than sitting in a warm patrol car, and the arrests you were likely to make while on foot would probably be of small-time offenders that would not do much to advance your police career.

The research showed that the police chiefs were right: Foot patrol did not cut crime. But it showed something else as well: The citizens loved it.

Explaining this puzzle is why we wrote the article. Were the citizens just fooling themselves by liking foot patrol? Did the whole project mean that the cops got better public relations just by conning the voters? Or maybe the citizens were right. Maybe they valued public order as much as they valued less crime. Perhaps public order would later on reduce the chances of crime rates rising if enough good folk used the streets and fewer roughnecks did.

We think the citizens were right. Getting rid of graffiti, aggressive panhandling, and wandering drunks made the citizens happier and increased their support for the police. Moreover, the cops on foot actually liked the work because they got to meet a lot of decent people and learn how they thought instead of just getting out of a patrol car to arrest a crook. We went on to offer the speculation—and at the time it was only a guess—that more orderly neighborhoods would, over the long haul, become less dangerous ones.

Our idea survived the predictable onslaught. Many civil rights organizations began to protest against efforts to control panhandling. Such efforts, they argued, were directed at the poor, blacks and the homeless. The ACLU filed suits in some cities against aspects of broken-windows policing. They must have forgotten, or perhaps they never knew, that broken-windows policing was first tested in poor black neighborhoods that enthusiastically endorsed it.

Civil libertarians also complained that stopping begging in the New York subways denied people free speech, and even got a federal judge to agree with them. But the appeals court threw out the argument because begging was not speech designed to convey a message, it was simply solicitation for money.

Slowly our idea grew until now it is hard to find a police department that does not claim to practice community-oriented policing and follow a broken-windows strategy. Just what the police chief means by these terms is not always very clear; to some extent, these words have become buzz phrases, backed up by a federal government policy of giving money to cities if they practice community policing, somehow defined.

In 1996, Mr. Kelling and his wife, Catherine Coles, published a book, "Fixing Broken Windows," that reviewed what has been done by Robert Kiley, David Gunn, and William Bratton to restore decency and safety to the New York subways and Bratton's later efforts to cut crime citywide after he became commissioner of the New York Police Department. Similar efforts took place in Baltimore, San Francisco, and Seattle.

The New York Transit Authority experience was especially telling. Long before he became the NYPD commissioner, Mr. Bratton, working with Messrs. Kiley and Gunn, had cut crime dramatically in the city's subways by holding his subordinates accountable for reducing offenses and getting rid of the graffiti. The people and the editorial writers cheered and in time the number of cops on duty underground could be safely cut.

Everyone in New York will recall the key steps whereby the subway success became the whole city's achievement. Rudolph Giuliani got elected mayor after a tough anti-crime campaign. One of the first things the NYPD did after he took office was to emphasize a policy begun by former police commissioner Raymond Kelly (who is now commissioner again) to get tough on "squeegee-men," males who extort money from motorists by pretending to wash (and sometimes spitting on) their car windows. Traditionally, officers would at best give only tickets to squeegeers, who would usually ignore the tickets or at worst pay a small fine. But then the NYPD began issuing warrants for the arrest of squeegee-men who ignored their tickets. Getting the warrant for non-appearance meant jail time for the recipient, and suddenly squeegee harassment stopped.

It may have been a little thing, but every New York motorist noticed it. Almost overnight, the city seemed safer. No one can say it was safer from serious crime, but it appeared safer and the people loved it.

After Mr. Giuliani took office, the crime rate plummeted. Lots of criminologists think that this happened automatically or as a result of some demographic change. No doubt serious crime fell in a lot of cities, but it fell faster and more in New York than almost anywhere else.

I do not assume that broken-windows policing explains this greater drop. Indeed, my instinct is to think that Mr. Bratton's management style, and especially his effort to hold precinct commanders accountable by frequently reviewing their performance in rigorous CompStat hearings, was the chief factor.

But Mr. Kelling has gathered a lot of evidence that a broken-windows strategy also made a difference. He measured that strategy by counting the number of misdemeanor arrests in New York precincts and showing that an increase in such arrests was accompanied by a decrease in serious crime, even in areas where unemployment rates rose, drug use was common, and the number of young men in their crime-prone years had increased.

So maybe a broken-windows strategy really does cut crime. But we know that it draws people back into urban life. And that is no trivial gain.

Critical Thinking

1. How did enforcement under broken-windows policing help to establish new standards of public conduct of just what would and would not be tolerated in New York City?

2. According to Wilson, how did broken-windows enforcement help to change the public culture in New York, paving the way for the city's economic comeback?

Mr. Wilson is an emeritus professor at UCLA and a lecturer at Pepperdine University.

California Cities Gang Prevention Network Promising Developments for Sustainability of Local Efforts

ANDREW MOORE

Since 2007, teams of mayors, police chiefs and a broad range of local partners from 13 cities have made comprehensive, collaborative efforts to reduce gang violence, with support from their peers and colleagues in the California Cities Gang Prevention Network. Member cities include Fresno, Los Angeles, Oakland, Oxnard, Richmond, Sacramento, Salinas, San Bernardino, San Diego, San Francisco, San José, Santa Rosa, and Stockton. The National League of Cities Institute for Youth, Education and Families and the National Council on Crime and Delinquency have co-sponsored the network with support from the California Endowment, California Wellness Foundation and other local philanthropies.

As the California Cities Gang Prevention Network marks its first five years of peer learning and sharing, promising practices have emerged in several cities that point the way toward increased sustainability for local efforts. Embedding a comprehensive approach to gang violence reduction balanced among prevention, intervention, and enforcement in the practices of city governments and their partners has constituted a network priority from the start. Also of high importance for sustainability is to change the way city governments and their nonprofit and county partners "do business" when it comes to reducing gang impact, typically working in far more coordinated and collaborative ways.

This policy and practice brief offers a snapshot of the emerging and promising developments, and changed ways of doing business, in several cities. These developments, growing organically from cities' comprehensive plans, offer various routes to sustaining local youth and gang violence prevention efforts. Los Angeles is migrating toward a family focus, allowing the city to direct and evaluate its comprehensive services in a consistent manner. San José has stepped up its involvement in reentry and strengthened its collaboration with the county to prepare for the impending realignment of criminal justice responsibilities among state and county governments in California. Salinas is changing policing practices in one high-violence neighborhood to build trust between law enforcement and the community.

Santa Rosa is regionalizing its effort, knowing that gangs do not respect city boundaries. Sacramento has layered in a primary prevention emphasis through a focus on early literacy. Looked at across a continuum, these activities exemplify the dynamism within the network even as they suggest a trend toward greater permanence.

Salinas, a city of 150,000, faced a record-setting number of homicides in 2009, virtually all gang-related—twice the rate in the city as in Monterey County as a whole, and triple that of the rest of the state. With leadership from the mayor and police chief, as well as substantial assistance from the California Cities Gang Prevention Network and the U.S. Naval Postgraduate School, the Community Alliance for Safety and Peace (CASP) of Salinas/Monterey County incubated and implemented the Salinas Comprehensive Strategy for Community-Wide Violence Reduction. Under the vision of creating a "Peaceful Community," the plan sought to address six significant problem areas identified through community listening sessions, research, and the California Endowment's Building Healthy Communities initiative. These areas included: social and economic conditions, engaging and supervising youth, environmental design and urban planning, law enforcement, education and schools, and the impact of drugs and alcohol.

Of note, the Naval Postgraduate School (NPS), under the leadership of retired Colonel Hy Rothstein and colleagues, contributed facilitation and data analysis skills to the formulation of the plan. NPS' initial "counterinsurgency" framing triggered controversy, especially in the Hispanic community where many residents viewed police with mistrust and some perceived them as an occupying or predatory force. The controversy abated when city leaders stressed that the focus of the "counterinsurgency" strategy was not to overcome the violence problem with force, but to strengthen neighborhoods, communities and families and thereby build and sustain an environment where violent gangs could not thrive.

Whereas the plan has a citywide scope, CASP, the city's newly formed community safety division, and the police department determined to focus early efforts on the Hebbron neighborhood, known for its high crime rates. The assignment of two police officers exclusively to Hebbron to do whatever it takes to bring back the community—from neighborhood beautification to getting to know the families and, in essence, rebuilding after decades of mistrust—signals a readiness on the part of the police to conduct their business in a different way. This policy and practice change in turn suggests new directions that police and their partners in other hard-hit neighborhoods could take in California and across the nation.

Indeed, changes in the law enforcement sector may represent seismic shifts in how Salinas responds to its youth violence and gang issues. Over the past five years, budget cuts have meant the loss of 40 officer positions, a 21 percent reduction in force. Nevertheless, Deputy Chief of Police Kelly McMillin has played a central role in representing the police department in the overall planning effort, and in altering police department policy and practice to respond better to the needs of a frightened community. Deputy Chief McMillin's redeployment of two officers to Hebbron transcends budget strictures: "We're going to fight this fight whether we're fully funded or half funded or not funded at all," said McMillin in a January 2012 interview with *The New York Times*.

The core rationale for McMillin's redeployment strategy is not primarily enforcement, but trust building. While trust can lead to better and more frequent crime reporting, that is not the focus either. Neighborhood leaders and service agencies meet in Hebbron's family center where the police department has opened an office staffed by Officers Rich Lopez and Jeffrey Lofton. According to the Monterey Herald, Lopez and Lofton walk the streets and "hope to become familiar, trusted faces as they knock on every door in the area defined as Census Tract 5.01." Says McMillin, the officers "spend their days doing whatever is needed, like mediating disputes between sixth grade girls and helping people in the neighborhood write petitions to have street lights repaired." Community Safety Director Georgina Mendoza reports that the community sees them as "my cop, my officer." Over the long term, McMillin observes, "What do we want to leave behind in Hebbron? Not a structure, but a capacity, a sense of trust in the city, that the city is there for them."

Reinforcing the new orientation, the Salinas Police Managers' Association, composed of sergeants, commanders and deputy chiefs, nominated Officer Lopez as "Officer of the Year." The honor typically goes to a top performing officer with an impressive résumé that includes high-profile arrests, multiple firearm recoveries and completion of complex investigations. Lopez' nomination stemmed from outstanding efforts on patrol and, notes McMillin, "the work he's been doing in Hebbron as a 'CASP Cop.' . . . Staff recognized the importance of the outreach he's been doing, the trust building, the time and effort he's put into understanding the neighborhood and community members he's been assigned to serve."

Other agencies have stepped forward to complement the police redeployment. CASP, with the county's behavioral health division in the lead, organizes "charlas" (chats) two Friday evenings each month in Hebbron. In an interview with Lynn Graebner of the California Health Report, Mendoza commented on another example of increasing trust between residents and officials. "At first, CASP members brought the food and provided the space," said Mendoza. "Now the residents are saying, 'Don't bring your food. We have better food, and we'll decide where to meet.'" The faith community has weighed in as well. Pastor Frank Gomez has opened his church to about 50 second through seventh graders for tutoring four days per week. "We give up our facility four days a week, but it's a no brainer for me," Gomez said in a newspaper interview.

What are the results of Salinas' comprehensive plan to date? Citywide crime numbers have been going the right way: There were 51 shootings and 11 gang-related homicides in 2011, down from 151 shootings and 29 gang-related homicides in 2009. At the neighborhood level, public health nurses, police, probation officers, and recreation staff rub shoulders with each other and residents in Hebbron, and local partners note substantial improvements in building trust and community. "I see changes," says Brian Contreras, director of Second Chance Family and Youth Services in Salinas. "Kids are coming back to this area. There are new faces."

After passing through an era of mayoral transition and severe fiscal straits, Sacramento was among the most recent of the 13 network cities to coalesce around a comprehensive plan. With strong leadership from Mayor Kevin Johnson and by embracing a diverse group of partners, the city emerged with a "new paradigm" plan that focuses on prevention through early literacy as one strategy for reducing high rates of violence and incarceration. Whereas all network cities' comprehensive plans include a prevention plank—and many cities have sought in recent years to increase coordination of prevention activities with community-based organizations and county agencies—Sacramento stands at the vanguard with its heavy concentration on prevention. The city has advocated for this strategy and now, through implementation, has the opportunity to serve as a beacon for other communities.

The "Mayor's Strategic Plan for Gang Prevention 2012–2015" is the product of a Mayor's Gang Prevention Task Force appointed following high-profile, gang-related shootings in Sacramento. Building blocks for the plan emerged from a positive youth development framework, focusing on "protective factors" that youth can accumulate to guard against gang involvement rather than a primary examination of "risk factors." Attending school regularly, reading on grade level by the end of third grade, and building strong connections with caring adults through after-school programs all constitute examples of the protective factors that Sacramento seeks to strengthen. Further informing this focus is a concern for establishing stronger connections within the community "to get in front of the gang issue by addressing the root causes that lead to the individual, school, peer, and family disconnectedness." City Councilmember Jay Schenirer comments, "Prevention—it's what we should be doing for all kids. A large group do not get [prevention services] now."

Based on principles such as meaningful community engagement, enhanced cross-system efficacy, accountability, and a public health approach to gang prevention, the Sacramento plan sets out goals and strategies in four areas: (1) increase school-based supports and enrichment activities; (2) strengthen community capacity to address gang involvement and create safe neighborhoods; (3) provide workforce readiness and other positive alternatives for at-risk youth; and (4) develop regional collaboration in areas of enforcement, awareness, evaluation and implementation of the Mayor's Gang Prevention Task Force goals and objectives. The plan establishes specific targets to reduce gang violence by 30 percent in three years, improve the Academic Performance Index and school attendance rates, and reduce recidivism among gang-involved youth.

The Sacramento Police Department is one of the agencies adopting a new approach. The department assigned Lieutenant Kathy Lester to supervise school resource officers (SROs) as a unified force, and also made her time available to assist with preparation of the city's recently submitted CalGRIP (California Gang Reduction, Intervention and Prevention Initiative) proposal. Lester explains how the department and other team members proceeded: "The chief's question was, what can we do with existing resources? We didn't want to duplicate, so we did an inventory of what we already had. . . . We saw what was missing, observed a significant waiting list for afterschool programs, and so, focused our newest effort on children in kindergarten through sixth grade. We identified Project Learn [early literacy curriculum and tools] as an evidence-based practice, and we didn't have enough funding [from the city] for it, so we brought in partners." As Lester explains, "We don't get anything done these days unless we have collaboration, coordination, and partnership. No one single agency can act in a bubble. Everything is moving toward regionalization. We also work with traffic engineering and county animal control. The SRO program is specific to the city, but we meet with other SROs in the area as well."

Change has also come to the mayor's office, with Mayor Johnson as chief fundraiser and assembler of resources. Nik Howard spearheads the Sacramento READS! Third Grade Literacy Campaign as a centerpiece of the new plan, operating as a member of the mayor's staff from a privately-funded base at the Stand Up nonprofit organization. Support to date has come from national and regional sources such as the W.K. Kellogg, Tides, and Sierra Health Foundations and the multinational education company, Knowledge Universe. Howard describes part of the plan's impetus: "We wanted to make sure to engage kids from birth to age eight in early reading interventions, and middle and high school kids at risk of gang involvement as tutors and volunteers. . . . By focusing energy on early intervention, we are not only going to solve the literacy gap, we will also get at ancillary issues."

As another feature of plan implementation in Sacramento, Councilmember Schenirer has launched the multipurpose Way Up initiative out of his district office to establish "a proof point for what works—everything we do [in the Oak Park neighborhood] is scalable citywide." As a parallel to early literacy efforts, for instance, Way Up arranges medical screening to ensure connection to a "medical home" for 6,500 students in nine schools. "We will track emergency room visits, and hope to see a drop in usage," said Councilmember Schenirer. Way Up also operates a leadership development program and arranges "Summer in City Hall" stipended internships. Notably, the Oak Park pilot neighborhood constitutes half of the South Sacramento focus area of The California Endowment's

Building Healthy Communities project, and close coordination is in place among these geographically-focused efforts.

Maureen Price of the Sacramento Boys and Girls Clubs describes additional features of the plan in action. "We have adopted a more comprehensive literacy program for children in first through third grades," says Price. "We got a new grant to identify kids who are not proficient in reading. . . . We are conducting pilot projects in two school sites, and may implement Project Learn in club houses next fall. Also, the United Way supports the Star Readers program [in the clubs]."

As Sacramento proceeds with plan implementation, a variety of voices remind city leaders of key issues to consider. Vidal Gonzalez of La Familia, a youth development and employment organization, commented, "A general approach is not going to work. [You have to take into account] cultural and ethnic differences, particularly with Latino gangs. . . . The family has a lot to do with it. Some gang participation crosses generations." One of La Familia's contributions to the early literacy efforts in the plan is the development of a community lending library with donated books by multicultural authors for young readers. The organization also identifies older youth who will read to younger children.

Greg King of the grassroots neighborhood group Always Knocking, who will chair the community engagement effort under the plan, says, "On paper you can see it. Actions remain to be seen. City officials are on the right path." King looks forward to leveraging the plan to accomplish several infrastructure priorities, including "keeping the doors open at youth centers even in the face of budget cuts, establishing a screening policy for volunteers while still making them feel welcome, and giving people in the community a chance to feel heard." King adds, "While educating the kids, we have to bring in the parents. I say PIESE—Parent Involvement Equals Success for Education." Initially, King is coordinating an effort to support parents to spend at least 30 minutes per month in their child's school.

Alicia Ross, a leader with the Sacramento ACT faith-based community organizing group, worked closely with the police department to bring the Boston Ceasefire intervention program to the city. She sees the plan as "a good baseline tool to keep pushing collectively on prevention and intervention, [especially if we muster] real resources behind it and set benchmarks for how the city will implement the plan." Meanwhile, the combination of federal, state, and foundation grants that have supported Ceasefire to date will run out later in 2012. Thus, fundraising will proceed for continued intervention activities as well as the proposed, scaled-up prevention planks.

Councilmember Schenirer captures the sense of determination and commitment that undergirds the city's efforts. "We're going to figure out how to do this as we go," says Schenirer. "For instance, we're placing interns in the city's neighborhood services division. And we're working with parks and recreation on summer food programs . . . this may lead to a new structure in city government." He notes, "We want to be ready with infrastructure and results before we seek a dedicated [public] funding source." Specifically, Councilmember Schenirer will pay attention to "the standard indicators of youth and gun violence. On the school side, [we'll look at] attendance and graduation rates from the third grade on, reading scores from third grade forward, middle and high school suspensions and expulsions, and [ultimately] persistence rates in community colleges and California state universities."

Looking ahead, Police Lieutenant Lester says the plan shows that "we have actual commitment on a theoretical level from the mayor, councilmembers, agency heads, and schools. Now we can bring in Kaiser Permanente (the region's largest health provider) and community-based organizations for support and conduct a constant evaluation of what we're doing. We'll continue looking for best practices. And, if we're not succeeding, we'll change the plans." For other cities developing new strategies, Lester recommends: "Assess the problem and do a resource inventory. . . . Typically, you'll find a lot of agencies working independently. These can be much more effective if you pull them together. . . . Get the community involved, do outreach, take a community-oriented policing approach. . . . From there, report findings and implement programs with evidence behind them."

The City of San José—long known for its highly collaborative approach to gang violence reduction—faced a new reality in 2011, brought on by impending changes in prison sentencing and probation policy. "Realignment" is the all-purpose term Californians use to describe a suite of new policies and budget shifts designed to reduce prison populations, shift responsibility for supervision of individuals on probation and parole to the county level, and lower costs. Implications across Santa Clara County, where 60 percent of county residents reside within the city of San José, included a sudden uptick in the number of adult probationers returning to the community, challenges to the adequacy of reentry service and support systems, an increased need for jail beds and related services, and potentially closer connections between prison and street gangs. San José expects to receive some 70 percent of former prisoners released to the county. The county holds responsibility for juvenile and adult probation, prosecution, courts, and corrections. City and county leaders realized when realignment was announced that neither had a formal reentry plan in place.

To confront this wave of reform, the city once again applied its key "multi-purpose tool," the Mayor's Gang Prevention Task Force (MGPTF), which has been in place since 1991 with an expansive membership of city, county, and community and faith-based organization leaders. The response of the task force and its early experience implementing reentry plans constitute an emerging, promising practice for policymakers across the state and the nation to consider as states grapple with the balance between prisons and community supervision in an era of fiscal austerity. Specifically, the task force reoriented and reorganized itself to confront new challenges, added a reentry plank to its guiding three-year plan, and joined forces with the county to avoid duplicating oversight structures for reentry. Viewed as a whole, the city's response serves as yet another local model of evolving collaboration for the community's benefit.

Longtime task force staff lead Angel Rios, deputy director of the city's Department of Parks, Recreation, and Neighborhood Services, provides a helpful view on how realignment events unfolded within the task force structure:

The city doesn't have to play this prominent a role, based on regulations or statute. . . . The task force put briefings and reports on the [bimonthly] agenda as to what the probation department and police department expected would happen. Briefings evolved into an updated strategic goal area focused on reentry/realignment. Unlike all other goals which are city-driven, this one is county-led with support from the city. . . . The topic came up in open forum comments from the community, as in, "Is it true all these releases are coming? They're going to release all these criminals into our neighborhoods, and that's dangerous." There was a lot of incomplete [information] or misinformation. We made sure [other] people spoke at the meeting who were going to be involved so as to understand the issues better. This helped to demystify the issue, even though we didn't have all the answers [in advance]. Overall, this resulted in the city and county taking a more comprehensive approach, with more partners, and also mitigated the community outcry.

Cora Tomalinas, a leader among faith-based community organizers in San José and a longtime task force member, comments, "At the outset of the task force, we had prevention, intervention, enforcement, and aftercare [as watchwords]. . . . Up until recently, we have given minimal attention to aftercare." Tomalinas welcomes realignment for three reasons: "the problem of minority overrepresentation, the needs for health and mental health care, and the need to help families and the community [readjust]."

County Supervisor George Shirakawa, a task force member and former city councilmember, provides an analytical description of conditions when the county first learned that realignment was coming: "We were already looking at reentry, yet we had never pointed an instrument at ourselves to look at the effectiveness of what we were doing. We were still in silos, had no formal reentry plan that brought everybody together. When realignment came along, we needed to scale up." Assistant District Attorney Marc Buller added, "We saw high recidivism rates of 70–80 percent."

The task force's interagency collaboration subcommittee emerged as a helpful structure for joint planning. Rios explains, "We saw the county mirroring the efforts of the MGPTF, calling the same stakeholders together for its reentry network. The mayor invited Supervisor Shirakawa to sit on the policy team, and asked him to co-chair the subcommittee [with me]. . . . We made reentry and realignment a standing agenda item. Through that subcommittee, we agree to link reentry efforts under the MGPTF umbrella. This reduced some of the redundancy, and kept the county in the lead."

Through the subcommittee, notes Shirakawa, "I ensure that collaboration between our [county] departments and the city happens . . . [and on the policy team] I'm there with the mayor at the dais. . . . As assets dwindle, we're trying to be efficient. It's the same families that we deal with in our systems, which the city identifies [through its outreach]." Tomalinas, also a member of the subcommittee, comments that "the experience of residents helped shape the reentry plan and how we treat our young people who are coming back." She adds that the experience of ever-closer city–county collaboration on realignment may lead the task force to take on a new regional identity and set of functions, beyond its longstanding city focus.

From another countywide perspective, Chief Probation Officer Sheila Mitchell—stipulated by statute to chair the county corrections partnership to develop realignment plans—recalls involving the San José police chief and a mayoral aide in the deliberations of the partnership and working with them to prepare and make a presentation to the San José City Council. The partnership group continues to meet regularly, with a city team member also involved in implementation. Notably, city services and influence touch two of Mitchell's top priorities for assistance to reentering former prisoners—housing and employment.

Operationally, Buller notes:

> The MGPTF brings partnerships, additional resources, collaboration—everyone is at the table. . . . MGPTF will be a partner in how we go about providing services to those on probation. . . . If people coming out of prison have jobs and services, they will be less likely to commit crimes and become involved with gangs. MGPTF has to look at broad prevention programs. It doesn't necessarily affect just gang members. . . . MGPTF has been flexible enough to move in different directions. It still has enough momentum to keep going even in bad economic times. With realignment, what we're seeing is just another morphing, [a collective opportunity to say] "let's put some ideas together and figure out how we're going to do this."

Jermaine Hardy of the county juvenile probation department confirms that the task force also plays this role for juvenile reentry:

> We're changing the way we're reintegrating youth to create a seamless transition back into the community. We have been failing on recidivism rates, [and are now building a structure through which] intensive supervision, services and support will enable youth to be more successful. We're trying to establish ties and connections and work much better with families and community supports. . . . MGPTF [and its service provider partners constitute a] network that has resources and supports, so that when we identify a gap in services, we know where to turn. We expect to find challenges and unmet needs. Having MGPTF there, with its connections and a diversity of community-based partners, we'll be able to fill those gaps. Also, MGPTF provides oversight and adds a degree of accountability, ensuring collaboration, coordination, and sharing of information.

With the realignment process underway for only a few months, some voices acknowledge the relative strength of the structure while advising a "wait and see" approach to the details of implementation. Michael Pritchard of the Pathway behavioral health organization notes that the selection of inmates for release to community supervision does not take into account mental health and drug and alcohol dual diagnoses and the concomitant need for ongoing medication. Adds Pritchard, "We need to allow this [realignment] to work; we can't scrap it after the first bump" and can't withdraw funding after only one year. Sarah Gonzalez, a community advocate with the Parole Action Community Team, points to a need to transfer capacity once focused on parolees to the expanded probationer population. Assistant Police Chief Rikki Goede notes that, with a possible uptick in property crimes, "our biggest concern is [that realignment comes with] no additional funding for police officers. . . . It will be important to 'follow the money.' . . . If it's working, the people who are released won't be arrested again and will participate in programs."

Those most closely involved with collaborative realignment efforts in San José offer a few recommendations for leaders in other cities and counties. Supervisor Shirakawa says, "I would encourage other counties to visit San José and tailor what works for them. . . . Any time you can create any kind of inter-agency venue and ensure you have reporting across agencies, it is better." Lead staffer Rios adds three points:

> First, talk about the good, bad, and ugly of realignment. Make the subject a topic that you discuss in an inter-organizational setting. Second, talk about it in a way that moves the discussion toward action that is driven or assigned to specific organizations. Here's the role of probation, the police department, the nonprofit community, churches. . . . Develop a plan that incorporates all those roles. Then, develop a community goal or philosophical statement about what you want to accomplish. Is it mainly suppression, or rehabilitation, or a combination? Third, make sure the right message gets out there. Take this joint community strategy and message to the rest of the community that hasn't attended the meetings. . . . It is important to engage residents in assisting with reintegration.

Buller counsels, "[Working together on realignment] may be more difficult when long-term relationships [between city and county] are not in place. We [at the county level] see the benefit of the task force and its programs in the long range, in terms of community protection. And it's helpful to be able to work with the largest city in the county."

Based on solid anchoring and demonstrable results in Santa Rosa, as well as the desire of neighboring communities to learn from and coordinate with Sonoma County's largest city, what were once local efforts have evolved toward a regional strategy. This progression of events has assumed greater importance because of the state's recent turn toward realignment. Realignment discussions have brought city officials in contact with the wider law enforcement and human service provider communities. As such, regionalization represents a natural outgrowth of Santa Rosa's work, and serves as a potential model for other cities across the state.

With a Mayor's Gang Prevention Task Force (MGPTF) in place for nearly 10 years, a quarter-cent sales tax that provides dedicated funds for police, fire, and gang prevention and intervention activities, and a five-year strategic work plan effective since 2008, Santa Rosa has emerged as a leader among medium-sized cities pursuing a comprehensive gang reduction strategy. The city's plan ably blends prevention, intervention and enforcement strategies, and sets out criminal justice goals—such as cutting gang violence in half in five years—alongside quality of life goals, such as increasing school attendance rates.

Several factors contributed toward the regionalization push in Santa Rosa. City and county leaders recognized that youth violence and gang activity does not stop neatly at a city's borders. Santa Rosa's gangs become Petaluma's problem, as Petaluma's become Santa Rosa's. Witnessing success, other jurisdictions such as Sonoma, Windsor, and Rohnert Park have requested help from the Santa Rosa team. In addition, the composition of the MGPTF policy team, which includes the sheriff, the district attorney and the chief probation officer, as well as joint participation in the county Law Enforcement Chief's Association, meant that key county officials knew intimately of and backed Santa Rosa's work. The county also recognized the need to plan for the future before its jail became severely overcrowded and before it faced an unaffordable bill for new construction.

Another factor that fostered regional collaboration was the State of California's commitment to shift responsibility from the state to the county for the custody, treatment and supervision of individuals convicted of specific non-violent, non-serious, non-sex offenses. Furthermore, the joint city–county membership of the county's Asset Forfeiture Allocation Committee—including the chief probation officer, Santa Rosa police chief, and district attorney, who are also members of the MGPTF—provides an ideal perch from which to envision and help fund regional initiatives. Last but hardly least among elected officials, the Sonoma County Board of Supervisors and Santa Rosa City Council pledged full, coordinated support for countywide youth violence prevention efforts.

Examining how joint actions flowed from these factors helps paint a multi-dimensional picture of regionalization as it develops. For example, Santa Rosa's Police Chief Tom Schwedhelm's participation in the Sonoma County Law Enforcement Chief's Association (SCLECA) provided a venue for spreading news of Santa Rosa's successes among other police and sheriffs' departments in the county. "The relationships are extraordinary. We share a mission. There is an easy sharing of information," says Robert Ochs, Sonoma County Chief Probation Officer. In addition, the county had committed itself to an "Upstream" initiative chaired by the former director of human services, in parallel to the SCLECA, which would help ensure that prevention and intervention initiatives receive equal attention. "We're going to enforce the law, but we've made a commitment to keep people out of the criminal justice system. Our county has a rich tradition of collaboration and making changes for the better," adds Ochs.

The availability of asset forfeiture funds has enabled the city and county to buttress state realignment funds. Early priorities have included opening a day reporting center (DRC) to help handle the influx of returning former prisoners, accomplished in January 2012. The county continues to seek funding for a proposed community corrections center to complement the DRC. The Sonoma County Probation Department receives funding from the state Juvenile Justice Crime Prevention Act (JJCPA) for three school probation officers and two gang probation officers active in portions of the county beyond Santa Rosa city limits. Additionally, a juvenile probation officer is funded by the state's Youthful Offenders Block Grant specifically to handle mental health cases.

Ochs believes that the sound links among the city, county supervisors and county administrators have enabled the county to attract grants from a number of sources. City and county leaders had put together what they believed to be a winning application for federal funds from the Office of Juvenile Justice and Delinquency to develop a countywide effort. Some of its key provisions included implementing or enhancing evidence-based gang prevention, intervention, and suppression programs and hiring a multi-strategy gang coordinator to expand the regionalization efforts by coordinating existing community-based anti-gang programs and strategies that are closely aligned with local law enforcement efforts. Although cutbacks in federal funding forced the withdrawal of the request for proposals, city and county officials have pledged to implement the plan to the extent possible with available resources.

In fulfillment of one aspect of the city's strategic plan and one of seven Santa Rosa City Council goals, the MGPTF hosted a regionalization forum in June 2010 to broaden and strengthen community gang prevention and intervention efforts. Invitees included all city councilmembers and police chiefs from around Sonoma County, law enforcement leaders from probation and the district attorney's office, members of the county board of supervisors, and representatives from the faith-based and non-profit communities. More than 80 community leaders from across the county participated. The agenda for this "regional gang summit" included a panel of local representatives from law enforcement, education, city council and a community-based organization that provides services to former gang members. This panel shared how the efforts of the city MGPTF have changed how they function. In addition, representatives from the City of San Pablo shared their current efforts to adopt a similar gang prevention and intervention model. The forum produced commitments to work together even more closely across the county.

The City of Los Angeles Office of Gang Reduction and Youth Development (GRYD) directs and oversees the implementation of the Gang Reduction and Youth Development comprehensive strategy, an evolving "road map" that combines prevention, intervention, suppression, and community engagement activities to reduce risk factors associated with gang membership and violence. Following recommendations from The Advancement Project—a nonprofit, "public policy change organization"—and the city controller, Los Angeles created GRYD as an office that would oversee the implementation of all of its gang violence reduction strategies and ensure that these strategies were effective and efficient.

Increasingly, GRYD places gang-affected families and communities at the center of its comprehensive activities.

As Deputy Mayor Guillermo Cespedes and GRYD Research Director Denise Herz noted in a December 2011 summary of the city's comprehensive strategy, GRYD activities "are focused on building community-level support systems to alter norms that tolerate violence and support healthy children, youth, and families." GRYD's conceptual framework emphasizes that families and communities can develop and apply their strengths to reduce at-risk behavior and grow from adversity. Following this framework allows GRYD to evaluate its gang reduction efforts and identify the interventions most likely to build community resiliency, reduce risk factors for joining gangs, and stop gang violence.

When Los Angeles Mayor Antonio Villaraigosa established GRYD in 2008, he tasked the new office with implementing Los Angeles' gang violence reduction efforts and evaluating those efforts' impact. GRYD's evaluation revealed that the city's comprehensive strategy lacked a unified framework to guide implementation. Cespedes recalls that, "in the beginning, the comprehensive plan appeared disjointed." Furthermore, since existing literature on comprehensive strategies did not provide much specific direction on service delivery, it was not clear "what types of services should be delivered, how services should be delivered, and how services across strategic approaches should be coordinated."

GRYD subsequently consulted with service providers working with Los Angeles' gang-impacted communities and all parties agreed upon the necessity of working with families to help high-risk and gang-involved youth. In response to this driving principle, a team of researchers fashioned GRYD's unified conceptual framework based on family systems theory, which views social context (such as family and community) as the starting point for making change. GRYD's prevention and intervention activities are designed to focus and build on the strengths of the individual, community, and family. By building their strengths, the expectation is that the risk factors associated with gang violence and involvement will decline.

With this new, clear, conceptual framework, GRYD found itself able to direct and evaluate its comprehensive services in a more consistent and cohesive manner. GRYD used this framework to establish a set of guiding principles to drive practice and ensure the coordinated and effective implementation of all activities directed at the community, as well as the individual, family, and peer system. Furthermore, the framework established the components necessary to conduct process and outcome evaluations of its comprehensive strategy, such as goals, objectives, activities, and performance and outcome measures.

GRYD's unique structure enhances its ability to evaluate and direct service delivery in accordance with its conceptual framework. As a city office overseen by the Los Angeles mayor, the GRYD has the flexibility to take on multiple roles, make funding decisions, and take action quickly. With the support of the mayor and the approval of the city council, GRYD acts as a policy maker, able to address policy needs to support sustainable, comprehensive efforts and decide how to allocate funds. As a funder, GRYD promotes efficient distribution of resources and contracts with service providers working in Los Angeles

neighborhoods most affected by gang violence to implement prevention and intervention services that correspond with the GRYD strategies' conceptual framework.

Furthermore, GRYD is itself a program developer and service provider. It develops programming and implementation models for city-contracted service providers to follow. For example, the GRYD developed the Gang Prevention Model of Practice, an eight-phase prevention strategy based on coaching multiple generations of families in problem-solving techniques to reduce the risk factors associated with youth gang involvement. As a service provider, GRYD provides gang-impacted communities with direct services such as the Summer Night Lights initiative, a violence reduction effort coordinated by the GRYD office and designed to engage the family and community in prevention and intervention activities.

GRYD also supports city-contracted service providers with trainings and tools for delivering services that correspond with the goals and needs of the GRYD strategy. By providing ongoing training, GRYD increases the ability of service providers to implement effective and consistent practices. Moreover, this training ensures that, over time, all GRYD staff working with service providers can reinforce and support the GRYD strategy's conceptual framework and promote the strategy's sustainability.

Indeed, GRYD has a consistent message about its work and services that is important to sustaining the GRYD strategy: Los Angeles has a place-based, data-driven, family-focused plan to address gang violence. To disseminate and reinforce its message, GRYD works with the mayor and the communities affected by gangs. Whenever the mayor speaks about the GRYD strategy, he reiterates this message and utilizes findings from its data-driven efforts to highlight successes. Furthermore, when working with neighborhoods, GRYD utilizes its community education campaign to provide information about its services. GRYD's messaging campaign establishes a language and culture for the way Los Angeles thinks about gangs, gang-impacted communities, and the GRYD strategy.

Los Angeles provides one key recommendation for cities interested in directing and coordinating comprehensive strategies in a more cohesive manner: Ask city staff and local experts (e.g., service providers) what framework is driving programs. Identifying an existing framework—or building a preferred framework—will enhance the ability of cities to coordinate and drive their comprehensive plans and to evaluate their strategy.

Conclusion

The five cities profiled here have made substantial progress toward sustaining their comprehensive work by changing how city and county agencies do business and expanding comprehensive efforts more deeply into prevention and regional strategies. Other cities in California and nationwide may "take a page" from one or more of the California Cities Gang Prevention Network sites, directly borrowing and adapting approaches. Additional cities may draw inspiration from the five examples to develop their own innovations toward sustainability.

City-Specific Resources

Los Angeles Gang Reduction

http://mayor.lacity.org/Issues/GangReduction/index.htm

The City of Los Angeles Mayor's Office of Gang Reduction and Youth Development (GRYD) Comprehensive Strategy, December 2011

Mayor's Strategic Plan for Gang Prevention, City of Sacramento 2012–2015. Draft of January 6, 2012

Sacramento Reads! Third Grade Literacy Campaign

www.sacramentoreads.com

Sacramento Youth Development Services

www.cityofsacramento.org/Youth-Development/youth-and-gang-violence.cfm

Salinas Comprehensive Strategy for Community-wide Violence Reduction

www.ci.salinas.ca.us/pdf/SalinasSWP.pdf

Salinas-Monterey County Community Alliance for Safety and Peace

www.future-futuro.org

San José Mayor's Gang Prevention Task Force

www.sanjoseca.gov/Mayor/goals/pubsafety/mgptf/mgptf.asp

Santa Rosa Mayor's Gang Prevention Task Force

http://ci.santa-rosa.ca.us/departments/recreationandparks/programs/MGPTF/Pages/default.aspx

Way Up Sacramento

http://wayupsacramento.org

General Resources

California Cities Gang Prevention Network

www.ccgpn.org

National League of Cities Institute for Youth, Education, and Families

www.nlc.org/iyef

National Forum on Youth Violence Prevention

www.findyouthinfo.gov

Prevention Institute/UNITY Coalition

www.preventioninstitute.org/unity

Critical Thinking

1. How do the anti-gang efforts of California cities represent an alternative to more conventional policing strategies aimed at curtailing gang activity?

2. How are partnerships an essential component of the gang prevention strategies of California cities?

UNIT 8

A Suburban Nation: Suburban Growth, Diversity, and the Possibilities of "New Urbanism" and "New Regionalism"

Unit Selections

Learning Outcomes

After reading this unit, you should be able to:

- Describe the evolution of suburbia, how suburbia has changed over the decades.

- Explain how zoning works.

- Identify the "costs" of anti-density zoning (also called "exclusionary zoning).

- Differentiate between communalism and autonomy, two often antagonistic political attitudes that are often associated with suburban living.

- Define "First Suburbs" and identify First Suburbs in your region.

- Propose policies that can help strengthen First Suburbs.

- Identify the opportunities for creative coalition-building that may exist among cities and suburbs.

- List and summarize the major guiding principles of New Urbanism.

- Explain how the architects of New Urbanism seek to reinvigorate a sense of community that many observers feel is missing in contemporary suburbia.

- Assess the degree to which the New Urbanism can be expected to build "better" suburban communities.

Student Website

Internet References

The Brookings Institution: First Suburbs
www.brookings.edu/topics/first-suburbs

Congress for a New Urbanism
www.cnu.org

First Suburbs Coalition
www.marc.org/firstsuburbs

National Geographic Magazine, Urban Sprawl
http://ngm.nationalgeographic.com/ngm/data/2001/07/01/html/ft_20010701.3.html

Newurbanism.org
www.newurbanism.org

Sierra Club, Stopping Sprawl
www.sierraclub.org/sprawl

Smart Communities Network: Urban Growth Boundaries
www.smartcommunities.ncat.org/landuse/urban.shtml

Sprawl Watch Clearinghouse
www.sprawlwatch.org

The United States is a suburban nation. As the 1970 census first indicated, the number of Americans who live in suburbs surpasses the number in central cities. Today about a half of all Americans reside in suburbs.

Lang, LeFurgy, and Nelson (Article 32, "The Six Suburban Eras of the United States") trace the evolution of suburbia. In the early years of the nation's history, communities located on the edge of cities were quite small and largely rural in character. These farming hamlets were not really suburbs but protosuburbs, rural villages that lacked any strong connection to the central city. By the early 1900s, population pressures on central cities coupled with new transportation technology led urban populations to expand outward, transforming once-rural communities into suburbs. The first major transportation innovation was the electric streetcar; hence the growing suburbs of this period were known as streetcar suburbs. During the post–World War II years, especially the 1950s and 1960s, the automobile fundamentally altered the shape of metropolitan areas, allowing the growth of bedroom communities (commuter suburbs). By the end of the twentieth century, continuing advances in telecommunications and transportation produced a New Metropolis dominated by the suburban office parks, shopping gallerias, and entertainment centers of edge cities. Affluent and highly educated technoburbs became new centers of employment. Edgeless development in nondescript "strip" shopping plazas and small office complexes dispersed urban growth still further.

In the mid-twentieth century, suburbia was stereotyped as a string of faceless and boring bedroom communities. Clearly that portrait does not accurately describe suburbia today; in fact, the 1950s stereotype was never totally accurate. Contemporary suburbia encompasses a diversity of communities: leafy and wealthy bedroom communities; working- and middle-class communities with rows of tract housing; gritty industrial suburbs centered around factories; minority suburbs with large concentrations of South Asian, East Asian, African-American, and Latino families; booming edge cities; quickly growing boomburbs, which suffer from overcrowded schools and a lack of quality public services; and even disaster suburbs where

Exactostock / SuperStock

conditions are not all that different from the troubled central cities that they border.

Many suburbanites value the privileges and comforts of suburban living. More affluent communities rely on zoning and land-use regulations to protect the local quality of life and to keep out unwanted people and activities (Article 33, "Why Regions Fail: Zoning as an Extractive Institution"). These communities enact exclusionary zoning ordinances that essentially drive up the costs of buying a home or renting an apartment in more privileged suburbs, an effective means for ensuring that only people of wealth will be able to move into the community. Exclusionary ordinances typically limit (or even ban) the construction of apartments and affordable housing units. Such ordinances also require that new single-family homes be built on large lots of an acre or more. Exclusionary ordinances serve to trap lower-income and minority families in the inner city and in declining inner-ring communities, away from the growing job opportunities and better schools of better-off suburbs. Exclusionary zoning and land-use ordinances also help to reinforce patterns of class and racial stratification in the metropolis.

Local control of land uses also impairs effective environmental planning. Certain rim communities seek to expand their tax bases by allowing the construction of automobile-reliant shopping malls and suburban office parks. Other, more privileged communities located close to the city actually restrict housing construction, forcing populations to search for more affordable housing in communities located on the far edges of the metropolis.

David Brooks (Article 34, "Patio Man and the Sprawl People: America's Newest Suburbs") observes the diversity of communities and political attitudes that can be found in suburbia. While some residents moved to the suburbs in search of a sense of "community," Brooks's Patio Man rejects communitarian pressures and instead seeks the enjoyment and privacy of life in his home and back yard. While many social critics and even popular filmmakers castigate the relative insularity of such suburban lives (see the Academy Award–winning film *American Beauty* and the Emmy Award–winning television series *Mad Men*), Brooks reminds us that a great many suburbanites are quite satisfied with their lives and resent government efforts directed at social change.

In his essay on Patio Man, Brooks describes the life and general prosperity of the boomburbs, especially the fast-growing sprinkler cities of the American Southwest. Such relatively new suburbs, however, often have very little in common with America's first suburbs, the older or inner-ring communities located adjacent to the central city. As Bruce Katz and Robert Puentes of The Brookings Institution describe (Article 35, "Affluent, but Needy [First Suburbs]"), at one time many of these inner-ring communities were once quite well off; they were home to a region's factory owners, bankers, and other members of the local elite. Today, however, these communities are exhibiting new vulnerabilities as they suffer an aging infrastructure, job losses with factory closings, population stagnation, and the sudden appearance of housing vacancies and closed shops that dot once-thriving shopping strips. Younger Americans do not especially value these aging communities but instead seek newer homes with more modern facilities located further from the city center. Businesses, too, have moved out to suburban locations along a metropolitan area's ring road or beltway or perimeter highway. Urban decline is no longer confined to central cities but also characterizes the situation of numerous inner-ring suburban communities. Katz and Puentes urge the adoption of policies to prevent the first suburbs from sliding further downhill.

American metropolitan areas are, with very few exceptions, characterized by extensive political fragmentation. There exists no regional authority to plan and enact laws that will serve the needs of the entire region. Instead, the region's governing authority is parceled out among a variety of smaller governmental pieces or fragments—cities, counties, villages, townships, special districts, and school districts, just to name the more obvious ones—with each piece possessing the autonomy to pursue its own interests. Fragmented local governments do not cooperate willingly with one another, unless they find it in their mutual interest to do so. But actions that can reverse a region's economic decline or construct a mass transit system that can provide effective alternatives to automobile commutes throughout the region, however, often requires the sort of broad-scale action that is often impeded by the unwillingness of various small-box governments (to use the phrase coined by David Rusk) to cooperate.

As a result, many urbanists call for enhanced regionalism. These observers note the cost savings that come when services are provided on a large-scale basis. They also observe how cities and suburbs can work together to market a region

to new employers. Regionalists also observe the importance of developing a mass transit system that can serve the entire region, not only to combat air pollution but also to alleviate the traffic jams that pose a barrier to continued economic development of communities throughout the region.

In the 1950s and 1960s, numerous academic experts sought to restructure local governments by establishing new metropolitan governments that would possess clear authority to govern a regional or at least a large subregional area. A few important city–county consolidations or mergers took place, most notably in greater Jacksonville, Nashville, Indianapolis, and, more recently, Louisville. New metropolitan governing bodies or empowered counties were created in Minneapolis–St. Paul, Portland, Seattle, and Miami. But in recent decades, the wave of such far-reaching metropolitan restructuring has largely come to an end. In most metropolitan areas, powerful forces—including local officeholders and suburban citizens who are unwilling to surrender their privileges—resist ceding local autonomy for the goal of creating a strong, centralized metropolitan government. Citizens also worry that a large metropolitan body could not be fully responsive to the variation of local and individual needs.

Urbanists have come to recognize the virtual political impossibility of creating strong metropolitan governments in the face of such opposition. As a consequence, one school of thought no longer pays great attention to the impossible dream of creating centralized regional authorities. Instead, the school of New Regionalism seeks deeper and greater collaboration among the existing governments in the metropolis. The New Regionalism seeks to create new incentives for cities and suburbs to initiate joint power agreements and share resources in program efforts that cross normal city and suburban boundary lines. The New Regionalism is also embodied in the efforts of local Chambers of Commerce and other business councils that push for new visions that will guide a region's future economic development.

Myron Orfield argues that the opportunities for joint city–suburban action are greater than is usually recognized (Article 36, "Regional Coalition-Building and the Inner Suburbs"). Once political strategists recognize the diversity of suburban communities, they can discover new opportunities for creative coalition building among central cities, suburbs, and other potential partners. According to Orfield, many suburbs do not share in the benefits of a region's growth, which is disproportionately concentrated in the metropolitan area's favored quarter communities. The central city, declining inner-ring suburbs, and low-property-tax-base working-class suburbs are largely bypassed when new investment is concentrated in the technoburbs and more prestigious communities in a region. Orfield urges that a region's central city, aging first suburbs, and low-resource working-class communities unite to fight for their fair share of infrastructure support, governmental assistance, and new investment. The dividing line in the metropolis does not need to be "suburbs versus the central city." Instead, a coalition comprised of central cities, first suburbs, working-class communities—and even farmers and environmentalists—may discover that they all share in the benefits of programs (especially state policies) that help to direct growth back toward the urban core. Orfield even raises the possibility of regional tax-base sharing, a program enacted in the Twin Cities region that ensures that all communities in a region will receive a share of the benefits derived from new growth, no matter where in the region a development is situated.

Churches and faith-based groups have a special role to play in pushing for more equitable patterns of regional growth.

Another school of thought, the New Urbanism, seeks to reshape suburbia in order to promote ecologically sensitive development and to create living patterns that revive residents' sense of neighborliness and community. New Urbanists promote sustainable development, including relatively dense clusters of housing that allow for the preservation of surrounding green areas. Compact development also encourages walking, diminishing the reliance of residents on the automobile (Article 37, "Principles of New Urbanism"). New Urbanists seek to eliminate driveway cuts that add to the distance between homes and businesses, impeding walkability. New Urban planning also embraces traffic-calming measures to reduce driving speeds, making streets safer for leisurely pedestrian strolls. New Urban communities typically feature homes built close to the street and often with front porches, facilitating daily interaction and the development of a sense of community among neighbors.

The New Urbanism is a powerful critique of conventional suburbs. Its principles have been copied and adapted by developers in countries around the world. The design principles of the New Urbanism have also been applied to inner-city developments, an effort to build more livable alternatives to the high-rise slums of public housing that were torn down.

New Urbanists have succeeded in building a number of wonderful communities. Yet, the New Urbanism does not constitute a challenge capable of refashioning suburbia or curbing suburban sprawl (Article 38, "New Urbanism: A Limited Revolution"). Few Americans choose to buy homes in New Urban communities. Instead, home seekers continue to buy the most home they can find for their money. They prefer large detached homes with sizeable back yards and the convenience of multi-car garages that allow direct entry through the garage to the home. The vast majority of developers will continue to build, as Americans will continue to buy, homes in conventional automobile-dominated developments.

The Six Suburban Eras
of the United States

ROBERT LANG, JENNIFER LEFURGY, AND ARTHUR C. NELSON

Introduction

The Metropolitan Institute at Virginia Tech (MI) proposes a timeline to show the flow of suburban eras and types. The timeline defines six periods of U.S. suburban development in order to establish more common base years for historical data analysis. As the field of suburban studies matures into a formal academic sub-discipline, these suggested eras can help guide research projects.

The current standard split in suburban history, proposed by New Urbanists such as Andres Duany, offers a rather crude division into pre- and post-World War II periods (Duany, Plater-Zyberk, and Speck 2000). But this simple pre/post-war dichotomy is a caricature of suburban history. It can be argued that one suburban era actually spans the immediate pre- and post-war decades, which are labeled "Mid-Century Suburbs" (or the years 1930 to 1970) in this note. In addition, the post-war period is now so long, at 60 plus years, that it too can be divided into eras. Consider, for example an article by Robert Lang, Edward Blakely, and Meghan Gough (2005) that looks at the "new suburban metropolis" period from 1970 to 2010.

This timeline is not meant to be definitive. There are no clean breaks in history. Thus the timeline is depicted as a meandering river to indicate the continuous flow of events. The dates show stops along the way where the river course shifts, implying a directional change in history.

This note divides American suburban history into six eras. It finds that the United States is now in the fifth era and will soon enter a sixth one. The timeline also indicates some exemplar suburbs of each period and touches on key political changes and technological innovations. However, this argument does not subscribe to the notion of technological or economic determinism. Previous efforts to categorize historic eras focused especially on advances in transit technology (Stern and Massengale 1981), but multiple forces propel suburban change, and this proposed timeline also considers how cultural influences shaped the course of evolution.

The timeline reflects current thinking on the suburbs and incorporates the work of many historians including James Borchert (1996), Robert Fishman (1987, 1990), Dolores Hayden (2003), Kenneth Jackson (1985), Chester Liebs (1985), Richard Longstreth (1998, 1999), and Sam Bass Warner, Jr. (1962, 1972). The understanding of the three later eras is driven mostly by the current work of researchers at MI and The Brookings Institution's Metropolitan Policy Program. The labels attached to these eras were developed by MI and reflect its conceptualization of how the suburbs have evolved since the mid-19th century.

Before 1850: Proto Suburbs

Prior to 1850, U.S. suburbs were mostly extensions of cities (Jackson 1985, Warner 1972). They featured street plans and housing that closely resembled the urban core. In this era, the urban fringe featured dense row houses that abruptly give way to open fields and farms. However, some historians have documented the fact that the residents of early U.S. suburbs such as Brooklyn already had a different demographic character than residents of the central city (Jackson 1985). At first, these borderlands were poorer than the core. But with the introduction of ferry service around New York harbor, neighborhoods such as Brooklyn Heights emerged that catered to middle-income commuters. Henry Binford (1988) finds a similar development pattern at the fringe of Boston in the first half of the 19th century.

The earliest distinctly non-urban looking suburbs began in the United Kingdom in the early 19th century (Fishman 1987). They appeared first in London (Clapham Common—1800) and later Manchester (Victoria Park—1830s). These same kinds of "picturesque" suburbs did not emerge in the United States until the second half of the 19th century.

1850 to 1890: Town and Country Suburbs

The notion of suburbs as distinct physical places from cities became evident in the United States by the 1850s (Fishman 1987). The earliest documented English-style American suburb was Llewellyn Park, NJ, designed by Frederick Law Olmsted in 1857. Olmsted's work captured in design and spirit an entire mid-19th century U.S. movement that elevated domesticity and the nuclear family. This movement, along with the picturesque landscape architecture, had its roots in England.

But note that we do not refer to this suburban era as "picturesque" as some others have (Hayden 2003). That is because these suburbs are only part of the suburban story of the period. The flip side of the affluent picturesque places was a more moderate-income and city-like suburb based on horse-drawn streetcars (Hayden 2003). These streetcars were a big improvement over horse-drawn omnibuses because they were faster and carried more load (Warner 1962). They helped change the course of urban development in places such as New York, where suburbs now spread north on Manhattan Island instead of only crossing the East River to Brooklyn (Jackson 1985).

The horse-drawn streetcar suburbs were much denser and more traditionally urban that their picturesque counterparts—thus they were the "town" in the "town and country suburbs." But they also were now distinct from the urban core. In places such as the Jamaica Plains neighborhood of Boston, the architecture began to shift in the 1850s from the tight row houses such as those found on Beacon Hill to a looser configuration with side alleys (Warner 1962). In many cases, the houses were fully detached but remained on small narrow lots. To a modern eye, this does not seem as important a distinction, but it signaled a much larger change. Also note that many of the "town" suburbs had been annexed by the central city and appeared for all intents and purposes to be "urban neighborhoods" (Rusk 1993). Yet in the context of the mid-to-late 19th century American metropolis, these places were suburbs. The best example of a neighborhood built in this style was Gross Park in Chicago, dating from the 1880s (Hayden 2003).

1890 to 1930: Streetcar Suburbs

By the late 1880s, the first electric streetcars—or trolleys—were in use. The trolleys were a turbo version of the horse-drawn streetcars (Warner 1962). They were much bigger and faster and helped spread development for miles past the old urban core. Many of the trends that began in the horse-drawn era were greatly accentuated and extended by trolleys—the suburban houses spread out more (especially in places such as Los Angeles) and differences between the look and feel of the edge and the core grew (Fishman 1987). The streetcars so dominated the construction and speculation of this period that many historians use them to label this suburban era (Warner 1962). Suburban diversity, which began in earlier eras, continues and intensifies with the emergence of large-scale residential "city suburbs" (Borchert 1996).

Suburban retail and commercial districts also began to change radically in the streetcar suburbs (Liebs 1985). The old, dense form of Main Street now took on an elongated appearance. Storefronts stretched to reflect the fact that people might now window shop from a fast-moving trolley. These extended main streets, also referred to as "taxpayer strips," were the forerunner of the auto-based strip (Liebs 1985; Lang, LeFurgy, and Hornburg 2005). Many of these places exist today, threading through the edges of central cities and older suburbs, and are to the modern eye "traditional looking." But in their era, these strips represented a sharp break with commercial districts in the urban core.

Automobiles were invented around the same time as trolleys, but had much less immediate impact on urban development in the early years of the 20th century. They were expensive, hard to store, and poorly accommodated in urban places. Yet the streetcars began to loosen up the American metropolis so effectively that cars began to find navigating suburbs easier with each passing year. The first commercial districts to begin building parking lots were the trolley-based taxpayer strips. By the 1920s, the west side of Los Angeles began to develop fully auto-based shopping (Longstreth 1998, 1999).

1930 to 1970: Mid-Century Suburbs

Key developments during this era include the creation of Federal Housing Administration loans in the 1930s, which greatly improved middle-income access to suburban housing, and the beginning of the interstate highways in 1956 (Jackson 1985). Suburban architecture grew even more distinct from both traditional urban and even earlier suburbs (Hayden 2003). The dominant housing type was the one-story ranch-style home with a minimally classic exterior and a modern open floor plan. The scale of development expanded, especially after World War II in projects such as Levittown and Lakewood (Hayden 2003). The modest suburban shopping centers of the early 20th century exploded into massive malls that, beginning in 1956, were mostly enclosed and climate-controlled (Liebs 1985).

The New Urbanists, such as Andres Duany (Duany, Plater-Zyberk, and Speck 2000) and James Kunstler (1993), argue that a clean break in history exists between the pre- and post-World War II eras. In their view, all development before the war was pedestrian-oriented and traditional in form. After the war came an auto-dominated environment of subdivisions and shopping malls. However, the historical literature does not support this simplistic view (Harris 1988) and instead indicates that many early 20th century suburbs began a slow, decades-long adoption of automobiles (Liebs 1985). By the 1930s, cars were poised to significantly remake the American metropolis, but first a depression and then war greatly slowed the pace of urban change (Jackson 1985). Yet in the few places that still grew during the depression and war, such as the Los Angeles and Washington, DC, regions, the car made its mark (Longstreth 1998, 1999). These places, along with select parts of suburban New York, contain many examples of 1930s auto suburbs complete with proto tract-style subdivisions and early auto-oriented shopping centers.

Thus, a new suburban style emerged at the mid-20th century. This style existed both immediately before and after the war. There is just so much more development occurring after the war, that Mid-Century Suburbs were said to have a "post-war" style.

1970 to 2010:
New Metropolis Suburbs

The interstate beltways, constructed mostly in the 1960s, paved the way for a boom in suburban commercial development by the 1970s. A new suburban-dominated metropolis emerged during this period (Fishman 1990; Sharpe and Wallock 1994). The amount of suburban office space surpassed that of central cities, giving rise to Edge Cities and even more commonly Edgeless Cites (Lang 2003)—a more sprawling style of commercial development. Suburbs now typically had the region's balance of people, shopping, and business, yet they maintained a distinct non-urban look (Lang, Blakely and Gough 2005). They became cities in function, but not in form (Fishman 1990; Lang 2003).

The suburbs also grew diverse (Lang and LeFurgy 2006). The 1965 reform in immigration law led to a surge in the foreign-born population of the United States by the 1980s. The cities no longer had a monopoly on attracting immigrants. By the first decade of the 21st century, the suburbs equaled cities as immigrant magnets (Frey 2003). The suburbs also attracted growing numbers of nontraditional households, including single and even gay residents (Brekhus 2003; Frey and Berube 2003). In fact, the suburbs grow so diverse in this era that a whole new language was needed to describe the multiple types of communities and their complicated forms of development.

The suburban split between upscale and more modest development, detectable even in the 19th century, intensified in this era (Orfield 1997, 2002). Many older suburbs from the streetcar, and even mid-century, periods were in decline (most town and country era suburbs have been annexed by central cities). The amount of suburban poverty dramatically increased in places that fall outside the "favored quarter" (Leinberger 1997), or the most affluent wedge of the metropolis. Places in the favored quarter boomed. Newer suburbs at the edge of the region featured "McMansions" as the average house size in new construction nearly doubled from 1970 to the end of the century (Lang and Danielsen 2002). Closer-in suburbs within this quarter became cosmopolitan and competed directly with fashionable urban neighborhoods for the region's arts and intellectual communities (Lang, Hughes, and Danielsen 1997).

2010 and beyond:
Megapolitan Suburbs

A new suburban era may emerge after 2010. It likely will be characterized by an enlarging exurban belt that stretches so far from the original urban core that its residents may have a choice of directions in which to commute. For example, people living around Fredericksburg, VA, 50 miles south of Washington, DC, now have the option of commuting south to Richmond or north to the District of Columbia or booming Northern Virginia. The commuter sheds in the "Megapolitan Suburbs" will link up vast networks of cities (Carbonell and Yaro 2005). The scale of the building also will be enormous as the nation adds at least 30 million new residents each decade until mid-century (Nelson 2004).

Lang and Dhavale (2005) developed a new trans-metropolitan geography that labels vast urban zones "Megapolitan Areas." The first one emerged in the Northeast between Maine and Virginia (Gottmann 1961), but now nine others reach into all regions of the United States. By 2005, Megapolitans captured more than two in three Americans, and the share will grow significantly by 2050 (Lang and Dhavale 2005).

A wave of suburban gentrification will occur post-2010, especially in the favored quarter. Many of the new developments will intensify the urban look and feel of many suburbs. A new urbanity will sweep the suburbs—they will still not look like traditional cities, but may incorporate more urban elements than Edge Cities of the past. Many first-generation Edge Cities will lose their edge as traditional cores revive and more distant suburbs explode with new development (Lang 2003). The scale of urbanity may shift away from mega projects in the suburbs—like Edge Cities—and into smaller scale town centers. The new town centers will have less concentrated office space than Edge Cities, but will be more mixed-use and pedestrian-oriented than the current form of suburban commercial development.

References

Binford, Henry, C. 1988. *The First Suburbs: Residential Communities on the Boston Periphery, 1815–1860.* Chicago: University of Chicago Press.

Borchert, James. 1996. Residential City Suburbs: The Emergence of a New Suburban Type, 1880–1930. *Journal of Urban History* 22: 283–307.

Brekhus, Wayne. 2003. *Peacocks, Chameleons, Centaurs: Gay Suburbia and the Grammar of Social Identity.* Chicago: University of Chicago Press.

Carbonell, Armando and Robert Yaro. 2005. American Spatial Development and the New Megalopolis. *Landlines* 17(2): 2–5.

Duany, Andres, Elizabeth Plater-Zyberk, and Jeff Speck. 2000. *Suburban Nation.* New York: North Point Press.

Fishman, Robert. 1987. *Bourgeois Utopias: The Rise and Fall of Suburbia.* New York: Basic Books.

Fishman, Robert. 1990. America's New City: Megalopolis Unbound. *Wilson Quarterly* 14(1): 24–45.

Frey, William. 2003. Melting Post Suburbs: A Study of Suburban Diversity. In Bruce Katz and Robert E. Lang (eds.), *Redefining Cities and Suburbs: Evidence from Census 2000,* Volume I, pp. 155–180. Washington, DC: The Brookings Institution Press.

Frey, William and Alan Berube. 2003. City Families and Suburban Singles: An Emerging Household Story. In Bruce Katz and Robert E. Lang (eds.), *Redefining Cities and Suburbs: Evidence from Census 2000,* Volume I, pp. 257–288. Washington, DC: The Brookings Institution Press.

Gottmann, Jean. 1961. *Megalopolis: The Urbanized Northeastern Seaboard of the United States.* New York: Twentieth-Century Fund.

Harris, Richard. 1988. American Suburbs: A Sketch of a New Interpretation. *Journal of Urban History* 15: 98–103.

Hayden, Dolores. 2003. *Building Suburbia: Green Fields and Urban Growth, 1820.* New York: Vintage Books.

Jackson, Kenneth. 1985. *Crabgrass Frontier: The Suburbanization of the United States.* New York: Oxford University Press.

Kunstler, James H. 1993. *Geography of No-where: The Rise and Decline of America's Man-made Landscape.* New York: Free Press.

Lang, Robert. 2003. *Edgeless Cities: Exploring the Elusive Metropolis.* Washington, DC: Brookings Institution.

Lang, Robert E. and Karen A. Danielsen. 2002. Monster Homes. *Planning* (5): 2–7.

Lang, Robert and Dawn Dhavale. 2005. "Beyond Megalopolis: Exploring America's New 'Megapolitan' Geography." Census Report Series: 05:01. Alexandria, VA: Metropolitan Institute at Virginia Tech.

Lang, Robert E. and Jennifer LeFurgy. 2006. *Boomburbs: The Rise of America's Accidental Cities.* Washington, DC: The Brookings Institution Press.

Lang, Robert E., Edward J. Blakely, and Meghan Z. Gough. 2005. Keys to the New Metropolis: America's Big, Fast-Growing Suburban Counties. *Journal of the American Planning Association* 71(4): 381–391.

Lang, Robert E., James W. Hughes, and Karen A. Danielsen. 1997. Targeting the Suburban Urbanites: Marketing Central City Housing. *Housing Policy Debate* 8(2): 437–470.

Lang, Robert, Jennifer LeFurgy, and Steven Hornburg. 2005. From Wall Street to Your Street: New Solutions for Smart Growth Finance. Coral Gables, FL: Funders' Network for Smart Growth and Livable Communities.

Leinberger, Christopher. 1997. The Favored Quarter; Where the Bosses Live, Jobs and Development Follow. *Atlanta Journal Constitution,* June 8.

Liebs, Chester. 1985. *Main Street to Miracle Mile: American Roadside Architecture.* Boston: Little, Brown.

Longstreth, Richard. 1998. *City Center to Regional Mall: Architecture, the Automobile, and Retailing in Los Angeles, 1920–1950.* Cambridge, MA: MIT Press.

Longstreth, Richard. 1999. *The Drive-In, the Supermarket, and the Transformation of Commercial Space in Los Angeles, 1914–1941.* Cambridge, MA: MIT Press.

Nelson, Arthur C. 2004. Toward a New Metropolis: The Opportunity to Rebuild America. Washington, DC: The Brookings Institution Metropolitan Policy Program Survey Series (December).

Orfield, Myron. 1997. *Metro Politics: A Regional Agenda for Community and Stability.* Washington, DC: The Brookings Institution Press.

Orfield, Myron. 2002. *American Metropolitics.* Washington, DC: The Brookings Institution Press.

Rusk, David. 1993. *Cities Without Suburbs.* Washington, DC: Woodrow Wilson Center Press.

Sharpe, William and Leonard Wallock. 1994. Bold New City or Built-Up 'Burb? Redefining Contemporary Suburbia. *American Quarterly* 46(1): 1–30.

Stern, Robert A.M. and John M. Massengale. 1981. The Anglo-American Suburb, Architectural Design Profile 37, Vol. 51, No. 10/11. New York: St. Martin's Press.

Warner, Sam Bass, Jr. 1962. *Streetcar Suburbs: The Process of Growth in Boston, 1870–1900.* Cambridge, MA: Harvard University Press.

Critical Thinking

1. Explain how a series of transportation and technological advancements led to the growth of suburbia.

2. How do Edge Cities differ from a more sprawling style of suburban development of an earlier era?

ROBERT E. LANG is the Director of the Metropolitan Institute at Virginia Tech and is an Associate Professor in the school's Urban Affairs and Planning Program. He is also co-editor of *Opolis.* **JENNIFER LEFURGY** is the Deputy Director of the Metropolitan Institute at Virginia Tech. Along with Robert Lang, she is authoring *Boomburbs: The Rise of America's Accidental Cities* for The Brookings Institution Press. She is also doctoral candidate in Virginia Tech's Urban Affairs and Planning program. **ARTHUR C. NELSON** is professor and founding director of Virginia Tech's Urban Affairs and Planning Program at the Alexandria Center. He was formerly professor of city and regional planning, and public policy at Georgia Tech and adjunct professor of law at Georgia State University.

From *Opolis: An International Journal of Suburban and Metropolitan Studies,* vol. 2, no. 1, 2006, pp. 65–72. Copyright © 2006 by Robert Lang, Jennifer LeFurgy, and Arthur C. Nelson. Reprinted by permission.

Why Regions Fail: Zoning as an Extractive Institution

Jonathan Rothwell

The hottest topic in economic development theory right now is the role of institutions. In their new book, *Why Nations Fail,* social scientists Daron Acemoglu and James Robinson argue that institutions—the rules of society—have long-lasting implications on national prosperity.

Specifically, they contrast "extractive institutions" that concentrate power and hamper development, such as slavery (at the extreme) and limited voting, civil, or property rights, with open institutions that diffuse power and opportunity, providing universal incentives to invest and innovate.

Urban scholars and policymakers have much to learn from such institutional analysis. While most political economists think of institutions operating at the national or even state level, there is one essential but overlooked institution operating at and within the metro scale: zoning.

In a new report I argue that its impacts are destructive. Zoning laws are keeping poor children out of high-scoring schools, degrading education, and weakening economic opportunity. (View the paper's interactive feature to compare data on test scores, housing, and income.)

Anti-density zoning—embodied in lot-size and density regulations—is an extractive institution par excellence. Through the political power of affluent homeowners and their zoning boards, it restricts private property rights—the civic privilege to freely buy, sell, or develop property—for narrow non-public gains. Property owners in a jurisdiction benefit from zoning through higher home prices (because supply is artificially low) and lower tax rates (because population density is kept down, as school-age children are kept out), while everyone else loses.

Take New Jersey, which by any measure of zoning is one of the most restrictive, anti-density states. In 1970, two Rutgers professors did a survey of zoning in eight northeastern New Jersey counties. They found that only 8 percent of developable land was zoned for multi-family housing, and 90 percent of land required at least a half acre or more per housing unit; by contrast, the typical single-family house in the United States sits on roughly a quarter acre today. In 2010, the median home value in New Jersey is 80 percent higher than the average for all 50 states, and it has the third highest median home values behind Hawaii and California (which also has extensive zoning laws, albeit less onerous in their opposition to density, as examined recently).

The effects within the state are even more important. Compare two counties in 1970: Somerset and Camden. Zoning laws in Somerset County prohibited multi-family housing on developable land in 1970. Moreover, 85 percent of developable land was zoned so as to require at least one acre of land per housing unit—land plots roughly four times larger than the median U.S. home. In Camden County, by contrast, 46 percent of land was zoned for multi-family use and only 21 percent was zoned for large lots—on one acre or more. Today, homes cost 1.8 times more in Somerset County than in Camden County—a $180,000 difference.

These high housing costs prevent poor people living in Camden, Trenton, Newark, or elsewhere from moving to Somerset County, where they would otherwise benefit from higher-quality schools. Indeed, public school test scores in Somerset County are nearly 30 percentage points higher (on a 1–100 scale) than they are in Camden County. Moreover, while 40 percent of public school students in Camden are eligible for free or reduced lunch—an indicator of low-income status—only 15 percent of students meet that standard in Somerset. Despite multiple New Jersey Supreme Court cases declaring that all municipalities must meet their fair share of affordable housing requirements, these rulings have never had the power to overcome the protectionist incentives of the affluent and iron-willed townships.

The New Jersey case is by no means isolated. These laws are common across the country.

Dragging down the quality of education available to poor children is not only unjust, it hobbles national economic gains and therefore harms even affluent people. Young black and Latino adults earn thousands of dollars more each year, and are far more likely to obtain a college education, if they grow up in metro areas where blacks or Latinos attend high-scoring schools—like in Raleigh or San Jose—compared to their counterparts in metro areas with low-scoring schools—as in Philadelphia or New Haven. Impressive research from Raj Chetty and other economists has also found that the quality of one's school environment—measured by teacher or peer performance—causes large long-term gains in earnings and labor market performance.

Previously, my work has found that zoning laws inflate metro-wide housing costs, limit housing supply, and exacerbate segregation by income and race. Other work faults these laws for their damaging effect on the environment, since they make public transportation infeasible and extend commuting times. With a few possible exceptions (see Michelle Alexander), it's hard to think of an existing political institution in the United States that is more destructive of human and social capital.

Critical Thinking

1. What are the "destructive" effects of zoning?
2. What are the various zoning and land-use regulations that more affluent communities utilize in their efforts to exclude less affluent residents?
3. Rothwell argues that anti-density zoning is a violation of property rights. Do you agree?
4. Would the elimination of anti-density zoning serve to improve communities or hasten their decline?

JONATHAN ROTHWELL Associate Fellow and Senior Research Analyst

Patio Man and the Sprawl People
America's Newest Suburbs

DAVID BROOKS

I don't know if you've ever noticed the expression of a man who is about to buy a first-class barbecue grill. He walks into a Home Depot or Lowe's or one of the other mega hardware complexes and his eyes are glistening with a faraway visionary zeal, like one of those old prophets gazing into the promised land. His lips are parted and twitching slightly. Inside the megastore, the grills are just past the racks of affordable-house plan books, in the yard-machinery section. They are arrayed magnificently next to the vehicles that used to be known as rider mowers but are now known as lawn tractors, because to call them rider mowers doesn't really convey the steroid-enhanced M-1 tank power of the things.

The man approaches the barbecue grills and his face bears a trance-like expression, suggesting that he has cast aside all the pains and imperfections of this world and is approaching the gateway to a higher dimension. In front of him are a number of massive steel-coated reactors with names like Broilmaster P3, The Thermidor, and the Weber Genesis, because in America it seems perfectly normal to name a backyard barbecue grill after a book of the Bible.

The items in this cooking arsenal flaunt enough metal to suggest they have been hardened to survive a direct nuclear assault, and Patio Man goes from machine to machine comparing their features—the cast iron/porcelain coated cooking surfaces, the 328,000-Btu heat-generating capacities, the 1,600-degree-tolerance linings, the multiple warming racks, the lava rock containment dishes, the built-in electrical meat thermometers, and so on. Certain profound questions flow through his mind. Is a 542-square-inch grilling surface really enough, considering that he might someday get the urge to roast an uncut buffalo steak? Though the matte steel overcoat resists scratching, doesn't he want a polished steel surface on his grill so he can glance down and admire his reflection as he is performing the suburban manliness rituals, such as brushing tangy sauce on meat slabs with his right hand while clutching a beer can in an NFL foam insulator ring in his left?

Pretty soon a large salesman in an orange vest who looks like a human SUV comes up to him and says, "Howyadoin'," which is, "May I help you?" in Home Depot talk. Patio Man, who has so much lust in his heart it is all he can do to keep from climbing up on one of these machines and whooping rodeo-style with joy, manages to respond appropriately. He grunts inarticulately and nods toward the machines. Careful not to make eye contact at any point, the two manly suburban men have a brief exchange of pseudo-scientific grill argot that neither of them understands, and pretty soon Patio Man has come to the reasoned conclusion that it really does make sense to pay a little extra for a grill with V-shaped metal baffles, ceramic rods, and a side-mounted smoker box. Plus the grill he selects has four insulated drink holders. All major choices of consumer durables these days ultimately come down to which model has the most impressive cup holders.

Patio Man pays for the grill with his credit card, and is told that some minion will forklift his machine over to the loading dock around back. It is yet another triumph in a lifetime of conquest shopping, and as Patio Man heads toward the parking lot he is glad once again that he's driving that Yukon XL so that he can approach the loading dock guys as a co-equal in the manly fraternity of Those Who Haul Things.

He steps out into the parking lot and is momentarily blinded by sun bouncing off the hardtop. The parking lot is so massive that he can barely see the Wal-Mart, the Bed Bath & Beyond, or the area-code-sized Old Navy glistening through the heat there on the other side. This mall is in fact big enough to qualify for membership in the United Nations, and is so vast that shoppers have to drive from store to store, cutting diagonally through the infinity of empty parking spaces in between.

As Patio Man walks past the empty handicapped and expectant-mother parking spots toward his own vehicle, wonderful grill fantasies dance in his imagination: There he is atop the uppermost tier of his multi-level backyard patio/outdoor recreation area posed like an admiral on the deck of his destroyer. In his mind's eye he can see himself coolly flipping the garlic and pepper T-bones on the front acreage of his new grill while carefully testing the citrus-tarragon trout filets that sizzle fragrantly in the rear. On the lawn below he can see his kids, Haley and Cody, frolicking on the weedless community lawn that is mowed twice weekly by the people who run Monument Crowne Preserve, his town-home community.

Haley, 12, is a Travel Team Girl, who spends her weekends playing midfield against similarly pony-tailed, strongly calved soccer marvels. Cody, 10, is a Buzz Cut Boy, whose naturally blond hair has been cut to a lawn-like stubble and dyed an almost phosphorescent white. Cody's wardrobe is entirely derivative of fashions he has seen watching the X-Games.

In his vision, Patio Man can see the kids enjoying their child-safe lawn darts with a gaggle of their cul de sac friends, a happy gathering of Haleys and Codys and Corys and Britneys. It's a brightly colored scene: Abercrombie & Fitch pink spaghetti-strap tops on the girls and ankle length canvas shorts and laceless Nikes on the boys. Patio Man notes somewhat uncomfortably that in America today the average square yardage of boys' fashion grows and grows while the square inches in the girls' outfits shrink and shrink, so that while the boys look like tent-wearing skateboarders, the girls look like preppy prostitutes.

Nonetheless, Patio Man envisions his own adult softball team buddies lounging on his immaculate deck furniture watching him with a certain moist envy in their eyes as he mans the grill. They are fit, sockless men in dock siders, chinos, and Tommy Bahama muted Hawaiian shirts. Their wives, trim Jennifer Aniston women, wear capris and sleeveless tops that look great owing to their many hours of sweat and exercise at Spa Lady. These men and women may not be Greatest Generation heroes, or earthshaking inventors like Thomas Edison, but if Thomas Edison had had a Human Resources Department, and that Human Resources Department had organized annual enrichment and motivational conferences for mid-level management, then these people would have been the marketing executives for the back office outsourcing companies to the meeting-planning firms that hooked up the HR executives with the conference facilities.

They are wonderful people. And Patio Man can envision his own wife, Cindy, a Realtor Mom, circulating amongst them serving drinks, telling parent-teacher conference stories and generally spreading conviviality while he, Patio Man, masterfully runs the grill—again, to the silent admiration of all. The sun is shining. The people are friendly. The men are no more than 25 pounds overweight, which is the socially acceptable male paunch level in upwardly mobile America, and the children are well adjusted. It is a vision of the sort of domestic bliss that Patio Man has been shooting for all his life.

And it's plausible now because two years ago Patio Man made the big move. He pulled up stakes and he moved his family to a Sprinkler City.

Sprinkler Cities are the fast-growing suburbs mostly in the South and West that are the homes of the new style

American Dream, the epicenters of Patio Man fantasies. Douglas County, Colorado, which is the fastest-growing county in America and is located between Denver and Colorado Springs, is a Sprinkler City. So is Henderson, Nevada, just outside of Las Vegas. So is Loudoun County, Virginia, near Dulles Airport. So are Scottsdale and Gilbert, Arizona, and Union County, North Carolina.

The growth in these places is astronomical, as Patio Men and their families—and Patio retirees, yuppie geezers who still like to grill, swim, and water ski—flock to them from all over. Douglas County grew 13.6 percent from April 2000 to July 2001, while Loudoun County grew 12.6 percent in that 16-month period. Henderson, Nevada, has tripled in size over the past 10 years and now has over 175,000 people. Over the past 50 years, Irving, Texas, grew by 7,211 percent, from about 2,600 people to 200,000 people.

The biggest of these boom suburbs are huge. With almost 400,000 people, Mesa, Arizona, has a larger population than Minneapolis, Cincinnati, or St. Louis. And this sort of growth is expected to continue. Goodyear, Arizona, on the western edge of the Phoenix area, now has about 20,000 people, but is projected to have 320,000 in 50 years' time. By then, Greater Phoenix could have a population of over 6 million and cover over 10,000 square miles.

Sprinkler Cities are also generally the most Republican areas of the country. In some of the Sprinkler City congressional districts, Republicans have a 2 or 3 or 4 to 1 registration advantage over Democrats. As cultural centers, they represent the beau ideal of Republican selfhood, and are becoming the new base—the brains, heart, guts, and soul of the emerging Republican party. Their values are not the same as those found in either old-line suburbs like Greenwich, Connecticut, where a certain sort of Republican used to dominate, or traditional conservative bastions, such as the old South. This isn't even the more modest conservatism found in the midwestern farm belt. In fact, the rising prominence of these places heralds a new style of suburb vs. suburb politics, with the explosively growing Republican outer suburbs vying with the slower-growing and increasingly Democratic inner suburbs for control of the center of American political gravity.

If you stand on a hilltop overlooking a Sprinkler City, you see, stretched across the landscape, little brown puffs here and there where bulldozers are kicking up dirt while building new townhomes, office parks, shopping malls, AmeriSuites guest hotels, and golf courses. Everything in a Sprinkler City is new. The highways are so clean and freshly paved you can eat off them. The elementary schools have spic and span playgrounds, unscuffed walls, and immaculate mini-observatories for just-forming science classes.

The lawns in these places are perfect. It doesn't matter how arid the local landscape used to be, the developers come in and lay miles of irrigation tubing, and the sprinklers pop up each evening, making life and civilization possible.

The roads are huge. The main ones, where the office parks are, have been given names like Innovation Boulevard and Entrepreneur Avenue, and they've been built for the population levels that will exist a decade from now, so that today you can cruise down these flawless six lane thoroughfares in traffic-less nirvana, and if you get a cell phone call you can just stop in the right lane and take the call because there's no one behind you. The smaller roads in the residential neighborhoods have pretentious names—in Loudoun County I drove down Trajan's Column Terrace—but they too are just as smooth and immaculate as a blacktop bowling alley. There's no use relying on a map to get around these places, because there's no way map publishers can keep up with the construction.

The town fathers try halfheartedly to control sprawl, and as you look over the landscape you can see the results of their ambivalent zoning regulations. The homes aren't spread out with quarter-acre yards, as in the older, close-in suburbs. Instead they are clustered into pseudo-urban pods. As you scan the horizon you'll see a densely packed pod of townhouses, then a stretch of a half mile of investor grass (fields that will someday contain 35,000-square-foot Fresh-Mex restaurants but for now are being kept fallow by investors until the prices rise), and then another pod of slightly more expensive detached homes just as densely packed.

The developments in the southeastern Sprinkler Cities tend to have Mini-McMansion Gable-gable houses. That is to say, these are 3,200-square-foot middle-class homes built to look like 7,000-square-foot starter palaces for the nouveau riche. And on the front at the top, each one has a big gable, and then right in front of it, for visual relief, a little gable jutting forward so that it looks like a baby gable leaning against a mommy gable.

These homes have all the same features as the authentic McMansions of the mid-'90s (as history flows on, McMansions come to seem authentic), but significantly smaller. There are the same vaulted atriums behind the front doors that never get used, and the same open kitchen/two-story great rooms with soaring palladian windows. But in the middle-class knockoffs, the rooms are so small, especially upstairs, that a bedroom or a master-bath suite would fit inside one of the walk-in closets of a real McMansion.

In the Southwest the homes tend to be tile and stucco jobs, with tiny mousepad lawns out front, blue backyard spas in the back, and so much white furniture inside that you have to wear sunglasses indoors. As you fly over the Sprinkler Cities you begin to see the rough pattern—a little pseudo-urbanist plop of development, a blank field, a plop, a field, a plop. You also notice that the developers build the roads and sewage lines first and then fill in the houses later, so from the sky you can see cul de sacs stretching off into the distance with no houses around them.

Then, cutting through the landscape are broad commercial thoroughfares with two-tier, big-box malls on either side. In the front tier is a line of highly themed chain restaurants that all fuse into the same Macaroni Grill Olive Outback Cantina Charlie Chiang's Dave & Buster's Cheesecake Factory mélange of peppy servers, superfluous ceiling fans, free bread with olive oil, and taco salad entrees. In the 21st-century migration of peoples, the food courts come first and the huddled masses follow.

Then in the back row are all the huge, exposed-air-duct architectural behemoths, which are the big-box stores.

Shopping experiences are now segregated by mood. If you are in the mood for some titillating browsing, you can head over to a Lifestyle Center, which is one of those instant urban streetscapes that developers put up in suburbia as entertainment/retail/community complexes, complete with pedestrian zones, outdoor cafés, roller rinks, multiplexes, and high-attitude retail concepts such as CP Shades, a chain store that masquerades as a locally owned boutique.

If you are buying necessities, really shopping, there are Power Malls. These are the big-box expanses with Wal-Marts, K-Marts, Targets, price clubs, and all the various Depots (Home, Office, Furniture, etc.). In Sprinkler Cities there are archipelagoes of them—one massive parking lot after another surrounded by huge boxes that often have racing stripes around the middle to break the monotony of the windowless exterior walls.

If one superstore is in one mall, then its competitor is probably in the next one in the archipelago. There's a Petsmart just down from a Petco, a Borders nearby a Barnes & Noble, a Linens 'n' Things within sight of a Bed Bath & Beyond, a Best Buy cheek by jowl with a Circuit City. In Henderson, there's a Wal-Mart superstore that spreads over 220,000 square feet, with all those happy greeters in blue vests to make you feel small-town.

There are also smaller stores jammed in between the mega-outlets like little feeder fish swimming around the big boys. On one strip, there might be the ostentatiously unpretentious Total Wine & More, selling a galaxy of casual Merlots. Nearby there might be a Michaels discount women's clothing, a bobo bazaar such as World Market that sells raffia fiber from Madagascar, Rajasthani patchwork coverlets from India, and vermouth-flavored martini onions from Israel, and finally a string of storefront mortgage bankers and realtors serving all the new arrivals. In Sprinkler Cities, there are more realtors than people.

People move to Sprinkler Cities for the same reasons people came to America or headed out West. They want to leave behind the dirt and toxins of their former existence—the crowding and inconvenience, the precedents, and the oldness of what suddenly seems to them a settled and unpromising world. They want to move to some place that seems fresh and new and filled with possibility.

Sprinkler City immigrants are not leaving cities to head out to suburbia. They are leaving older suburbs—which have come to seem as crowded, expensive, and stratified as cities—and heading for newer suburbs, for the suburbia of suburbia.

One of the problems we have in thinking about the suburbs is that when it comes to suburbia the American imagination is motionless. Many people still have in their heads the stereotype of suburban life that the critics of suburbia established in the 1950s. They see suburbia as a sterile, dull, Ozzie and Harriet retreat from the creative dynamism of city life, and the people who live in the suburbs as either hopelessly shallow or quietly and neurotically desperate. (There is no group in America more conformist than the people who rail against suburbanites for being conformist—they always make the same critiques, decade after decade.)

The truth, of course, is that suburbia is not a retreat from gritty American life, it is American life. Already, suburbanites make up about half of the country's population (while city people make up 28 percent and rural folk make up the rest), and America gets more suburban every year.

According to the census data, the suburbs of America's 100 largest metro areas grew twice as fast as their central cities in the 1990s, and that was a decade in which many cities actually reversed their long population slides. Atlanta, for example, gained 23,000 people in the '90s, but its suburbs grew by 1.1 million people.

Moreover, newer suburbs no longer really feed off cities. In 1979, 74 percent of American office space was located in cities, according to The Brookings Institution's Robert Puentes. But now, after two decades in which the biggest job growth has been in suburban office parks, the suburbs' share of total office space has risen to 42 percent. In other words, we are fast approaching a time when the majority of all office space will be in the suburbs, and most Americans not only will not live in cities, they won't even commute to cities or have any regular contact with city life.

Encompassing such a broad swath of national existence, suburbs obviously cannot possibly be the white-bread places of myth and literature. In reality, as the most recent census shows, suburbs contain more non-family houses—young singles and elderly couples—than family households, married couples with children. Nor are they overwhelmingly white. The majority of Asian Americans, half of Hispanics, and 40 percent of American blacks live in suburbia.

And so now there are crucial fault lines not just between city and suburb but between one kind of suburb and another. Say you grew up in some southern California suburb in the 1970s. You graduated from the University of Oregon and now you are a systems analyst with a spouse and two young kids. You're making $65,000 a year, far more than you ever thought you would, but back in Orange County you find you can't afford to live anywhere near your Newport Beach company headquarters. So your commute is 55 minutes each way. Then there's your house itself. You paid $356,000 for a 1962 four-bedroom split level with a drab kitchen, low ceilings, and walls that are chipped and peeling. Your mortgage—that $1,800 a month—is like a tapeworm that devours the family budget.

And then you visit a Sprinkler City in Arizona or Nevada or Colorado—far from the coast and deep into exurbia—and what do you see? Bounteous roads! Free traffic lanes! If you lived here you'd be in commuter bliss—15 minutes from home on Trajan's Column Terrace to the office park on Innovation Boulevard! If you lived here you'd have an extra hour and a half each day for yourself.

And those real estate prices! In, say, Henderson, Nevada, you wouldn't have to spend over $400,000 for a home and carry that murderous mortgage. You could get a home that's brand new, twice the size of your old one, with an attached garage (no flimsy carport), and three times as beautiful for $299,000. The average price of a single-family home in Loudoun County, one of the pricier of the Sprinkler Cities, was $166,824 in 2001, which was an 11 percent increase over the year before. Imagine that! A mortgage under 200 grand! A great anvil would be lifted from your shoulders. More free money for you to spend on yourself. More free time to enjoy. More Freedom!

Plus, if you moved to a Sprinkler City there would be liberation of a subtler kind. The old suburbs have become socially urbanized. They've become stratified. Two sorts of people have begun to move in and ruin the middle-class equality of the development you grew up in: the rich and the poor.

There are, first, the poor immigrants, from Mexico, Vietnam, and the Philippines. They come in, a dozen to a house, and they introduce an element of unpredictability to what was a comforting milieu. They shout. They're less tidy. Their teenage boys seem to get involved with gangs and cars. Suddenly you feel you will lose control of your children. You begin to feel a new level of anxiety in the neighborhood. It is exactly the level of anxiety—sometimes intermingled with racism—your parents felt when they moved from their old neighborhood to the suburbs in the first place.

And then there are the rich. Suddenly many of the old ramblers are being knocked down by lawyers who proceed to erect 4,000-square-foot arts and crafts bungalows with two-car garages for their Volvos. Suddenly cars in the neighborhoods have window and bumper stickers that never used to be there in the past: "Yale," "The Friends School," "Million Mom March." The local stores are changing too. Gone are the hardware stores and barber shops. Now there are Afghan restaurants, Marin County bistros, and environmentally sensitive and extremely expensive bakeries.

And these new people, while successful and upstanding, are also . . . snobs. They're doctors and lawyers and journalists and media consultants. They went to fancy colleges and they consider themselves superior to you if you sell home-security systems or if you are a mechanical engineer, and in subtle yet patronizing ways they let you know it.

I recently interviewed a woman in Loudoun County who said she had grown up and lived most of her life in Bethesda, Maryland, which is an upscale suburb close to Washington. When I asked why she left Bethesda, she hissed "I hate it there now" with a fervor that took me by surprise. And as we spoke, it became clear that it was precisely the "improvements" she hated: the new movie theater that shows only foreign films, the explosion of French, Turkish, and new wave restaurants, the streets choked with German cars and Lexus SUVs, the doctors and lawyers and journalists with their educated-class one-upmanship.

These new people may live in the old suburbs but they hate suburbanites. They hate sprawl, big-box stores, automobile culture. The words they use about suburbanites are: synthetic, bland, sterile, self-absorbed, disengaged. They look down on people who like suburbs. They don't like their lawn statuary, their Hallmark greeting cards, their Ethan Allen furniture, their megachurches, the seasonal banners the old residents hang out in front of their houses, their untroubled attitude toward McDonald's and Dairy Queen, their Thomas Kinkade fantasy paintings. And all the original suburbanites who were peacefully enjoying their suburb until the anti-suburban suburbanites moved in notice the condescension, and they do what Americans have always done when faced with disapproval, anxiety, and potential conflict. They move away. The pincer movements get them: the rich and the poor, the commutes and the mortgages, the prices and the alienation. And pretty soon it's Henderson, Nevada, here we come.

George Santayana once observed that Americans don't solve problems, they just leave them behind. They take advantage of all that space and move. If there's an idea they don't like, they don't bother refuting it, they just go somewhere else, and if they can't go somewhere else, they just leave it in the past, where it dies from inattention.

And so Patio Man is not inclined to stay and defend himself against the condescending French-film goers and their Volvos. He's not going to mount a political campaign to fix the educational, economic, and social woes that beset him in his old neighborhood. He won't waste his time fighting a culture war. It's not worth the trouble. He just bolts. He heads for the exurbs and the desert. He goes to the new place where the future is still open and promising. He goes to fresh ground where his dreams might more plausibly come true.

The power of this urge to leave and create new places is really awesome to behold. Migration is not an easy thing, yet every year 43 million Americans get up and move. And it sets off a chain reaction. The migrants who move into one area push out another set of people, who then migrate to another and push out another set of people, and so on and so on in one vast cycle of creative destruction. Ten years ago these Sprinkler Cities didn't really exist. Fifteen years ago the institutions that dot them hadn't been invented. There weren't book superstores or sporting goods superstores or Petsmart or Petco, and Target was just something you shot arrows at. And yet suddenly metropolises with all these new stores and institutions have materialized out of emptiness.

It's as if some Zeus-like figure had appeared out of the ether and slammed down a million-square-foot mall on the desert floor, then a second later he'd slammed down a 5,000-person townhome community, then a second later an ice rink and a rec center and soccer fields and schools and community colleges. How many times in human history have 200,000-person cities just materialized almost instantaneously out of nowhere?

The people who used to live in these empty places don't like it; they've had to move further out in search of valleys still pristine. But the sprawl people just love it. They talk to you like born-again evangelists, as if their life had undergone some magical transformation when they made the big move. They talk as if they'd thrown off some set of horrendous weights, banished some class of unpleasant experiences, and magically floated up into the realm of good climate, fine people, job opportunities, and transcendent convenience. In 2001, Loudoun County did a survey of its residents. Ninety-eight percent felt safe in their neighborhoods. Ninety-three percent rated their county's quality of life excellent or good. Only a third of the county's residents, by the way, have lived there for more than 10 years.

These people are so happy because they have achieved something that human beings are actually quite good at achieving. Through all the complex diversity of society, they have managed to find people who want pretty much the same things they want.

This is not to say they want white Ozzie and Harriet nirvana. The past 40 years happened. It never occurs to them to go back before rock, rap, women working, and massive immigration. They don't mind any of these things, so long as they complement the core Sprinkler City missions of orderly living, high achievement, and the bright seeking of a better future.

Recently three teams from the Seneca Ridge Middle School in Loudoun County competed in the National Social Studies Olympiad. The fifth grade team finished fifth out of 242 teams, while the eighth grade team finished twenty-third out of 210. Here are some of the names of the students competing for Loudoun: Amy Kuo, Arshad Ali, Samanth Chao, Katie Hempenius, Ronnel Espino, Obinna Onwuka, Earnst Ilang-Ilang, Ashley Shiraishi, and Alberto Pareja-Lecaros. At the local high school, 99 percent of seniors graduate and 87 percent go on to higher education.

When you get right down to it, Sprinkler Cities are united around five main goals:

- *The goal of the together life.* When you've got your life together, you have mastered the complexities of the modern world so thoroughly that you can glide through your days without unpleasant distractions or tawdry failures. Instead, your hours are filled with self-affirming reminders of the control you have achieved over the elements. Your lawn is immaculate. Your DVD library is organized, and so is your walk-in closet.

Your car is clean and vacuumed, your frequently dialed numbers are programmed into your cell phone, your telephone plan is suited to your needs, and your various gizmos interface without conflict. Your wife is effortlessly slender, your kids are unnaturally bright, your job is rewarding, your promotions are inevitable, and you look great in casual slacks.

You can thus spend your days in perfect equanimity, the Sprinkler City ideal. You radiate confidence, like a professional golfer striding up the 18th fairway after a particularly masterful round. Compared with you, Dick Cheney looks like a disorganized hothead. George W. Bush looks like a self-lacerating neurotic. Professionally, socially, parentally, you have your life together. You may not be the most intellectual or philosophical person on the planet, but you are honest and straightforward. You may not be flamboyant, but you are friendly, good-hearted, and considerate. You have achieved the level of calm mastery of life that is the personality equivalent of the clean and fresh suburban landscape.

- *The goal of technological heroism.* They may not be stereotypical rebels, and nobody would call them avant-garde, but in one respect many Sprinkler City dwellers have the souls of revolutionaries. When Patio Man gets out of his Yukon, lowers his employee-badge necklace around his neck, and walks into his generic office building, he becomes a technological radical. He spends his long workdays striving to create some technological innovation, management solution, or organizing system breakthroughs that will alter the world. Maybe the company he works for has one of those indecipherable three-initial names, like DRG Technologies or SER Solutions, or maybe it's got one of those jammed together compound names that were all the rage in the 1990s until WorldCom and MicroStrategy went belly up.

Either way, Patio Man is working on, or longs to be working on, a project that is new and revolutionary. And all around him there are men and women who are actually achieving that goal, who are making that leap into the future. The biotech revolution is being conducted in bland suburban office parks by seemingly unremarkable polo-shirt-and-chino people at firms like Celera and Human Genome Sciences. Silicon Valley is just one long string of suburban office parks jutting out from San Jose. AOL is headquartered in Loudoun County. You walk down a path in a Sprinkler City corporate center and it leads you to a company frantically chasing some market-niche innovation in robotics, agricultural engineering, microtechnology, or hardware and software applications.

There are retail-concept revolutionaries, delivery-system radicals, market-research innovators, data-collection pioneers, computer-game Rembrandts, and weapons-systems analysts. They look like bland members of some interchangeable research team, but many of them are deeply engrossed in what they consider a visionary project, which if completed will help hurtle us all further into the Knowledge Revolution, the Information Millennium, the Age of MicroTechnology, the Biotech Century, or whatever transplendent future it is you want to imagine. They have broken the monopoly that cities used to have, and they have made themselves the new centers of creativity.

- *The goal of relaxed camaraderie.* The critics of suburbia believe that single-family homeowners with their trimmed yards and matching pansies are trying to keep up with the Joneses. But like most of what the critics assert, that's completely wrong. Sprinkler City people are competitive in the marketplace and on the sports field, but they detest social competition. That's part of why these people left inner-ring suburbs in the first place.

They are not emulating the rich; they are happy to blend in with each other. One of the comforts of these places is that almost nobody is far above you socially and almost nobody is far below. You're all just swimming in a pond of understated success.

So manners are almost aggressively relaxed. Everybody strives overtime to not put on airs or create friction. In style, demeanor, and mood, people reveal the language and values they have in common. They are good team members and demonstrate from the first meeting that they are team-able. You could go your entire life, from home to church to work to school, wearing nothing but Lands' End—comfortable, conservative, non-threatening activewear for people with a special fondness for navy blue. The dominant conversational tone is upbeat and friendly, like banter between Katie Couric and Matt Lauer on the "Today" show. The prevailing style of humor is ironic but not biting and owes a lot to ESPN's "SportsCenter."

- *The goal of the active-leisure lifestyle.* Your self-esteem is based on your success at work, but since half the time it's hard to explain to people what the hell it is you do, your public identity is defined by your leisure activities. You are the soccer family, engrossed by the politics and melodrama of your local league, or you are the T-ball coach and spend your barbecue conversations comparing notes on new $200 titanium bat designs (there's a new bat called The Power Elite—even C. Wright Mills has been domesticated for the Little League set). You are Scuba Woman and you converse about various cruises you have taken. You are Mountain Bike Man and you make vague references to your high altitude injuries and spills. Or you are a golfer, in which case nobody even thinks of engaging you in conversation on any topic other than golf.

Religion is too hot a subject and politics is irrelevant, so if you are not discussing transportation issues—how to get from here to there, whether the new highway exit is good or bad—you are probably talking about sports. You're talking about your kids' ice hockey leagues, NBA salary levels, or the competition in your over-70 softball league—the one in which everybody wears a knee brace and it takes about six minutes for a good hitter to beat out a double. Sports sets the emotional climate of your life. Sports provides the language of easy camaraderie, self-deprecating humor, and (mostly) controlled competition.

- *The goal of the traditional, but competitive, childhood.* Most everything in Sprinkler Cities is new, but much of the newness is in the service of tradition. The families that move here are trying to give their children as clean and upright and traditional a childhood as they can imagine. They're trying to move away from parents who smoke and slap their kids, away from families where people watch daytime TV shows about transvestite betrayals and "My Daughter is a Slut" confessions, away from broken homes and, most of all, away from the company of children who are not being raised to achieve and succeed.

They are trying to move instead to a realm of clean neighborhoods, safe streets, competitive cheerleading, spirit squads, soccer tots academies, accelerated-reader programs, and adult-chaperoned drug-free/alcohol-free graduation celebrations.

For the fifth consecutive year, the Henderson, Nevada, high school Marine Corps Junior ROTC squad has won the National Male Armed Drill Team championship. The Female Unarmed Drill Team has come in first six out of the past eight years. In Loudoun County the local newspaper runs notices for various travel team tryouts. In one recent edition, I counted 55 teams announcing their tryouts, with names like The Loudoun Cyclones, the Herndon Surge, the Loudoun Volcanoes. (It's not socially acceptable to name your team after a group of people anymore, so most of the teams have nature names.) As you drive around a Sprinkler City you see SUVs everywhere with cheers scrawled in washable marker on the back windows: "Go Heat!" "#24 Kelly Jones!" "Regional Champs!"

The kids spend their days being chaperoned from one adult-supervised activity to another, and from one achievement activity to the next. They are well tested, well trophied, and well appreciated. They are not only carefully reared and nurtured, they are launched into a life of high expectations and presumed accomplishment.

The dominant ideology of Sprinkler Cities is a sort of utopian conservatism. On the one hand, the people who live here have made a startling leap into the unknown. They have, in great numbers and with great speed, moved from their old homes in California, Florida, Illinois, and elsewhere, to these brand new places that didn't really exist 10 years ago. These places have no pasts, no precedents, no settled institutions, very few longstanding groups you can join and settle into.

Their inhabitants have moved to towns where they have no family connections, no ethnic enclaves, and no friends. They are using their imaginations to draw pictures for themselves of what their lives will be like. They are imagining their golf club buddies even though the course they are moving near is only just being carved out of the desert. They are imagining their successful children's graduation from high school, even though the ground around the new school building is still rutted with the tracks of construction equipment. They are imagining outings with friends at restaurants that are now only investor grass, waiting to be built.

And when they do join groups, often the groups turn out to be still in the process of building themselves. The migrants join congregations that meet in school basements while raising the money to construct churches. They go to office parks at biotech companies that are still waiting to put a product on the market. They may vote, or episodically pay attention to national politics, but they don't get drawn into strong local party organizations because the local organizations haven't been built.

But the odd thing is that all this imaginative daring, these leaps into the future, are all in the service of an extremely conservative ideal. You get the impression that these people have fled their crowded and stratified old suburbs because they really want to live in Mayberry. They have this image of what home should be, a historical myth or memory, and they are going to build it, even if it means constructing an old fashioned place out of modern materials.

It's going to be morally upstanding. It's going to be relaxed and neighborly. It's going to be neat and orderly. Sprinkler City people seem to have almost a moral revulsion at disorder or anything that threatens to bring chaos, including out-of-control immigration and terrorist attacks. They don't think about the war on terror much, let alone some alleged invasion of Iraq, but if it could be shown that Saddam Hussein presented a threat to the good order of the American homeland, then these people would support his ouster with a fervor that would take your breath away. "They have strong emotions when dealing with security," says Tom Tancredo, a congressman from suburban Denver. "Border security, the security of their families, the security of their neighborhoods."

Of course, from the moment they move in, they begin soiling their own nest. They move in order to get away from crowding, but as they and the tens of thousands like them move in, they bring crowding with them. They move to get away from stratification, snobbery, and inequality, but as the new towns grow they get more stratified. In Henderson, the $200,000 ranch homes are now being supplemented by gated $500,000-a-home golf communities. People move for stability and old fashioned values, but they are unwilling to accept limits to opportunity. They are achievement oriented. They are inherently dynamic.

For a time they do a dance about preserving the places they are changing by their presence. As soon as people move into a Sprinkler City, they start lobbying to control further growth. As Tancredo says, they have absolutely no shame about it. They want more roads built, but fewer houses. They want to freeze the peaceful hominess of the town that was growing when they moved there five minutes before.

But soon, one senses, they will get the urge to move again. The Hendersons and the Douglas Counties will be tomorrow what the Newport Beaches and the Los Altoses and the White Plainses are today, places where Patio Man no longer feels quite at home. And the suburban middle-class folks in these places will again strike out as the avant-garde toward new places, with new sorts of stores and a new vision of the innocent hometown.

So the dynamism and volatility will continue—always moving aggressively toward a daring future that looks like an imagined picture of the wholesome past, striving and charging toward that dream of the peaceful patio, the happy kids, the slender friends, and, towering over it all, the massive barbecue grill.

Critical Thinking

1. Where does Patio Man live? What are the political attitudes of Patio Man that can be seen as typical of a great many suburbanites?

2. The concept of "suburbia" often masks a surprising diversity of communities. What different types of suburbs can you identify?

DAVID BROOKS is a senior editor at *The Weekly Standard.*

Affluent, but Needy (First Suburbs)

As they grow and change, the nation's first suburbs, Nassau County included, show signs of stress ahead.

BRUCE KATZ AND ROBERT PUENTES

The problems of America's older, inner-ring first suburbs, Nassau County being among the most prominent, are finally beginning to draw national attention. And not a moment too soon. Warning signs loom.

A new analysis of statistics comparing population growth and demographic changes in these areas from 1950 to 2000, to be formally released by The Brookings Institution this week, shows that across the country first suburbs are undergoing a series of changes that threaten their ability to remain vital and prosperous communities during the long term.

While still largely affluent and suburban in character, these places, which are adjacent to central cities and were identified as standard metropolitan areas by 1950, are beginning to take on some of the characteristics of urban areas. An influx of lower-income minority and foreign-born residents means that, like cities, these first suburbs increasingly will need more state and federal aid to keep up with a growing need for social services and affordable housing.

At the moment, however, they fall through the cracks in a nation where government assistance has been directed for years at urban or rural areas. As Sen. Hillary Clinton said in a speech last month at Adelphi University, "Long Island is the victim of its own success."

Nassau, as we all know, possesses major assets—proximity to New York City, extensive parkland and beaches, quality neighborhoods, a large number of highly educated residents with high income levels and a highly developed transportation network for commuting to the city. Its home values are among the highest in the nation. But a number of trends suggest that stress lies ahead.

The population has remained stagnant since the 1960s in terms of size, yet is much more diverse than even 20 years ago. Racially, the nonwhite percentage of the population has grown nearly 15 percent since 1970; the percentage of foreign-born has more than doubled, and the elderly population has risen nearly 400 percent since 1950, compared with the U.S. average of 185 percent.

Amid great wealth, growing pockets of poverty and communities of poorer and older residents are presenting needs that weren't an issue in earlier years, when incomes and education levels were not as dissimilar as they are today. A county built as a haven for young, middle-class families with automobiles, most of whom who could afford single-family houses, is now home to a growing population with limited access to cars, a need for cheaper housing and a greater need for social services in order to succeed as members of the community.

Just as we have seen in cities, as their numbers increase, foreign-born populations will put new demands on schools unaccustomed to non-English speakers and on health care systems designed to serve much smaller numbers of lower-income clients. The growing numbers of elderly also will need more health and social services.

Across the country, other first-ring suburbs such as Newark's Essex County, Chicago's Cook County, Seattle's King County and Atlanta's Fulton County also are dealing daily with these issues. The risk for the nation is that their relatively small local governments—which not only have to serve a changing population but maintain an aging system of highways and bridges—will leave them vulnerable to a rapid decline once they start to run out of resources. The suburbs' underdiversified commercial bases add to the risk.

As Nassau County Executive Thomas Suozzi warned in his State of the County address last year, "We have stopped growing. America's first suburb has reached middle age. We now have little open space left to grow, and we want to preserve what we have left. Meanwhile, traffic worsens, and under current zoning laws we can't redevelop those places that could sustain more density. With no new construction or new business, with rising expenses and a flat tax base, local government will be forced to raise property taxes even further or dramatically cut existing services. To continue on that course would be a catastrophe for Nassau. It would mean not simply no new business, but a loss of business and a shrinking tax base to pay higher and higher taxes."

The long-run problem Nassau faces is really a national problem, and it deserves a national solution.

You'd expect the first suburbs to have the political clout to demand one. They are home to about 20 percent of the nation's population. In some states like Maryland, Connecticut and New Jersey, about half the residents live in first suburbs. New York State, the city and first suburban populations together constitute a super majority: Two-thirds of all New Yorkers live in these places. At least a third of congressional districts represent all or part of first suburbs.

The trouble is that these suburbs are not organized to deliver on this political power. Rather, they operate independently or as part of a vast suburban bloc. We tend to think of Nassau and Suffolk as a bloc, for instance, even though most of Suffolk County is a good deal newer.

As a consequence, first suburbs are caught in a policy blind spot between the benefaction long directed toward central cities for problems like housing and economic investment and the new attention being lavished on fast-growing outer suburbs, where demands for new infrastructure and services take precedence.

The first suburbs are often not poor enough to participate in economic programs like empowerment zones or other housing and urban redevelopment efforts. They are frequently too small to qualify for direct funding. With populations less than 50,000, for example, Garden City, Wantagh, West Hempstead and others are not entitled to receive direct funding from the federal Community Development Block Grant program, which pays for improving housing, streets, infrastructure and downtowns.

What can the first suburbs do to get the attention they need from federal and state governments?

First, they need to encourage more research that can help state and federal policy makers understand the urgency of the demographic and market trends in first suburbs and re-envision how these places can continue to thrive. Unfortunately, scant data exist. Institutions such as Hofstra University have begun to fill this gap—in Hofstra's case, with its new Center for Suburban Studies—as have metropolitan organizations in places like Philadelphia and St. Louis. Much more research is needed in many localities.

Second, these first suburbs need to build coalitions and share experiences and lessons, in order to develop and articulate an agenda that focuses specifically on their needs. Successful regional alliances have emerged in Cuyahoga County, near Cleveland, and in Los Angeles County. Some leaders like Suozzi are seeking to build alliances statewide.

The groundwork for reform already is being laid in a number of areas:

On the federal level, Sen. Clinton and Rep. Peter King (R-Seaford) have introduced the Suburban Core Opportunity, Restoration and Enhancement Act in the Senate and House. This bill would set aside $250 million for first

Changing with Age

Nassau and older suburbs are developing differently from cities and newer suburbs.

Nassau County
Percent change in population, 1950–2000 **98.4**
Percentage point change in share of population other than non-Hispanic white, 1980–2000 **14.7**
Percent change in foreign-born population, 1970–2000 **108.5**
Percent change in population age 65 and older, 1950–2000 **398.3**
Percent change in population younger than 15, 1970–2000 **-28.8**

First Surburbs
Percent change in population, 1950–2000 **161.3**
Percentage point change in share of population other than non-Hispanic white, 1980–2000 **17.0**
Percent change in foreign-born population, 1970–2000 **263.7**
Percent change in population age 65 and older, 1950–2000 **341.7**
Percent change in population younger than 15, 1970–2000 **1.7**

Primary Cities
Percent change in population, 1950–2000 **5.3**
Percentage point change in share of population other than non-Hispanic white, 1980–2000 **15.8**
Percent change in foreign-born population, 1970–2000 **138.1**
Percent change in population age 65 and older, 1950–2000 **44.3**
Percent change in population younger than 15, 1970–2000 **-13.1**

Newer Surburbs
Percent change in population, 1950–2000 **75.1**
Percentage point change in share of population other than non-Hispanic white, 1980–2000 **10.8**
Percent change in foreign-born population, 1970–2000 **208.2**
Percent change in population age 65 and older, 1950–2000 **131.1**
Percent change in population younger than 15, 1970–2000 **32.5**

United States
Percent change in population, 1950–2000 **86.0**
Percentage point change in share of population other than non-Hispanic white, 1980–2000 **10.4**
Percent change in foreign-born population, 1970–2000 **223.4**
Percent change in population age 65 and older, 1950–2000 **185.2**
Percent change in population younger than 15, 1970–2000 **4.1**

suburbs nationwide to help fund reinvestment and revitalization projects.

Several states, including Pennsylvania, Michigan and Illinois, are directing infrastructure dollars to cities and established suburbs. This gives priority to the maintenance and rehabilitation needs of existing infrastructure before building new.

Efforts are under way to foster cooperation between first suburbs and central cities. Cleveland's new mayor has promised, for example, to create a post in his administration to oversee regional issues.

First suburbs in Pittsburgh's Allegheny County and Boston's Middlesex County are collaborating to jointly assemble parcels of land with uniform tax rates, codes and streamlined approvals to encourage redevelopment.

Such federal, state and regional efforts are still early in formation and, to date, limited in effect. They raise the potential, however, of first suburbs' flexing their political muscle.

Whether Nassau County and the other first suburbs will emerge as a powerful, focused and disciplined force remains one of the great political questions of a young century.

Critical Thinking

1. What is a First Suburb?

2. How do the conditions of a First Suburb generally differ from those of the suburb in which Patio Man lives?

3. Are there opportunities for city-suburban political alliances? What sort of suburbs would find it in their interest to form an alliance with central cities? On what issues?

As seen in *Newsday,* February 12, 2006, p. A44. Copyright © 2006 by Bruce Katz and Robert Puentes, Brookings Institution-Metropolitan Policy Program. Reprinted by permission of Brookings Institute and the authors.

Regional Coalition-Building and the Inner Suburbs

Myron Orfield

In response to growing social and economic polarization, between 1993 and 1997 Minnesota's Twin Cities jump-started a long-dormant regional debate. In three years, the area reorganized its regional planning council, moving it from a $40-million-a-year coordinating agency to a $600-million-a-year regional governance structure for transit and transportation, sewers, land use, airports, and housing policy. It enacted an important regional affordable-housing bill, strengthened the regional land-use system, and the legislature passed (but the governor vetoed) a major addition to regional tax-base sharing and a measure to elect the Metropolitan Council, a regional planning and operating agency. Energy for regional reform is growing.

In the process of reenergizing regionalism and ranging metropolitan issues on our negotiating table, we have discovered that our problems are not unique and that the suburban monolith, thought to prevent all progress on regional issues, is a myth. Every metropolitan region in the United States faces the same problems. Coalition-building efforts that emphasize the links between core cities and suburbs can bring about reforms to increase equity for an entire region.

Local Metropolitan Subregions

Over generations of urban growth, four distinct types of suburban communities have emerged in the Twin Cities metropolitan area.

The "inner suburbs" are a collection of fully developed working- and middle-class communities just outside the inner city, where 26 percent of the metropolitan population lives. Many of these communities are beginning to feel the effects of socioeconomic changes spreading outward from the city and are ill equipped to handle new problems. Politically, the inner suburbs house a mix of Democrats and Republicans.

Middle-class, and particularly working-class, inner suburbs are less stable than central cities for economic, organizational, and cultural reasons. Older suburbs are often a collection of smaller houses without a significant commercial industrial base and without the central city's amenities, significant police force and social welfare presence.

"Mid-developing suburbs," the low-tax-capacity but developing suburbs beyond the beltways, tend to be extensions of middle- and working-class neighborhoods. These rapidly developing communities, with a property tax base resting mainly on inexpensive single-family homes and apartment buildings, have insufficient resources to support basic public services. The older suburbs and mid-developing suburbs are classic swing districts, leaning toward Democrats on economic issues and Republicans on social issues.

The "commercial high-tax-capacity developing suburbs" in the Twin Cities form the "favored quarter" of the area's south and west. To the east lie the "residential, high-tax capacity developing suburbs," with a broad, rich property tax base and comparatively few socioeconomic needs. The crime rate is low in the south and west, and even lower in the east.

More than half the cities in this area had smaller concentrations of poor children at the end of the decade than at the beginning, possibly as a result of local zoning and metropolitan transportation policies restrictive to poor residents. Over time, households that cannot make it over suburban housing barriers tend to collect in the central cities and the older suburbs. The high-tax capacity suburbs have a median household income almost twice as high as in the central cities, 23 percent higher than in the inner ring, and 10 percent higher than in the mid-developing suburbs. They have about one-third more tax wealth than the other subregions.

Income Polarization and Politics

Underlying this spatial polarization has been the polarization of household income. Throughout the United States in the 1980s, those in the bottom three quintiles of household income lost ground, those in the fourth stayed even, and those in the top fifth saw their household income increase by nearly one-third.

These shifts in income have exacerbated tension between people in the second and third economic quintiles and those on the bottom. In the late 1960s, in older, larger regions of the country, poor people had rolled into these suburbs, fleeing the declining core city. People in the second- and third-quintile groups felt a deep threat to the value of their houses—their main assets—and to their neighborhoods—the center of their world. As residents resisted these incursions, they aligned with more conservative economic and political forces than their economic circumstances would normally indicate. These increasingly conservative, working class inner suburbanites outside of large cities feared for their homes and neighborhoods. Their racism was wrong, but their fear that disorderly metropolitan change would severely hurt their communities was well founded.

Spatial and income polarizations marry in unpredictable and angry politics. In the older, more divided regions of the country, the divide-and-conquer tactics of 1960s politics succeeded in working-class city neighborhoods and older suburbs undergoing social changes. In his book *Middle Class Dreams,* Stan Greenberg writes of the inner suburbs, the land of the second and third quintiles. While central cities have traditionally voted Democratic and white-collar suburbs Republican, many people in the middle groups, who had voted for Kennedy in 1960 and Johnson in 1964, switched to Nixon and the Republicans by 1968. These communities of middle-class whites, raised with the union movement and the New Deal, now had homes and neighborhoods to protect—homes and communities directly in the path of metropolitan decline.

Although this trend continued with the "Reagan revolution" of the 1980s, in 1992, during an economic recession, the middle class supported Bill Clinton and, to some degree, Ross Perot. In Minnesota, the lowest three income quintiles supported Clinton, but in declining numbers as income rose; George Bush's strength lay in the top two quintiles. Perot took 20 percent of the vote of each group. The central cities, inner suburbs, and low-tax capacity suburbs went Democratic in both statewide and legislative elections; the affluent, high-tax capacity suburbs supported Bush and the Republicans. But in 1994, many middle-income voters throughout the country again turned to the Republican Party, not so much because of the inherent force of the Contract with America—which few voters had even heard of—but perhaps because their economic prospects were not improving.

In the end, spatial polarization and income polarization augment each other. As social and economic polarization spreads throughout the Twin Cities, instability is growing. The intensity of debate on schools and crime is a good indicator of the scope and depth of middle-class anxiety. It is the rapid increase of poor children in local schools, however, that sounds the first warning of imminent middle-class flight.

In another part of suburbia, in their insulated, exclusive neighborhoods, people in the upper quintiles have watched those in the lower and mid-quintiles fighting among themselves. The more they have fought, the more insulated and affluent the top economic group has become. In some ways, the desperate struggle for exclusivity in the affluent suburbs is part and parcel an effort by the upper class to reduce its responsibilities to society in terms of a progressive tax policy. As the privileged have less and less contact with those less fortunate, their attitudes harden. Their intensely exclusive zoning practices may be a last-ditch effort to act through municipal government before opting for private "gated" communities, as the affluent have already done in many older, more polarized regions of the United States—and in the third world.

In light of this polarization of residential areas, the challenges of regionalism are substantial:

- To unite the central cities with the middle- and lower middle-class voters in the declining and low-property tax value suburbs;
- To show them that tax-base sharing lowers their taxes and improves local services, particularly schools; and
- To convince them that fair housing will limit their commitment to poor citizens to manageable regional standards and thereby stabilize residential change in their communities.

For middle-class inner suburban neighborhoods—which have their fair share of the region's poor residents already—regionalism promises to limit their commitment to affordable housing and end overwhelming waves of poor people arriving from the city. Once inner-suburban legislators understand this message, they can become powerfully supportive. For years, however, they have campaigned against the city in elections. At the outset, these inner suburbs are not disposed to believe that an alliance with their previous enemy is either wise or politically expedient.

Coalition Building in the Twin Cities

In the Twin Cities, the coalition built to pass recent fair housing and tax-base sharing bills included suburban leaders, church groups, environmental advocates, 'good government' groups, and concerned citizens. Though each group traditionally had different agendas, the issue of fiscal equity brought them together. Some of the older suburbs supported this legislation because they were overburdened with affordable housing and believed their decline would be more precipitous unless the newer suburbs stepped up to the plate. The churches supported it because of the moral dimension: many higher-income communities—particularly job rich communities—have restrictive zoning laws that keep large classes of people from social and economic opportunity. Environmental advocates supported the legislation because affordable housing gets people closer to jobs and requires less commuting. 'Good government' groups backed the measure for all these reasons, but with less passion than those with a more direct stake in the process.

As the debate continued over three legislative sessions, which heightened public awareness on these issues, a particularly restrictive Twin Cities suburb, Maple Grove, went through convulsions over the siting of an affordable housing project. The scenes on the evening news, much like the early civil rights movement, galvanized the public and local officials in support of a plan to equitably distribute tax burdens and benefits throughout the region. Finally, after the governor vetoed two bills, came the Livable Communities Act of 1995.

The Fair Tax Base Act was designed to redistribute taxes collected from high valued homes in the region. The bill would benefit 83 percent of the area's population. These communities, particularly the property-poor northern suburbs, unified with the central cities to support this measure, and along the way religious and 'good government' groups joined in. The issue was intensely controversial, as the high-property wealth suburbs—about one fourth of the region—strongly opposed the bill. However, self-interest and strong public policy carried the day, and the legislature approved the bill after a lengthy debate. Although it was vetoed in 1995, it signaled the growing strength of the coalition and led to a significantly more equitable school funding formula, and the Minneapolis and Saint Paul school districts are now spending significantly more per student than the suburban averages.

Such issues are difficult and controversial but of mutual concern to inner-cities and suburbs. And efforts to find solutions that will unite communities within the Twin Cities region hold lessons for other regions facing similar circumstances.

Lessons in Coalition Building

Understand the Region's Demographics and Make Maps

Develop the most accurate and comprehensive picture of the region possible. Look for the declining older, low tax-base developing, and favored-quarter suburbs. Understand the local fiscal equity issue and the local barriers to affordable housing. Measure road spending and land use. Finance and conduct regional studies, and seek other regions' studies. Bring in the best scholars from area universities.

Use color maps to show trends. Politicians, newspaper reporters, citizens groups, and other potential allies will not necessarily read reports or speeches, but they will look at color maps, over and over again.

Reach Out and Organize on a Personal Level

Political reform is about ideas, but individuals who organize others bring it about. Political persuasion is about selling an idea to another person or group that has power. Once regional trends are satisfactorily described, some individual or group of people has to reach out, person to person, to make contact with the individuals and groups affected by these trends. Do not announce problems and disparities until after meeting with the groups who will be affected by your work.

Invite broad input from these individuals. Then lay out broad themes and the areas where regional progress is necessary—namely, affordable housing, tax-base sharing, and land-use planning. Talk about the experience of other states. Engage all affected constituencies in crafting legislation. This gives them all ownership and allows for adjustment to the peculiarities of the local terrain they know best—economic, physical, cultural, and political.

Build a Broad, Inclusive Coalition

The coalition should stress two themes: It is in the long-term interest of the entire region to solve the problems of polarization, and it is in the immediate short-term interest of the vast majority of the region. The first argument is important for the long haul; the second gets the ball rolling.

A regional agenda, at the beginning, finds few elected altruistic supporters. The early political support for regional reform in the Twin Cities came entirely from legislators who believed their districts would benefit immediately or soon from part or all of our policy package.

"It's the Older Suburbs, Stupid"

Regional reformers should tape this message to their mirrors: The inner and low-tax-base suburbs are the pivot point in American politics and are the reformers' key political allies. They were instrumental in electing Presidents Nixon, Carter, Reagan, and Clinton and an endless procession of officials in state office. The support of these suburbs alters the political dynamics. When regionalism becomes a suburban issue, it becomes possible. As long as regionalism is portrayed as a conflict between city and suburbs, the debate is over before it starts.

Do not accept early rejection by working-class, inner, older suburbs. These communities have been polarized for over a generation. Residential turnover and the growing impoverishment of their communities, the downturn in the U.S. economy for low-skilled workers, and relentless class- and raced-based political appeals have made many residents callous. Underneath they will soon realize that they need regionalism to have healthy, stable communities. They will come around as they come to see that a better future is possible, their alternatives are limited, cooperation will produce measurable benefits, and they have long-term, trustworthy friends in those who promote regionalism.

Reach into the Central Cities to Make Sure the Message Is Understood

Central cities have a volatile political landscape. Without person-to-person contact in the inner city, the message will be misunderstood. Regionalism, if misperceived, threatens the power base of officials elected by poor, segregated constituencies. In this light, as in the older suburbs, the patterns of regional polarization must be reemphasized and the hopelessness of the present course revealed. Metropolitan reforms must not be presented as alternatives to existing programs competing for resources and power. Instead, they need to be seen as complements that would gradually reduce overwhelming central-city problems to manageable size and provide resources for community redevelopment through metropolitan equity. Fair housing is not an attempt to force poor minority communities to disperse but to allow individuals to choose—whether to remain or seek opportunity, wherever it may be.

Seek the Religious Community

Politicians and arguments appealing to people's self-interest can move the agenda forward in the city and older suburbs, but they will not build a base of understanding of affluent communities, whose determined opposition will slow progress. Churches and other houses of worship and religious organizations can bring a powerful new dimension to the debate—the moral dimension. How moral is it, they will ask, to divide a region into two communities, one prospering and enjoying all the benefits of metropolitan citizenship while the other bears most of its burdens? How moral is it to strand the region's poor people on a melting ice cube of resources at the region's core or to destroy forests and farmland while older cities decline? Churches will broaden the reach of a regional movement. They can provide a legitimacy for its message in distrustful blue-collar suburbs, and understanding and a sense of responsibility and fair play in more affluent ones. Without the churches, the Twin Cities housing bill would not have been signed.

Seek the Philanthropic Community, Established Reform Groups, and Business Leaders

Every day philanthropic organizations face the consequences of regional polarization, and their mission statements are often in line with regional reform. They can be important sources of financing for research and nonprofit activities in support of regional solutions. The League of Women Voters can be helpful, as can the National Civic League and established reform groups. These groups can confer establishment respectability to the regional cause. Many of these groups, by themselves, have been working on regional reform for a generation. Seek their counsel as well as their support. Business leaders, particularly in the central business district and the older suburbs, can also be helpful and influential.

Include Distinct but Compatible Issues and Organizations

In addition to the churches, communities of color have a deep stake in this agenda, as do land use groups and a broad variety of environmental organizations that can reach into affluent suburbia. Women's and senior citizens' organizations, for example, want a variety of housing types in all communities for single mothers and retired people who cannot remain in their homes. These groups also want better transit. Regionalism is a multifaceted gemstone. In the power of its comprehensive solutions, it can show a bright face to many different constituencies to build broad support.

With the Coalition, Seek Media Attention

Using factual information, suburban officials, churches, philanthropists, reform groups, and business leaders, seek out editorial boards, which by necessity must have a broad, far-reaching

vision for the region. Reporters who have covered the same political stories over and over will be interested in something new and potentially controversial. They will like the maps, and straightforward news releases without too much theoretical discussion will get the message across.

Prepare for Controversy

Over the years professional regionalists have explained away Minnesota's and Oregon's success with reforms as being the result of people having reached some happy consensus. This is not true. Each reform was a tough battle, and each group of leaders had to build coalitions to weather intense opposition and controversy. This is how any important reform in politics comes about—from labor reform, to civil rights, to the women's movement. Reform never happens effortlessly or overnight. It entails building coalitions, creating power, and engaging in strenuous political struggle.

The agenda sketched here to deal with growing regional instability and disparities will evolve in the negotiation, reformulation, and synthesis that make up the political process. Essential to this discussion is the realization that our metropolitan areas are suffering from a set of problems too massive for an individual city to confront alone—the same problems that have caused the decline and death of some of our largest urban centers. Unless we concentrate on finding new solutions, we can expect no better outcome in the future.

Critical Thinking

1. How does New Regionalism differ from the Old Regionalism that dominated metropolitan reform in the 1960s and 1970s?

2. What is a metropolitan region's "favored quarter" communities?

3. What types of communities in a metropolitan area might find it in their interest to join together in building a coalition to fight for policies that better address their needs?

MYRON ORFIELD is an adjunct professor of law at the University of Minnesota and Minnesota state representative, 612-296-9281. This article has been adapted from *Metropolitics: A Regional Agenda for Community and Stability,* The Brookings Institution/Lincoln Institute for Land Policy 1997.

Principles of New Urbanism

The principles of New Urbanism can be applied increasingly to projects at the full range of scales from a single building to an entire community.

1. Walkability

- Most things within a 10-minute walk of home and work.
- Pedestrian friendly street design (buildings close to street; porches, windows & doors; tree-lined streets; on street parking; hidden parking lots; garages in rear lane; narrow, slow speed streets).
- Pedestrian streets free of cars in special cases.

2. Connectivity

- Interconnected street grid network disperses traffic & eases walking.
- A hierarchy of narrow streets, boulevards, and alleys.
- High quality pedestrian network and public realm makes walking pleasurable.

3. Mixed-Use & Diversity

- A mix of shops, offices, apartments, and homes on site. Mixed-use within neighborhoods, within blocks, and within buildings.
- Diversity of people—of ages, income levels, cultures, and races.

4. Mixed Housing

A range of types, sizes and prices in closer proximity.

5. Quality Architecture & Urban Design

Emphasis on beauty, aesthetics, human comfort, and creating a sense of place; Special placement of civic uses and sites within community. Human scale architecture & beautiful surroundings nourish the human spirit.

6. Traditional Neighborhood Structure

- Discernable center and edge.
- Public space at center.
- Importance of quality public realm; public open space designed as civic art.

- Contains a range of uses and densities within 10-minute walk.
- Transect planning: Highest densities at town center; progressively less dense towards the edge. The transect is an analytical system that conceptualizes mutually reinforcing elements, creating a series of specific natural habitats and/or urban lifestyle settings. The Transect integrates environmental methodology for habitat assessment with zoning methodology for community design. The professional boundary between the natural and man-made disappears, enabling environmentalists to assess the design of the human habitat and the urbanists to support the viability of nature. This urban-to-rural transect hierarchy has appropriate building and street types for each area along the continuum.

7. Increased Density

- More buildings, residences, shops, and services closer together for ease of walking, to enable a more efficient use of services and resources, and to create a more convenient, enjoyable place to live.
- New Urbanism design principles are applied at the full range of densities from small towns, to large cities.

8. Smart Transportation

- A network of high-quality trains connecting cities, towns, and neighborhoods together.
- Pedestrian-friendly design that encourages a greater use of bicycles, rollerblades, scooters, and walking as daily transportation.

9. Sustainability

- Minimal environmental impact of development and its operations.
- Eco-friendly technologies, respect for ecology and value of natural systems.
- Energy efficiency.
- Less use of finite fuels.
- More local production.
- More walking, less driving.

10. Quality of Life

Taken together these add up to a high quality of life well worth living, and create places that enrich, uplift, and inspire the human spirit.

Benefits of New Urbanism
1. Benefits to Residents

Higher quality of life; Better places to live, work, & play; Higher, more stable property values; Less traffic congestion & less driving; Healthier lifestyle with more walking, and less stress; Close proximity to main street retail & services; Close proximity to bike trails, parks, and nature; Pedestrian friendly communities offer more opportunities to get to know others in the neighborhood and town, resulting in meaningful relationships with more people, and a friendlier town; More freedom and independence to children, elderly, and the poor in being able to get to jobs, recreation, and services without the need for a car or someone to drive them; Great savings to residents and school boards in reduced busing costs from children being able to walk or bicycle to neighborhood schools; More diversity and smaller, unique shops and services with local owners who are involved in community; Big savings by driving less, and owning fewer cars; Less ugly, congested sprawl to deal with daily; Better sense of place and community identity with more unique architecture; More open space to enjoy that will remain open space; More efficient use of tax money with less spent on spread out utilities and roads.

2. Benefits to Businesses

Increased sales due to more foot traffic & people spending less on cars and gas; More profits due to spending less on advertising and large signs; Better lifestyle by living above shop in live-work units—saves the stressful & costly commute; Economies of scale in marketing due to close proximity and cooperation with other local businesses; Smaller spaces promote small local business incubation; Lower rents due to smaller spaces & smaller parking lots; Healthier lifestyle due to more walking and being near healthier restaurants; More community involvement from being part of community and knowing residents.

3. Benefits to Developers

More income potential from higher density mixed-use projects due to more leasable square footage, more sales per square foot, and higher property values and selling prices; Faster approvals in communities that have adopted smart growth principles resulting in cost/time savings; Cost savings in parking facilities in mixed-use properties due to sharing of spaces throughout the day and night, resulting in less duplication in providing parking; Less need for parking facilities due to mix of residences and commercial uses within walking distance of each other; Less impact on roads/traffic, which can result in lower impact fees; Lower cost of utilities due to compact nature of New Urbanist design; Greater acceptance by the public and less resistance from NIMBYS; Faster sell out due to greater acceptance by consumers from a wider product range resulting in wider market share.

4. Benefits to Municipalities

Stable, appreciating tax base; Less spent per capita on infrastructure and utilities than typical suburban development due to compact, high-density nature of projects; Increased tax base due to more buildings packed into a tighter area; Less traffic congestion due to walkability of design; Less crime and less spent on policing due to the presence of more people day and night; Less resistance from community; Better overall community image and sense of place; Less incentive to sprawl when urban core area is desirable; Easy to install transit where it's not, and improve it where it is; Greater civic involvement of population leads to better governance.

Ways to Implement New Urbanism

The most effective way to implement New Urbanism is to plan for it, and write it into zoning and development codes. This directs all future development into this form.

New Urbanism Is Best Planned at All Levels of Development

- The single building.
- Groups of buildings.
- The urban block.
- The neighborhood.
- Networks of neighborhoods.
- Towns.
- Cities.
- Regions.

Increasingly, regional planning techniques are being used to control and shape growth into compact, high-density, mixed-use neighborhoods, villages, towns, and cities. Planning new train systems (instead of more roads) delivers the best results when designed in harmony with regional land planning—known as Transit Oriented Development (TOD). At the same time, the revitalization of urban areas directs and encourages infill development back into city centers.

Planning for compact growth, rather than letting it sprawl out, has the potential to greatly increase the quality of the environment. It also prevents congestion problems and the environmental degradation normally associated with growth.

Obstacles to Overcome

The most important obstacle to overcome is the restrictive and incorrect zoning codes currently in force in most municipalities. Current codes do not allow New Urbanism to be built, but do allow sprawl. Adopting a TND ordinance and/or a system of 'smart codes' allows New Urbanism to be built easily without having to rewrite existing codes.

An equally important obstacle is the continuous road building and expansion taking place in every community across America. This encourages more driving and more sprawl which has a domino effect increasing traffic congestion across the region. Halting road projects and building new train systems helps reverse this problematic trend. Read more.

"Only when humans are again permitted to build authentic urbanism—those cities, towns, and villages that nurture us by their comforts and delights—will we cease the despoiling of Nature by escaping to sprawl"—Andres Duany.

Critical Thinking

1. How does New Urbanism seek to build better suburban communities?

2. List what you think are the four most important guiding principles of New Urbanism.

From NewUrbanism.org, 2008. Copyright © 2008 by New Urbanism. Reprinted by permission. www.newurbanism.org.

The New Urbanism:
A Limited Revolution

MYRON A. LEVINE

The New Urbanism "is arguably the most influential movement in city design in the last half-century."[1] New Urbanist developers and planners have reacted against the environmental degradation and the perceived lost sense of communal life in suburbia. The New Urbanism seeks to build better suburbs—sustainable communities that offer alternatives to reliance on the automobile. The New Urbanism embraces the more efficient use of land, reducing the vast acreage that is lost to wide roadways, access ramps and a sea of parking lots that surround suburban shopping malls and office galleries. Just as significantly, New Urbanist design seeks to re-inject a sense of community into suburbia reestablishing the small-town connections among citizens that, as critics charge, have been lost to privatization of lives in backyards and big houses separated by side yards and driveways.

The New Urbanism promises a better alternative to the traditional suburb. But just how realistic and viable is this new and better vision of suburbia? Before this question can be answered, we must first review the core principles and promises of the New Urbanist movement.

The Guiding Principles of the New Urbanism[2]

In its attempt to offer an alternative to both the sprawl and anomie of suburbia, the New Urbanism emphasizes such principles as compact development, walkable communities, identifiable town centers, and the integration of suburban communities in regional mass-transit systems. New Urbanists seek to get Americans out of their cars and back on the streets and in touch with their neighbors. Conventional suburbs, designed for the convenience of the automobile, place virtually insurmountable barriers in the way of walking. Homes are located far from commercial destinations. High schools and office centers are situated on virtual islands surrounded by acres of parking that are not easily traversable on foot. Multi-lane highways and access ramps are nearly impossible for pedestrians to cross; they pose virtual moats that separate one office building and retail development from another. The workers in a suburban

office tower simply cannot walk to a café or convenience store; they have no alternative but to get into their cars and drive across one parking lot into another. The highway- and parking-dominated landscape of suburbia further lacks visual attractions and walkable destinations; it is "an incredibly boring place to walk."[3]

New Urbanist design encourages people to return to the streets. Homes can be built close to sidewalks and located within a five-minute walk to schools, convenience stores, and other key facilities that serve as neighborhood focal points. Town homes and apartments are included in suburban developments, as their existence helps to provide the population densities needed to support walkable neighborhood facilities and town centers. With more people walking and with more homes being built with front porches (town homes can even share porches) located close to the street, residents are encouraged to interact and learn and care about their neighbors.

Front porches also help to restore the "eyes" that watch over streets, making streets safe and free of crime. In commercial areas, "live-works," where owners reside above their stores, help to restore 24-hour-a-day surveillance and a sense of life necessary for the vitality of shopping areas. Just as walkability can be promoted (and the sense of suburban isolation reduced) by having homes located close to one another with parking moved to the rear, stores are similarly located, one abutting another in order to promote walking.

Narrow and tree-lined streets, lower speed limits, and the preservation of on-street parallel parking to protect pedestrians in shopping districts from the flow of automobile traffic and various other traffic calming measures, all serve to make communities more walkable. A conventional street grid, as opposed to dead-end suburban *cul-de-sacs,* further allows residents to choose from a variety of paths, adding to the interest of walking from one destination to another. Walkways and bike paths provide pleasant alternatives to the automobile.

The New Urbanism also emphasizes the construction of attractive, old-style town centers with cafés and interesting shops that serve to promote a leisurely, community lifestyle. Where central facilities require automobile access, parking is pushed to rear garages so that pedestrian-friendly shopping and an environment conducive to civic activity can be maintained in the town center.

New Urbanists emphasize diversity as an alternative to the insularity of life in more conventional (especially exclusive) suburbs, where homogeneity is rigidly enforced through zoning. At its visionary best, the New Urbanism seeks to blend well-designed and visually-attractive apartments into communities with single-family homes. New Urbanists even accept subsidized housing, again stressing the "blending in" concept so that the subsidized units are made part of the community as their appearance is not easily distinguishable from market-rate apartments. These New Urbanist principles have also been applied to the creation of better public housing environments in Chicago, Atlanta, Baltimore, Pittsburg, Charlotte, and other cities across the nation.[4]

New Urbanist communities are not meant to be isolated developments. Rather the New Urbanism seeks an environmentally sustainable vision of communities embedded in a larger metropolis As a result, New Urbanists propose greater residential densities around a rail station, with the goal of establishing a transit-oriented village that provides shopping and other conveniences as well as a mass-transit connection to work.[5] In Portland, Oregon, transit stations have served as the nodes for new development and pedestrian-friendly activity. The sustainability of New Urbanist communities enmeshed in their larger surroundings depends, to a great extent, on the existence of a well-funded and functioning regional mass transit system.

Preliminary evidence from Orenco Station, an affluent New Urban subdivision in Portland, shows that residents exhibit a higher sense of community or "within-neighborhood cohesion" than do the residents of more typical Portland communities. Orenco Station citizens, however, do not exhibit any great sense of responsibility to citizens who live outside, beyond the borders of the local community.[6] The question remains as to what extent New Urbanist design can truly increase a community's stock of social capital.

Limitations and Criticisms of the New Urbanism

Does the New Urbanism provide a viable alternative to conventional suburban development? Can the New Urbanism, as celebrated as it is, reshape suburbia?

One obvious limitation is that the New Urbanism cannot greatly alter patterns of land use that have taken root over time. New Urbanist developers and planners have been most successful where they have had the freedom to design new housing developments according to their community-oriented principles; but, overall, they have not been able to greatly reduce automobile commutes, as residents choose to travel to jobs, shopping centers, and strip malls located outside the borders of the ideal New Urban community.

The New Urbanism creates highly desirable communities for those who choose, and those with the buying power, to live in them. But the New Urbanism lacks the ability to change the suburban preference of the vast majority of Americans. Homeowners in conventional suburbs express a great deal of satisfaction with their lives. As a result, the vast majority of Americans can be expected to continue to use their buying power to purchase big homes with spacious backyards and a sense a privacy; they are satisfied with the escape and exclusiveness that affluence and the automobile have placed within their grasps.

Not only does the New Urbanism lack the power to reverse the suburban housing choices that most Americans have made, but also this architectural and design movement does little to alter the provision of road-building subsidies and homeowner tax breaks that continue to promote sprawl development. As a result, New Urban developments often fail to attract the population densities necessary to support neighborhood facilities and thriving town centers.

Compared to most New Urban developments, Celebration, Florida, is noteworthy for its attractive town center with a town hall, bank, post office, upscale grocery store, theater, trendy cafés, and a lakeshore path; yet, the residents of Celebration routinely drive to supermarkets, shopping malls, power stores, and restaurants in the suburban shopping strips beyond its borders. Celebration, like other New Urban communities, lacks the population density to support major stores of its own. For a long while, Celebration was able to maintain its town center only as a result of the subsidized store leases offered by the Disney Corporation.[7]

In Kentlands, Maryland (located within Gaithersburg, a suburb of Washington, D.C.), there was no deep-pockets Disney Corporation to subsidize store leases. In Kentlands and similar communities, developers had to respond to market forces, compromising New Urbanist ideals where the market required. Indeed, Kentlands Square is like any other strip mall, only a bit more aesthetically pleasing. The stores facing the parking area have proved economically viable; but vacancies quickly appeared in areas of the center that were not visible to, or easily accessible from, the parking lot.[8]

Constrained by market forces and reliant on private developers, the New Urbanism has not produced communities with great social balance. Seaside, Florida, in the state's panhandle, is a New Urban community much celebrated for its small-town appearance—white picket fences, front porches, gabled roofs, narrow streets, walkways to the beach, homes of architectural distinction, public spaces, and striking beach pavilions. The setting for Jim Carrey's film, *The Truman Show,* Seaside is pleasant and attractive. But Seaside fails to represent an authentic revival of small-town life. Seaside is little more than a fashionable beachfront community, with housing that sells at high prices attesting to the community's aesthetically-pleasing qualities. Seaside's homes mainly cater to short-term vacationers, not permanent town residents.

The decline in federal subsidies for the new construction of subsidized housing has seriously impaired the ability of New Urbanist developers to achieve their ideal vision of social balance. In the absence of government subsidies to build extensive affordable housing, New Urbanist developers have found that their efforts to design ideal communities are still highly constrained by a market in which many homebuyers value exclusivity and distance from lower classes. Even where New Urban communities have offered affordable housing, the lower-income units tend to be relatively few and are usually separated from the more high-status and attractive residential developments. As a result of these constraints, New Urbanists "are producing only slightly less exclusive suburbs than the ones they dislike."[9]

Celebration, Florida, developed by the Disney Corporation, is not strictly a New Urban community yet is noteworthy for a number of its New Urban design features. As already noted, the development, just south of Disney World, contains an attractive, upscale town center with cafés, a theater, and a community store, but no full-scale supermarket. The development also contains different neighborhoods with different housing styles. Yet, Celebration has only the most limited class diversity. Disney did not support the construction of affordable housing within the community; instead, the developer chose to meet its obligations under state law by contributing to a fund to assist people with rents and housing down payments outside of Celebration's borders. Celebration's housing is priced beyond the reach of the area's Hispanic service workers: "It's true that Celebration does have some mix of housing, but it's a mixing of the upper class."[10] Despite its aesthetically pleasing appearance, in important ways, Celebration is not all that different from other exclusive suburbs.

"You Say You Want a Revolution, Well, You Know, We All Want to Change the World."

—The Beatles

Regardless of the shortcomings and incompleteness of the New Urbanism, the residents of New Urban communities often express great satisfaction with their lives—with biking and hiking trails, with the sense of freedom that comes with the ability of children to walk safely to schools and recreation, and with the sense of community that they report they have found. Homeowners in Celebration, for instance, report that they value community and neighborliness: "You *can* be isolated in Celebration, but unlike in traditional suburbs, you have to work at it."[11]

Overall, the New Urbanism offers a relative few citizens, who desire it, a more aesthetically-pleasing alternative to the conventional suburb. The movement, however, falls short of achieving its goal of offering residents a revival of small-town community life with a respect for true social diversity. The goal of having a community in which residents "live, work, shop, and play in close proximity" is "more theory than reality," especially as New Urbanists have been unable to build at high densities and have failed to counter Americans' automobile-oriented lifestyles.[12] The New Urban communities that have been built fall far short of the ideal vision of compact, socially-balanced, mixed-use, transit-oriented communities. Instead, New Urbanists have succeeded in building only "a slightly reconfigured suburb," an "automobile-oriented subdivision dressed up to look like a small pre-car-centered town."[13]

The practitioners of the New Urbanism have created a number of highly desirable communities. Residents often express great satisfaction with life there. Still, the movement, despite the overstated claims of its enthusiasts, promises no great reshaping of suburbia. While the New Urbanism does offer a more sustainable alternative to the conventional suburb, it is a choice that the great majority of Americans will resist. Rather than revolutionize suburbia, the New Urbanism poses only the smallest of counterweights to continued sprawl.

Notes

1. Alex Marshall, *How Cities Work: Suburbs, Sprawl, and the Roads Not Taken* (Austin, TX; University of Texas Press, 2000), p. xix.

2. For a good review of the guiding principles of The New Urbanism, see Andres Duany, Elizabeth Plater-Zyberk, and Jeff Speck, *Suburban Nation: The Rise of Sprawl and the Decline of the American Dream* (New York: North Point Press, 2000); Peter Katz, *The New Urbanism: Toward an Architecture of Community* (New York: McGraw-Hill, 1994); Congress for The New Urbanism, *Charter of The New Urbanism* (New York: McGraw-Hill, 2000); Calthorpe and Fulton, *The Regional City.*

3. Duany et al, *Suburban Nation,* p. 30.

4. Calthorpe and Fulton, *The Regional City,* pp. 253–265; Janet L. Smith, "HOPE VI and The New Urbanism, Eliminating Low-Income Housing to Make Mixed-income Communities," *Planner's Network* 151 (Spring 2002): 22–25; Sabrina Deitrick and Cliff Ellis, "New Urbanism in the Inner City: A Case Study of Pittsburgh," *Journal of the American Planning Association* 70, 4 (Autumn 2004); 426–442.

5. Michael Bernick and Robert Cervero, *Transit Villages in the 21st Century* (New York: McGraw-Hill, 1997); Peter Newman and Jeffrey Kenworthy, *Sustainability and Cities: Overcoming Automobile Dependence* (Washington, DC: Island Press, 1999).

6. Bruce Podobnik, "The New Urbanism and the Generation of Social Capital: Evidence from Orenco Station," *National Civic Review* 91, 3 (Fall 2002): 245–55. F. Kaid Benfield, Jutka Terris and Nancy Vorsanger, *Solving Sprawl: Models of Smart Growth in Communities across America* (Washington, DC: Island Press, 2001) present Orenco Station as a model "smart growth" community. Also see Thomas H. Sander, "Social Capital and The New Urbanism: Leading a Civic Horse to Water?" *National Civic Review* 91, 3 (Fall 2002): 213–34.

7. Marshall, *How Cities Work,* pp. 8–14.

8. Alexander Garvin, *The American City: What Works, What Doesn't,* 2nd ed. (New York: McGraw-Hill, 2002), pp. 415–416.

9. Susan F. Fainstein, "New Directions in Planning Theory," *Urban Affairs Review* 35(4), (March 2000), p. 464.

10. Marshall, p. 27. For a more detailed and nuanced discussion of life in Celebration, see Douglas Frantz and Catherine Collins, *Celebration, U.S.A.: Living in Disney's Brave New Town* (New York: Owl Books/Henry Holt, 2000), pp. 74–77 and 219–225.

11. Frantz and Collins, *Celebration, U.S.A.,* p. 313; also see pp. 255–56.

12. Garvin, *The American City: What Works, What Doesn't,* pp. 336–337.

13. Marshall, *How Cities Work,* pp. xx and 6. Also see Alex Krieger, "Arguing the 'Against' Position: The New Urbanism as a Means of Building and Rebuilding Our Cities," in *The Seaside Debates: A Critique of The New Urbanism,* ed. Todd W. Bressi (Rizzoli, 2002), pp. 51–58. For a defense of The New Urbanism that attempts to rebut many of the critiques, see Cliff Ellis, "The New Urbanism: Critiques and Rebuttals," *Journal of Urban Design* 7, 3 (2002): 261–291. For a most useful overview of The New Urbanism movements, the international reach of The New Urbanism, and the potential and limitations inherent in The New Urbanism, see Jill Grant, *Planning the Good Community: The New Urbanisms in Theory and Practice* (London: Routledge, 2006).

Critical Thinking

1. What are the limitations of the New Urbanism? Despite its admirable ideas, why won't the New Urbanism lead to a revolution that reshapes suburbia?

UNIT 9

Toward Sustainable Cities and Suburbs?

Unit Selections

Learning Outcomes

After reading this unit, you should be able to:

- Define "sustainability" and "sustainable development."

- Explain why patterns of urban and suburban growth in the United States are often viewed as unsustainable.

- Identify the various policy measures that can help reduce highway congestion.

- Describe how a system of congestion pricing, as seen in London and other cities around the world, works and is enforced.

- Assess the various arguments for and against a system of congestion pricing.

- Identify the various steps that the State of California and its communities have taken in an effort to reduce automobile tailpipe emissions and thermal pollution.

Student Website

www.mhhe.com/cls

Internet References

The Brookings Institution: Transportation
www.brookings.edu/topics/transportation.aspx
London First
www.londonfirst.co.uk
Green Cities
http://greencities.com
International Transport Forum
www.internationaltransportforum.org
The Keep NYC Congestion Tax Free
www.keepnycfree.com
London (England) Chamber of Commerce
www.londonchamber.co.uk/lcc_public/home.asp
Our Green Cities, Dr. Kent Portney, Tufts University
http://ourgreencities.com

Planner's Web: Sprawl and Growth
www.plannersweb.com/articles/sprawl-articles.html
Reason Foundation
http://reason.org
Resources for the Future (RFF): Transportation and Urban Land
www.rff.org/Focus_Areas/Pages/Transportation_and_Urban_Land.aspx
Sierra Club: Stopping Sprawl
www.sierraclub.org/sprawl
Smart Growth America
http://smartgrowthamerica.org
Sustainable Cities
http://sustainablecities.net

Are patterns of urban and suburban development ecologically sound? Given the high price of energy, can present-day patterns of urban living be sustained over time?

Hundreds of cities across the United States have already launched important initiatives regarding sustainability; these cities seek to promote development that respects ecological and energy concerns. American cities and states have legislated construction codes to ensure that new homes meet or surpass LEED (Leadership in Energy and Environmental Design) standards. Such ordinances seek to ensure that homes have proper insulation, low-flow toilets, energy-efficient appliances, and landscaping that minimizes runoff and groundwater contamination. Governmental programs also seek to have home builders include solar panels and use recycled wood products and repurposed materials obtained from the local "deconstruction depot," which salvages material from homes that have been torn down. Chicago and Dayton have even installed a "green roof" (a patch of grass or vegetation) atop of city hall, modeling an innovative way by which private builders can minimize a structure's thermal loss and thereby reduce energy consumption.

Sustainability also entails reduced reliance on pollution-spewing automobiles. Freiburg, Germany (Article 39, "New German Community Models Car-Free Living"), has created a pedestrian- and mass-transit-oriented community where automobile ownership and usage is actively discouraged. In Freiburg, parking is quite limited, ride-sharers receive free transit passes, and trails separated from traffic serve to promote bicycling. Car-sharing programs in Freiburg and in cities throughout Europe make automobiles available to persons who value city living and mass transit but who require a car for the occasional weekend or shopping trip. San Francisco and other Bay Area communities have similarly tried to promote car-sharing, setting aside priority and discounted parking places for Zip-Car users.

Anthony Downs (Article 40, "Traffic: Why It's Getting Worse, What Government Can Do") applies the rational-actor logic of an economist to show why cities and states cannot easily reduce urban traffic and clogged freeways. When a government constructs wider roads and undertakes other measures to alleviate congestion, traffic flow improves, but only in the short run. As more and more drivers discover the improved road, the highway once again fills up and traffic jams return. Downs identifies the various steps—including ramp metering, the creation of high-occupancy vehicle (HOV) and high-occupancy toll (HOT) lanes, and the use of computers to speed traffic flows—that government can take to reduce, but not to eliminate, urban traffic woes.

London, Stockholm, and Singapore are among the cities in Europe and Asia that have had implemented a system of congestion pricing, imposing a steep fee on vehicles that enter the business sectors of the city during peak hours. The fee, which is levied primarily in an attempt to discourage traffic at peak hours, can vary with the hour of day and the day of the week. Much like the E-Z Pass system on major U.S. toll roads, drivers

© Sam Diephuis/Getty Images

can even set up accounts where they pay in advance. Cameras and digital technology enable municipal authorities to bill drivers who bring a car into the city. Drivers face steep fines for failing to pay the daily entrance fee.

Many downtown businesses object that the imposition of such a fee will make it difficult for downtown firms to attract customers and even to recruit good workers who travel by car. But the advocates of congestion pricing point out that central London and Stockholm have thrived economically even with the imposition of commuting charges (Article 41, "Is Congestion Pricing Ready for Prime Time?"). Congestion fees also yield revenues that can be used to finance improvements in mass transit. Nonetheless, when Mayor Michael Bloomberg sought to bring the system of congestion pricing to New York City, the state legislature refused to allow it.

California, a state famed for its highways and car-dependent lifestyle, has recently become the nation's leader in introducing measures to reduce automobile emissions and avert climate change (Article 42, "California's Pioneering Transportation Strategy"). State decision makers spurned the high taxes on gasoline, a policy used in Europe to reduce driving and to force consumers to buy fuel-efficient cars. Instead, California has enacted a mix of regulation and incentives intended to spur advances in automobile design (including the production of a zero-emission vehicle [ZEV]). California has also expanded carpool lanes and provided new subsidies for mass transit. Still, the California approach has its limits. It contains no strong measures capable of curbing sprawled development in order to promote more compact and less automobile-intensive patterns of land use.

New German Community Models Car-Free Living

ISABELLE DE POMMEREAU

I t's pickup time at the Vauban kindergarten here at the edge of the Black Forest, but there's not a single minivan waiting for the kids. Instead, a convoy of helmet-donning moms—bicycle trailers in tow—pedal up to the entrance.

Welcome to Germany's best-known environmentally friendly neighborhood and a successful experiment in green urban living. The Vauban development—2,000 new homes on a former military base 10 minutes by bike from the heart of Freiburg—has put into practice many ideas that were once dismissed as eco-fantasy but which are now moving to the center of public policy.

With gas prices well above $6 per gallon across much of the continent, Vauban is striking a chord in Western Europe as communities encourage people to be less car-dependent. Just this week, Paris unveiled a new electric tram in a bid to reduce urban pollution and traffic congestion.

"Vauban is clearly an offer for families with kids to live without cars," says Jan Scheurer, an Australian researcher who has studied the Vauban model extensively. "It was meant to counter urban sprawl—an offer for families not to move out to the suburbs and give them the same, if better quality of life. And it is very successful."

There are numerous incentives for Vauban's 4,700 residents to live car-free: Carpoolers get free yearly tramway passes, while parking spots—available only in a garage at the neighborhood's edge—go for € 17,500 (US $23,000). Forty percent of residents have bought spaces, many just for the benefit of their visiting guests.

As a result, the car-ownership rate in Vauban is only 150 per 1,000 inhabitants, compared with 430 per 1,000 inhabitants in Freiburg proper.

In contrast, the US average is 640 household vehicles per 1,000 residents. But some cities—such as Davis, Calif., where 17 percent of residents commute by bike—have pioneered a car-free lifestyle that is similar to Vauban's model.

Vauban, which is located in the southwestern part of the country, owes its existence, at least in part, to Freiburg—a university town, like Davis—that has a reputation as Germany's ecological capital.

In the 1970s, the city became the cradle of Germany's powerful antinuclear movement after local activists killed plans for a nuclear power station nearby. The battle brought energy-policy issues closer to the people and increased involvement in local politics. With a quarter of its people voting for the Green Party, Freiburg became a political counterweight in the conservative state of Baden-Württemberg.

At about the same time, Freiburg, a city of 216,000 people, revolutionized travel behavior. It made its medieval center more pedestrian-friendly, laid down a lattice of bike paths, and introduced a flat rate for tramways and buses.

Environmental research also became a backbone of the region's economy, which boasts Germany's largest solar-research center and an international center for renewable energy. Services such as installing solar panels and purifying wastewater account for 3 percent of jobs in the region, according to city figures.

Little wonder then, that when the French Army closed the 94-acre base that Vauban now occupies in 1991, a group of forward-thinking citizens took the initiative to create a new form of city living for young families.

"We knew the city had a duty to make a plan. We wanted to get as involved as possible," says Andreas Delleske, then a physics student who led the grass-roots initiative that codesigned Vauban. "And we were accepted as a partner of the city."

In 1998, Freiburg bought land from the German government and worked with Delleske's group to lay out a master plan for the area, keeping in mind the ecological, social, economic, and cultural goals of reducing energy levels while creating healthier air and a solid infrastructure for young families. Rather than handing the area to a real estate developer, the city let small homeowner cooperatives design and build their homes from scratch.

In retrospect, "It would have been much simpler to give a big developer a piece of land and say, 'Come back five years later with a plan,' " says Roland Veith, the Freiburg city official in charge of Vauban.

But the result is a "master plan of an ecological city . . . unique in its holistic approach," says Peter Heck, a professor of material-flow management at Germany's University of Trier, pointing out that this was a community-wide effort involving engineers, politicians, city planners, and residents—not just an environmental group's pilot program.

Today, rows of individually designed, brightly painted buildings line streets that are designed to be too narrow for cars. There are four kindergartens, a Waldorf school, and plenty of playgrounds—a good thing, because a third of Vauban's residents are under age 18, bucking the trend in a graying country.

As Germany's population ages—and shrinks—experts say Vauban's model will become more important as officials increasingly tailor-make communities in an effort to attract citizens.

"We have fewer young people. What you need now is a good quality of life with good services, a good infrastructure for kids and older people," says Thomas Schleifnecker, a Hannover-based urban planner.

Across Europe, similar projects are popping up. Copenhagen, for instance, maintains a fleet of bikes for public use that is financed through advertising on bicycle frames.

But what makes Vauban unique, say experts, is that "it's as much a grass-roots initiative as it is pursued by the city council," says Mr. Scheurer. "It brings together the community, the government, and the private sector at every stage of the game."

As more cities follow Vauban's example, some see its approach taking off. "Before you had pilot projects. Now it's like a movement," says Mr. Heck. "The idea of saving energy for our landscape is getting into the basic planning procedure of German cities."

Critical Thinking

1. What policies in Germany seek to limit reliance on the automobile?
2. How does Vauban, Germany, promote car-free living?

From *The Christian Science Monitor,* December 20, 2006. Copyright © 2006 by Isabelle de Pommereau. Reprinted by permission of the author.

Traffic: Why It's Getting Worse, What Government Can Do

ANTHONY DOWNS

Rising traffic congestion is an inescapable condition in large and growing metropolitan areas across the world, from Los Angeles to Tokyo, from Cairo to São Paolo. Peak-hour traffic congestion is an inherent result of the way modern societies operate. It stems from the widespread desires of people to pursue certain goals that inevitably overload existing roads and transit systems every day. But everyone hates traffic congestion, and it keeps getting worse, in spite of attempted remedies.

Commuters are often frustrated by policymakers' inability to do anything about the problem, which poses a significant public policy challenge. Although governments may never be able to eliminate road congestion, there are several ways cities and states can move to curb it.

The Real Problem

Traffic congestion is not primarily a problem, but rather the solution to our basic mobility problem, which is that too many people want to move at the same times each day. Why? Because efficient operation of both the economy and school systems requires that people work, go to school, and even run errands during about the same hours so they can interact with each other. That basic requirement cannot be altered without crippling our economy and society. The same problem exists in every major metropolitan area in the world.

In the United States, the vast majority of people seeking to move during rush hours use private automotive vehicles, for two reasons. One is that most Americans reside in low-density areas that public transit cannot efficiently serve. The second is that privately owned vehicles are more comfortable, faster, more private, more convenient in trip timing, and more flexible for doing multiple tasks on one trip than almost any form of public transit. As household incomes rise around the world, more and more people shift from slower, less expensive modes of movement to privately owned cars and trucks.

With 87.9 percent of America's daily commuters using private vehicles, and millions wanting to move at the same times of day, America's basic problem is that its road system does not have the capacity to handle peak-hour loads without forcing many people to wait in line for that limited road space. Waiting in line is the definition of congestion, and the same condition is found in all growing major metropolitan regions. In fact, traffic congestion is worse in most other countries because American roads are so much better.

Coping with the Mobility Problem

There are four ways any region can try to cope with the mobility challenge. But three of them are politically impractical or physically and financially impossible in the United States.

There are many good reasons to expand the nation's public transit systems to aid mobility, but doing so will not notably reduce either existing or future peak-hour traffic congestion.

Charging peak-hour tolls. Governments can charge people money to enter all the lanes on major commuting roads during peak hours. If tolls were set high enough and collected electronically with "smart cards," the number of vehicles on each major road during peak hours could be reduced enough so that vehicles could move at high speeds. That would allow more people to travel per lane per hour than under current, heavily congested conditions.

Transportation economists have long been proponents of this tactic, but most Americans reject this solution politically for two reasons. Tolls would favor wealthier or subsidized drivers and harm poor ones, so most Americans would resent them, partly because they believe they would be at a disadvantage.

The second drawback is that people think these tolls would be just another tax, forcing them to pay for something they have already paid for through gasoline taxes. For both these reasons, few politicians in our democracy—and so far, anywhere else in the world—advocate this tactic. Limited road-pricing schemes that have been adopted in Singapore, Norway, and London only affect congestion in crowded downtowns, which is not the kind of congestion on major arteries that most Americans experience.

Greatly expanding road capacity. The second approach would be to build enough road capacity to handle all drivers who want to travel in peak hours at the same time without delays. But this "cure" is totally impractical and prohibitively expensive. Governments would have to widen all major commuting roads by demolishing millions of buildings, cutting down trees, and turning most of every metropolitan region into a giant concrete slab. Those roads would then be grossly underutilized during non-peak hours. There are many occasions when adding more road capacity is a good idea, but no large region can afford to build enough to completely eliminate peak-hour congestion.

Greatly expanding public transit capacity. The third approach would be to expand public transit capacity enough to shift so many people from cars to transit that there would be no more excess demand for roads during peak hours. But in the United States in 2000, only 4.7 percent of all commuters traveled by public transit. (Outside of New York City, only 3.5 percent use transit and 89.3 percent use private vehicles.) A major reason is that most transit commuting is concentrated in a few large, densely settled regions with extensive fixed-rail transit systems. The nine U.S. metropolitan areas with the most daily transit commuters, when taken together, account for 61 percent of all U.S. transit commuting, though they contain only 17 percent of the total population. Within those regions, transit commuters are 17 percent of all commuters, but elsewhere, transit carries only 2.4 percent of all commuters, and less than one percent in many low-density regions.

Even if America's existing transit capacity were tripled and fully utilized, morning peak-hour transit travel would rise to 11.0 percent of all morning trips. But that would reduce all morning private vehicle trips by only 8.0 percent—certainly progress, but hardly enough to end congestion—and tripling public transit capacity would be extremely costly. There are many good reasons to expand the nation's public transit systems to aid mobility, but doing so will not notably reduce either existing or future peak-hour traffic congestion.

Living with congestion. This is the sole viable option. The only feasible way to accommodate excess demand for roads during peak periods is to have people wait in line. That means traffic congestion, which is an absolutely essential mechanism for American regions—and most other metropolitan regions throughout the world—to cope with excess demands for road space during peak hours each day.

Although congestion can seem intolerable, the alternatives would be even worse. Peak-hour congestion is the balancing mechanism that makes it possible for Americans to pursue other goals they value, including working or sending their children to school at the same time as their peers, living in low-density settlements, and having a wide choice of places to live and work.

The Principle of Triple Convergence

The least understood aspect of peak-hour traffic congestion is the principle of triple convergence, which I discussed in the original version of *Stuck in Traffic* (Brookings/Lincoln Institute of Land Policy, 1992). This phenomenon occurs because traffic flows in any region's overall transportation networks form almost automatically self-adjusting relationships among different routes, times, and modes. For example, a major commuting expressway might be so heavily congested each morning that traffic crawls for at least thirty minutes. If that expressway's capacity were doubled overnight, the next day's traffic would flow rapidly because the same number of drivers would have twice as much road space. But soon word would spread that this particular highway was no longer congested. Drivers who had once used that road before and after the peak hour to avoid congestion would shift back into the peak period. Other drivers who had been using alternative routes would shift onto this more convenient expressway. Even some commuters who had been using the subway or trains would start driving on this road during peak periods. Within a short time, this triple convergence onto the expanded road during peak hours would make the road as congested as it was before its expansion.

Experience shows that if a road is part of a larger transportation network within a region, peak-hour congestion cannot be eliminated for long on a congested road by expanding that road's capacity.

The triple convergence principle does not mean that expanding a congested road's capacity has no benefits. After expansion, the road can carry more vehicles per hour than before, no matter how congested it is, so more people can travel on it during those more desirable periods. Also, the periods of maximum congestion may be shorter, and congestion on alternative routes may be lower. Those are all benefits, but that road will still experience some period of maximum congestion daily.

> **If a region's population is growing rapidly, as in Southern California or Florida, any expansions of major expressway capacity may soon be swamped by more vehicles generated by the added population.**

Triple Convergence and Other Proposals

Triple convergence affects the practicality of other suggested remedies to traffic congestion. An example is staggered work hours. In theory, if a certain number of workers are able to commute during less crowded parts of the day, that will free up space on formerly congested roads. But once traffic moves faster on those roads during peak hours, that will attract other drivers from other routes, other times, and other modes where conditions have not changed to shift onto the improved roads. Soon the removal of the staggered-working-hour drivers will be fully offset by convergence.

The same thing will happen if more workers become tele-commuters and work at home, or if public transit capacity is expanded on off-road routes that parallel a congested express-way. This is why building light rail systems or even new sub-ways rarely reduces peak-hour traffic congestion. In Portland, where the light rail system doubled in size in the 1990s, and in Dallas, where a new light rail system opened, congestion did not decline for long after these systems were up and running. Only road pricing or higher gasoline taxes are exempt from the principle of triple convergence.

How Population Growth Can Swamp Transportation Capacity

A ground transportation system's equilibria can also be affected by big changes in the region's population or economic activity. If a region's population is growing rapidly, as in Southern California or Florida, any expansions of major expressway capacity may soon be swamped by more vehicles generated by the added population. This result is strengthened because America's vehicle population has been increasing even faster than its human population. From 1980 to 2000, 1.2 more auto-motive vehicles were added to the vehicle population of the United States for every 1.0 person added to the human popula-tion (though this ratio declined to 1 to 1 in the 1990s). The nation's human population is expected to grow by around 60 million by 2020—possibly adding another 60 million vehi-cles to our national stock. That is why prospects for reducing peak-hour traffic congestion in the future are dim indeed.

Shifts in economic activity also affect regional congestion. During the Internet and telecommunications boom of the late 1990s, congestion in the San Francisco Bay Area intensified immensely. After the economic "bubble" burst in 2000, con-gestion fell markedly without any major change in popula-tion. Thus, severe congestion can be a sign of strong regional prosperity, just as reduced congestion can signal an economic downturn.

The most obvious reason traffic congestion has increased everywhere is population growth. In a wealthy nation, more people means more vehicles. But total vehicle mileage traveled has grown much faster than population. From 1980 to 2000, the total population of the United States rose 24 percent, but total vehicle miles traveled grew 80 percent because of more inten-sive use of each vehicle. The number of vehicles per 1,000 per-sons rose 14 percent and the number of miles driven per vehicle rose 24 percent. Even without any population gain in those two decades, miles driven would have risen 47 percent.

One reason people drove their vehicles farther is that a com-bination of declining real gas prices (corrected for inflation) and more miles per gallon caused the real cost of each mile driven to fall 54 percent from 1980 to 2000. That helped raise the frac-tion of U.S. households owning cars from 86 percent in 1983 to 92 percent in 1995.

Furthermore, American road building lagged far behind increases in vehicle travel. Urban lane-miles rose by 37 percent versus an 80 percent increase in miles traveled. As a result, the amount of daily traffic that was congested in the 75 areas ana-lyzed in studies by the Texas Transportation Institute went from 16 percent in 1982 to 34 percent in 2001.

Another factor in road congestion is accidents and incidents, which some experts believe cause half of all traffic congestion. From 1980 to 2000, the absolute number of accidents each year has remained amazingly constant, and the annual number of traffic deaths in the United States fell 18 percent, in spite of the great rise in vehicle miles traveled. So accidents could only have caused more congestion because roads were more crowded, and each accident may now cause longer back-ups than before.

Incidents are non-accident causes of delay, such as stalled cars, road repairs, overturned vehicles, and bad weather. No one knows how many incidents occur, but it is a much greater num-ber than accidents. And the number of incidents probably rises along with total driving. So that could have added to greater congestion, and will in the future.

Severe congestion can be a sign of strong regional prosperity, just as reduced congestion can signal an economic downturn.

Low-Density Settlements

Another crucial factor contributing to traffic congestion is the desire of most Americans to live in low-density settlements. In 1999, the National Association of Homebuilders asked 2,000 randomly-selected households whether they would rather buy a $150,000 townhouse in an urban setting that was close to public transportation, work, and shopping or a larger, detached single-family home in an outlying suburban area, where dis-tances to work, public transportation, and shopping were longer. Eighty-three percent of respondents chose the larger, farther-out suburban home. At the same time, new workplaces have been spreading out in low-density areas in most metropolitan regions.

Past studies, including one published in 1977 by Boris S. Pushkarev and Jeffery M. Zupan, have shown that public transit works best where gross residential densities are above 4,200 persons per square mile; relatively dense housing is clustered close to transit stations or stops; and large numbers of jobs are concentrated in relatively compact business districts.

But in 2000, at least two thirds of all residents of U.S. urban-ized areas lived in settlements with densities of under 4,000 persons per square mile. Those densities are too low for public transit to be effective. Hence their residents are compelled to rely on private vehicles for almost all of their travel, including trips during peak hours.

Recognizing this situation, many opponents of "sprawl" call for strong urban growth boundaries to constrain future growth into more compact, higher-density patterns, including greater reinvestment and increased densities in existing neighborhoods. But most residents of those neighborhoods vehemently oppose raising densities, and most American regions already have densities far too low to support much public transit. So this strategy would not significantly reduce future traffic congestion.

Possible Improvements

While it's practically impossible to eliminate congestion, there are several ways to slow its future rate of increase:

Create High Occupancy Toll (HOT) lanes. Peak-hour road pricing would not be politically feasible if policymakers put tolls on all major commuter lanes, but HOT lanes can increase traveler choices by adding new toll lanes to existing expressways, or converting underused high-occupancy vehicle (HOV) lanes to HOT lanes, and leaving present conventional lanes without tolls. True, HOT lanes do not eliminate congestion. But they allow anyone who needs to move fast on any given day to do so, without forcing all low-income drivers off those same roads during peak periods. In some regions, whole networks of HOT lanes could both add to overall capacity and make high-speed choices always available to thousands of people in a hurry.

Respond more rapidly to traffic-blocking accidents and incidents. Removing accidents and incidents from major roads faster by using roving service vehicles run by government-run Traffic Management Centers equipped with television and electronic surveillance of road conditions is an excellent tactic for reducing congestion delays.

Build more roads in growing areas. Opponents of building more roads claim that we cannot build our way out of congestion because more highway capacity will simply attract more travelers. Due to triple convergence, that criticism is true for established roads that are already overcrowded. But the large projected growth of the U.S. population surely means that we will need a lot more road and lane mileage in peripheral areas.

Install ramp-metering. This means letting vehicles enter expressways only gradually. It has improved freeway speed during peak hours in both Seattle and the Twin Cities, and could be much more widely used.

Use Intelligent Transportation System devices to speed traffic flows. These devices include electronic coordination of signal lights on local streets, large variable signs informing drivers of traffic conditions ahead, one-way street patterns, Global Positioning System equipment in cars and trucks, and radio broadcasts of current road conditions. These technologies exist now and can be effective on local streets and arteries and informative on expressways.

Create more HOV (High Occupancy Vehicle) lanes. HOV lanes have proven successful in many areas such as Houston. More regions could use HOV lanes effectively if there were more lanes built for that purpose, rather than trying to convert existing ones. Merely converting existing lanes would reduce overall road capacity.

Adopt "parking cash-out" programs. Demonstration programs have shown that if firms offer to pay persons now receiving free employee parking a stipend for shifting to carpooling or transit, significant percentages will do so. That could reduce the number of cars on the road. However, this tactic does not prevent the offsetting consequences of triple convergence.

Restrict very low-density peripheral development. Urban growth boundaries that severely constrain all far-out suburban development will not reduce future congestion much, especially in fast-growing regions. And such boundaries may drive up peripheral housing prices. But requiring at least moderate residential densities—say, 3,500 persons per square mile (4.38 units per net acre)—in new growth areas could greatly reduce peripheral driving, compared to permitting very low densities there, which tend to push growth out ever farther. In 2000, thirty-six urbanized areas had fringe area densities of 3,500 or more. Those thirty-six urbanized areas contained 18.2 percent of all persons living in all 476 U.S. urbanized areas.

Transit Oriented Developments (TODs) would permit more residents to commute by walking to transit, thereby decreasing the number of private vehicles on the roads.

Cluster high-density housing around transit stops. Such Transit Oriented Developments (TODs) would permit more residents to commute by walking to transit, thereby decreasing the number of private vehicles on the roads. However, the potential of this tactic is limited. In order to shift a significant percentage of auto commuters to transit, the number of such "transit circles" within each region would have to be very large, the density within each circle would have to be much greater than the average central city density in America's fifty largest urbanized areas, and the percentage of workers living in the TODs who commuted by transit would have to greatly exceed the 10.5 percent average for central cities in 2000. Even so, developing many of these high-density clusters might make public transit service more feasible to many more parts of large regions.

Give regional transportation authorities more power and resources. Congress has created Metropolitan Planning Organizations to coordinate ground transportation planning over all modes in each region. If these were given more technical assistance and power, more rational systems could be created. Without much more regionally focused planning over land uses as well as transportation, few anti-congestion tactics will work effectively.

Raise gasoline taxes. Raising gas taxes would notably slow the rate of increase of all automotive travel, not just peak-hour commuting. But Congress has refused to consider it because it is politically unpopular and fought by industry lobbyists. Despite Americans' vocal complaints about congestion, they do not want to pay much to combat it.

Conclusion

Peak-hour traffic congestion in almost all large and growing metropolitan regions around the world is here to stay. In fact, it is almost certain to get worse during at least the next few decades, mainly because of rising populations and wealth. This will be true no matter what public and private policies are adopted to combat congestion.

But this outcome should not be regarded as a mark of social failure or misguided policies. In fact, traffic congestion often results from economic prosperity and other types of success.

Although traffic congestion is inevitable, there are ways to slow the rate at which it intensifies. Several tactics could do that effectively, especially if used in concert, but nothing can eliminate peak-hour traffic congestion from large metropolitan regions here and around the world. Only serious economic recessions—which are hardly desirable—can even forestall an increase.

For the time being, the only relief for traffic-plagued commuters is a comfortable, air-conditioned vehicle with a well-equipped stereo system, a hands-free telephone, and a daily commute with someone they like.

Congestion has become part of commuters' daily leisure time, and it promises to stay that way.

Critical Thinking

1. Why does the construction or widening of a highway seldom reduce traffic congestion for long? Why does congestion soon reemerge?

2. What is a TOD (transit-oriented development)? Explain how a TOD looks different from conventional suburban developments.

3. What policies or steps can you propose that would help to reduce automobile commuting or otherwise alleviate traffic congestion?

ANTHONY DOWNS is a senior fellow in Economic Studies at The Brookings Institution.

All data in this policy brief concerning population and travel behavior are from the Census Bureau, primarily from the 2000 Census, unless otherwise noted.

Is Congestion Pricing Ready for Prime Time?

A controversial approach comes to the fore.

MICHAEL A. REPLOGLE

For decades now, traffic congestion and transportation-related greenhouse gas pollution have been growing in most cities around the world—seemingly as much out of control as the weather. In the U.S., leaders from across the political spectrum—including the mayor of New York, the Bush administration's transportation secretary, and the top official of King County, Washington—have responded with a controversial solution: congestion pricing.

Their model is London, which in 2004 imposed a central area congestion charge. But there are other examples as well, including Singapore, which introduced a similar $3 congestion charge way back in 1975. Oslo, Bergen, and five other Norwegian cities adopted their own charges between 1986 and 2004, both to manage traffic and to finance transportation projects. Stockholm, Milan, Rome, and other cities have similar initiatives.

Meanwhile, political resistance to higher fuel taxes has led to renewed interest in tolls to finance highways. High-occupancy toll (HOT) lanes took hold in southern California in the 1990s as an alternative to public financing, then spread rapidly to Texas, Minnesota, Utah, Colorado, and Virginia. Germany in 2005 pioneered a nationwide system of emission-based truck tolls on its 7,500-mile autobahn network, collected with the help of global positioning system satellites. The tolls raised over $4.5 billion in 2006, cut greenhouse emissions from trucks by seven percent, and doubled the rate at which old trucks are replaced by newer, cleaner models.

Last year, the Dutch government announced it was phasing out charges for owning motor vehicles in favor of motorist charges based on distance driven, with higher rates for using busy roads during peak hours and for more polluting vehicles. The new, GPS-based road charges will start with trucks in 2011 and gradually extend to passenger vehicles.

Closer to home, the Puget Sound region is completing a federally funded study of a similar GPS-based traffic-management system. Preliminary findings are promising: They show that road-pricing incentives caused a sample of Seattle-area households to voluntarily cut their driving by one fourth. A similar result comes from a federally sponsored test of mileage-based fees in Oregon; it suggests that such a system could be phased in over several years to replace motor fuel taxes.

Habits Are Hard to Change

Tolls are being used to finance a growing share of new road capacity worldwide. Increasingly such tolls are higher at times and locations where demand is greatest—the core idea of congestion pricing. But applying such tolls to existing free roads is a lot tougher, even after half a century of promotion by transportation economists.

Even in the U.K., where London is a model of congestion pricing, there is resistance. Last year, 1.5 million people signed a petition opposing a central government plan for nationwide road pricing. In the U.S., proposals for congestion pricing on existing roads face political hurdles in New York, northern California, Colorado, and elsewhere. Throughout the world, the same concerns surface: Will congestion pricing harm the poor? Will it intrude on personal privacy? Is it double taxation for roads? Where will revenues go?

Research suggests that traffic, sprawl, and pollution tend to increase when tolls are used simply to expand roads. In addition, more jobs are put out of reach of the poor. In contrast, low-income households benefit and traffic and pollution are cut when tolls are used to manage congestion on existing roads.

A synthesis of public attitudes on congestion pricing prepared last year by Joanne Zmud of NuStats, an Austin-based research company, found that, while the public generally supports tolling and pricing, populist politics make it harder to implement—and to evaluate—such programs. Effective public education and leadership are needed to raise public understanding of the complex policy issues associated with congestion pricing.

Acceptance is increasing, however, prompted by the growing awareness of gridlock, local governments' well-publicized fiscal distress, and a broadening knowledge of climate change.

Leadership in London

Congestion pricing in London, as elsewhere, resulted only from decisive political leadership; after years of studies, Ken Livingstone made congestion pricing a key issue in his 2000 mayoral campaign. On taking office, he quickly put a special team into place to design and implement a system. The new charge—about $8—went live in early 2003; 26 months after the process started. The initiative initially affected about 200,000 vehicles a day operating weekdays from 7 A.M. to 6:30 P.M. in a congested 13-square-mile area of central London. Motorists may pay in retail outlets, online, via text messaging, or by phone. Scoffers face escalating penalties.

Opposition ran two to one at first, but support grew as the results came in. Congestion dropped by 30 percent in 2003 and 2004, bus speed and reliability rose 20 percent or more, and emissions fell by 15 percent. Bicycle use rose 43 percent within the congestion charging zone. To encourage participation, more than 500 buses were added during morning rush hours shortly before the charge began, and extensive improvements benefited pedestrians and cyclists.

Livingstone won reelection by a decisive margin in 2004, after promising to broaden the zone, which in February 2007 was doubled in size to include the West End. The fees (all for driving in the congestion charge zone) were boosted to $16 in July 2005. The most fuel-inefficient vehicles will pay $50 per day starting in October, even those of zone residents (who otherwise enjoy a 90 percent discount). Fees are waived for drivers of the most fuel-efficient, cleanest vehicles. Nearly half of the $520 million in annual revenues are used to administer the charging system, with the rest dedicated to public transportation.

In February of this year, a new, citywide low-emission zone went into effect. This one is based on the experience of Berlin, Germany, and Malmo, Sweden, both of which have smaller low-emission zones. In London's zone, heavy trucks that fail to meet recent European Union emission standards now pay $400 a day to drive anywhere in the city. Similar charges will extend to buses, minibuses, large vans, and ambulances this summer.

"It's an effort to save the lives of 1,000 Londoners a year who die prematurely because of the worst air quality in Western Europe," Mayor Livingstone said just before the initiative's launch. The zone is projected to cut pollution 16 percent by 2012 and save health costs of $500 million.

Transport for London, the agency that overseas the city's trains, buses, and roads, is spending $98 million to set up the new zone and $20 million a year to operate it, with annual revenue projected at $92 million. In the first month, the city counted about 50,000 trucks a week entering the zone. Eight percent failed to meet the emissions standard. Fees are refundable if the vehicle is upgraded with better pollution controls.

The new low-emission zone uses cameras to check license plate numbers against lists. If the vehicle is certified as exempt or registered as having paid the appropriate fee, the photo is discarded. If not on the list, the image is processed for billing. The city plans to adopt a toll transponder system like the U.S. EZPass to simplify toll payments. According to the *Times of London,* if Ken Livingstone wins a tough reelection campaign this May, he intends to introduce charges on congested roads outside the existing zone.

The idea is simple enough: Charge fees based on where and when motorists drive, with discounts offered during times of low demand. Used in that way, congestion pricing matches demand more closely to available road space, and boosts the efficiency, reliability, and speed of an area's transportation system. Revenues can be used to increase travel choices.

It works in Singapore. There, electronic toll charges—on the outer ring road, major arterials, and entry roads to both the central business district and a newer commercial center—are adjusted periodically for each location by hour of the week based on what is needed to keep traffic flowing freely at least 85 percent of the time.

Now try putting this idea into practice in the U.S. A major stumbling block is the common belief that inflation-eroded gas taxes have already paid for "freeways" and other roads. For many drivers, the idea of a toll conjures up images of being stuck in a long traffic jam waiting to throw your money out the window.

The Debate Continues

The HOT lanes that opened in 1995 in the median of southern California's State Road 91 broke new ground in many ways. The project demonstrated that private investment could succeed in delivering road improvements years ahead of the public sector. It significantly boosted vehicle occupancy and traffic flow along the corridor. And it showed how automated time-of-day road pricing could guarantee free-flowing traffic in a congested corridor. All that with no toll booths in sight.

During the most congested hours, SR-91's two managed lanes carry as many vehicles as four adjacent unmanaged lanes, at three times the speed. But getting to that point was not easy.

The contract for SR-91 included a non-compete agreement that barred public investment in parallel transportation improvements by state and local governments. This provision proved so unacceptable to Riverside County that the original agreement had to be renegotiated in 2002, a painful and costly process. Like many other HOT lanes, those on SR-91 were not designed to boost public transportation and actually facilitated sprawl development. After gaining temporary relief from congestion, many drivers were still stuck on clogged freeway lanes.

In contrast, the I-15 HOT lane project that opened in San Diego in 1996 offered an example of a more transit-friendly approach to managed lanes. The San Diego Association of

Governments dedicated toll revenue from the new HOT lanes (created from existing lanes) to improved public transportation. A dynamic pricing system allowed tolls to be adjusted every seven minutes, helping to keep the managed lanes flowing. With polls showing 80 percent approval of the system, San Diego is now building a regional system of managed lanes with express bus services.

Back East

Pressure to introduce congestion pricing has also been building in metropolitan New York—where more than half of all tolls in the U.S. are collected. William Vickery, a Nobel Prize-winning economist at Columbia University, first proposed the idea in 1952. In the early 1970s, he and other civic advocates actually convinced Mayor John Lindsay to try congestion pricing on the East River bridges, but the authority to do so was blocked in court.

In 2000, the political stars aligned just as the Port Authority of New York and New Jersey was set to issue a toll increase. Thanks to the efforts of a civic coalition, the Tri-State Transportation Campaign, the governors of both states supported a staff recommendation to increase peak-period Hudson River bridge and tunnel tolls, while keeping charges the same for non-peak-hour EZPass toll transponder users.

The $1.50 time-of-day toll differential was enough to shift about seven percent of the traffic from peak hour, yielding a substantial reduction in congestion. With nearly half the Port Authority's net toll revenues dedicated to improving trans-Hudson PATH passenger rail service, this initiative became a milestone on the path toward wider congestion pricing. Soon after, modest time-of-day toll differentials were introduced by the New Jersey Turnpike, the Garden State Parkway, and the New York Thruway Authority as new toll increases took effect.

Meanwhile, other states were advancing HOT lanes under the federal Congestion/Value Pricing Pilot Program, which in 1991 opened a door for states to circumvent the 35-year ban on imposing tolls on interstate highways. In the debate over the 2005 federal transportation law, opposition from U.S. trucking interests—long opposed to tolls except to build new roads—was overcome by an unusual alliance of transportation industry, state, metropolitan, and environmental interests. The states won much greater flexibility to add tolls to new or existing roads.

Fast forward to 2006, when a national congestion initiative was launched by U.S. Department of Transportation Secretary Norman Mineta and carried forward by his successor, Mary Peters. One piece of that, the Urban Partnership Agreements, promised federal funding from a dozen discretionary programs to a few cities with the most ambitious implementation plans: congestion pricing of existing roads combined with improved public transportation and traffic management. Thanks to a reduction in earmarking of transportation funds when the Democrats took over Congress, DOT was able to award $852 million to five cities under the initiative—New York, San Francisco, Seattle, Minneapolis, and Miami.

Go-Getters

Of the two dozen applications, the most ambitious was the proposal by New York Mayor Michael Bloomberg, who in 2003 submitted a budget to put congestion tolls on East River bridges but was forced to back down because he lacked needed approvals from the governor and legislature.

Last year, Bloomberg made congestion pricing a central piece of his PlaNYC vision for New York—a long-term plan to house a million more residents, enhance livability and public health, cut congestion, and trim greenhouse gas emissions by 30 percent by 2030. Bloomberg sought a green light from the state to implement his plan, which would impose a congestion charge of $8 a day on cars and $21 on trucks ($7 on low-emission trucks) entering the city's central core.

Despite opposition from key legislators, the mayor got approval to further refine the plan. The city also won a $354 million Urban Partnership grant, which it plans to use for congestion pricing, bus rapid transit initiatives, and improvements in traffic operations. But this grant is conditioned on approval by the city council and the state legislature of key planning goals—to cut Manhattan traffic by at least 6.3 percent by 2009 and to raise more than $250 million a year for transit. That condition could make the New York plan a model for future performance-based federal transportation funding.

Months of hearings led to a refined (and simpler) pricing plan that would shift the proposed zone boundaries and exemptions, produce more revenue, and lower collection costs. Polls showed that a majority of city residents supported congestion pricing so long as toll revenues would be dedicated to improving public transportation. A strong campaign by a coalition of business, civic, and environmental groups led to a 30-to-20 vote in favor of the plan by the city council, and support by the governor and state senate leader. But the plan died April 7 in the State Assembly when the deadline for action expired, a victim of election-year politics and failed deal making.

The plan's failure in Albany leaves an added $4.5 billion hole in the Metropolitan Transportation Authority's $29.5 billion, five-year capital budget, portending higher taxes and service cuts in addition to the loss of the $352 million federal grant.

With leadership from Mayor Gavin Newsom, San Francisco also won a matching $159 million DOT grant under the Urban Partnership agreement, conditioned on implementation of congestion pricing. The Bay Area Toll Authority's approval this month of a peak-period toll hike of $1 (to $6) on the bridge should be enough to guarantee the grant, which would help to cover some of the $1.1 billion cost of replacing Doyle Drive, the structurally unstable connector road south of the Golden Gate Bridge.

This is a breakthrough for a region that has for years tried to implement congestion pricing on bridges but been blocked by state legislative leaders. While suburban officials continue to resist the pricing proposal, charging that it amounts to a commuter tax, area transportation planners are making plans to implement new parking, transit, and HOT lanes under the partnership agreement. Planners in the San Francisco region

Stockholm Experiment

After a decade of studies, proposals, and other setbacks, Stockholm in January 2006 launched a seven-month congestion tax pilot project with a goal of reducing traffic and pollution. The Swedish Green Party pushed its Social Democratic coalition partners to implement the initiative, which had been held up for two years by challenges regarding legal authority and procurement.

The government invested $200 million in the revenue collection system and $300 million in related public transportation improvements. Charges were imposed between 6 A.M. and 7 P.M. weekdays at the 18 entry points surrounding the central core. Residents of a small part of the city accessible only through the charging zone were exempt; so were taxis, foreign-registered cars, the handicapped, and extremely low-emission vehicles. Others faced fees up to $3.50 for each entry or exit from the zone. The toll collection system is based primarily on automated license plate recognition.

Twelve new express bus lines, improved rail service, and 1,800 new park-and-ride spaces were designed to win over public opinion (although opponents outnumbered proponents by two to one on opening day). The results were good: Traffic fell by 15 percent, congestion delay fell by up to 50 percent, and greenhouse gases and other pollution dropped by 14 percent in the core area and by two to three percent in the region. Public transportation ridership rose by 45,000. When the charge ended, traffic quickly went back to the old, higher charge levels.

In September 2006, a non-binding referendum was held to determine whether the charge would be reinstated. The ayes had it. Although most of the parties that formed a new government following that election had campaigned against the charge, they promptly decided to restore the central area charge with minor modifications. Today, the charge generates annual revenues of over $150 million; about a fifth of the gross revenues are required to administer the system.

Last year, President Bush cited Stockholm's success in discussing his own congestion initiative. Recent Stockholm polls show nearly two-to-one public support for congestion charging.

Singapore Transformed

Pictures taken in Singapore in the mid-1970s show a city mired in congestion, with cars, trucks, buses, and motorbikes stalled for hours on hopelessly crowded roads. It's a scene reminiscent of Jakarta or Bangkok today.

No more. Singapore is a city transformed. Its roads are largely free of congestion, public transportation is outstanding, and the economy is booming. Congestion pricing is certainly part of that success story.

The world's first congestion charging system was instituted in Singapore's Central Business District in 1975. The system cut private car traffic into the core by more than half. Carpooling rose by more than a third, and bus use doubled. As Singapore's income has skyrocketed to $32,500 per capita, the number of cars has grown 2.5 times, and public transportation's share of travel has risen from four out of 10 trips to over six in 10, thanks to road pricing, a vehicle quota system that manages the number of motor vehicles, and high levels of investment in public transportation and transit-oriented development. Singapore is also a leader among the world's affluent major cities for its very low personal transportation greenhouse gas emissions.

Singapore started with a central area charge in morning peak hours, which it later extended to the evening peak and midday hours. In 1990, congestion pricing was applied to the city's ring road expressway. In 1998, Singapore implemented electronic tolling, retrofitting all vehicles with toll transponders, which work with cash cards to deduct a fee automatically when a vehicle passes a charging gantry. Different reader devices correspond to each vehicle class, with higher fees for larger vehicles. Tolls are now imposed at 55 locations, and the number will grow to 70 by the end of the year.

With electronic tolling, Singapore was able to adjust rates by hour of the week, cutting fees in some cases by half or more below what they had been with a flat $2.15 peak/$1.45 midday charge per gantry passage. Toll rates are adjusted accordingly to keep traffic generally free flowing. In July, the base toll will double to $1.45, as will the increment by which tolls are raised for particular locations and times. Road pricing now contributes over $60 million per year to Singapore's general budget, with operating costs accounting for only seven percent of that; the most efficient of any urban congestion charging system.

are also studying a central area cordon charge modeled after London, Stockholm, and Singapore.

A third winner was Seattle, where King County Executive Ron Sims and the Washington State DOT have strongly supported congestion pricing. A nearly completed federally supported study estimates that it would cost about $750 million to create a GPS satellite-based tolling system in the region and about $288 million a year to operate it, potentially generating annual revenues of $3 billion and a 6:1 benefit-to-cost ratio.

The study concludes that the technology needed for such toll collection is mature, noting that public understanding and acceptance are the keys to moving forward. In the near term, the region intends to convert State Road 167's high-occupancy vehicle lane into a HOT lane, and plans are proceeding to finance and manage the failing SR 520 Lake Washington bridge with congestion tolls.

Other initiatives for adding tolls to existing interstate highways (restriping lanes and using shoulders, for instance) are advancing in Minneapolis and Miami, which won $133 million and $63 million respectively under the Urban Partnerships program. They have agreements for HOT lane projects on I-35 and I-95, which also support new express bus services.

Other federal grants are expected this year for Congestion Reduction Demonstration pilot projects, which encourage integrated initiatives for transit, traffic operations, and congestion pricing on existing roads. More than 20 regions applied late last year for this latest round of grants. Funding levels depend on the appropriations process and the level of congressional earmarks.

U.S. federal transportation policy is at a crossroads, with widespread perception that the system is both broke and broken as the current federal transportation law expires next year and the highway trust fund runs out of money. With bridges falling down, gas prices soaring, and traffic congestion getting worse, public confidence in the current system is low. Debate is growing about how to fund and focus transportation investments, how to curb transportation-related greenhouse gas emissions, and how to boost system performance and accountability.

With dozens of new congestion pricing initiatives launched across America last year, and even more across the rest of the world, the genie conjured up by William Vickery seems finally to be out of the bottle. But just what will we ask that genie to do?

Critical Thinking

1. Explain how a system of congestion pricing would work in a city.
2. What possible criticisms can be made against the desirability of a system of congestion pricing?

MICHAEL A. REPLOGLE, a civil engineer, is transportation director for the Environmental Defense Fund and president and founder of the Institute for Transportation and Development Policy.

California's Pioneering Transportation Strategy

DANIEL SPERLING AND MARY NICHOLS

The state that has become identified with freeways and smog now aspires to become the leader in reducing motor vehicles' carbon footprint and changing the way people travel.

No place in the world is more closely associated with the romance of the automobile and the tragedy of its side effects than California. Having faced the problem of traffic-damaged air quality, the state became a leader in policies to reduce auto emissions. Now that transportation is the source of 40% of the state's contribution to climate change, California has become a pioneer in the quest to shrink its transportation footprint and a possible trailblazer for national policy.

Two political circumstances favor California's climate policy leadership. First, it has unique authority and political flexibility. Because California suffered unusually severe air quality problems as early as the 1940s and adopted requirements for vehicles and fuels before Congress was moved to act, the U.S. Congress in 1970 preserved the state's authority over vehicle emissions, as long as its rules were at least as strong as the federal ones. California has continued in a leadership role for over 40 years, launching many of the world's first emission controls on internal combustion engine vehicles, reformulated gasoline, and zero-emission vehicles. Since the 1977 amendments to the U.S. Clean Air Act, other states have enjoyed the option of following the more stringent California standards instead of the federal standards. The California legislature took advantage of this authority in 2002 when it directed the California Air Resources Board (CARB) to adopt limits on vehicular emissions of greenhouse gases (GHGs), designating these emissions as a form of air pollution.

Second, California has been able to act in advance of the national government because it has more political space to maneuver. The Detroit car companies have relatively small investments in California, and coal companies are absent. California is home to leading research universities, innovators, and entrepreneurs, as well as a diverse resource base of solar, wind, ocean, and geothermal energy resources. The state is also home to the world's largest venture capital industry, which favors clean energy policy. California politicians feel freer to pursue aggressive energy and climate policies than do their counterparts in many other states.

In 2005, Governor Schwarzenegger issued an executive order requiring the state to reduce GHGs emitted by 80% from 1990 levels by 2050. This goal has also been adopted by the European Union and many other governments. By acting early, California has launched a policy experiment that could produce valuable lessons for the United States and other countries.

The 80% goal cannot be met without dramatic change in driver behavior and transportation technology. Researchers and companies have made rapid technological progress in recent years in improving conventional and advanced technologies. Performance-based regulations for gasoline-powered cars are expected to double fuel economy between 2010 and 2025, and rapid advances are being made with advanced lithium batteries and vehicular fuel cells. With greater emphasis on energy efficiency and low-carbon technologies, dramatic reductions in oil use and GHG emissions will occur. A key ingredient in reaching this goal will be government policy to stimulate innovation, encourage consumer behavior changes, and direct society toward large reductions in oil use and GHG emissions.

Emphasize Regulation

The California strategy departs from the common approach to climate change in two notable ways: It does not depend on international agreements, and although it incorporates market instruments, it relies primarily on performance-based regulatory actions. Both elements are critical to its success.

Although climate change is a global problem that will require global action, transportation is essentially a local concern. International cooperation will be necessary to resolve problems in maritime and air transport, but action on cars and trucks can be taken at a national or state level.

In addition, although many experts say that the solution to our energy and climate problems is sending the correct price signals to industry and consumers, the transport sector's behavior is highly inelastic in that it does not change significantly in response to changes in fuel prices, at least in the range that is politically acceptable. Europe has gasoline taxes over $4 per gallon and still finds the need to adopt aggressive performance standards for cars to reduce GHGs and oil use. These high fuel taxes certainly have an effect in reducing the average size and power of vehicles and leading people to drive less, but the resulting reductions in fuel use and GHGs still fall far short of the climate goals.

Large carbon (and fuel) taxes are efficient in an economic sense, but their effect on vehicles, fuels, and driving is modest. The European experience suggests that huge taxes would be needed to motivate significant changes in investments and consumer behavior, but U.S. public opinion is hostile to even small energy tax increases. Moreover, the energy market is distorted by a number of factors, including the failure to internalize the total cost of pollution and climate change, the market power of the OPEC cartel, technology lock-in, and the fact that many energy users such as apartment renters and drivers of company cars are insulated from the price of energy because they do not pay the bills.

We are not saying that getting the prices right and adopting international climate agreements and carbon taxes are irrelevant and unimportant. But we are saying that much progress can, and probably will, be made in the transport sector in the next decade without international agreements and without getting the prices right. California is leading the way with policies that address three critical elements of the transportation system: vehicles, fuels, and mobility.

Vehicles

Americans like their cars big and powerful. U.S. fuel economy standards remained stagnant for 30 years, until 2010, while Japan, Europe, and even China adopted increasingly aggressive standards to reduce oil use and GHGs. California played a leadership role in breaking the paralysis in U.S. efficiency standards. In 2002, California passed the so-called Pavley law, which required a roughly 40% reduction in vehicle GHG emissions by 2016. The car companies filed lawsuits against California and states that followed California's lead. When those lawsuits failed, the Bush administration refused to grant a waiver to California to proceed, even though waivers were granted routinely for previous vehicle emissions regulations by California. In 2009, President Obama not only agreed to grant a waiver, but committed the entire country to the aggressive California standards.

And then in August 2011, at the request of President Obama, the Department of Transportation, Environmental Protection Agency, and CARB announced an agreement with the major automakers to sharply reduce fuel consumption and GHG emissions by another 4 to 5% per year from 2017 to 2025. California was recognized as playing an instrumental role by threatening to adopt its own more stringent rules if the federal government and automakers did not agree to strong rules. CARB expects to adopt these rules in January, with the federal government following suit in summer 2012.

The California strategy departs from the common approach to climate change in two notable ways: it does not depend on international agreements, and although it incorporates market instruments, it relies primarily on performance-based regulatory actions. Both elements are critical to its success.

These regulations requiring automakers to reduce oil consumption and GHG emissions are central to California's GHG reduction efforts and are expected to elicit larger reductions than any other policy or rule, including carbon cap and trade. The reductions are also expected to be the most cost-effective, with consumers actually earning back at least twice as much from fuel savings over the life of their vehicle than they would be paying for the added cost of the efficiency improvements, even after discounting future fuel cost savings.

The federal government has recently asserted leadership in supporting the commercialization of electric vehicles (EVs), with the Obama administration offering tax credits of $7,500 per car and billions of dollars in loan guarantees and grants to EV and battery manufacturers. In addition, in 2009 the federal government adopted vehicle GHG standards that provide strong incentives to automakers to sell EVs.

But California has a much more ambitious long-term policy commitment to EVs. In 1990, California adopted a zero-emission vehicle (ZEV) requirement, mandating that the seven largest automotive companies in California "make available for sale" an increasing number of vehicles with zero tailpipe emissions. The initial sales requirement was 2% of car sales in 1998 (representing about 20,000 vehicles at the time), increasing to 5% in 2001 and 10% in 2003.

The intent was to accelerate the commercialization of electric (and other advanced) technology, but batteries and fuel cells did not advance as fast as regulators hoped. The ZEV rule, after surviving industry litigation and multiple adjustments to reflect the uneven progress of hybrid, fuel cell, and battery technologies, now bears little resemblance to the original. Although some consider the ZEV mandate a policy failure, others credit it with launching a revolution in clean automotive technology.

The actual numbers of vehicles sold to consumers as a result of the ZEV program are certainly not what CARB originally expected. Only a few thousand EVs were sold in the United States in the first decade of this century, most of them by start-ups such as Tesla. But 2011 could mark a breakthrough, because for the first time major automakers have made firm commercial commitments to the technology. Nissan began selling its all-electric Leaf, and General Motors its plug-in hybrid EV, the very first commitment of major car companies to mass-produce plug-in vehicles in over a century. Sales of the two vehicle models amounted to fewer than 20,000 worldwide in 2011 (about half of which were in California), but both companies are expanding factory capacity in anticipation of each selling 50,000 or more in 2012, and virtually all major car companies have plans to sell plug-in vehicles in the next couple of years.

Could another policy have accomplished the same at less cost with less conflict? Who knows? What's certain is that the ZEV program accelerated worldwide investment in electric-drive vehicle technology. The benefits of those accelerated investments continue to sprout throughout the automotive world, and California policy was the catalyst. In addition to the ZEV mandate, California has enacted various other incentives in recent years to support the introduction of fuel-efficient and low-GHG vehicles, including allowing access to carpool lanes and providing rebates to buyers of EVs.

Fuels

California has also taken steps to encourage the development and use of low-carbon alternative fuels, and the federal government has followed with its own aggressive actions. The federal Renewable Fuel Standard (RFS) requires the production of 36 billion gallons of biofuels by 2022, and Congress and President Obama have enacted a series of provisions that promote EVs. But these efforts have serious shortcomings.

The RFS biofuels mandate has led to the annual production of more than 12 billion gallons of corn-based ethanol, but almost no low-carbon, non–food-based biofuels. Corn ethanol is roughly similar to gasoline in terms of life-cycle carbon emissions. The EPA has repeatedly given waivers to oil companies that allow them to defer investments in lower-carbon advanced biofuels.

California has gone further in pioneering a regulation that provides a durable framework for the transition to low-carbon fuel alternatives. Its low-carbon fuel standard (LCFS), adopted in 2009 and taking effect in 2011, applies to all fuel alternatives, unlike the biofuels-only RFS, and it allows oil companies to trade credits among themselves and with other suppliers such as electric utilities. Also, unlike the federal RFS, it provides incentives to make each step in the energy pathway, from the growing of biomass to the processing of oil sands in Canada, more efficient and less carbon-intensive. The LCFS provides a framework for all alternatives to compete. Versions of California's LCFS are being enacted in other places, including British Columbia and the European Union, and many states are in the advanced stages of review and design of an LCFS.

Because the LCFS is novel, casts such a wide net, and requires major investments in low-carbon alternative fuels, it has been controversial. Economists argue that a carbon tax would be more economically efficient. Energy security advocates and producers of high-carbon petroleum, such as that from the Canadian oil sands, are concerned that it will discourage investments in unconventional energy sources and technologies that could extend the world's supply of oil. Oil companies correctly argue that the imposition of the LCFS in one state will encourage the shuffling of high-carbon ethanol and petroleum to regions that don't discourage those fuels. And corn ethanol producers complain about the details of how emissions are calculated. Moreover, administering this seemingly simple rule requires vast amounts of technical information and great transparency in the calculation of life-cycle emissions.

GHG emissions will be reduced if people drive less, and people can be nudged to drive less by cities that reduce urban sprawl, enhance public transportation, and raise the price of travel to incorporate externalities of carbon emissions, pollution, and energy security.

The LCFS is a powerful policy instrument that is already stimulating innovation. Oil company executives in Europe and North America acknowledge privately that the LCFS has motivated their companies to reduce the carbon footprint of their investments and to reassess their long-term commitment to high-carbon fuels such as fuel from oil sands. But to realize the full benefits of an LCFS policy, more governments must adopt similar policies to minimize fuel shuffling. Also, as with low-carbon vehicles, additional complementary policies are needed to target the many market failures and market conditions that inhibit the transition to low-carbon fuels. For example, investments in hydrogen stations are needed to reassure car companies and early buyers of hydrogen fuel cell cars that fuel will be available. It is a classic chicken-and-egg dilemma. California is considering a requirement that oil companies build a certain number of hydrogen stations in accordance with the number of hydrogen cars sold.

Mobility

The third major factor in transportation is the vehicle user. GHG emissions will be reduced if people drive less, and people can be nudged to drive less by cities that reduce urban sprawl, enhance public transportation, and raise the price of travel to incorporate externalities of carbon emissions, pollution, and energy security. Still other user-related strategies to reduce GHG emissions include better driving habits, keeping tires properly inflated, and removing unneeded roof racks that increase wind resistance. Better road maintenance and traffic management can also reduce energy waste and excess emissions.

Efforts to alter vehicle use have enjoyed little success. Indeed, vehicle use has increased substantially, despite decades of federal initiatives such as "Transportation System Management," "Transportation Control Measures," and "Transportation Demand Management," as well as the construction of networks of carpool lanes and increased subsidies for public transportation. After all these efforts, the number of vehicles per licensed driver has increased to 1.15, public transport has shrunk to less than 3% of passenger miles, carpooling has also shrunk, and vehicle miles per capita have steadily increased. Cars have vanquished competitors and become ever more central to daily life. Reversing this trend, while providing a high level of access to work, school, health care, and other services, is a daunting challenge. It requires a vast swath of changes related to the imposition and disbursement of sales and property taxes, land-use zoning, transportation funding formulas, parking supply, innovative mobility services (such as demand-responsive transit and smart car sharing), pricing of vehicle use, and much more.

As noted, California pioneered car-dependent cities and living and took it to an extreme, creating a highly expensive and resource-intensive transportation system. It has overindulged. Most of the world has followed California's car-dependent path, but none have gone as far as California. Other countries have been far more innovative and determined at restraining vehicle use. But perhaps because it has gone so far to the extreme, California is now showing policy leadership in reversing the pattern.

In 2008, California passed the Sustainable Communities law, known as SB375, to reduce sprawl and vehicle use. It led to the creation of a new policy framework for cities to guide the transition to a less resource-intensive and car-intensive future. It provides a more robust and performance-based approach than did previous efforts to reduce vehicle use. It is just the beginning, but it does provide a good policy model for others.

In implementing the law, CARB established distinct targets for each metropolitan area in the state. Those targets range from 6 to 8% reduction in GHGs per capita for major regions by 2020 and 13 to 16% by 2035. The targets are applied to regional associations of governments that then work with individual cities and counties within their region to attain those targets. One strength of SB375 is that local governments are free to choose what strategies and mechanisms will work best in their situation.

The downside of SB375 is that it imposes no penalties for noncompliance and only weak incentives and rewards. The rationale for the absence of penalties is that the responsible parties are cities, most of which are in desperate financial straits. The challenge is to provide incentives that are compelling enough for the cities to assert themselves. Two options under consideration are diverting cap-and-trade revenues to cities that comply with reduction targets and restructuring transport funding formulas to reward complying cities. Current formulas are tied primarily to population and vehicle use, with the result that having more vehicles earns cities more money. The incentives should be just the opposite.

One lesson learned during the early implementation of the program and the development of the GHG targets was that local politicians and transportation managers came to support the targets when they realized that strategies to achieve the GHG targets are the same strategies they were already pursuing for other reasons, such as infrastructure cost reduction, livability, and public health. In fact, having a formal policy framework aids their efforts in governing their cities. But whatever the motivation, behavioral change is difficult.

Carbon Cap and Trade

Perhaps surprisingly, California's adoption of a carbon cap-and-trade rule as the capstone of its plan for meeting the goals of AB32, the state's overarching climate law, will not have much impact on transportation. A cap-and-trade program imposes shrinking carbon caps on factories, oil refineries, cement producers, electricity-generating facilities, and other large GHG sources. If companies cannot or choose not to shrink their emissions, they can purchase "allowances" from companies that are overperforming. With carbon trading, a market is created for carbon reductions, with carbon gaining a market value. The carbon price will be low if everyone is successful in reducing their emissions and no one needs to buy allowances from others, but it will be high if they are not successful. When carbon has a market value, polluters know exactly how much it costs them to pollute and can make economically rational decisions about how to reduce GHG emissions.

The European Union preceded California by a few years in implementing a cap-and-trade system, and the northeastern and mid-Atlantic states followed Europe in instituting a carbon cap-and-trade program for their electric utilities. But California's policy is broader than the eastern utilities program by including all large industrial and electricity-generation facilities, and broader than the European program by capping transport fuels.

The cap-and-trade program is valuable in creating a price for carbon, but it is not central to reducing transportation emissions. The California cap-and-trade program covers oil refineries, and beginning in 2015 the carbon content of the fuels themselves. The program is designed with floor and ceiling prices of $10 and $70 per ton of carbon through 2020. Although $70 is likely to motivate large changes in electricity generation, the effect will be far less for transportation, where $70 per ton translates into $0.70 per gallon of gasoline. That is not enough to motivate oil companies to switch to alternative fuels or to induce consumers to significantly reduce their oil consumption, but it is still important to establish the principle of placing a price on carbon.

Replicable?

California has put in place a unique, comprehensive, and largely coherent set of policies to reduce GHGs and oil use in transportation. Although it includes a carbon cap-and-trade policy that injects a price of carbon into the economy, more important is the mix of policy instruments that target specific vehicle, fuel, and mobility activities. Most of these policies are regulatory, though they are largely performance-based and many, such as the LCFS and its credit-trading component, have a pricing component to them.

This California model has the benefit of minimal cost to taxpayers, extensive use of performance-based standards, and some harnessing of market forces. Most important of all, it has survived political challenge. Even in the midst of a severe recession and 12% unemployment, California voters defeated an initiative measure to suspend implementation of the program.

The plan does suffer from some theoretical and practical defects. One concern is that many of the policies shield consumers from price increases and will thus slow the behavioral response. One future option might be to impose a system of fee-bates for vehicles, whereby car buyers pay an additional fee for those that consume more oil and produce more GHGs, and less for those that consume and emit less. A fee-bate reconciles regulations with market signals. Another way to create more transparency and boost the effectiveness of the price signal might be to convert the carbon cap imposed on fuels into a fee or carbon tax.

Another major weakness is the absence of policies addressing most air, maritime, and freight activities, leaving significant chunks of the economy untouched by carbon policy. These activities can be much more effectively addressed at the federal level. Emissions leakage and fuel shuffling—whereby fuel suppliers send their "good" fuel to California and their high-carbon fuel elsewhere—is a particular challenge for California and for any small jurisdiction, whether the policies are based on market or regulatory instruments.

In a broad sense, perhaps the biggest challenge is the complex interplay of the many regulations and incentives, and the involvement by various government bodies. For example, large-scale adoption of EVs depends on whether the design of the cap-and-trade program by CARB and the Public Utilities Commission encourages electricity generation that replaces high-carbon petroleum in the transportation sector. The Public Utilities Commission also enacts rules regarding who can or cannot sell electricity to vehicles. Meanwhile, the federal government and CARB determine how much credit EVs receive as part of vehicle performance standards. Are full upstream emissions from utilities considered, even though they are not for petroleum-fueled vehicles? And should automakers be given more or less credit for EVs relative to fuel cell vehicles in the ZEV mandate? It is important to make sure that the many rules are aligned and send consistent signals. This will be a challenging task, exacerbated by the involvement of numerous government agencies and legislative bodies.

One might argue that California has no business in pioneering climate policy, that it contributes a small part of the world's total GHG emissions, and that it is a global problem that should be left to global agreements. Although it is true that California contributes only about 2% of the world's total GHG emissions, there are few entities with larger shares. More important, although it is clear that top-down approaches contained in international treaties and even national rules will be required to achieve substantial climate change mitigation, a bottom-up approach that more directly engages individuals and businesses is also needed. California is providing the bottom-up model for others to follow.

Recommended Reading

National Research Council, Driving and the Built Environment:
    The Effects of Compact Development on Motorized Travel,
    Energy Use, and CO2 Emissions (Washington, DC:
    Transportation Research Board of the National Academies,
    Special Report 298, 2009).

National Research Council, Policy Options for Reducing Energy Use and Greenhouse Gas Emissions from U.S. Transportation (Washington, DC: Transportation Research Board of the National Academies, Special Report 307, 2011).

Joan Ogden and Lorraine Anderson, Sustainable Transportation Energy Pathways: A Research Summary for Decision Makers (Davis, CA: Institute of Transportation Studies, University of California, Davis, 2011).

Andreas Schäfer, J. B Heywood, H. D. Jacoby, and A. Waitz, Transportation in a Climate-Constrained World (Cambridge, MA: MIT Press, 2009).

Daniel Sperling and Deborah Gordon, Two Billion Cars (New York: Oxford University Press, 2010).

Daniel Yergin, The Quest: Energy, Security, and the Remaking of the Modern World (New York: Penguin Press, 2011).

Critical Thinking

1. What policies has California initiated in its efforts to reduce tailpipe emissions and global warming?
2. How will these efforts affect California's communities?

DANIEL SPERLING (dsperling@ucdavis.edu) is a professor and the director of the Institute of Transportation Studies at the University of California Davis and a member of the California Air Resources Board. **MARY NICHOLS** is chair of the California Air Resources Board.

UNIT 10

Cities and Urban Problems Around the Globe

Unit Selections

Learning Outcomes

After reading this unit, you should be able to:

- Explain how global economic competition affects local decision making.

- Illustrate how Japan and its cities have responded to the pressures of global competition.

- Show what is lost or ignored when a country like Japan reshapes its major cities to be "national champions" in the global economic competition.

- Describe how Shanghai has been transformed as China's leaders seek to have the city grow as a center of factories, offices, and foreign investment.

- Explain how cities like Rio de Janeiro use the Olympic Games and other megaevents as part of a strategy to modernize and restructure local communities.

- Evaluate the slum demolition and pacification programs of cities like Delhi and Rio.

- Identify alternatives to slum demolition and how government can enact more humane policies when dealing with the problems posed by squatter settlements and slum communities.

- Explain how the needs of women, especially low-income and working women, in a city differ somewhat from those of men.

- Document the horror of femicides in Ciudad Juárez and explain how femicides in that city are related to the growth of *maquiladoras* and the globalization of economic activity.

Student Website
www.mhhe.com/cls

Internet References

Planetizen
www.planetizen.com
Planum
www.planum.net
Rio On Watch
http://rioonwatch.org

Squatter City, the blog of Robert Neuwirth, author of
Shadow Cities: A Billion Squatters, A New Urban World
http://squattercity.blogspot.com
United Nations Human Settlements Programme
www.unhabitat.org

Cities continue to be the places to where people migrate in search of a better life. But the lives of city residents, especially newcomers, can be quite difficult. Just how well do cities serve their residents, especially their more vulnerable residents?

The earlier units of this book observed how the intercity and global competition for economic development often leads local leaders to give a special primacy to the demands of investors. To maintain their economic health, cities must attract and retain businesses. Even Tokyo, a city that clearly sits at the top of the global-city hierarchy, has had to act proactively in the face of rising economic challenges from Hong Kong, Shanghai, Mumbai, Singapore, and other Pacific office centers (Article 43, "Japan's Cities Amid Globalization"). Tokyo has torn down traditional low-rise neighborhoods in order to clear land for modernistic high-rise developments that house global corporations and their upscale workforces.

Each city initiates actions to capture new development. In the historic capital of Japan, Kyoto, a city of temples and shrines, municipal leaders built a soaring glass, rail station–hotel–shopping complex as the centerpiece of the city's effort to modernize the downtown and attract new investment. Critics argue that such growth-oriented developments defile Japan's cultural heritage, replacing tradition with a modern international architecture.

Shanghai, China, a megacity region of 23 million people, has been reshaped for economic competition. Shanghai, today, bears little resemblance to the gray anti-capitalist city that it was during the long rule of Communist Party chairman Mao Zedong (Article 44, "Shanghai Gets Supersized"). Modern Shanghai has over 200 office towers and is experiencing rapid transformation, as a result of national government policies that see cities as the growth engines of a dynamic Chinese economy. In order to attract foreign investment, the Chinese government has constructed an entirely new international banking, finance, and hotel district at Pudong, on the grasslands just across the river from the Bund, the city's historic business center. An extraordinarily expensive magnetic levitation bullet train has only two stations; it speeds the officials of multinational corporations arriving at the region's distant international airport to the towering skyscrapers of Pudong. Shanghai has torn down residential neighborhood after neighborhood, with their narrow lanes and crammed-tight low-rise housing, in order to build the high-rise towers capable of accommodating the growing number of workers with the skills prized by the city's growing businesses.

In lesser developed countries (LDCs), cities are overburdened by the seemingly never-ending flood of newcomers arriving from the countryside. In the giant megacities of LDCs, the poor can often be found in slums and shantytowns (also called favelas in Brazil) that lack adequate housing and basic municipal services—clean drinking water, electricity, toilets and sewer facilities, trash pickup, and public schools. Squatters settle on whatever piece of land they can find in the city. In more established squatter communities, a resident may even fix up and expand a dwelling unit, offering space that is then rented to another family. The residents of squatter communities, who cannot afford to reside elsewhere, often live with the constant fear of

© David Zurick

eviction, that they can be forced from their homes as they lack legal land tenure, that is, the legal right to occupy the dwellings in which they reside.

Public officials face conflicting pressures when dealing with shantytowns and squatter communities. The governments of LDCs lack the resources to address the full range of needs of slum communities. But oftentimes governments do not even do all that they can reasonably do to improve slum conditions. Public officials may even reject calls to build new housing and to extend water provision, sanitation, and public schooling to squatter communities; local officials argue that any improvement in slum conditions will only serve to attract still additional residents to these areas, overwhelming the city still further.

Some LDCs have sought to alleviate the population pressures on megacities by constructing major new towns to divert economic activity and population growth away from the congested urban core. In the mid-twentieth century, Brazil sought to relieve the pressure on Rio de Janeiro by shifting the nation's political capital to Brasilia, a new city developed inland, on the edge of the Amazon. More recently, Nigeria has similarly sought to relieve some of the pressure on Lagos, possibly the world's most overburdened megacity, by moving the country's political capital to Abuja, a new city constructed 300 miles northeast of Lagos.

In Egypt, public officials built two giant new towns, or satellite cities, in the desert, 20 miles outside of Cairo, in order to relieve some of the overload and congestion of that country's megacity (Article 46, "To Catch Cairo Overflow, 2 Megacities Rise in Sand"). The new towns present attractive housing and corporate sites to international investors, offering a safe and pleasant alternative to central poverty-laden, polluted Cairo. The new towns contain luxury gated communities and even feature green golf courses, an expensive luxury in the desert. The satellite communities also provide new housing for poor families relocated from the slums of Cairo. But it was not clear that the poor desire to live in housing located in relatively remote areas, making it difficult for them to reach their jobs (whatever they did for survival) in central Cairo.

In many instances, public leaders have not sought to improve slum conditions but instead have yielded to the urging of business leaders, bulldozing squatter communities. Delhi is just one of a great many LDC cities that has forcibly evicted squatters from their homes, razing their makeshift dwellings and destroying their possessions, in order to clear sites for commercial and industrial projects (Article 47, "Demolishing Delhi: World Class City in the Making").

Around the globe, cities have sought to increase their competitive edge through the visibility that can be obtained by hosting megaevents such as the Olympic Games and the FIFA soccer World Cup. Local leaders use these events to brand the city, to establish a global image that will attract tourism and new investment. As seen in Brazil and other countries, however, such megaevents also generate pressures that lead to the displacement and pacification of squatter communities (Article 48, "Reinventing Rio"). Megaevents are often used as vehicles to transform a city, or at least its poorer neighborhoods.

Many local governments, of course, take a more humane approach: they launch initiatives to alleviate the squalor of slum conditions by providing underserved areas with electricity, clean drinking water, sewerage, regular trash pickup, public schools, and improved public transit. Progressive policies also seek to regularize the status of squatters, providing quasi-legal protection to persons who lack legal title or right to their dwelling. Such protection affords residents a degree of permanency that enables residents to invest their own money and labor (called "sweat equity") in making improvements to the places in which they reside. Where governments lack the money to provide quality housing for the urban poor, public authorities can still act to improve housing conditions by enacting supportive policies that enable the poor themselves to upgrade and expand a city's stock of housing (Article 49, "No Excuses Slum Upgrading").

The discussion of service provision in squatter communities invites a larger question: Just how well do cities serve their more vulnerable residents? But it is not just the poor who are often neglected. Cities also overlook the needs of women.

As the field of gender studies has clearly articulated, women (especially low-income women) in the city have problems that are a bit distinct from those faced by men. Cities intent on attracting new investment may be more inclined to meet the concerns of business firms rather than raise taxes to ensure the provision of affordable day care, quality public transportation, and other essential services needed by poorer working women and female-headed families. Of even greater significance, we can ask: Do cities adequately provide for the physical safety of women who have a greater fear of physical violence and rape?

Ciudad Juárez, Mexico, just across the border from El Paso, Texas, has received considerable coverage in the news media as a result of the city's deadly gang wars and the battles between drug lords and government forces. Yet, Juárez's history of femicides—the murder of hundreds of women—actually predates the surge in drug-related violence (Article 50, "Femicide in Ciudad Juárez: *What Can Planners Do?*"). In Juárez and other border communities, women make up the bulk of the labor force in the *maquiladoras,* the factories that have sprouted up on the Mexican side of the border as a result of economic globalization. The North American Free Trade Agreement (NAFTA) eliminated many of the trade barriers between the U.S. and Mexico, spurring the shift of production to low-wage sites located on the Mexican side of the border. Goods that are produced in such factories in Mexico can be seamlessly shipped to markets in the United States. The owners of the *maquiladoras* rely on the work of women, recently arrived from the countryside, who are seen as more reliable and docile than men. But these women must often travel long distances across unsafe, unlighted streets and vacant lots in order to reach the factories and to return home, often late at night.

By 2012, activist groups estimated that over 700 Juárez women had been murdered. The city's response to the revelations of rape, torture, and murder has been slow and inadequate. Women's advocacy groups turned to feminist groups in other countries and to international tribunals, investigatory bodies that issue reports that will help keep the murders in the public spotlight. They hope that global pressure will convince public authorities in Mexico to give greater priority to the provision of safe transportation and the protection of women.

Japan's Cities Amid Globalization

Myron A. Levine

Global pressures and influences have altered spatial planning in Japan and have reshaped the face of Japan's cities. In the years following World War II and for much of the remaining twentieth century, Japan pursued the goal of spatial deconcentration; various policies sought to preserve the population and economic stability of smaller cities across Japan by limiting the overconcentration of population and economic activity in Tokyo. In the 1960s, the public's concern over dirty air and other environmental problems strengthened the demand to limit the growth of giant Tokyo.

The various policy efforts did not fully work, and Tokyo continued to grow. Nonetheless, the central government built peripheral housing and steered R&D (research and development) activities to high-amenity regional science and technology centers in Osaka, Nagoya, and new suburban technopoles. By steering supportive economic activities to the periphery, the deconcentration policy produced an important side benefit: in the age of intensified global competition that would soon follow, the government's deconcentration policy helped to free up space in overcrowded central Tokyo, space that would be a valuable asset in the national effort to secure prime office development (Edgington 1999; Saito 2004; Sorensen 2004).

Rising competition from other office centers in the Pacific Hong Kong, Singapore, Shanghai, Bangkok, and Kuala Lumpur—eventually led Japan to abandon spatial concentration in favor of a national economic strategy that sought to build on the assets and attractiveness of Tokyo. Tokyo would be the "national champion" (Jessop and Sum 2000, 2295–2296) in the increasingly intense global battles for development. The 2001 collapse of the "bubble economy" only reinforced the sense of national urgency in transforming Tokyo for the global competition.

Both the TMG (Tokyo Metropolitan Government) and the central government sought to create new areas of the city, particularly in the southern and western sectors, that would be attractive to international firms and their high-end workforces. Traditional low-rise neighborhoods had to be cleared in order to create new spaces for global firms. The 1988 Special District Plan for Redevelopment relaxed the country's strict land-use restrictions in order to facilitate the construction of new corporate skyscrapers and condominiums. Pursuing the dense development of corporate spaces, Tokyo borrowed New York City's "bonus" system, permitting developers to build additional floors and at greater density in return for open space, plazas, and other public facilities (Sorensen 2004; Saito 2003). The City Planning Acts of 1992, 1995, and 1999 permitted a level of local initiative that was previously unseen. Tokyo and other cities were no longer merely "agents" of central planning; "planning became a local government function (jichi jimu) instead of a delegated function" (Sorensen 2004, 299; also see Jacobs 2003a and 2004; Muramatsu 1997).

The rise of local initiative marked an important change in a planning system that, until that point in time, had been characterized as highly central-state directed, a system of "vertical administrative control" (Muramatsu 1997, 16 and 28; also, see Gilman 1997 and Edgington 1999; Fujita 2003). Tokyo (and other cities) gained new leeway to modernize their infrastructure and to pursue economic development initiatives that would work to the nation's advantage. Local governments in Japan pushed for local economic growth projects, working within the confines of a hierarchical state-planning system.

The construction of Roppongi Hills exemplifies the upgrading of land uses and the transformation of Tokyo's cityscape. Governmental officials helped to facilitate the efforts of developers to tear down a low-rise Tokyo neighborhood to make way for a 27-acre office-residential-shopping-complex. At the time of its 2003 opening, Roppongi Hills was the largest private development in the country and included a 54-story central office tower (with Goldman Sachs, Lehman Brothers, and Yahoo! Japan as anchor tenants), over 200 shops and restaurants (including Louis Vuitton, Wolfgang Puck's, and Starbucks), a 9-screen, all-reserved-seats cinemaplex, a Hyatt Hotel, a headquarters building for Asahi Television, an outdoor concert venue, and four residential buildings with over 840 units. Roppongi Hills was meant to be exclusive. Monthly rents (2006 figures) were high: an unfurnished one-bedroom went for $5,000 (600,000 Yen); a four-bedroom apartment rented for $50,000 (5,500,000 Yen) a month.

As we shall see, the TMG pushed for the creation of other major economic megadevelopment projects, including the construction of a virtual new quarter of the city, the Rainbow Town subcenter built on an artificial island in Tokyo Bay. Other cities responded to Tokyo's success by initiating development projects of their own. In contemporary Japan, local governments "take the policy initiative and play the role of trend-setter within the state policy structure" (Fujita 2003, 265; also see Jacobs 2005). Local chambers of commerce, relatively new actors in

Japan's local arena, even joined with municipal and prefectural officials in pushing local development projects.

A Tale of Four Cities

A brief review of key development projects in Tokyo, Kyoto, Kobe, and Fukuoka will reveal the degree to which local governments have taken the initiative and are often the "drivers" of major development projects. In contemporary Japan, the pressures for development are often bottom-up and no longer just top-down and fully controlled by the central-state. Such bottom-up efforts are inconsistent with the portrayal of Japan as a central-bureaucracy-dominated developmental state. In an age of heightened global competition, the national government has welcomed the new local initiatives.

Tokyo Pushes the Creation of a Tokyo Bay Subcenter: The Development of Teleport/Rainbow Town

Over the years, the Tokyo Metropolitan Government (TMG) has rebuilt entire sections of the city to facilitate economic growth. One of the most significant TMG projects was the construction of a massive waterfront city subcenter, known over the years as Teleport Town and Rainbow Town. Located just two miles from the commercial heart of downtown Tokyo, to which it is connected by highway and train running across the Rainbow Bridge, the megadevelopment is projected to have an eventual working population of 70,000 and a residential population of 42,000 (TMG 2002, 31).

The artificial island contains striking corporate buildings (the offices of Panasonic, Suntory, and Fuji), an iconic exhibition center, hotels, teleport and business support facilities, themed multi-level shopping malls (with indoor reconstructions of the streets of "Little Hong Kong" and Renaissance Italy), concert venues, museums, and amusement complexes (including a giant Ferris wheel). The island's Odaiba shopping/entertainment area has arguably emerged as Tokyo's most important tourist destination, drawing visitors from the rest of Japan to the island's shopping malls and to the dramatic view of the Rainbow Bridge cast against the backdrop of the city's downtown.

Local officials helped initiate the Tokyo Bay project, expanded its scope, and provided political and financial support for it during the years of economic difficulty when the enthusiasm of the central government waned. In the 1980s, TMG governor Shunichi Suzuki proposed the construction of a Tokyo Bay "teleport town," a concentration of the most up-to-date satellite and telecommunications facilities that would help draw information-age businesses to Japan (Saito 2003). Amid the optimism that characterized the bubble economy, TMG officials expanded their vision to a full-fledged city subcenter with residences, shopping, and entertainment. By 1987, only two years after the initial announcement of the project, plans for the island mushroomed to 11 times the original project acreage; its budget swelled by a factor of four (Yipu 2005).

When the bubble economy burst, few observers saw the need for new office and commercial space proposed for the island. A new national government sought to cut unnecessary expenditures on an unneeded project. During that period, local officials—the TMG—kept the project alive, continuing to pour local money into roadways, rail, and infrastructure support. Even when populist national leaders criticized the project's size and extravagance, TMG careerists continued to lend their support to the project (Saito 2003; Yipu 2005). Local planners promised that the island's "lively atmosphere and broad-based appeal" (TMG 2002, 15) would help make Tokyo attractive to the managers and to workers in cutting-edge industries (Saito 2003). A new administration would eventually adopt Tokyo's perspective.

Traditional Kyoto Builds an Ultra-Modern Train Station and Gateway to the Global Economy

In Kyoto, local officials and business leaders initiated the construction of a massive rail station project from the fear that their city was being eclipsed by the construction boom in nearby Osaka and Kobe and by the opening of Osaka's new Kansai International Airport:

> A task force (composed of representatives from the city, prefecture, the Chamber of Commerce and Industry, and JR West [the West Japan Railway company] organized an international competition for the design of a new station for Kyoto. The winner, the Japanese architect Hiroshi Hara, was announced in 1991. This type of competition is uncommon in Japan and shows how much was at stake in this ambitious project. (Tiry 2001)

In a city of temples and shrines, Kyoto's leaders sought an architecturally distinguished, monumental project to signal that Kyoto was no longer merely a quiet, sleepy tourist destination but a modern city that welcomed business. The striking multi-functioned megaplex (opened in 1997) contains a shopping mall, hotels, exhibition space, various support facilities, and a multi-screen theater. The "Cube" is the 16-story, two-winged heart of the project, with an open-air "Grand Staircase" that rises from below ground.

The project serves as a symbol of Kyoto's economic vitality and provides the city with an important gateway to the global economy. As Kyoto has no airport of its own (a critical impediment to the city's ability to attract international corporations), local elites sought a rail facility that would serve *de facto* as the city's airport, offering "seamless" travel to executives who can check their bags at the station without having to recheck them at Kansai Airport (Tiry 2001). The Cube abuts the high-speed Shinkansen bullet trains that connect the city to Tokyo.

Kobe Seeks Its Niche in the New Economy: From "Port City" to "International City"

Kobe's leaders followed a somewhat different development path, choosing a strategy that sought to market the city's livability, building on Kobe's environmental assets. In the wake of the Great Hanshin-Awaji Earthquake of 1995 (4,500 deaths and 120,000 damaged buildings), planners did more than just rebuild the city; they pursued a strategy for long-term economic diversification and growth. Kobe no longer promotes itself solely as the home of Japan's most active seaport. Instead, Kobe advertises itself as an "international city" with "facilities and amenities established by and for such foreign communities" (City of Kobe, 2004). Kobe residents enjoy greater green space per capita (17 square meters per person) than do the residents of any other major Japanese city (Hinrichsen, 2002).

Kobe built attractive new residential environments and promoted the city's international schools and close proximity to both the mountains and the sea. A greenbelt helps to prevent the recreational space of the Rokko Mountains, preventing new development incursions. Given its assets, municipal officials boast that "Kobe is uniquely qualified to support a comfortably refined lifestyle for just about any company or individual from any country" (City of Kobe, 2004). The striking waterfront skyline of Harborland, the large complex of office buildings, shopping malls, hotels, cinemas, restaurants, and an amusement park built on the site of the city's old freight yards, provides Kobe with the future-oriented imagery that is used to market the city to an international community.

Kobe occupies an extremely narrow strip of land between the Rokko Mountains and the Seto Inland Sea, a geographical situation that greatly restricted the supply of developable land. Before the great earthquake, Kobe had adopted an aggressive strategy of creating new sites for growth and development. Sites for Suma residential town, Kobe academic town (a university center), and the Seishin new town and high-tech park were obtained by flattening parts of the Rokko Mountain region. The removed earth was then used as fill to help create two large man-made harbor islands which were created to expand port-related activities and to create new residential opportunities.

Port Island was constructed in 1992 as a center of new facilities to alleviate bottlenecks in the old port area. But the island also became the site of residential and lifestyle activities. Port Island is envisioned to have an eventual population of 20,000, many attracted to the island's extensive sports and recreational facilities. A dozen years after its initial opening, a "second stage" expansion project was announced "to meet the needs of this new age of globalization and foreign companies" (City of Kobe, 2004). The expanded island houses the Kobe Medical Industry Development Project, a biomedical research-and-development complex and the first "Life Science super-cluster in Japan" (City of Kobe, 2004).

Kobe's effort to reposition itself as an international city with an attractive living environment—no longer just a port city—is even more clearly evident in the "new town" development at Rokko Island, the city's second large man-made island. Situated only 4 miles from downtown Kobe and 12 miles from downtown Osaka, the island is linked to the mainland by a driverless train. The new town is projected to house a residential population of 30,000. The island offers corporate offices, hotels, a convention center, a western-style cinema complex, fitness clubs, international schools, and a water amusement park.

With its tree-lined pedestrian walkways that wind along a narrow man-made "river," Rokko Island is marketed as offering a setting that is attractive to both foreign corporations

and expatriate families. Procter & Gamble chose the island as the site for its offices. With its fashion center and fashion museum, the island has also become the center of Kobe's fashion industry.

Fukuoka: Building on Links to Asia, but Influenced by the United States

Faced with the decline of the regions' coal-producing and ship-building economies, Fukuoka (population 1.3 million) turned to a tourism-based strategy designed to attract visitors from nearby South Korea and mainland Asia. In terms of miles, Fukuoka actually lies closer to Seoul, South Korea, than to Tokyo! The city's Asian Art Museum, built as part of the plush Riverain shopping complex with its high-end fashion stores, is designed to appeal to visitors from South and East Asia.

A mile away, however, an American-themed shopping mall and entertainment center serves as the lure for tourism. Private developer Fukuoka Jisho acquired 9 acres of land bordering the Naka River in the city's dilapidated Hakata warehouse district. After the collapse of his initial development plans, he turned to Jon Jerde, the California designer of Horton Plaza in San Diego and the Mall of America in the Twin Cities, as the Japanese-American partnership built a fantasy/shopping theme park.

At the time of its 1996 opening, Canal City was the largest private development in Japan. A computer-orchestrated "symphony of fountains" and performing acrobats, trapeze artists, and jugglers (who perform on a small island in an artificial central canal) entice customers to the complex's shops and eateries. With bold primary colors and curved lines, Canal City was meant to stand out. In contrast to the traditional Japanese model of station-centered development (a model which still shapes the development of Tenjin, Fukuoka's rail-centered downtown), Canal City has no direct rail access; instead, customers arrive much like they do in the United States, by car as they enter the complex through a multi-decked parking structure. Canal City is Japan's version of the city as a "theme park" (Sorkin 1992).

The Refashioning of Tokyo Continues

This brief review of Tokyo's Rainbow Town, Kyoto's train station, Kobe's livability, and Fukuoka's Canal City projects all reveal that local actors have become driving forces behind major development projects in Japan. In Japan, a central-state renowned for top-down guidance and planning, gave local officials new discretion to pursue economic development, so much so that one authority on urban Japan says the word "centralized" can no longer be accurately used to describe the contemporary development system in Japan (Jacobs 2003a; also see Hein and Pelletier 2006; and Hill and Fujita 2003).

The collapse of the bubble economy heightened national government's sense of urgency in rebuilding Tokyo as a global center. Even Tokyo, clearly a top-tier city in the global hierarchy, had to be reshaped to maintain its primacy. Traditional low-rise neighborhoods were displaced to create new areas that would meet the needs of multinational corporations and their workforces.

The concern that Japanese national policy once gave to preserving regional balance in development fell by the wayside. Central authorities announced that the goal of spatial deconcentration was no longer relevant. The nation's global economic competitiveness required "compact urban structures with centripetal force" (Prime Minister of Japan and his Cabinet 2002). Faced with new competition from Shanghai, Hong Kong, Singapore and other Pacific office sites, Japan sought to strengthen Tokyo as the "global financial capital gateway to the world" (Saito 2004, 9).

With office space in Tokyo almost fully occupied (Takahashi and Sugiura 1995), planners had to create or free up new space for global-oriented development. Rainbow Town was only one of a ring of new city subcenters created for different economic functions. Shinjuku emerged as a virtual second downtown, a dense development of skyscrapers housing the government and back-office functions. Shibuya became a center of fashion and youth culture; Ikebukuro as a locus of retail activity. The new subcenters freed up space in the Marunouchi central business district for high-value corporate development. Even the fabled Tsukiji wholesale fish market, situated only a half mile from Ginza and in the shadow of the Shiodome skyscrapers, was relocated to the city's outskirts in order to make way for higher-valued land uses in the center of the city (Bestor 2004; Makino 2003) that looked increasingly toward an international corporate audience and less toward preserving tradition.

Tokyo's traditional neighborhoods were swept aside in the new global undertaking. The TMG announced Tokyo Plan 2000 to make the city a "Peerless International City" (TMG 2002, 21). The national Koizumi government sought to fast-track the "redevelopment of inner city sites into high-rise global space," allowing development authorities new leeway to sidestep "the protests of local residents and the sometimes extended processes of public consultation" (Sorensen 2003, 528). The result was a transformation of these areas and "the rapid loss of traditional townscapes" (Sorensen 2004, 334), Tokyo neighborhoods with narrow streets, small shops, and roofs slanted to the street to permit sunshine.

Roppongi Hills, in conjunction with similar mixed-use complexes that had been built nearby at ARK Hills and Izumi Garden, formed a concentration of megadevelopments that was designed to transform the Tokyo ward of Minato-ku, already a center of embassies and expatriate life, into "a magnet for the global business community" (Frederick 2003). At Roppongi Hills, English-speaking residents enjoyed a 24-hour bilingual concierge service and a Borders-type café and bookstore where half of the books are in English. Roppongi Hills, like other TMG-led entrepreneurial projects in southwestern Tokyo, resulted in new patterns of income stratification by *ku* (or ward), patterns that until recently were atypical of Japanese cities (Jacobs 2005). Japanese cities have tended to lack the degree of class stratification, and city-suburban social distance that characterizes U.S. communities. Japanese housing, land-use, and zoning policies have traditionally encouraged a mixing of social classes (Dimmer and Klinkers 2004; Fujita and Hill 1997). The new globally-oriented megadevelopments in Tokyo represent a relatively new and important exception, government-approved developments of exclusive living and work environments that violate the Japanese model of class mixing.

The transformation of Japanese cities continues. New urban forms emerge, and, in major cities, traditional urban patterns and neighborhoods are disappearing amid global influences and competitive pressures.

References

Ahlert, D., M. Blut, and H. Evanschitzky. 2006. Current status and future evolution of retail formats. In *Retailing in the 21st century: Current and future trends,* edited by M. Krafft and M. Mantrala, 289–308. Berlin: Springer.

Bestor, T. C. 2004. *Tsukiji: The fish market at the center of the world.* Berkeley: Univ. of California Press.

City of Kobe. 2004. Overview of Kobe. Retrieved January 9, 2006, from www.city.kobe.jp/cityoffice/17/020/en/outline.

Dimmer, C., and K. Klinkers. 2004. Downtown Tokyo revisited: Restructuring and urban renaissance. University of Tokyo, Department of Urban Engineering, Urban Design Lab.

Edgington, D. W. 1999. Firms, governments and innovation in the Chukyo region of Japan. *Urban Studies 36* (2): 305–339.

Frederick, J. 2003. TomorrowLand: Tycoon Minoru Mori wants to make Tokyo a more livable city. *Time-Asia,* August 4.

Fujita, K. 2003. Neo-industrial Tokyo: Urban development and globalization in Japan's state-centered developmental capitalism. *Urban Studies 40* (20): 249–281.

Fujita, K., and R. C. Hill. 1993. *Japanese cities in the world economy.* Philadelphia: Temple Univ. Press.

——. 1997. Together and equal: Place stratification in Osaka. In *The Japanese city,* edited by P. P. Karan and K. Stapleton, 106–133. Lexington: Univ. Press of Kentucky.

Gilman, T. J. 1997. Urban redevelopment in Omuta, Japan, and Flint, Michigan: A comparison. In *The Japanese city,* edited by P. P. Karan and K. Stapleton, 176–220. Lexington: Univ. Press of Kentucky.

Hein, C., and P. Pelletier, eds. 2006. *Cities, Autonomy and Decentralization in Japan.* Abingdon, UK: Routledge.

Hill, R. C., and K. Fujita. 2003. The nested city: Introduction. *Urban Studies 40* (2): 207–217.

Hill, R. C., and J. W. Kim. 2000. Global cities and developmental states: New York, Tokyo and Seoul. *Urban Studies, 37* (12): 2167–2195.

Hinrichsen, D. (2002). Kobe rises from the ashes. *PeopleandPlanet .net.* Retrieved January 9, 2006, from: www.peopleandplanet .net/doc.php?id=1799.

Jacobs, A. J. 2002. Integrated development planning, supportive public policies, and corporate commitment: A recipe for thriving major cities in Aichi, Japan. *Journal of Urban Affairs,* 24 (2): 175–196.

——. 2003a. Devolving authority and expanding autonomy in Japanese prefectures and municipalities. *Governance: An International Journal of Policy, Administration, and Institutions 16* (4): 601–623.

——. 2003b. Embedded autonomy and uneven metropolitan development: A comparison of the Detroit and Nagoya auto regions, 1969–2000. *Urban Studies, 40* (2): 335–360.

——. 2004. Federations of municipalities: A practical alternative to local government consolidations in Japan? *Governance: An International Journal of Policy, Administration, and Institutions,* 17 (2): 247–274.

———. 2005. Has central Tokyo experienced uneven development? An examination of Tokyo's 23 Ku relative to America's largest urban centers. *Journal of Urban Affairs, 27* (5): 521–555.

Jessop, B., and N.-L. Sum. 2000. An entrepreneurial city in action: Hong Kong's emerging strategies in and for (inter)urban competition. *Urban Studies, 37* (12): 2287–3313.

Kamo, T. 2000. An aftermath of globalisation? East Asian economic turmoil and Japanese cities adrift. *Urban Studies, 37* (12): 2245–2265.

Lathom, A. 2006. Anglophone urban studies and the European city: Some comments on interpreting Berlin. *European Urban and Regional Studies 13* (1): 88–92.

Makino, C. 2003. Eviction notice for tuna. *Christian Science Monitor.* December 10.

Muramatsu, M. 1997. *Local power in the Japanese state,* translated by B. Scheiner and J. White. Berkeley: Univ. of California Press.

Saito, A. 2003. Global city formation in a capitalist developmental state: Tokyo and the waterfront sub-centre project. *Urban Studies, 40* (2): 283–308.

———. 2004. Global city in developmental state: Urban restructuring in Tokyo.

Sorensen, A. 2003. Building world city Tokyo: Globalization and conflict over urban space. *Annals of Regional Science 37* (3): 519–531.

———. 2004. *The making of urban Japan: Cities and planning from Edo to the twenty-first century.* London: Routledge Japanese Studies Series.

Sorkin, M., ed. 1992. *Variations on a theme park: The new American city and the end of public space.* New York: Hill and Wang.

Takahashi, J., and N. Sugiura. 1995. The Japanese urban system and the growing centrality of Tokyo in the global economy. In *Emerging world cities in Pacific Asia,* edited by F-c. Lo and Y-m. Yeung, 101–143. Tokyo: United Nations Univ. Press.

Tiry, C. 2001. Stations help define urban image: Kyoto and Lille-Europe. *Japan Railway and Transport Review 28:* 18–21. Online at www.jrtr.net/jrtr28/f18_tir.html, retrieved January 2006.

Tokyo Metropolitan Government, Bureau of City Planning. 2002. *Planning of Tokyo.* Tokyo: TMG.

Yipu, Z. 2005. *Selling props, playing stars: Virtualising the self in the Japanese mediascape.* Doctoral dissertation, University of Western Sidney, Centre for Cultural Research. Available at http://library.uws.edu.au/adt-NUWS/uploads/approved/adt-NUWS20060210.104650/public/01Front.pdf, retrieved February 2006.

Critical Thinking

1. What was the goal of Japan's spatial planning policies during the half century that followed World War II? Just where did Japan seek to promote—and to limit—growth?

2. Why has Japan welcomed new mega-developments such as Tokyo's Roppongi Hills and the construction of a new Rainbow Town city subcenter? How do such projects represent Japan's response to globalization and a reversal of earlier spatial planning objectives?

3. Why did city leaders in Kyoto, the historical capital of Japan, push for the development of an ultra-modern rail station and shopping/hotel complex?

4. What is lost when Tokyo, Kyoto, and Fukuoka pursue globally-oriented developments?

Shanghai Gets Supersized

Boasting 200 skyscrapers, China's financial capital has grown like no other city on earth—and shows few signs of stopping.

DAVID DEVOSS WITH ADDITIONAL REPORTING BY LAUREN HILGERS

When building projects grew scarce in the United States a few years ago, the California architect Robert Steinberg opened an office in Shanghai. He says he didn't understand the city until the night he dined with some prospective clients. "I was trying to make polite conversation and started discussing some political controversy that seemed important at the time," he recalls. "One of the businessmen leaned over and said, 'We're from Shanghai. We care only about money. You want to talk politics, go to Beijing.'"

When I visited Steinberg's Shanghai office, he led me past cubicles packed with employees working late into the evening. "We talk acres in America; developers here think kilometers," he said. "It's as if this city is making up for all the decades lost to wars and political ideology."

Over the past decade or more, Shanghai has grown like no other city on the planet. Home to 13.3 million residents in 1990, the city now has some 23 million residents (to New York City's 8.1 million), with half a million newcomers each year. To handle the influx, developers are planning to build, among other developments, seven satellite cities on the fringes of Shanghai's 2,400 square miles. Shanghai opened its first subway line in 1995; today it has 11; by 2025, there will be 22. In 2004, the city also opened the world's first commercial high-speed magnetic levitation train line.

With more than 200 skyscrapers, Shanghai is a metroplex of terraced apartments separated by wide, tree-lined boulevards on which traffic zooms past in a cinematic blur. At the 1,381-foot-tall Jin Mao Tower, whose tiered, tapering segments recall a giant pagoda, there's a hotel swimming pool on the 57th floor, and a deck on the 88th floor offers a view of scores of spires poking through the clouds. I had to look up from there to see the top of the 101-story World Financial Center, which tapers like the blade of a putty knife. The Bank of China's glass-curtained tower seems to twist out of a metal sheath like a tube of lipstick.

The last time I'd been to Shanghai, in 1994, China's communist leaders were vowing to transform the city into "the head of the dragon" of new wealth by 2020. Now that projection seems a bit understated. Shanghai's gross domestic product grew by at least 10 percent a year for more than a decade until 2008, the year economic crises broke out around the globe, and it has grown only slightly less robustly since. The city has become the engine driving China's bursting-at-the-seams development, but it somehow seems even larger than that. As 19th-century London reflected the mercantile wealth of Britain's Industrial Revolution, and 20th-century New York showcased the United States as commercial and cultural powerhouse, Shanghai seems poised to symbolize the 21st century.

This is quite a transformation for a port whose name became synonymous with "abducted" after many a sailor awoke from the pleasures of shore leave to find himself pressed into duty aboard an unfamiliar ship. Shanghai lies on the Huangpu River, about 15 miles upstream from where the mighty Yangtze, the lifeblood of China's economy for centuries, empties into the East China Sea. In the middle of the 19th century, the Yangtze carried trade in tea, silk and ceramics, but the hottest commodity was opium. After defeating the Qing dynasty in the first Opium War (1839–42), the British extracted the rights to administer Shanghai and to import opium into China. It was a lucrative franchise: about one in ten Chinese was addicted to the drug.

Opium attracted a multitude of adventurers. American merchants began arriving in 1844; French, German and Japanese traders soon followed. Chinese residents' resentment of the Qing dynasty's weakness, stoked partially by the foreigners' privileged position, led to rebellions in 1853 and 1860. But the principal effect of the revolts was to drive half a million Chinese refugees into Shanghai; even the International Settlement, the zone where Westerners stayed, had a Chinese majority. By 1857 the opium business had grown fourfold.

The robust economy brought little cohesion to Shanghai's ethnic mix. The original walled part of the city remained Chinese. French residents formed their own concession and filled it with bistros and *boulangeries*. And the International Settlement remained an English-speaking oligarchy centered on a municipal racecourse, emporiums along Nanjing Road and Tudor and Edwardian mansions on Bubbling Well Road.

The center of old Shanghai was known as the Bund, a mile-long stretch of banks, insurance companies and trading houses on the western bank of the Huangpu. For more than a century, the Bund boasted the most famous skyline east of Suez. Bookended by the British consulate and the Shanghai Club, where foreign entrepreneurs sat ranked by their wealth along a 110-foot-long bar, the Bund's granite and marble buildings evoked Western power and permanence. A pair of bronze lions guarded the Hongkong and Shanghai Bank building. The bell tower atop the Customs House resembled Big Ben. Its clock, nicknamed "Big Ching," struck the Westminster chime on the quarter-hour.

Beneath the opulent façade, however, Shanghai was known for vice: not only opium, but also gambling and prostitution. Little changed after Sun Yat-sen's Republic of China supplanted the Qing dynasty in 1912. The Great World Amusement Center, a six-story complex packed with marriage brokers, magicians, earwax extractors, love-letter writers and casinos, was a favorite target of missionaries. "When I had entered the hot stream of humanity, there was no turning back had I wanted to," the Austrian-American film director Josef von Sternberg wrote of his visit in 1931. "The fifth floor featured girls whose dresses were slit to the armpits, a stuffed whale, story tellers, balloons, peep shows, masks, a mirror maze . . . and a temple filled with ferocious gods and joss sticks." Von Sternberg returned to Los Angeles and made *Shanghai Express* with Marlene Dietrich, whose character hisses: "It took more than one man to change my name to Shanghai Lily."

While the rest of the world suffered through the Great Depression, Shanghai—then the world's fifth-largest city—sailed blissfully along. "The decade from 1927 to 1937 was Shanghai's first golden age," says Xiong Yuezhi, a history professor at Fudan University in the city and editor of the 15-volume *Comprehensive History of Shanghai.* "You could do anything in Shanghai as long as you paid protection [money]." In 1935 *Fortune* magazine noted, "If, at any time during the Coolidge prosperity, you had taken your money out of American stocks and transferred it to Shanghai in the form of real estate investments, you would have trebled it in seven years."

At the same time, Communists were sparring with the nationalist Kuomintang for control of the city, and the Kuomintang allied themselves with a criminal syndicate called the Green Gang. The enmity between the two sides was so bitter they did not unite even to fight the Japanese when long-running tensions led to open warfare in 1937.

Once Mao Zedong and his Communists came to power in 1949, he and the leadership allowed Shanghai capitalism to limp along for almost a decade, confident that socialism would displace it. When it didn't, Mao appointed hard-line administrators who closed the city's universities, excoriated intellectuals and sent thousands of students to work on communal farms. The bronze lions were removed from the Hongkong and Shanghai Bank, and atop the Customs House, Big Ching rang in the day with the People's Republic anthem "The East Is Red."

The author Chen Danyan, 53, whose novel *Nine Lives* describes her childhood during the Cultural Revolution of the 1960s and '70s, remembers the day new textbooks were distributed in her literature class. "We were given pots full of mucilage made from rice flour and told to glue all the pages together that contained poetry," she says. "Poetry was not considered revolutionary."

I first visited Shanghai in 1979, three years after the Cultural Revolution ended. China's new leader, Deng Xiaoping, had opened the country to Western tourism. My tour group's first destination was a locomotive factory. As our bus rolled along streets filled with people wearing Mao jackets and riding Flying Pigeon bicycles, we could see grime on the mansions and bamboo laundry poles festooning the balconies of apartments that had been divided and then subdivided. Our hotel had no city map or concierge, so I consulted a 1937 guidebook, which recommended the Grand Marnier soufflé at Chez Revere, a French restaurant nearby.

Chez Revere had changed its name to the Red House, but the elderly maître d' boasted that it still served the best Grand Marnier soufflé in Shanghai. When I ordered it, there was an awkward pause, followed by a look of Gallic chagrin. "We will prepare the soufflé," he sighed, "but Monsieur must bring the Grand Marnier."

Shanghai today offers few reminders of the ideology that inspired the Cultural Revolution. After the city's Mao Museum closed in 2009, leftover statues of the Great Helmsman stood on a shuttered balcony like so many lawn jockeys. By contrast, many of Shanghai's precommunist buildings look almost new. The former villa of the Green Gang leader lives on as the Mansion Hotel, whose Art Deco lobby doubles as a memorial to the 1930s, filled with period furnishings and sepia photographs of rickshaw pullers unloading cargo off sampans. The reopened Great World Amusement Center provides a venue for Chinese opera, acrobats and folk dancers, though a few bars are allowed.

As for the Bund, it has been restored to its original Beaux-Arts grandeur. The Astor House, where plaques commemorate Ulysses S. Grant's post-presidential visit, and where Charlie Chaplin and Paulette Goddard were summoned to dinner by liveried butlers bearing golden trumpets, is once again receiving guests. Across Suzhou Creek, the Peace Hotel (known as the Cathay when Noel Coward wrote *Private Lives* there during a four-day bout with the flu in 1930) recently underwent a $73 million restoration. The Shanghai Pudong Development Bank now occupies the Hongkong and Shanghai Bank building. Bronze lions have returned to guard duty at the entrance.

With the Chinese well into their transition to what they call a "socialist market economy," it seems that they look upon the city not as an outlier, but as an example. "Every other city is copying Shanghai," says Francis Wang, a 33-year-old business reporter who was born here.

Shanghai's makeover began haphazardly—developers razed hundreds of tightly packed Chinese neighborhoods called *lilongs* that were accessed through distinctive stone portals called *shikumen*—but the municipal government eventually imposed limitations on what could be destroyed and built in its place. Formerly a two-block-long lilong, Xintiandi (New Heaven and

Earth) was torn down only to be rebuilt in its 19th-century form. Now the strip's chic restaurants such as TMSK serve Mongolian cheese with white truffle oil to well-heeled patrons amid the cyberpunk stylings of Chinese musicians.

Nobody arrives at Xintiandi on a Flying Pigeon, and Mao jackets have about as much appeal as whalebone corsets. "Shanghai is a melting pot of different cultures, so what sells here is different from other Chinese cities," says fashion designer Lu Kun, a Shanghai native who numbers Paris Hilton and Victoria Beckham among his clients. "No traditional cheongsams or mandarin collars here. Sexy, trendy clothes for confident, sophisticated women; that's Shanghai chic."

Xia Yuqian, a 33-year-old migrant from Tianjin, says she knows "lots of Shanghainese women who save all their money to buy a [hand] bag. I think it's strange. They want to show off to other people." But Xia, who moved to the city in 2006 to sell French wine, also relies on Shanghai's reputation for sophistication in her work. "When you go to other cities, they automatically think it's a top product," she says. "If you said you were based in Tianjin, it wouldn't have the same impact."

In Tian Zi Fang, a maze of narrow lanes off Taikang Road, century-old houses are now occupied by art studios, cafés and boutiques. The Cercle Sportif Français, a social club in the colonial era and a *pied-à-terre* for Mao during the communist regime, has been grafted onto the high-rise Okura Garden Hotel. "A decade ago this structure would have been destroyed, but now the municipal government realizes that old buildings are valuable," says Okura general manager Hajime Harada.

The old buildings are filled with new people: Nine million of Shanghai's 23 million residents migrated to the city. When I met with eight urban planners, sociologists and architects at the Municipal Planning, Land and Resources Administration, I asked how many of them had come from outside the city. They greeted the question with silence, sidelong glances and then laughter as seven of the eight raised their hands.

Pudong, the district Deng had in mind when he spoke of the enormous dragon of wealth, was 200 square miles of farmland 20 years ago; today, it is home to Shanghai's skyscraper district and the Shanghai Stock Exchange, which has daily trading volumes of more than $18 billion, ranking seventh worldwide. The jade-colored stone used for curbing around the Jin Mao Tower may strike an outsider as a bit much, but for Kathy Kaiyuan Xu, Pudong's excess is a source of pride. "You must remember that ours is the first generation in China never to know hunger," says the 45-year-old sales manager for a securities company. Because of China's policy of limiting urban married couples to one child, she said, "families have more disposable income than they ever thought possible."

Materialism, of course, comes with a cost. A collision of two subway trains this past September injured more than 200 riders and raised concerns over transit safety. Increased industry and car ownership haven't helped Shanghai's air; this past May, the city started posting air-quality reports on video screens in public places. Slightly less tangible than the smog is the social atmosphere. Liu Jian, a 32-year-old folk singer and writer from Henan Province, recalls when he came to the city in 2001. "One

of the first things I noticed was there was a man on a bicycle that came through my lane every night giving announcements: 'Tonight the weather is cold! Please be careful,'" he says. "I had never seen anything like it! It made me feel that people were watching out for me." That feeling is still there (as are the cycling announcers), but, he says, "young people don't know how to have fun. They just know how to work and earn money." Still, he adds, "there are so many people here that the city holds lots of opportunities. It's hard to leave."

Even today, Shanghai's runaway development, and the dislocation of residents in neighborhoods up for renewal, seems counterbalanced by a lingering social conservatism and tight family relationships. Wang, the business reporter, who is unmarried, considers herself unusually independent for renting her own apartment. But she also returns to her parents' house for dinner nightly. "I get my independence, but I also need my food!" she jokes. "But I pay a price for it. My parents scold me about marriage every night."

In a society where people received their housing through their state-controlled employers not so long ago, real estate has become a pressing concern. "If you want to get married, you have to buy a house," says Xia, the wine seller. "This adds a lot of pressure"—especially for men, she adds. "Women want to marry an apartment," says Wang. Even with the government now reining in prices, many can't afford to buy.

Zao Xuhua, a 49-year-old restaurant owner, moved to Pudong after his house in old Shanghai was slated for demolition in the 1990s. His commute increased from a few minutes to half an hour, he says, but then, his new house is modern and spacious. "Getting your house knocked down has a positive side," he says.

When Zao starts talking about his daughter, he pulls an iPhone out of his pocket to show me a photograph of a young woman in a Disney-themed baseball hat. He tells me she's 25 and living at home. "When she gets married, she'll get her own apartment," he says. "We'll help her, of course."

Shanghai's development has created opportunities, Zao says, but he has kept his life simple. He rises early each day to buy supplies for the restaurant; after work he cooks dinner for his wife and daughter before trundling off to bed. "Every once in a while I'll go around the corner to get a coffee at the Starbucks," he says. "Or I'll go out to karaoke with some of our employees."

For others, the pace of change has been more unnerving. "I joke with my friends that if you really want to make money in China, you should open a psychiatric hospital," says Liu, the singer. And yet, he adds, "I have many friends who are really thankful for this crazy era."

Chen Danyan, the novelist, says, "People look for peace in the place where they grew up. But I come home after three months away and everything seems different." She sighs. "Living in Shanghai is like being in a speeding car, unable to focus on all the images streaming past. All you can do is sit back and feel the wind in your face."

DAVID DEVOSS profiled Macau for *Smithsonian* in 2008. LAUREN HILGERS is a freelance writer living in Shanghai. New Jersey native.

Critical Thinking

1. How is Shanghai today different than it was during the long rule of Communist Party chairman Mao Zedong?

2. What steps has China taken to increase Shanghai's competitiveness as an economic center?

3. What have been the social and environmental costs of Shanghai's makeover?

From *Smithsonian*, November 2011. Copyright © 2011 by David DeVoss and the additional readings provided by Lauren Hilgers. Reprinted by permission of the authors.

To Catch Cairo Overflow, 2 Megacities Rise in Sand

THANASSIS CAMBANIS

The highway west out of Cairo used to promise relief from the city's chaos. Past the great pyramids of Giza and a final spasm of traffic, the open desert beckoned, 100 barren miles to the northwest to reach the Mediterranean.

That, at least, was the case until recently. Now, the microbus drivers and commuters driving from Cairo cross 20 miles of nothingness to encounter a new city suddenly springing from the sand. A distressingly familiar jam of cars and a cluster of soaring high-rises herald the metropolis that is designed to relieve pressure on the historic center of Cairo, which city planners have deemed overtaxed beyond repair.

Welcome to the new Cairo, not entirely different from the old one.

Cairo has become so crowded, congested and polluted that the Egyptian government has undertaken a construction project that might have given the Pharaohs pause: building two megacities outside Cairo from scratch. By 2020, planners expect the new satellite cities to house at least a quarter of Cairo's 20 million residents and many of the government agencies that now have headquarters in the city.

Only a country with a seemingly endless supply of open desert land—and an authoritarian government free to ignore public opinion—could contemplate such a gargantuan undertaking. The government already has moved a few thousand of the city's poorest residents against their will from illegal slums in central Cairo to housing projects on the periphery.

Few Egyptians seriously expect the government to demolish the makeshift neighborhoods that comprise as much as half the capital, although many critics accuse the government of transferring Cairo's historical inequalities to the new cities.

But on one point almost everyone seems to agree: it is too late to change course.

Enormous subdivisions have sprung up in the dunes outside of Cairo, on an almost incomprehensible scale. Already a million people have moved to 6 October City, due west of Cairo, named for the date of the 1973 war between Egypt and Israel still hailed as a seminal Arab victory. A similar number have moved east of the city, to a settlement unimaginatively dubbed "New Cairo."

The government's original plans—which are widely considered more wishful than literal—conceived of 6 October City's expanding to 3 million by 2020 and New Cairo to 4 million, primarily as havens for working-class Cairenes. So far, however, the overwhelming majority of new residents come from Egypt's uppermost economic strata.

"These settlements represent the greed of the rich," said Abdelhalim Ibrahim Abdelhalim, an architect known for incorporating historic Islamic aesthetics into his contemporary public buildings and parks. Mr. Abdelhalim designed the American University of Cairo's new eastern campus, but he no longer works on elite housing projects.

The Egyptian government has spent untallied millions of dollars building new roads and power and water lines to the desert areas it designated for future development. It has sold huge parcels of land to developers in opaque deals, and built some low-income housing. But it has relied primarily on private developers to put up the cities' more expensive villas and condos, as well as the malls and offices.

Some of the earliest arrivals in the new cities are affluent Egyptians like Nisrine Alkbeissi, 29, who chose suburban quality of life over urban convenience. "I was torn between staying in Cairo, close to everything, or moving out here," said Ms. Alkbeissi on a recent weekend at Dandy Mall, a rare public space in 6 October City, a patchwork of luxury compounds and lower-income housing complexes that still is a city in name only.

Her mother had already moved to a nearby gated compound with palm trees and a swimming pool.

"I chose the house with the garden," Ms. Alkbeissi said, her saucer-size gold filigree earrings flapping as she propped her two-year-old daughter on her lap.

She was hosting two friends who had driven 50 miles for coffee. A few years ago, they lived only a few miles apart but hours away when they factored in Cairo's legendarily snarled traffic.

Now they drive along the ring road from New Cairo in the east to 6 October City in the west, never once getting close enough even to spot the old city in the distance.

Other pioneers include some of the richest Cairenes, who buy villas on golf courses and in gated compounds. They have been joined by some of the poorest, drawn by factory and construction jobs, or to serve the rich. Other poor people are shuttled in against their will by the government to isolated tracts of row houses.

The juxtaposition of rich and poor highlights one of Mr. Abdelhalim's greatest concerns. The new cities, he says, tend to highlight Egypt's already striking imbalance between rich and poor, and could sow the seeds of future troubles.

Consider Haram City, the first affordable housing development here built by a private company. Phase 1 was just completed this summer, and 25,000 people have moved in. When it is complete in two years, Haram City will house 400,000 people—a single project with the population of Miami.

Although it was designed for lower-income workers, some of Haram City's first residents are indigent Cairenes who were displaced by a rockslide and moved to this distant development by the government. They complain that they are isolated, and that it costs them nearly as much to take the bus into the city as they can earn in a day's work.

"We're in the middle of nowhere. We can't work or live," complained Saber Abdel Hady, 31, who relocated three months ago to a 400-square-foot apartment in Haram City with his pregnant wife and two children. They used to inhabit a spacious but illegal dwelling in Cairo's Manshiet Nasser neighborhood.

He slaughters chickens for $6 a day, but commuting consumes half his wages, so he has stopped going. For now, he's living on borrowed money, and recently broke into a larger, uninhabited apartment where he plans to squat with his family.

Haram City was conceived as an affordable neighborhood for lower-middle-class professionals, but the government has bought hundreds of units and is filling them with some of Cairo's poorest inhabitants—importing the city's historic class tensions to the replacement 6 October City.

Piecemeal development has created short-term hiccups as well. The new development lacks a subway, sufficient jobs, schools and medical services. Businesses, however, are relocating to the new city and the government plans to put many of its ministries and service buildings there.

Greater Cairo needs 2 million new housing units within the next 10 years, said Omar Elhitamy, managing director of Orascom Housing Communities, Haram City's developer. That demand can be met only if private companies like Orascom create a sizable volume of new homes at low cost, he added.

"It's not charity, it's a longer-term vision," Mr. Elhitamy said. "The project has to provide quality of life."

He envisions 6 October City's sprawl eventually meeting Cairo's western edge, "like Dallas–Ft. Worth or the Twin Cities."

A few miles farther out in the desert is the extreme side of replacement Cairo: an exclusive golf course community called Allegria, already half built, and the planned luxury development of Westown, flanking the main highway from Cairo to Alexandria. Developers are building a replica of downtown Beirut, which will serve as an urban hub for all the gated communities and other developments proliferating in the desert.

Well-off Egyptians who have moved to the desert cities rave about their new suburban lifestyles.

"Cairo is hot and packed," said Noha Refaat Elfiky, 33, a market researcher who moved a year ago to Palm Park from Heliopolis, itself built as a leafy getaway from downtown Cairo in the 19th century, but now swallowed by the city. "There will be nothing lost and much gained as everybody moves out of the city."

Nevertheless, Ms. Elfiky still spends a night or two a week in her family apartment in Cairo. "Sometimes," she said, "I miss the smell of pollution."

Critical Thinking

1. Why has Egypt built giant new towns, virtual satellite cities, outside of Cairo?

2. Whom do the new towns primarily benefit?

3. Should government force the relocation of the poor from the central city of Cairo to new housing built in the satellite cities?

Demolishing Delhi: World Class City in the Making

AMITA BAVISKAR

As London gentrifies its way toward the 2012 Olympics, social cleansing and riverine renewal proceed in parallel but more brutal form in Delhi. In preparation for the Commonwealth Games in 2010 the city's slum dwellers are being bulldozed out to make room for shopping malls and expensive real estate. Amita Baviskar reports on a tale of (more than) two cities and the slums they destroy to recreate.

Banuwal Nagar was a dense cluster of about 1,500 homes, a closely-built beehive of brick and cement dwellings on a small square of land in north-west Delhi, India. Its residents were mostly masons, bricklayers and carpenters, labourers who came to the area in the early 1980s to build apartment blocks for middle-class families and stayed on. Women found work cleaning and cooking in the more affluent homes around them. Over time, as residents invested their savings into improving their homes, Banuwal Nagar acquired the settled look of a poor yet thriving community—it had shops and businesses; people rented out the upper floors of their houses to tenants. There were taps, toilets, and a neighbourhood temple. On the street in the afternoon, music blared from a radio, mechanics taking a break from repairing cycle-rickshaws smoked bidis and drank hot sweet tea, and children walked home from school. Many of the residents were members of the Nirman Mazdoor Panchayat Sangam (NMPS), a union of construction labourers, unusual for India where construction workers are largely unorganised.

In April 2006, Banuwal Nagar was demolished. There had been occasions in the past when eviction had been imminent, but somehow the threat had always passed. Local politicians provided patronage and protection in exchange for votes. Municipal officials could be persuaded to look the other way. The NMPS union would negotiate with the local administration. Squatters could even approach the courts and secure a temporary stay against eviction. Not this time. Eight bulldozers were driven up to the colony. Trucks arrived to take people away. With urgent haste, the residents of Banuwal Nagar tore down their own homes, trying to salvage as much as they could before the bulldozers razed everything to the ground. Iron rods, bricks, doors and window frames were dismantled. TV sets and sofas, pressure cookers and ceiling fans, were all bundled up. The sound of hammers and chisels, clouds of dust, filled the air.

There was no time for despair, no time for sorrow, only a desperate rush to escape whole, to get out before the bulldozers.

But where would people go? About two-thirds of homeowners could prove that they had been in Delhi before 1998. They were taken to Bawana, a desolate wasteland on the outskirts of the city designated as a resettlement site. In June's blazing heat, people shelter beneath makeshift roofs, without electricity or water. Children wander about aimlessly. Worst, for their parents, is the absence of work. There is no employment to be had in Bawana. Their old jobs are a three-hour commute away, too costly for most people to afford. Without work, families eat into their savings as they wait to be allotted plots of 12.5 sq. m. Those who need money urgently sell their entitlement to property brokers, many of them moonlighting government officials. Once, they might have squatted somewhere else in Delhi. Now, the crackdown on squatters makes that option impossible. They will probably leave the city.

One-third of home owners in Banuwal Nagar couldn't marshal the documentary evidence of eligibility. Their homes were demolished and they got nothing at all. Those who rented rooms in the neighbourhood were also left to fend for themselves. One can visit Bawana and meet the people who were resettled, but the rest simply melted away. No one seems to know where they went. They left no trace. What was once Banuwal Nagar is now the site of a shopping mall, with construction in full swing. Middle-class people glance around approvingly as they drive past, just as they watched from their rooftops as the modest homes of workers were dismantled. The slum was a nuisance, they say. It was dirty, congested and dangerous. Now we'll have clean roads and a nice place to shop.

Banuwal Nagar, Yamuna Pushta, Vikaspuri—every day another *jhuggi basti* (shanty settlement) in Delhi is demolished. Banuwal Nagar residents had it relatively easy; their union was able to intercede with the local administration and police and ensure that evictions occurred without physical violence. In other places, the police set fire to homes, beat up residents and prevented them from taking away their belongings before the fire and the bulldozers got to work. Young children have died in stampedes; adults have committed suicide from the shock and shame of losing everything they had. In 2000, more than three million people, a quarter of Delhi's population, lived in 1160 *jhuggi bastis* scattered across town. In the last five years, about half of these have been demolished and the same fate awaits the rest. The majority of those evicted have not been resettled. Even among those entitled to resettlement, there are many who have got nothing. The government says it has no more land to give. Yet demolitions continue apace.

The question of land lies squarely at the centre of the demolition drive. For decades, much of Delhi's land was owned by the central government which parcelled out chunks for planned development. The plans were fundamentally flawed, with a total mismatch between spatial allocations and projections of population and economic growth. There was virtually no planned low-income housing, forcing poor workers and migrant labourers to squat on public lands. Ironic that it was Delhi's Master Plan that gave birth to its evil twin: the city of slums. The policy of resettling these squatter *bastis* into 'proper' colonies—proper only because they were legal and not because they had improved living conditions, was fitfully followed and, over the years, most *bastis* acquired the patina of de facto legitimacy. Only during the Emergency (1975–77) when civil rights were suppressed by Indira Gandhi's government, was there a concerted attempt to clear the *bastis*. The democratic backlash to the Emergency's repressive regime meant that evictions were not politically feasible for the next two decades. However, while squatters were not forcibly evicted, they were not given secure tenure either. Ubiquitous yet illegal, the ambiguity of squatters' status gave rise to a flourishing economy of votes, rents and bribes that exploited and maintained their vulnerability.

In 1990, economic liberalisation hit India. Centrally planned land management was replaced by the neoliberal mantra of public–private partnership. In the case of Delhi, this translated into the government selling land acquired for 'public purpose' to private developers. With huge profits to be made from commercial development, the real estate market is booming. The land that squatters occupy now commands a premium. These are the new enclosures: what were once unclaimed spaces, vacant plots of land along railway tracks and by the Yamuna river that were settled and made habitable by squatters, are now ripe for redevelopment. Liminal lands that the urban poor could live on have now been incorporated into the profit economy.

The Yamuna riverfront was the locale for some of the most vicious evictions in 2004 and again in 2006. Tens of thousands of families were forcibly removed, the bulldozers advancing at midday when most people were at work, leaving infants and young children at home. The cleared river embankment is now to be the object of London Thames-style makeover, with parks and promenades, shopping malls and sports stadiums, concert halls and corporate offices. The project finds favour with Delhi's upper classes who dream of living in a 'world-class' city modelled after Singapore and Shanghai. The river is filthy. As it flows through Delhi, all the freshwater is taken out for drinking and replaced with untreated sewage and industrial effluent. Efforts to clean up the Yamuna have mainly taken the form of removing the poor who live along its banks. The river remains filthy, a sluggish stream of sewage for most of

the year. It is an unlikely site for world-class aspirations, yet this is where the facilities for the next Commonwealth Games in 2010 are being built.

For the visionaries of the world-class city, the Commonwealth Games are just the beginning. The Asian Games and even the Olympics may follow if Delhi is redeveloped as a tourist destination, a magnet for international conventions and sports events. However wildly optimistic these ambitions and shaky their foundations, they fit perfectly with the self-image of India's newly-confident consuming classes. The chief beneficiaries of economic liberalisation, bourgeois citizens want a city that matches their aspirations for gracious living. The good life is embodied in Singapore-style round-the-clock shopping and eating, in a climate-controlled and police-surveilled environment. This city-in-the-making has no place for the poor, regarded as the prime source of urban pollution and crime. Behind this economy of appearances lie mega-transfers of land and capital and labour; workers who make the city possible are banished out of sight. New apartheid-style segregation is fast becoming the norm.

The apartheid analogy is no exaggeration. Spatial segregation is produced as much by policies that treat the poor as second-class citizens, as by the newly-instituted market in real estate which has driven housing out of their reach. The Supreme Court of India has taken the lead in the process of selective disenfranchisement. Judges have remarked that the poor have no right to housing: resettling a squatter is like rewarding a pickpocket. By ignoring the absence of low-income housing, the judiciary has criminalised the very presence of the poor in the city. Evictions are justified as being in the public interest, as if the public does not include the poor and as if issues of shelter and livelihood are not public concerns. The courts have not only brushed aside representations from *basti*-dwellers, they have also penalised government officials for failing to demolish fast enough. In early 2006, the courts widened the scope of judicial activism to target illegal commercial construction and violations of building codes in affluent residential neighbourhoods too. But such was the outcry from all political parties that the government quickly passed a law to neutralise these court orders. However, the homes of the poor continue to be demolished while the government shrugs helplessly.

Despite their numbers, Delhi's poor don't make a dent in the city's politics. The absence of a collective identity or voice is in part the outcome of state strategies of regulating the poor. Having a cut-off date that determines who is eligible for resettlement is a highly effective technique for dividing the poor. Those who stand to gain a plot of land are loath to jeopardise their chances by resisting eviction. Tiny and distant though it is, this plot offers a secure foothold in the city. Those eligible for resettlement part ways from their neighbours and fellow-residents, cleaving communities into two. Many squatters in Delhi are also disenfranchised by ethnic and religious discrimination. Migrants from the eastern states of Bihar and Bengal, Muslims in particular, are told to go back to where they came from. Racial profiling as part of the war on terror has also become popular in Delhi. In the last decade, the spectre of Muslim terrorist infiltrators from Bangladesh has become a potent weapon to harass Bengali-speaking

Muslim migrants in the city. Above all, sedentarist metaphysics are at work, such that all poor migrants are seen as forever people out of place: Delhi is being overrun by 'these people'; why don't they go back to where they belong? Apocalyptic visions of urban anarchy and collapse are ranged alongside dreams of gleaming towers, clean streets and fast-moving cars. Utopia and dystopia merge to propose a future where the poor have no place in the city.

Delhi, Mumbai, Kolkata and many other Indian cities figure prominently in what Mike Davis describes as a 'planet of slums'. Slum clearances may give India's capital the appearance of a 'clean and green Delhi' but environmental activism has simply shifted the problem elsewhere. The poor live under worse conditions, denied work and shelter, struggling against greater insecurity and uncertainty. Is Davis right? Has the late-capitalist triage of humanity already taken place? Even as demolitions go on around me, I believe that Davis might be wrong in this case. Bourgeois Delhi's dreams of urban cleansing are fragile; ultimately they will collapse under the weight of their hubris. The city still needs the poor; it needs their labour, enterprise and ingenuity. The vegetable vendor and the rickshaw puller, the cook and the carpenter cannot be banished forever. If the urban centre is deprived of their presence, the centre itself will have to shift. The outskirts of Delhi, and the National Capital Region of which it is part, continue to witness phenomenal growth in the service economy and in sectors like construction. Older resettlement colonies already house thriving home-based industry. The city has grown to encompass these outlying areas so that they are no longer on the spatial or social periphery. This longer-term prospect offers little comfort to those who sleep hungry tonight because they couldn't find work. Yet, in their minds, the promise of cities as places to find freedom and prosperity persists. In those dreams lies hope.

Critical Thinking

1. Describe the conditions of the Banuwal Nagar squatter community that was torn down in 2006. To where were they moved? Were the lives of the poor made better or worse by the relocation?

2. Why do cities like Delhi turn to programs of slum demolition instead of providing basic services to slum residents?

3. What does the author mean when he states that "New apartheid-style segregation is fast becoming the norm"?

AMITA BAVISKAR researches the cultural politics of environment and development. She is the author of *In the Belly of the River: Tribal Conflicts over Development in the Narmada Valley* and has edited *Waterlines: The Penguin Book of River Writings*.

Reinventing Rio

The Dazzling but Tarnished Brazilian City Gets a Makeover as It Prepares for the 2014 World Cup and 2016 Olympic Games

ALAN RIDING

When it comes to Rio de Janeiro there is no avoiding the obvious. The city may be as famous for its *Carnaval,* soccer, flesh and fun as it is infamous for its hillside slums and organized crime. Yet its defining feature remains its breathtaking setting. No visitor can ever forget viewing the city from on high for the first time. Even natives—the Cariocas—stand in awe of its grandeur. How could I feel different? I, too, was born there. As a writer friend, Eric Nepomuceno, put it, "only Paris comes close to matching Rio in self-love."

Mountains rise to the east and west and protrude like giant knuckles from inside the city itself. Stretching to the north is a vast bay, which Portuguese navigators evidently thought was a river when they first sighted it in January 1502. Hence the name Rio de Janeiro (River of January). For centuries, ferries carried people and cargo to and from the city of Niterói on the bay's eastern shore; today a seven-mile-long bridge crosses the bay. And standing guard at its entrance is the 1,300-foot-high granite mound known as the Pão de Açúcar—the Sugar Loaf.

To the west, two long curving beaches—Copacabana and Ipanema-Leblon—run along the city's Atlantic shoreline, only to be interrupted by twin mountains, the Dois Irmãos, or the Two Brothers. Behind the beaches lies a glistening lagoon, Lagoa Rodrigo de Freitas, and the Botanical Gardens. From there, thick tropical forest reaches up into the Tijuca National Park, "every square inch filling in with foliage," as the American poet Elizabeth Bishop put it a half-century ago. And rising 2,300 feet out of this vegetation is still another peak, the Corcovado, or the Hunchback, crowned by the 125-foot-tall—including the pedestal—statue of Christ the Redeemer.

Then there are the less sublime areas. Rio's North Zone, which begins at the city center and sprawls for miles inland, resembles many cities in developing countries, with crowded highways, run-down factories, crumbling housing projects and many of Rio's more than 1,000 shantytowns, or *favelas,* as they're known. Anyone landing at Antônio Carlos Jobim International Airport (named after the late bossa nova composer) is confronted with this unexpected, dismaying sight as they go to their likely destinations in the South Zone of the city.

Then suddenly another Rio comes into view. The bayside highway curves around the city center before dipping into the majestic Aterro do Flamengo park and sweeping past the Sugar Loaf. It then enters the tunnel leading to Copacabana and the broad Avenida Atlántica, which stretches nearly three miles along the beach. A different route south passes under the Corcovado and reappears beside the Lagoa Rodrigo de Freitas, following its shores to Ipanema-Leblon. (That was my way home when I lived in Rio in the 1980s.)

The Atlantic beaches are the city's playgrounds, with sunbathers crowding near the waves and soccer and volleyball occupying much of the rest. The beaches are also strikingly heterogeneous: people of all income levels and colors mix comfortably, while women and men of every shape feel free to wear the skimpiest of swimsuits. Actors, journalists, lawyers and the like have their favorite meeting places at beachside cafés selling beer, sodas, coconut milk and snacks. There is even a corridor for cyclists and joggers.

Away from the sea, though, the Copacabana neighborhood looks run-down and its streets are often clogged with traffic. Even the more elegant Ipanema and Leblon, one beach but two neighborhoods, coexist with those hillside favelas, highlighting the gulf between Rio's rich and poor. During violent storms in April this year it was mainly residents of the favelas who died—251 in greater Rio—as a result of landslides. Favelas are also routinely blamed for drug-related violence and all-too-frequent muggings. With the pleasures of living in the beauteous South Zone, then, comes the need for security.

Farther west, beyond Leblon and a smaller beach called São Conrado, is a third Rio, Barra da Tijuca, with 11 miles of sand and no encroaching mountains. Forty years ago, it seemed an obvious place to accommodate Rio's growing middle class. But what was intended as a model urban development has become a soulless expanse of apartment blocks, highways, supermarkets and, yes, more favelas, including the one, Cidade de Deus, that gave its name to Fernando Meirelles' award-winning 2002 movie, *City of God*.

So, for all their devotion to "the marvelous city," as they call Rio, Cariocas know full well that their hometown has been in decline. The slide began 50 years ago when Brazil's capital moved to Brasília. For two centuries before then, Rio was the capital of finance and culture as well as politics. To the rest of the world, Rio was Brazil. But once politicians, civil servants and foreign diplomats moved to the new capital in 1960, São Paulo increasingly dominated the nation's economy. Even important oil fields off the coast of Rio brought little solace. The state government received a share of royalties, but no oil boom touched the city. Rio was stripped of its political identity but found no substitute. Many Brazilians no longer took it seriously: they went there to party, not to work.

"I'd call Rio a ship adrift," says Nélida Piñón, a Brazilian novelist. "We lost the capital and got nothing in return. Rio's narcissism was once a sign of its self-sufficiency. Now it's a sign of its insecurity."

Lately, Rio has even fallen behind the rest of Brazil. For the first time in its history, Brazil has enjoyed 16 years of good government, first under President Fernando Henrique Cardoso and now under President Luiz Inácio Lula da Silva, who is to leave office on January 1, 2011. And the result has been political stability, economic growth and new international prestige. But during much of this time, Rio—both the city and the state that carries its name—has been plagued by political infighting, incompetence and corruption. And it has paid the price in poor public services and mounting crime.

Yet, for all that, when I recently returned to Rio, I found many Cariocas full of optimism. The city looked much as it did a decade ago, but the future looked different. And with good reason. Last October, Rio was chosen to host the 2016 Summer Olympics, the first to be held in South America and, after Mexico City in 1968, only the second in Latin America. As if in one fell swoop, Cariocas recovered their self-esteem. Further, Lula's strong support for Rio's Olympic bid represented a vote of confidence from Brazil as a whole. And this commitment looks secure with either of the main candidates to succeed Lula in general elections on October 3—Dilma Rousseff, Lula's hand-picked nominee, and José Serra, the opposition challenger. Now, with federal and state governments pledging $11.6 billion in extra aid to prepare the city for the Olympics, Rio has a unique chance to repair itself.

"Barcelona is my inspiring muse," Eduardo Paes, the city's energetic young mayor, told me in his downtown office, referring to how the Catalan capital used the 1992 Summer Olympics to modernize its urban structures. "For us, the Olympics are not a panacea, but they will be a turning point, a beginning of the transformation." And he listed some upcoming events that will measure the city's progress: the Earth Summit in 2012, known as Rio+20, two decades after the city hosted the first Earth Summit; the soccer World Cup in 2014, which will take place across Brazil, with the final to be held in Rio's Maracanã stadium; and the city's 450th anniversary in 2015.

For the Olympics, at least, Rio need not start from scratch. Around 60 percent of the required sports installations were built for the 2007 Pan American Games, including the João Havelange Stadium for athletics; a swimming arena; and facilities for gymnastics, cycling, shooting and equestrian events. The Lagoa Rodrigo de Freitas will again be used for the rowing competitions and Copacabana for beach volleyball, while the marathon will have numerous scenic routes to choose from. The Rio Olympics Organizing Committee will have a budget of $2.8 billion to ensure every site is in good shape.

But because many competition venues will be a dozen or more miles from the new Olympic Village in Barra da Tijuca, transportation could become an Olympic-size headache. Barra today is linked to the city only by highways, one of which goes through a tunnel, the other over the Tijuca Mountains. While about half the athletes will compete in Barra itself, the rest must be transported to three other Olympic "zones," including the João Havelange Stadium. And the public has to get to Barra and the other key areas.

To pave the way, the organizing committee is counting on a $5 billion state and municipal investment in new highways, improvements to the railroad system and an extension of the subway. The federal government has also committed to modernize the airport by 2014, a long overdue upgrade.

Yet even if the Olympics are a triumph for Rio, and Brazil does unusually well in medals, there is always the morning after. What will happen to all those splendid sports installations after the closing ceremony on August 21, 2016? The experience of numerous Olympic cities, most recently Beijing, is hardly encouraging.

"We're very worried about having a legacy of white elephants," said Carlos Roberto Osório, the secretary general of the Brazilian Olympic Committee. "With the Pan American Games, there was no plan for their use after the games. The focus was on delivering the installations on time. Now we want to use everything that is built and we're also building lots of temporary installations."

Rio already has one embarrassing white elephant. Before leaving office in late 2008, César Maia, then the mayor, inaugurated a $220 million City of Music in Barra, designed by French architect Christian de Portzamparc. It is still not finished; work on its three concert halls has been held up by allegations of corruption in construction contracts. Now the new mayor has the unhappy task of completing his predecessor's prestige project.

At the same time, Paes is looking to finance his own pet project. As part of a plan to regenerate the shabby port area on the Baía de Guanabara, he commissioned Spanish architect Santiago Calatrava, renowned for his sculptural forms, to design a Museum of Tomorrow, which would focus on the environment and, hopefully, be ready for the 2012 Earth Summit. His initial designs were unveiled this past June.

New museums with bold architecture have long been an easy way of raising a city's profile. Rio's Modern Art Museum on the Aterro do Flamengo did that in the 1960s. Since the 1990s, Oscar Niemeyer's UFO-like Contemporary Art Museum in Niterói has been the main reason for tourists to cross the bay. And construction will soon begin on a new Museum of Image and Sound, designed by the New York-based firm Diller Scofidio + Renfro, on Copacabana's Avenida Atlántica.

Culture is the one area where Rio holds its own in its decades-old rivalry with São Paulo, its larger and far richer neighbor. São Paulo boasts the country's most important universities, newspapers, publishing houses, recording companies, theaters and concert halls. But Rio remains the cradle of creativity; Brazil's dominant television network, Globo, is headquartered in the city and employs a small army of writers, directors and actors for its ever-popular soap operas. Also, Globo's nightly news is beamed across Brazil from its studios in Rio. But more importantly, as "a city that releases extravagant freedoms," in Piñón's words, Rio inspires artists and writers.

And musicians, who play not only samba, choro and now funk, but also bossa nova, the sensual jazz-influenced rhythm that gained international fame with such hits as Antônio Carlos Jobim's "Girl from Ipanema." One evening, I joined a crowd celebrating the reopening of the three cramped nightspots in Copacabana—Little Club, Bottle and Baccarat—where the bossa nova was born in the late 1950s.

"Rio remains the creative heart of Brazilian music," said Chico Buarque, who has been one of the country's most admired singer-composers for over 40 years and is now also a best-selling novelist. São Paulo may have a wealthier audience, he says, "but Rio exports its music to São Paulo. The producers, writers and performers are here. Rio also imports music from the United States, from the Northeast, then makes it its own. Funk, for instance, becomes Brazilian when it is mixed with samba."

Popular music can be heard across the city, but the downtown neighborhood of Lapa is the new hot spot. In the 19th century, it was an elegant residential district reminiscent of New Orleans and, while its terraced houses have known better days, many have been converted into bars and dance halls where bands play samba and choro and the forró rhythms of northeastern Brazil. In the weeks before the pre-Lenten Carnaval, attention turns to Rio's escolas de samba, or samba "schools," which are, in fact, large neighborhood organizations. During Carnaval, the groups compete for the title of champion, taking turns to parade their dancers and colorful floats through a noisy and crowded stadium known as the Sambódromo.

Rio is also a magnet for writers. As a legacy of its years as the country's capital, the city is still home to the Brazilian Academy of Letters, which was founded in 1897 and

modeled on the Académie Française. Among its 40 immortels today are Piñón, the novelists Lygia Fagundes Telles, Rubem Fonseca and Paulo Coelho and the author of popular children's books, Ana Maria Machado. But even Fonseca's novels, which are set in Rio's underworld, rely on São Paulo for their readership.

Except for music, Cariocas are not great consumers of culture. Alcione Araújo, a playwright and lecturer, thinks he knows why. "In a city with these skies, beaches and mountains, it is a crime to lock people inside a theater," he said. And he might have added movie theaters and art galleries. Walter Moreira Salles Jr., who directed the award-winning movies Central Station and The Motorcycle Diaries, lives in Rio, but looks beyond the city for his audience. A painter friend of mine, Rubens Gerchman, who died in 2008, moved to São Paulo to be close to his market.

But Silvia Cintra, who has just opened a new gallery in Rio with her daughter Juliana, prefers to be close to her artists. "São Paulo has more money, but I think that 80 percent of Brazil's most important artists live and work in Rio," she said. "São Paulo treats art as a commodity, while the Carioca buys art because he loves it, because he has passion. Rio has space, oxygen, energy, everything vibrates. The artist can work, then go for a swim. You know, I have never felt as happy about Rio as now."

Cariocas have long accepted the hillside favelas as part of the landscape. Writing in Tristes Tropiques, French anthropologist Claude Lévi-Strauss described what he saw in 1935: "The poverty-stricken lived perched on hills in favelas where a population of blacks, dressed in tired rags, invented lively melodies on the guitar which, during carnaval, came down from the heights and invaded the city with them."

Today, although many of Rio's favelas still lack running water and other basic necessities, many have improved. Brick and concrete houses have replaced wooden shacks, and most communities have shops; many have schools. Until around 20 years ago, the favelas were relatively tranquil, thanks to the power of the bicheiros, godfather-like figures who run an illegal gambling racket known as the "animal game." Then the drug gangs moved in.

In the late 1980s, Colombian cocaine traffickers opened new routes to Europe through Brazil. Homegrown gangsters stepped in to supply the local market, much of it found among the young and wealthy of the South Zone. Soon, protected by heavy weapons, they set up their bases inside favelas.

The response of the state government, which is in charge of security, was largely ineffective. Police would carry out raids, engage in furious gun battles with traffickers—kill some, arrest others—then leave. With most drug gangs linked to one of three organized crime groups, Comando Vermelho (Red Command), Amigos dos Amigos (Friends of Friends) and Terceiro Comando Puro (Pure Third Command), favela residents were routinely terrorized by bloody turf wars.

The reputation of Rio's police was little better. Many were thought to be on the traffickers' payroll. A December 2009 report by the New York City-based Human Rights Watch accused police officers of routinely executing detainees they claimed had been killed resisting arrest. In some favelas, police have driven out the traffickers—only to set up their own protection rackets.

Fernando Gabeira is one politician with direct experience of urban warfare. In the late 1960s, having joined leftist guerrillas fighting Brazil's military dictatorship, he participated in kidnapping the American ambassador, Charles Burke Elbrick. Elbrick was released after he was swapped for political prisoners, while Gabeira was himself arrested and then freed in exchange for another kidnapped foreign diplomat. When Gabeira returned to Brazil after a decade in exile, he was no longer a militant revolutionary and soon won a seat in Congress representing the Green Party. Having narrowly lost in Rio's mayoral elections in 2008, he plans to challenge Sérgio Cabral's bid for re-election as state governor in October.

"The principal characteristic of the violence is not drugs, but the occupation of territory by armed gangs," Gabeira said over lunch, still dressed in beach clothes. "You have 600,000 to 1 million people living in favelas outside the control of the government. And this is the state government's responsibility." Like many experts, he rejects the automatic link between poverty and violence. "My view is that we should combine social action and technology," he said. "I suggested we use drones to keep an eye on the traffickers. I was laughed at until they shot down a police helicopter."

The downing of the helicopter last October took place just two weeks after the city was chosen to host the 2016 Olympics, following Governor Cabral's assurances to the International Olympic Committee that army and police reinforcements would guarantee the security of athletes and the public. After the helicopter was shot down, Cabral threw his weight behind a new strategy designed by the state's security secretary, José Beltrame.

Starting in the South Zone, Cabral ordered the state government to establish a permanent police presence—so-called Police Pacification Units—in some favelas. After police were met by gunfire, they began a policy of leaking to the media which favela they would next target, giving traffickers time to leave and, it soon transpired, to invade favelas farther inland.

One morning I visited Pavão, Pavãozinho and Cantagalo, a three-community favela overlooking Copacabana and Ipanema, which has been peaceful since this past December. First settled a century ago, the favela has a population estimated at 10,000 to 15,000. A cable car built in the 1980s takes residents up the slope and returns with garbage in cans. It has a primary school, running water and some drainage. For years, it was also a drug stronghold. "There were constant gun battles," recalled Kátia Loureiro, an urban planner and financial director of a community organization called Museu de Favela. "There were times when we all had to lie on the floor."

Today, heavily armed police stand at the favela's entrance, while others patrol its narrow alleys and steep steps. After visiting the local school and a boxing club, I came across the Museu de Favela, which was founded two years ago to empower favela residents to develop their community and improve living conditions. Even during the bad times, it organized courses to train cooks, waiters, seamstresses, craftsmen and artists. Now it offers tours of its "museum," which is what it calls the entire favela. Says the group's executive director, Márcia Souza: "The idea is, 'My house is in the favela, so I am part of the museum.'"

My visit began with a rooftop performance by Acme, the stage name of a local rapper and Museu founder. "We don't need more cops," he told me, "we need more culture, more rap, more graffiti, more dance." The Museu sees social exclusion, not violence, as the problem in the favelas.

I took the cable car up to the home of Antônia Ferreira Santos, who was selling local handicrafts. She showed me her rooftop garden of herbs and medicinal plants. My final stop was at a little square where 11 boys and 5 girls of the local samba school were practicing drumming. With Carnaval only two weeks away, there was no time to waste.

Just how many of the city's roughly 1,000 favelas can be "pacified" by 2016 is unclear. Of course if Rio is to fully exploit its potential as a tourist destination, it must do more. It needs an up-to-date airport, better transportation and greater overall security, as well as new hotels and easier access to popular sites like the Corcovado.

One man who believes in getting things done is the city's new cheerleader, Eike Batista, an oil and mining magnate and reputedly Brazil's wealthiest man. After working mainly abroad for years, he returned home in 2000 and, unusually for a Brazilian industrialist, chose to live in Rio rather than São Paulo. "I said at the time, 'I'm going to spend my millions to fix this city,'" he recounted when I called on him at his home overlooking the Botanical Gardens. In a city with little tradition of individual philanthropy, he started by spending $15 million to help clean the lagoon.

In 2008, Batista bought the once-elegant Hotel Glória, which is now undergoing a $100 million makeover. He then acquired the nearby Marina da Glória, a port for leisure boats, and is modernizing it at a cost of $75 million. He is putting up two-thirds of the estimated $60 million it will take to build a branch of a top-flight São Paulo hospital and has invested $20 million in movie productions in Rio. Over a dinner with Madonna last November, he committed $7 million for her children's charity. He even built his own Chinese restaurant a mile from his home. "It's difficult to fly to New York once a week to eat well," he said with a laugh.

So, yes, things are stirring in Rio. Plans and promises are in the air, objectives are being defined and, thanks to the Olympics, a deadline looms to focus the mind. True, not all Cariocas support the Rio Olympics: they fear that massive public works will bring massive corruption. But the countdown has begun and Cariocas have six years to prove they can change their city for the better. When the Olympic flame is lit in Maracanã on August 5, 2016, a verdict will be returned. Only then will they know if the entire exercise was worthwhile.

Critical Thinking

1. How does Rio illustrate the urban dualism—the side-by-side existence of the rich and the poor—that characterizes major cities in Lesser Developed Countries?

2. How do Rio's hillside *favelas* defy many of the stereotypes of squatter communities?

3. What do social activists fear will be Brazil's response to the favelas as the country prepares to host the Olympic Games?

ALAN RIDING was the Brazil bureau chief for *The New York Times*. He now lives in Paris.

From *Smithsonian*, September 2010. Copyright © 2010 by Alan Riding. Reprinted by permission of Alan Riding.

No Excuses Slum Upgrading

In fast-urbanizing planet, São Paulo develops model toolkit to improve housing for poor, dispossessed.

FERNANDO SERPONE BUENO AND VERIDIANA SEDEH

Seventh largest among the world's metropolises and the linchpin of Brazil's booming economy, São Paulo presents a globally relevant case study of stepped-up efforts—but continued deep challenges—if cities are to correct the deep poverty and environmental perils of massive slum settlements.

Close to a third of São Paulo's 11 million people—in a metropolitan region of almost 20 million—live in slum-like conditions. There are some 1,600 favelas (private or public lands that began as squatter settlements), 1,100 "irregular" land subdivisions (developed without legally recognized land titles), and 1,900 cortiços (tenement houses, usually overcrowded and in precarious state of repair).

Government response has progressed light years from the brutal "eradication"—bulldozing of favelas—that began with Brazil's military dictatorship of the 1960s and continued for years as millions of rural families poured into São Paulo seeking industrial jobs. Today policy makers recognize that upgrading is a far wiser course—socially, economically and politically.

But the environment complicates the task: São Paulo has a monsoon-influenced humid subtropical climate with steep hillsides that create severe drainage problems, especially when storm water flows through sewerless slums, picking up loose debris that clogs drainage channels and can imperil local drinking water supplies. Environmental laws were passed in the 1980s to protect watersheds from construction projects—but settlements sprang up there anyway.

A Toolkit for Action— but Key Questions

Official Brazilian policy shifted in the 1980s toward slum upgrading instead of its eradication—recognizing it's easier and cheaper, not to mention more humane, to improve the conditions in a slum rather than try to remove it. But the new policy lacked much weight until the federal enactment, in 2001, of a "City Statute" requiring that cities enact master plans. It

also provided a set of tools that municipalities can use to control land transfer and seek to assure legal tenure for tenants—a process São Paulo formally integrated into its own master plan a year later. One of the most useful tools is letting cities create "zones of special interest" for disorganized slums, formally recognizing their existence and qualifying them for social services. Another tool authorizes joint citizen-government management councils both in new and more settled areas.

Moving to more legal tenure, experts on Brazilian slum upgrading suggest, requires three elements to be workable. First, is the location OK for human settlement—not a water pollution risk because its location is too steep or on a flood plain? Second, is the settlement legally registered, or at least in the database of city properties? And third, do its residents have legal title to the land? And if not, what can be done to assure them secure tenure?

There are clear rewards if a full process of regularization—providing clear legal tenure—can be achieved. If families can have their land title confirmed, or at least secure a certificate recognizing their occupancy rights, some taxes can be levied. Rules can be set (and enforced) to prevent building collapse. Regular streets, schools and clinics can be brought in, attracting investment. And it's easier to reduce litter by organizing residents to bring their own household waste to collection points for city pick-up.

But going the whole way continues to be difficult. While the city government works hard to give land tenure, property rights are only conceded by law once this possession is recorded in a register office. According to Nelson Saule, an Instituto Pólis lawyer, the complete process has occurred only with a few properties. In most cases dwellers received a document without clear legal value.

Allies Make a Difference

São Paulo government has clearly become more activist and attuned to long-term slum upgrading in recent years. It's also been aided since 2001 by Cities Alliance, a global alliance of national and city governments, UN-Habitat and the World Bank, focused on scaling up urban poverty solutions.

The São Paulo Municipal Housing Secretariat in 2006 created a management information system that's now able to track the status of favelas, other precarious settlements and site/flooding/water hazard areas citywide. With a priority of serving the city's most vulnerable populations, the tracking (developed in technical cooperation with Cities Alliance) provides a basis for effective targeting of upgrading efforts and environmental clean-ups. Before the system was implemented, notes Elisabete França, São Paulo's secretary of low-income housing, "data about our favelas and irregular private land subdivisions was unreliable, not reflecting the reality of these precarious settlements. The input of the new system resulted from a big field campaign, performed by our own technical staff in record time. The effort showed how people are as important as hardware and software. Now we can follow the dynamics of urban settlement. It is a new culture."

In 2008, São Paulo and Cities Alliance invited high-ranking officials from five other major cities—Cairo, Lagos, Manila, Mumbai and Ekurhuleni (South Africa)—to convene in São Paulo, examine its efforts, and discuss the broad challenges of slum upgrading. "The passion of São Paulo's technical staff in the slum upgrading process was clear for all to see," Godfrey Hiliza of the Ekurhuleni delegation noted at the end of the sessions.

Challenges

Still, São Paulo's reforms haven't come easily. Brazil's legal steps to establish clear land title are murky, unreformed nationally because of powerful rural land-holding interests fearing loss to squatters on their properties. Other pitfalls and barriers have included the high cost of land for building new housing, millions of families' lack of any credit history, and urban crime compounded by Brazil's notorious drug gangs.

And while the flow of new families from the countryside has subsided dramatically in recent years, São Paulo's deep social divisions and tenacious poverty, stemming from the late 20th century's immense in-migration of poor rural families remain. Still, the city claims that the housing issue in São Paulo can be "solved" by 2025 at current rates of city budget expenditure.

Islands of Progress

One example that inspires hope that São Paulo's slum upgrading works is Paraisopolis (literally Paradise City), São Paulo's second biggest slum, with 60,000 people. Residents express a strong desire to stay, not be relocated, says Violêta Kubrusly, senior technical adviser at the Municipality of São Paulo Social Housing Department. Upgrading solutions are working

and the city's long-term goals have shifted from 50 percent removal of the neighborhood's population to just 10 percent (those in risky areas like sharp slopes or drainage facilities).

One of São Paulo's goals is to bring electricity, sewage and clean water services to as many areas as it can afford. It is also seeking to enable "domicile swaps" so that the shack occupied by a family moving to a government-built apartment can be made available to a family living in a crowded, dangerous slum area.

There's a strong plus in Paraisopolis' location next to a high-income neighborhood that provides easy access to jobs (such as maid or watchman work).

Citywide, São Paulo is consciously seeking to recycle city areas left by relocated families into such common spaces as parks, playgrounds, soccer fields and skate parks—ways to help people socialize and build a sense of citizenship for remaining residents. With luck, community leadership emerges.

For example, the Jardim Iporanga neighborhood is located in a protected watershed with a stream that feeds São Paulo's main water reservoir. Before slum upgrading, the neighborhood's scattered housing without sewage treatment had been causing pollution. Then, following the environmentally-attuned upgrading, one resident constructed a house on the newly-protected space. But he quickly heard from Sandra Regina, the community's association president, that he was threatening the common good. He agreed to demolish his structure.

"Nowadays it's paradise here," Regina says. "There is clean, treated water, while before it was all sewage." The main need now, she says, is jobs—indeed across São Paulo, income generation is seen as a main challenge to a successful urbanization process. And there are some conscious job-creation efforts, with citizen groups playing a key role. In Jardim Iporanga, for instance, 30 women produce "eco-bags" made of recycled rags; they are mostly sold to the city government which uses them for booklets at seminars and congresses.

Key to Success: A Voice for the Community

There's growing agreement in São Paulo that local communities must themselves take part in the upgrading process, with a community leader acting as a mediator between the local residents and the government. Social worker Rosana Aparício says this mediation is crucial for slum upgrading to be successful.

Anaclaudia Rossbach, Cities Alliance regional advisor for Latin America and the Caribbean, reckons that to have a complete slum upgrading process, social work with the communities should continue after the construction and urbanization process is fully implemented.

There is a question: the array of housing and environmental cleanup policies in slum upgrading demand large investments. The outlays have been rising progressively over the past five years, thanks to combined efforts of federal, state and city governments, as well as contributions from international organizations.

But will they endure politically—through one or more changes of municipal administration? Rossbach believes the answer is yes. And why? Because, she insists, there's a Municipal Housing Council, created by the city in 2002, which acts as a watchdog and also has a direct role in deciding how housing fund moneys will be spent. Its members come from government agencies, unions, from socially attuned non-government organizations and from the universities. They're popularly elected in polls open to all São Paulo citizens. "The council helps to guarantee the policies' continuity," she notes.

Critical Thinking

1. What polices can a government adopt as an alternative to slum eradication and bulldozing?

2. What are the benefits of regularization, of providing squatters with a legal right to live in their housing?

3. What municipal services need to be provided and improved under a strategy of slum upgrading?

Femicide in Ciudad Juárez: *What Can Planners Do?*

MARÍA TERESA VÁZQUEZ-CASTILLO

Femicide is a word whose definition women in Ciudad Juárez can explain very well. They learned and appropriated the word in the process of trying to make sense of the more than 400 murders of women that have taken place in this Mexican border city since 1993. In the last thirteen years, mothers, friends, activists, students, academics and other sectors inside and outside Ciudad Juárez have organized what is now an international movement of women. Their main concerns have been to find the murderers and to claim justice, to find *who* is committing these heinous crimes against women. This article, however, urges progressive planners to focus on *what* needs to be done to stop the femicide in Ciudad Juárez. In this fast-growing region characterized by uneven urbanization processes, the *maquiladora* industry, the narco-economy and corrupt police, women's lives are endangered as they move through unsafe public space that lacks protective urban infrastructure.

Many different hypotheses have emerged about the femicide. Public officials have been appointed to "investigate" the cases, only to then be removed. None of these public officials was awarded decision-making power to act or prosecute. Researchers and journalists have even denounced and publicized the names of the culprits supposedly involved in the femicide, but the Mexican government has neither taken any legal action nor initiated a serious investigation. After thirteen years the gender violence continues, and it is now spreading to other urban areas, such as Chihuahua City.

Meanwhile, some people are in jail, accused of being the murderers even though they claim they are innocent. The mothers of the victims have denounced that some of those in jail are scapegoats, there to placate the public's outrage. Yet even with these people behind bars, the murders have continued. Two lawyers of the jailed have been killed and the lives of two journalists who have written books about the femicide in Juárez—*Huesos en el Desierto* (*Bones in the Desert*) and *Harvest of Women*—have been threatened, too. One of them was even kidnapped, severely beaten and hospitalized for several months.

In order to understand this femicide, it must be put in the context of the characteristics of the city, the urbanization that has taken place here, the profile of the women who've been murdered, and the responses that have emerged both to protest the femicide and to claim justice.

Ciudad Juárez

Ciudad Juárez is a border city of approximately 1.3 million inhabitants located across from El Paso, Texas. About 60 percent of the population is immigrants who are unable to cross the border into the United States and therefore stay in Ciudad Juárez. The city has become one of the fastest growing in Mexico, not only because of the immigration, but also because of the investment made here. In the 1960s the Border Industrialization Program started promoting assembly plants, or *maquiladoras*. In 1992, with the passage of the North American Free Trade Agreement (NAFTA), favorable conditions for foreign capital permitted the siting of further *maquiladoras*. According to the *Instituto de Estadística, Geografía e Informática* (INEGI), by 2000, about 308 *maquiladoras* employing 250,000 workers existed in Ciudad Juárez. Many of those employed are single young women migrating from other states. Sexist men in border states who resent the increasing presence of working females in public spaces call these women *maquilocas*, meaning flirtatious women who work in *maquiladoras*.

Race and Class of the Femicide

It is not difficult to infer the class and racial implications of the atrocious murders of the more than 400 women who have been reported kidnapped, raped, tortured, mutilated and killed. The murderers have been killing only young working-class women of a certain profile: short and thin with long, dark hair and brown skin. The victims have been between fifteen to thirty-nine years old, and many were originally from other Mexican states.

While the murderers enjoy impunity, public officials and the local police have accused the victims of being prostitutes, of leading double lives and of being the provokers of the assaults. The records, however, show that many of the victims were *maquiladora* workers, while others were students, housewives or workers in another economic sector.

Roles of the Urbanization, *Maquiladoras*, and the Narco-Economy

Many explanations for the femicide have been advanced. From a planning perspective, it is important to understand the urbanization of Ciudad Juárez and the roles of the *maquiladora* industry and the criminal economy. First, as new waves of immigrants, attracted by the possibility of crossing the border and by the jobs available in the *maquiladora* industry, have arrived in Ciudad Juárez, the pressures on housing and urban services have increased. As has been the case in other Mexican and Latin American cities, the new arrivals tended to relocate to the edge of city, where land was cheaper but infrastructure and urban services were lacking. The layout of Ciudad Juárez is sprawling, and many of the women kidnapped and murdered either lived in the "new" settlements on the edges of the city or their bodies were found in these newly urbanized areas.

The murderers have attacked women who are most vulnerable in the urban space of Ciudad Juárez—those who use public transportation, who do not have a car and who, in many cases, walk long distances in order to take a bus or a collective taxi. Thus, the rapid urbanization process prompted by the relocation of global capital to the border area has created an unsafe city that lacks urban infrastructure, some of the most important of which are affordable housing, appropriate transportation and public lighting.

Impunity in the city is rampant in this border area that is now known as one of the most dangerous cities for women. The criminal narco-economy has free rein and has taken the lives of both men and women in the region. Some of the names denounced as possible culprits have been identified as men belonging to the high society of Ciudad Juárez and to the business and economic elites in the region. In addition, some local journalists affirm that those potential murderers might be linked to the criminal economy in the area.

A Planning Point of View

From a gendered planning perspective, the built environment of this city contributes to the violation of human rights. You might ask: How can a city reproduce human rights violations of young low-income women? I recently saw the answer in one of the latest European documentaries about the murders in Ciudad Juárez. In this film, the filmmaker follows the routine of a young woman from the time she leaves home to the time she comes back home from work. The woman leaves home late at night to go to her job in the *maquiladora*. *Maquiladoras* have different shifts and her shift starts at midnight. In order to catch the bus, she needs to walk in the dark, with no sidewalks or streetlights to guide her way. She carries a flashlight to see where she is walking. Like many other people who go to Ciudad Juárez either looking for a job in the *maquiladoras* or trying to cross the border, this young woman lives in the informal settlements of Ciudad Juárez, many of which lack access to urban services. This lack of urban services has a gender component, that of not providing safety to women in Ciudad Juárez.

The work of the mothers, relatives, activists, academics, students and other men and women in the region and around the world has created a growing global movement of women protesting the femicide in Juárez. At the local level, the light posts in Ciudad Juárez, painted in pink with a black cross in the middle, serve as memorials for the murdered women. In some cases, those post have the legend: ¡iNi Una Más! Not one more!

Big crosses have been planted around the city as if the city itself had become a huge cemetery as well as a huge memorial site for the murdered women. In addition to crosses, the residents of Juárez witness the visits of women from around the globe who travel to take back the streets and participate in international demonstrations in Ciudad Juárez. In 2004, the US portion of a demonstration gathered in El Paso, Texas, the twin city of Ciudad Juárez, and marched, crossing the border to meet the women in Ciudad Juárez.

Different local and bi-national organizations have emerged to respond to the femicide. Some have survived the threats, intimidation and lack of resources for many years, while others have not. These organizations include: Justicia para Nuestras Hijas (Justice for Our Daughters); Nuestras Hijas de Regreso a Casa (Our Daughter Come Back Home); Comité Independiente de Derechos Humanos de Chihuahua (Independent Committee for Human Rights in Chihuahua); Casa Amiga (Friendly House); Amigos de las Mujeres de Juárez (Friends of the Women of Juárez); El Paso Coalition Against Violence on Women and Children at the Border; and other human rights organizations and NGOs.

These groups have organized conferences and meetings and presented two films about the femicide: *Señorita Extraviada* or *Missing Young Woman* (Lourdes Portillo) and *La Batalla de las Cruces* (Patricia Ravelo). The Mexico Solidarity Network organizes groups in the United States to periodically visit the mothers of the victims and learn about Juárez so as to serve as constant witness to the violence.

What Remains to Be Done?

The question always remains for progressive planners and planning academics as to what needs to be done by different social actors in the city and in the world to stop this femicide and to make both private and public spaces safer for the women of Juárez. The response needs to be informed by the twelfth demand of the Resolutions of the International Conference on the Killings of Women of Juárez hosted by the Chicano Studies Department at UCLA on November 1, 2003. The mothers and activists who attended the conference wrote these resolutions, the twelfth demand of which reads:

> 12. We demand that the government of Ciudad Juárez, its planning entities and major employers in the region work jointly to provide the necessary infrastructure that will make Ciudad Juárez a safer place for everybody, in which women can have the freedom of movement, as any other human being, without fearing for their lives and their safety.

After the failure of the political and legal entities to bring justice to the murders of the women of Juárez, women participating in this transnational and international women's movement have started pointing out some solutions, very basic in appearance: adequate street lighting, transportation provided for the *maquiladora* workers and affordable housing close to jobs. These solutions target the provision of safer urban infrastructure. This war against women is affecting all residents of the city as the impact of the tragedy has resulted in the disintegration of families, the departure of families from Juárez and, in some cases, the suicide of men close to the victims.

The call then is for progressive planners to get involved and support the women of Juárez. Through a participatory approach, and in conjunction with different community organizations inside and outside Juárez, progressive planners could help develop a city plan from the grassroots, a plan that includes elements to be implemented at both the individual and group levels in order to end the violence. This is a call for Planners Network to establish a relationship with the groups supporting the movement of the Women of Juárez in order to jointly organize a bilateral/international meeting to work out a grassroots plan for Ciudad Juárez. This plan, the purpose of which would be to make Juárez a safer city and to stop the femicide and the terror, could effectively be carried out by grassroots organizations and civil society actors in Juárez.

Conclusion

Roads, housing and other urban services are not in place to support the labor force that has emerged as a result of the infusion of global capital in the form of the *maquiladoras*. Therefore, men and women working in the *maquiladoras* look for shelter in areas that were previously undeveloped, but these areas lack services. Globalization, which has manifested itself in the movement of firms to other countries, has prompted an unplanned urbanization in Mexico for which the planning offices have not made the *maquiladoras* accountable. I am not saying

that we need to take away our eyes from the murderers, but I am saying that, in addition to finding *who* is responsible, we need to think about *what* can be done to create an infrastructure that makes Ciudad Juárez a safer city for all women and men. Although new infrastructure, an improved urban form and community development will not stop the femicide, these are powerful tools for creating safer urban spaces. In addition, women and men in Ciudad Juárez deserve a democratic, grassroots planning process led by their voices and their demands.

For socially responsible planners, to ignore the femicide in Ciudad Juárez is to ignore justice in cities, especially now that the femicide has spread to other countries like Guatemala, El Salvador and Honduras. These countries have also opened their doors to the *maquiladoras,* and the women murdered have been mostly indigenous women.

Critical Thinking

1. What is a *maquiladora*? What factors led to the growth of *maquiladoras*?

2. Why do you think that women make up the vast majority of the workforce in the *maquiladoras*?

3. How has the physical layout of work sites and housing in Ciudad Juárez and the operations of the *maquiladoras* added to the physical jeopardy faced by young women?

4. What can cities do to meet the needs of women, especially poor women? Why has the response of Juárez been far, far less than adequate?

MARÍA TERESA VÁZQUEZ-CASTILLO is an assistant professor in the Department of Urban Studies and Planning at California State University-Northridge.

UNIT 11

The Future of Cities and Suburbs: The United States and the World

Unit Selections

Learning Outcomes

After reading this unit, you should be able to:

- Identify the various policy steps that nations in Europe have taken in an effort to reduce automobile usage and to promote biking and mass transit.

- Explain which of the European urban policies have the best chance of being transferred to the United States and which of the strategies would be virtually impossible to adopt in the United States.

- Identify the "hidden urban policy" of the United States, its various programs and policies that have served to promote automobile use and suburban sprawled development.

- Detail the actions that Japan has begun to initiate as part of the nation's effort to turn away from nuclear energy in the wake of the Fukushima tsunami and reactor crisis.

- Identify the possible costs to cities of a national policy that spurns nuclear energy.

Student Website
www.mhhe.com/cls

Internet References

The Atlantic: Cities
    www.theatlanticcities.com
Livable Cities
    www.livablecities.org
Urban Visions: The Future of Cities
    www.scientificamerican.com/report.cfm?id=future-cities
Planetizen
    www.planetizen.com
Planum
    www.planum.net
United Nations Human Settlements Programme
    www.unhabitat.org

How well will cities and suburbs of the future be able to respond to the problems they will face? In the previous unit, we focused on the ability of LDCs to meet the human needs found in rapidly growing megacities. In this unit, we will give primary attention to matters related to sustainable development. Will cities be able to pursue policies of economic growth that also respect energy constraints and the natural environment?

A comparison of the United States and Europe reveals the importance of public policy, the choices that governments make. Compared to the United States, metropolitan areas in Europe are more compact with less sprawl. European cities are also less reliant on the automobile. European urban areas are also less stratified by social class than are communities in the United States.

These differences are not merely the result of historical accident; they are magnified by public policies. The United States provides extensive tax subsidies for the purchase of single-family homes and, hence, for suburban growth. In Europe, such extensive tax breaks and subsidies for homeowners are not available. Instead, European countries put greater emphasis on rail-focused development, providing more reliable mass transit, establishing pedestrian zones, and enacting various disincentives to the use of the automobile (Article 51, "Across Europe, Irking Drivers Is Urban Policy").

A number of U.S. cities have begun to take steps, similar to those seen in Europe, to make urban communities more livable. Portland, Oregon, for instance, is renowned for its urban growth boundary, a policy that effectively bars sprawled growth, promotes infill and transit-oriented development, and protects valuable green spaces in the region. Minneapolis ranks as the top city in the United States when it comes to commuting by bicycle to work, an achievement that is all the more amazing given the city's brutally cold winters (Article 52, "Lessons from a Surprise Bike Town"). How has greater Minneapolis achieved such distinction? Most significantly, planners in the Twin Cities have created a maze of safe bicycle paths, separated not just from automobiles but, in many places, also from walkers. Bike trails that follow the shoreline of the area's many lakes offer a pleasurable and safe commute.

Energy requirements, too, will affect the shape of future cities. The nuclear crisis in Fukushima, Japan, where a tsunami

© Punchstock/Japan-Tokyo vol. AI116

overwhelmed the cooling systems of nuclear reactors just north of the Tokyo megalopolis, underscores the connection between energy and continued urban development. In Japan, recognition of energy constraints has led both citizens and policymakers to confront tough choices (Article 53, "Japan's Remarkable Renewable Energy Drive—After Fukushima"). In Japan, where a much greater disaster was only narrowly averted, citizens have begun to question the desirability of the fabled Japanese development state and its support of energy-intensive growth. Japan has begun to explore a shift from nuclear to renewable energy, with a new emphasis on conservation and "green growth." Such policies promise to alter prevailing patterns of urban development in Japan.

The summer 2012 crisis in India, where collapse of the electricity "grid" left hundreds of millions of people—half of the giant country—without power, further underscores the fragility of unabated urban growth predicated on the existence of limitless supplies of energy. It remains to be seen if India, Japan, and other countries have the will to resolve the energy/development dilemma, especially when memories of crisis recede into the past and pro-growth and industry forces reassert themselves.

Across Europe, Irking Drivers Is Urban Policy

Elisabeth Rosenthal

Zurich—while American cities are synchronizing green lights to improve traffic flow and offering apps to help drivers find parking, many European cities are doing the opposite: creating environments openly hostile to cars. The methods vary, but the mission is clear—to make car use expensive and just plain miserable enough to tilt drivers toward more environmentally friendly modes of transportation.

Cities including Vienna to Munich and Copenhagen have closed vast swaths of streets to car traffic. Barcelona and Paris have had car lanes eroded by popular bike-sharing programs. Drivers in London and Stockholm pay hefty congestion charges just for entering the heart of the city. And over the past two years, dozens of German cities have joined a national network of "environmental zones" where only cars with low carbon dioxide emissions may enter.

Likeminded cities welcome new shopping malls and apartment buildings but severely restrict the allowable number of parking spaces. On-street parking is vanishing. In recent years, even former car capitals like Munich have evolved into "walkers' paradises," said Lee Schipper, a senior research engineer at Stanford University who specializes in sustainable transportation.

"In the United States, there has been much more of a tendency to adapt cities to accommodate driving," said Peder Jensen, head of the Energy and Transport Group at the European Environment Agency. "Here there has been more movement to make cities more livable for people, to get cities relatively free of cars."

To that end, the municipal Traffic Planning Department here in Zurich has been working overtime in recent years to torment drivers. Closely spaced red lights have been added on roads into town, causing delays and angst for commuters. Pedestrian underpasses that once allowed traffic to flow freely across major intersections have been removed. Operators in the city's ever expanding tram system can turn traffic lights in their favor as they approach, forcing cars to halt.

Around Löwenplatz, one of Zurich's busiest squares, cars are now banned on many blocks. Where permitted, their speed is limited to a snail's pace so that crosswalks and crossing signs can be removed entirely, giving people on foot the right to cross anywhere they like at any time.

As he stood watching a few cars inch through a mass of bicycles and pedestrians, the city's chief traffic planner, Andy Fellmann, smiled. "Driving is a stop-and-go experience," he said. "That's what we like! Our goal is to reconquer public space for pedestrians, not to make it easy for drivers."

While some American cities—notably San Francisco, which has "pedestrianized" parts of Market Street—have made similar efforts, they are still the exception in the United States, where it has been difficult to get people to imagine a life where cars are not entrenched, Dr. Schipper said.

Europe's cities generally have stronger incentives to act. Built for the most part before the advent of cars, their narrow roads are poor at handling heavy traffic. Public transportation is generally better in Europe than in the United States, and gas often costs over $8 a gallon, contributing to driving costs that are two to three times greater per mile than in the United States, Dr. Schipper said.

What is more, European Union countries probably cannot meet a commitment under the Kyoto Protocol to reduce their carbon dioxide emissions unless they curb driving. The United States never ratified that pact.

Globally, emissions from transportation continue a relentless rise, with half of them coming from personal cars. Yet an important impulse behind Europe's traffic reforms will be familiar to mayors in Los Angeles and Vienna alike: to make cities more inviting, with cleaner air and less traffic.

Michael Kodransky, global research manager at the Institute for Transportation and Development Policy in New York, which works with cities to reduce transport emissions, said that Europe was previously "on the same trajectory as the United States, with more people wanting to own more cars." But in the past decade, there had been "a conscious shift in thinking, and firm policy," he said. And it is having an effect.

After two decades of car ownership, Hans Von Matt, 52, who works in the insurance industry, sold his vehicle and now gets around Zurich by tram or bicycle, using a car-sharing service for trips out of the city. Carless households have increased from 40 to 45 percent in the last decade, and car owners use their vehicles less, city statistics show.

"There were big fights over whether to close this road or not—but now it is closed, and people got used to it," he said, alighting from his bicycle on Limmatquai, a riverside pedestrian zone lined with cafes that used to be two lanes of gridlock. Each major road closing has to be approved in a referendum.

Today 91 percent of the delegates to the Swiss Parliament take the tram to work.

Still, there is grumbling. "There are all these zones where you can only drive 20 or 30 kilometers per hour [about 12 to 18 miles an hour], which is rather stressful," Thomas Rickli, a consultant, said as he parked his Jaguar in a lot at the edge of town. "It's useless."

Urban planners generally agree that a rise in car commuting is not desirable for cities anywhere.

Mr. Fellmann calculated that a person using a car took up 115 cubic meters (roughly 4,000 cubic feet) of urban space in Zurich while a pedestrian took three. "So it's not really fair to everyone else if you take the car," he said.

European cities also realized they could not meet increasingly strict World Health Organization guidelines for fine-particulate air pollution if cars continued to reign. Many American cities are likewise in "nonattainment" of their Clean Air Act requirements, but that fact "is just accepted here," said Mr. Kodransky of the New York-based transportation institute.

It often takes extreme measures to get people out of their cars, and providing good public transportation is a crucial first step. One novel strategy in Europe is intentionally making it harder and more costly to park. "Parking is everywhere in the United States, but it's disappearing from the urban space in Europe," said Mr. Kodransky, whose recent report "Europe's Parking U-Turn" surveys the shift.

Sihl City, a new Zurich mall, is three times the size of Brooklyn's Atlantic Mall but has only 225 more parking spaces than Atlantic's 625, and as a result, 70 percent of visitors get there by public transport, Mr. Kodransky said.

In Copenhagen, Mr. Jensen, at the European Environment Agency, said that his office building had more than 150 spaces for bicycles and only one for a car, to accommodate a disabled person.

While many building codes in Europe cap the number of parking spaces in new buildings to discourage car ownership, American codes conversely tend to stipulate a minimum number. New apartment complexes built along the light rail line in Denver devote their bottom eight floors to parking, making it "too easy" to get in the car rather than take advantage of rail transit, Mr. Kodransky said.

While Mayor Michael R. Bloomberg has generated controversy in New York by "pedestrianizing" a few areas like Times Square, many European cities have already closed vast areas to car traffic. Store owners in Zurich had worried that the closings would mean a drop in business, but that fear has proved unfounded, Mr. Fellmann said, because pedestrian traffic increased 30 to 40 percent where cars were banned.

With politicians and most citizens still largely behind them, Zurich's planners continue their traffic-taming quest, shortening the green-light periods and lengthening the red with the goal that pedestrians wait no more than 20 seconds to cross.

"We would never synchronize green lights for cars with our philosophy," said Pio Marzolini, a city official. "When I'm in other cities, I feel like I'm always waiting to cross a street. I can't get used to the idea that I am worth less than a car."

Critical Thinking

1. What are the various steps that European planners take in their efforts to reduce automobile use and traffic congestion?

2. Which of these policy steps can U.S. communities borrow in their own efforts to promote more livable cities?

3. Which of these policy efforts, despite their popularity in Europe, would be a bad "fit" for U.S. cities? That is, which of the European policy initiatives would have little chance of being adopted in the United States?

Lessons from a Surprise Bike Town

How snowy Minneapolis beat out Portland
for the title of best bike city in America.

Jay Walljasper

It came as a surprise to many when *Bicycling* magazine last year named Minneapolis, Minnesota as America's "#1 Bike City" (unseating Portland, Oregon, which had claimed the honor for many years). Shock that the heartland could outperform cities on the coasts was matched by widespread disbelief that biking was even possible in a state famous for its ferocious winters.

But Minneapolitans weren't surprised. "Biking has become a huge part of what we are," Mayor R.T. Rybak recently told a delegation of transportation leaders from other cities who had come to learn from Minneapolis' example. According to census data, close to four percent of Minneapolis residents bike to work (that's far fewer than in, say, Japan, where some 15 percent bike to work, but well above the U.S. national average, which is barely over half a percent). In Minneapolis, the percentage of bike commuters has increased by 33 percent since 2007, and 500 percent since 1980.

A Biking Transformation

Thirty years ago, local bicyclists would have howled with laughter at the idea of Minneapolis being named America's best bike city. It was a frustrating and dangerous place to bike, crisscrossed by freeways and arterial streets that felt like freeways. Drivers were openly hostile to bike riders, some of them going the extra step to scare the daylights out of us as they roared past. Bike lanes were practically non-existent.

The goal is to make two-wheelers a central component of the transportation system.

But Minneapolis also had the makings of a great bike town—in part, as Dorian Grilley of the Bicycle Alliance of Minnesota noted, due to a "150-year tradition of civic involvement" that preserved the land bikers use today. In the late 19th century, city fathers wisely preserved land along lakes, creeks and the Mississippi River for public use. These became popular places to bike in the 1890s and again, eighty years later, when the second bike boom hit town. Grassroots activists convinced

political leaders to take the bold step of developing abandoned rail lines as bike trails rather than as condos or industrial zones.

The combination of cyclist pressure and good civic sense has led the city to make supporting safe biking a priority in its transportation planning.

In these lean economic times, Mayor Rybak stressed, cities need to be creative about how they spend transportation dollars. Big-ticket engineering projects to move ever more cars must give way to more efficient projects that move people by a variety of means—including foot, bike, transit. "We need to get more use from all the streets we already have," Rybak said. "It really is the idea that bikes belong."

What a Bike Town Looks Like

So what does it take to become a great bike city? In a city where bicyclists of all ages and backgrounds already ride recreational trails regularly, the goal is to make two-wheelers a central component of the transportation system by encouraging everyone to hop on their bikes for commuting or short trips around town. This is not a far-fetched dream, since nationally half of all automobile trips are three miles or less—a distance easily covered by bike in twenty minutes.

This year, Minneapolis is adding 57 new miles of bikeways to the 127 miles already built, and an additional 183 miles are planned over the next twenty years. By 2020, almost every city resident will live within a mile of an off-street bikeway and within a half-mile of a bike lane, vows city transportation planner Donald Pfaum.

Having the option to ride apart from heavy traffic encourages more people to try out biking as a form of transportation.

The visiting planners and city officials—from Columbus, Ohio, and Pittsburgh—inspected America's "first bike freeway," Cedar Lake Trail, which runs along an uninterrupted rail corridor from the western suburbs through downtown Minneapolis to the Mississippi River. They also rode the Midtown Greenway, another converted rail line, which cuts through the city's south side and carries as many as 3,500 bicyclists a day. Both connect to numerous other trails, creating an off-road network that reaches deep into St. Paul and surrounding suburbs. Intersections are infrequent along these routes, which boosts riders' speed along with their sense of safety and comfort.

Minneapolis also launched the first large-scale bikesharing system in the U.S.—called Nice Ride—and boasts arguably the nation's finest network of off-street bicycle trails.

Minneapolis bikers face the added challenge of cold, snowy winters. "We're colder than Montreal or Moscow," Steve Clark, program manager of Bike Walk Twin Cities, told the visitors, "but that doesn't stop people from riding their bikes in even the coldest, snowiest, darkest conditions." Clark's group found that one in three summertime bike commuters will also ride regularly on warmer, sunny winter days; one in five will be out on their bikes through snowstorms and temperatures below zero.

City workers clear snow from the off-road bikeways just as they do the streets. Studded snow tires and breakthroughs in cold-weather clothing make year-round biking easier than it looks, Clark said. A few tips for would-be winter bikers: install fenders, ride slower, lower your seat so you can use your boots as an emergency brake, and enjoy the Christmas-card scenery.

Clark emphasizes the importance of doing bike counts throughout the coldest months. "Actual data legitimizes winter biking as transportation, and debunks the idea that bike projects are frivolous because they are used only in the summer."

Making Biking Safer and More Accessible

Minneapolis is committed to creating separate rights-of-way for bikes (i.e., keeping them a safe distance from cars) wherever feasible. Research shows that most people—including many women, families, and older citizens—are wary of biking alongside motor vehicles on busy streets. Having the option to ride apart from heavy traffic encourages more people to try out biking as a form of transportation. Nationally, only a quarter of riders are women; in Minneapolis, 37 percent are.

Since the 1970s, Dutch city planners have separated bicyclists from motor vehicles on most arterial streets, with impressive results. The rate of biking has doubled throughout the country, now accounting for 27 percent of all trips. Women make up 55 percent of two-wheel traffic and citizens over 55 ride in numbers slightly higher than the national average. Nearly every Dutch schoolyard is filled with kids' bikes parked at racks and lampposts.

Statistics show that as the number of riders rises, their safety increases. Shaun Murphy, Non-Motorized Transportation Program Coordinator for the city of Minneapolis, notes that, though bicycle ridership is much higher, your chances of being in a car vs. bike crash in the city are 75 percent less than in 1993.

At a time when gasoline prices are high and transit service is being cut across the country, bikes can help fill the transportation gaps in poor communities.

The group from Columbus and Pittsburgh pedaled downtown along Minneapolis's first cycle track—a bike lane

separated from motorized traffic by parked cars. The configuration provides a better experience for people on bikes and in cars by creating a buffer between them. The Columbus delegation paid particularly close attention to this project, down to scrutinizing how the paint was applied to the pavement, because the street resembles one in their own downtown.

On the next block, shared-lane ("sharrow") markers were painted on Hennepin Avenue within a continuous green stripe running down the street to send a clear message to both bicyclists and motorists that road space is used by everyone.

The group then pedaled out of downtown, crossing another bike-and-pedestrian bridge over a busy street before landing on Bryant Avenue, which has been transformed into a bicycle boulevard—a residential street where pedestrians and bicyclists are given priority over cars.

Another innovation now common throughout the Twin Cities is known as a road diet: by converting four-way streets into three-way configurations with alternating center turn lanes, bike lanes can be added or sidewalks widened without diminishing capacity for cars. "When done in the course of regular road repair projects, they cost nothing more than what it takes for a community outreach campaign," he noted.

Minneapolis is working hard to challenge the notion that only upper-middle-class white folks ride bikes. The Major Taylor Bicycle Club, named for the African-American racer who claimed world records in the 1890s, organizes rides and bike events in minority communities. A half-dozen bike rodeos to excite kids about biking took place in inner city neighborhoods over the summer. In St. Paul, the Sibley Bike Depot offers a wide range of programs to introduce biking to immigrants and low-income families, including a shop that sells low-cost bikes and lets people work on their own bikes for free. They also run programs where kids can earn free bikes by taking bike repair classes, and a bike library where low-income families are loaned free bikes.

At a time when gasoline prices are high and transit service is being cut across the country, bikes can help fill the transportation gaps in poor communities. Nice Ride, with support from the McKnight Foundation, has extended service to lower-income areas of both Minneapolis and St. Paul this summer. Bill Dosset says the initiative aims to overcome cultural attitudes in some communities that bikes are only for kids or for people who can't afford any other way to get around.

Bike Walk Twin Cities launched a social marketing campaign to promote biking in the lower-income neighborhoods of Minneapolis's north side, where this year a new Bike Walk Center opens along with an extensive network of new bikeways.

Bike Sharing: Have a Nice Ride

Minneapolis is home to the nation's first major bikesharing program, which hit the streets in June 2010. It was quickly followed by Denver, Washington, D.C., Boston, and Toronto—with Seattle, Chicago, Portland, and other cities now readying plans.

Bill Dossett, executive director of Nice Ride Minnesota—the non-profit organization that runs the bikeshare program—

recounted the widespread skepticism that greeted the new system: Would bikesharing work outside Europe? Would it work in a city where a high percentage of people already own bikes? In a city that is low-density? Wouldn't inexperienced riders hurt themselves? Won't most of the bikes be stolen or vandalized?

But when the lime-green bikes were put away for the winter in November 2010, those questions had all been answered. Only one bike was stolen, only one accident reported, no major injuries suffered, and less than $5000 in damage from vandalism, far lower than the organization's projections.

More than 100,000 rides were taken from June to November last year, and Nice Ride operated in the black. This year the system added 500 more bikes and 51 more stations, expanding outward from the center of Minneapolis and moving into St. Paul. From April to September, Nice Ride had logged 172,000 rides. Amy Duncan had not been on a bike since the 1970s but joined Nice Ride to do errands downtown. "I learned to ride a bike again, and 100 percent of my success belongs to Ride," she said.

The bikes themselves feature adjustable seats, lights and a rack for carrying a briefcase or shopping bag. The system is particularly popular with out-of-town tourists, downtown office workers, university students, and residents of apartment buildings and condos. Many local users may actually own bikes, but find Nice Ride easy to use in certain circumstances, such as when they take transit downtown or to the university. Every Nice Ride bike you see likely represents one less car on the road.

Learning from Minneapolis

Even people who haven't ridden a bike in years cheered when Minneapolis was named America's #1 biking city—biking has now become part of our positive self-image.

It's a model other cities are excited to emulate—starting with Pittsburgh and Columbus, whose leaders and planners were inspired by their tour of Minneapolis' biking innovations. "You see right away how bikes are accepted as a mode of transportation," said Alan McKnight, the director of recreation and parks for Columbus, Ohio, as the tour came to a close. Yarone Zober, chief of staff to the mayor of Pittsburgh, was excited to find that "the bike facilities here are not all big, expensive infrastructure."

"Places famous for biking, like Copenhagen and even Portland, feel very far away," remarked Jeff Stephens, director of the Columbus advocacy organization Consider Biking, who came to Minneapolis looking for ideas he could apply back home. "It was exciting to see what they've accomplished in Minneapolis, which is a city that seems a lot like Columbus.

"Our mayor has said that he wants Columbus to become a 'bike town'," Stephens added, "and seeing what's been done here gives us a clearer sense of what that means."

Critical Thinking

1. What initiatives has Minneapolis taken that have made it America's "best bike city"?

2. Who do you think are the opponents of policies to support biking? What arguments do they make?

JAY WALLJASPER is author of the forthcoming book *All That We Share*, is a contributing editor to *National Geographic Traveler*, editor of OnTheCommons.org, a senior fellow of the Project for Public Spaces, and a contributor to Shareable.net, where this article originally appeared.

Japan's Remarkable Renewable Energy Drive—After Fukushima

ANDREW DEWIT

The looming shutdown of every single one of Japan's nuclear plants—previously the providers of nearly one-third of the nation's electricity—has accelerated the country's initiatives on conservation, renewable energy sources, and decentralization of electricity supply. It has also injected considerable momentum into Japan's "green cities" initiative.

These changes are being fought by those who insist that Japan cannot live without nuclear power. The opponents include not just the utilities, but the banks who lent so much to the utilities, Keidanren (the main business federation) and much of the national government.

However, the growing cost of energy and worries about power supply are pushing firms and local governments to find alternatives. Japan responded with surprisingly rapid success in conservation and efficiency after the oil crises of 1973 and 1979. It may do so again.

Nuke Shutdown

At present, only two of Japan's 54 nuclear reactors are operating. One of these will be shut down at the end of March, and the last one will go off-line in late April or early May. Minister of Economy, Trade and Industry (METI) Edano Yukio says that Japan seems likely to spend this summer with no nuclear reactors in operation at all.

Japanese reactors have regular, 13-month maintenance schedules, and the approval of national and local authorities is required before they can be restarted. In order to reassure a newly resistant public of their safety, the nuclear reactors were subject to new "stress tests" as of last year. But in late February, the stress tests were publicly deemed inadequate by Madarame Haruki, Chairman of the Nuclear Safety Commission and a long-time proponent of nuclear power. That criticism has only increased opposition to restarts by prefectural governors, who are in a position to veto them. Even supportive local leaders are now calling for a resolution of the waste-storage problem before any restarts are allowed.

Buying Expensive Carbon Fuels

To make up for the shortfall, a lot of gas, oil, and coal-fired power capacity is being ramped up, newly deployed or taken out of mothballs. Data from METI indicates that in December 2011 thermal power composed 86% of power generation, with 16% of that being oil-fired, 23% coal and 46% Liquefied Natural Gas (LNG). Nuclear reactors provided only 7.4% of total power. Compare that with April, when nuclear was 28.2% of power generation, and thermal power (5% oil, 20% coal, 38% LNG) was 63% of the remainder. Japan's total fuel imports in 2010 were valued at ¥17.4 trillion ($217 bil.) but increased by 25% to ¥21.8 trillion in 2011. Some was due to an actual increase in volume and some to sharp price increases. In any case, the imports rose from 3.6% of GDP to 4.6%. The increased costs seem likely to continue for the foreseeable future. As a result, the much-loathed utility TEPCO (Tokyo Electric Power Corporation) is slated to raise electricity prices for large-lot power consumers (those using more than 500 kilowatts) by an average of 17%.

Pushback by Nuclear Lobby

These threatened price increases have mobilized a significant push back by Keidanren-centered business interests that still view the nuclear reactors as a cheap source of safe, reliable, low-emissions power and want them restarted. Their desire dovetails with that of the three big financial institutions which hold trillions of yen in loans to TEPCO, the biggest slice in the corporate bond market, as well as financing for other utilities.

Their nightmare scenario surely envisions Japan making it through a nuclear-free summer with no major blackouts or supply-chain disruptions. Such a scenario would perhaps tip opinion toward seeing nuclear energy as dispensable even in the short term, and thus lead to trillions of yen in stranded assets.

The banks have tried to forestall this outcome by securing reactor restarts as a pre-condition for their advancing any additional finance to a nationalized TEPCO. The financial sector and many large-lot power consumers have put forward a tsunami of arguments that the electricity price increases, resulting from costly purchases in international markets, and uncertainty of supply will exacerbate Japan's already grim problem of hollowing out. Japan's rising yen, shrinking population, huge public-sector debt, and other handicaps already pose significant disincentives to business investment, and the power issue clearly does not help.

Conservation: A Different Answer

While some push nuclear restarts as the answer to the problems of availability and cost, others are accelerating moves towards greater energy efficiency and conservation as well as creating big incentives for the rapid deployment of renewable power. There were startling advances in conservation and energy efficiency last year, driven by compulsory power reductions as well as subsidies and other encouragement.

For example, a recent study by market research firm GfK reported that less than 2.2% of household ceiling lights were LED (light-emitting diodes) in January of last year, but by the week of February 13 to 19 of this year had taken a 49.4% share of the market. Falling prices through this mass production also bode well for Japanese electronics makers hard-pressed in international markets by the strong yen.

The power-consumption data suggest policy support for efficiency had significant effects. The figures of the Federation of Electric Power Companies in Japan (FERC) for the summer months of 2011 show total nationwide electricity sales, relative to the previous year, down 5% in July, 11.3% in August, and 11.4% in September. Data for January 2012 indicate that power generation was down 3.7% compared to January of 2011.

Conservation and efficiency were already a growth industry before the nuclear crisis. But the new, unforeseeable spurs to innovation and diffusion may see Japan overshoot "New Growth Strategy" targets for 2020. These were established in June 2010, and aim at a "green innovation" market totaling ¥50 trillion ($625 billion, or 10% of 2011 GDP) and 1.4 million new workers. One example of the growing scale of the conservation incentives is that 80% of 104 major Japanese firms surveyed in late February by the Yomiuri planned to reduce power purchases from TEPCO. More than half (54) of the firms declared that they would invest in conservation, and 14 of the 104 replied that they would deploy some form of in-house power-generation capacity. To respond to this increasing demand for conservation, firms are rushing energy-management systems to market. Toray Engineering for example announced February 29 that it was opening sales on its "Eco-Plant EMS," an energy management system for use in factories. The system comes with a ¥40 million ($500,000) price tag, but in on-site tests apparently achieved a 30% power reduction of air conditioning and a 10–20% reduction in factory power use overall.

Moving to Renewables

Moreover, Japan has increasingly robust policies in place for diffusing renewable alternatives. In particular, its feed-in tariff (FIT)—a long-term subsidy guaranteeing producers a certain rate on the supply of electricity—has been expanded from solar to include wind, biomass, small hydro and geothermal, and will take effect by July 1.

Price setting and periods of guarantee are being determined by a five-member consultative committee that held its first meeting on March 6. The pro-renewable majority on the committee suggests these crucial elements of the policy will be robust, perhaps driving rapid diffusion and concomitant price declines in this market as well. Marubeni, NTT, Mitsui, and a host of local governments and other organizations are already committed to large-scale mega-solar, wind, and related projects. The most recent data indicate that the total of mega-solar projects announced over the past year is twice what the utilities were planning to install up to 2020. This is strong evidence of how much low-hanging fruit there was in Japan, on renewables. We seem likely to find a similar story in efficiency and conservation.

Decentralization

Local governments have been particularly aggressive in responding to the crises driven and exacerbated by the Fukushima shock. The effective collapse of national energy policy has seen many rethink their growth strategies and revamp their intergovernmental organizations, both among themselves as well as between them and the central government. The Fukushima shock was profound for most local governments due to the existential threat to power supplies as well as the central government's abysmal crisis management in the weeks following the disaster.

Major local governments such as Metropolitan Tokyo and Osaka are especially concerned by their vulnerability to highly centralized power generation and transmission as well as its clearly incompetent governance by the national administration. One of their responses to this threat from centralized, overly complex energy institutions dominated by vested interests has been to increase local resilience and autonomy via decentralized power generation. Tokyo, for example, determined that it needed its own generation capacity in order to maintain subway transport and other critical functions in the event of an emergency. So it is installing gas-fired power and a small-scale smart grid separate from the TEPCO utility. Also, Osaka City and Osaka Prefecture have banded together to launch an energy commission, which met on February 27. They are explicitly committed to ramping up conservation and renewables in the face of the central government's immobilism. Kobe and Kyoto have joined Osaka as partners in the effort.

Other prefectures, including Kanagawa and Saitama, are also explicitly aiming their policymaking at efficiency and fostering an energy shift to renewable power so as to enhance self-reliance, employment and business opportunities, as well as international competitiveness. As of late February, local governments' Fiscal 2012 initial budget compilations have a combined ¥52 billion ($650 million) investment aimed at fostering renewable power projects. While not tallied yet, the locals' investments in conservation and energy efficiency are many multiples of the budget for renewables. The central government's feed-in-tariff adds to these kinds of generalized incentives to enhance local resilience.

National Government Divided

The central government seems deeply conflicted. On the one hand, it appears to be waiting for a crisis in power supply to drive restarts. On the other hand, it is using the ongoing crisis to act rapidly to reshape the power economy and thus leverage green growth prospects. So, Prime Minister Noda Yoshihiko, partial to MOF and the banks, repeatedly calls for restarts while distracting himself with crafting visions for raising the consumption tax, though such fiscal austerity killed a recovery back in 1997. And his METI Minister, Edano Yukio, announced in a January 26 press conference that restarts might be unavoidable, yet failed to outline any serious initiatives for further incentivizing efficiency. Surely both understand that the longer they dawdle, allowing uncertainty free reign, the more damage is done to incentives to invest in Japan. As we have seen repeatedly over the past year, the nuclear lobby will say almost anything to keep their assets from becoming stranded. And that is what they are doing now, while the Noda Cabinet is preoccupied with papering over its divisions.

However, at the same time, central agencies are also rushing to keep up with events by deregulating so as to foster new industry as well as to open farmland, waterways, and parks to renewable power projects. Among recent moves, the METI is indicating that it will exempt solar from the factory site regulations on green space as well as include solar in calculations of peak-power supply. Even the EU countries don't do the latter as their peak demand is at night. But Japan's peak is in daytime in the summer due to air-conditioning demand, and this coincides well with peak insolation and solar output. Also, the Ministry of Agriculture, Forestry and Fisheries recently announced 1000 regional sites for small hydro and other renewable projects. There is more than a little irony in seeing the political class that was elected on a promise to displace bureaucrats being outclassed by them in a crisis.

New Deregulatory Efforts

These new deregulatory efforts are worth watching. They carry on from the flagship comprehensive special zone law, which was passed on June 22, 2011. The zone initiative was billed as a means to "concentrate resources of central and local government in areas of high pioneering potential." It is not simply a relaxation of rules but also an overall package of support that includes regulatory exemptions, tax breaks, financial aid and loans, and other mechanisms aimed at innovation. The major types of comprehensive special zones are the international strategic zones and the regional revitalization zones. The strategic zones are aimed at clustering industry and related intellectual

and other resources so as to increase growth opportunities in the environment, next-generation energy, bio life science, and other areas. These zones include a "Green Asia International Strategy comprehensive special zone," which groups Fukuoka City and Prefecture with Kitakyushu City in an initiative to position their region in western Japan as the gateway to Asia.

There are seven special zones as of February 2012. In total, they comprise budgetary requests of ¥153.9 billion yen ($1.9 billion) which are expected to lead to ¥6.97 trillion ($85 billion) in new economic activity and 298,000 new jobs.

There are at present 26 regional revitalization zones. The ambit of this zone program includes disaster prevention and mitigation, environment and next-generation industry, tourism and culture, agriculture, biomass, finance and social business, healthcare and nursing. The total fiscal scale of the zones is ¥63 billion ($0.7 billion) that is expected to lead to ¥2.15 trillion ($26 billion) in new business activity and 67,000 new jobs.

The tax breaks in the international strategy zone are focused on lowering the corporate tax in order to foster competitiveness in international markets, while those in the regional revitalization zones centre on deductions for individual investment in enterprises that are part of the strategy.

Green Cities Initiative

This flurry of deregulation policies is increasingly being funneled into the larger environmental "future city" initiative. This latter policy regime carries on from the "eco-model city" program that was put in place in the summer of 2008, and has helped environmental award-winning cities like Kitakyushu in Fukuoka Prefecture deepen their green business and expand their overseas sales. Kitakyushu last year became the first Asian city for the OECD's Green City Program. It is also exporting its expertise on recycling to such Chinese cities as Dalian and Qingdao. And it is expanding its reach in the global water business that in 2007 was assessed at ¥36.2 trillion ($440 billion) and is expected to reach ¥86.5 trillion ($1.05 trillion) in 2025. Kitakyushu's water-management business is finding purchasers in Cambodia's Phnom Penh as well as Vietnam's Hai Phong. The future city policy that Kitakyushu is part of was adopted as one of the 21 national strategic projects of the "new growth strategy" passed on June 18, 2010.

This initiative is not simply for green growth; it also includes measures for dealing with rapidly aging societies and disseminating policy lessons learned from within the eco-model cities. The initiative seeks synergies among these categories as well as from among the recipient cities. On December 22, 11 cities were selected as eco-model cities. Five were outside of Tohoku, the area hit by the earthquake. These five include Kitakyushu and Yokohama among those previously designated as eco-model cities. But after March 11, 2011, the national authorities expanded the group to include six from the affected area. These six cities include hard-hit Minamisoma and Kamaishi.

The inclusion of these cities in the larger initiative indicates that the government is drawing on outstanding successes of the eco-model city initiative, and expanding it to devastated areas. These successes include the realization of targets for such aspects as recycling, international engagement, and the demonstration of energy management systems. The core devastated areas are being rebuilt as renewable-centered smart cities with funding from the ¥19 trillion ($237 billion) fund for reconstruction. Japanese policymakers clearly see including them in the overall green-city project as a way to encourage application of lessons learned from both the cities initially involved in the eco-city project as well as those that are trying to rebuild from the tsunami. It is a means of speeding the dissemination of policy learning among local governments in general as well as to overseas markets.

Japan Seeks Lead in New Global Market

Japan is seeking to use its policy tools and experience as a means to gain leadership in the export of green-city models. This is a new and rapidly growing market. The University of Westminster's authoritative International Eco Cities Initiative reports that its most recent (September, 2011) international survey found "an unprecedented mushrooming of various kinds of eco-city initiatives and projects across the world," with a total of 174 eco-cities projects catalogued. Japan's initiative is not just a bureaucratic talking shop. The eco-city initiative was institutionalized on December 14, 2008 and included 130 organizations. Of these organizations 70 were "highly motivated municipalities," along with 39 prefectures, 12 related government ministries, and 19 related organs of government. As of November, 2011, these ranks had swelled to 89 cities, 46 prefectures, 12 governmental offices, 29 public organizations, and 28 organizations from the private sector for a total of 204 organizations. The private sector members include Japan IBM, Mitsubishi Automobiles, Pacific Consulting, and Nikkei BP. The latter is very strongly interested in a global "smart city" market that it expects to reach a cumulative ¥4,000 trillion ($49 trillion) by 2030.

The Tug of War

To what extent will these nice-sounding initiatives actually bear fruit? That remains to be seen. But to make an assessment of the chances, we need to get back to the context for all these policy moves. The potential for a zero-nuclear summer certainly presents risks to Japan. But it also affords an opportunity to ramp up the diffusion of cutting edge conservation and renewable technologies as well as to accelerate other focused action in this existing set of policies for fostering sustainable growth in green cities.

With powerful pressure from subnational governments, the green cities policy regime may become the agency for driving the Japanese political economy onto a sustainable growth track. The more Japan is pressed to rapidly innovate models of green city growth, the greater its prospects of realizing the national strategy of expanding green-city exports.

The problem with implementing this national strategy hitherto has been the enormous weight of vested interests in the power and Keidanren-centered manufacturing sector. They seek to shape green growth to accord with their own institutional interests which have long been bound up with nuclear power and TEPCO. Among other unwise things, that meant maintaining power monopolies and suppressing the diffusion of renewables and smart grids. Such interests are incompatible with the most competitive and sustainable green city model. Rather, the weight of vested interests has threatened to produce something of a "Galapagos effect," referring to an environment found nowhere else, giving Japan a hamstrung green city model unsuited to most of the potential green-city markets in rapidly growing Asia and other regions.

But with the FIT and local initiatives, some of Japan's most innovative providers of capital, including Softbank, have increasingly robust incentives and opportunities to wreak creative destruction in power and other strategic markets. Through deploying the most advanced technology and business practices, they increase the pressure on others, including the central government, to move faster and smarter. Perhaps this conjunction of daunting incentives and capable players in Japan's power sector can help make the country's green-city policy regime truly world class.

This is a revised and expanded version of an article that appeared in *The Oriental Economist*, March 2012.

Critical Thinking

1. What are the steps that Japan has taken in order to reduce its dependence on nuclear power?

2. Who do you think are the opponents of Japan's attempt to move away from nuclear power?

3. What are the costs to reducing reliance on nuclear power? How will reduced reliance on nuclear power affect life in Japan's cities?

4. How can cities provide jobs for people if the shift away from nuclear power winds up lessening economic growth?

ANDREW DEWIT is Professor in the School of Policy Studies at Rikkyo University and an Asia-Pacific Journal coordinator. With Iida Tetsunari and Kaneko Masaru, he is coauthor of "Fukushima and the Political Economy of Power Policy in Japan," in Jeff Kingston (ed.) *Natural Disaster and Nuclear Crisis in Japan.*

Test-Your-Knowledge Form

We encourage you to photocopy and use this page as a tool to assess how the articles in *Annual Editions* expand on the information in your textbook. By reflecting on the articles you will gain enhanced text information. You can also access this useful form on a product's book support website at www.mhhe.com/cls.

NAME: DATE:

_____

TITLE AND NUMBER OF ARTICLE:

_____

BRIEFLY STATE THE MAIN IDEA OF THIS ARTICLE:

_____

LIST THREE IMPORTANT FACTS THAT THE AUTHOR USES TO SUPPORT THE MAIN IDEA:

_____

WHAT INFORMATION OR IDEAS DISCUSSED IN THIS ARTICLE ARE ALSO DISCUSSED IN YOUR TEXTBOOK OR OTHER READINGS THAT YOU HAVE DONE? LIST THE TEXTBOOK CHAPTERS AND PAGE NUMBERS:

_____

LIST ANY EXAMPLES OF BIAS OR FAULTY REASONING THAT YOU FOUND IN THE ARTICLE:

_____

LIST ANY NEW TERMS/CONCEPTS THAT WERE DISCUSSED IN THE ARTICLE, AND WRITE A SHORT DEFINITION:

NOTES

NOTES

NOTES

NOTES

NOTES

NOTES

NOTES